MANAGING HURRICANE KATRINA

MANAGING HURRICANE KATRINA

LESSONS FROM A MEGACRISIS

Arjen Boin, Christer Brown, and James A. Richardson

LOUISIANA STATE UNIVERSITY PRESS   BATON ROUGE

Published by Louisiana State University Press
Copyright © 2019 by Louisiana State University Press
All rights reserved
Manufactured in the United States of America
First printing

Designer: Barbara Neely Bourgoyne
Typeface: Whitman
Printer and binder: Sheridan Books

Library of Congress Cataloging-in-Publication Data
Names: Boin, Arjen, author. | Brown, Christer, 1980– author. | Richardson, James A., author.
Title: Managing Hurricane Katrina : lessons from a megacrisis / Arjen Boin, Christer Brown, and
    James A. Richardson.
Description: Baton Rouge : Louisiana State University Press, [2019] | Includes bibliographical
    references and index.
Identifiers: LCCN 2018036777 | ISBN 978-0-8071-7044-1 (cloth : alk. paper) | ISBN 978-0-8071-
    7092-2 (epub) | ISBN 978-0-8071-7091-5 (pdf)
Subjects: LCSH: Hurricane Katrina, 2005. | Emergency management—Gulf Coast (U.S.) |
    Disaster relief—Government policy—Gulf Coast (U.S.) | Crisis management in government—
    United States.
Classification: LCC HV551.4.G85 B65 2019 | DDC 976/.044—dc23
LC record available at https://lccn.loc.gov/2018036777

CONTENTS

PREFACE   vii | ABBREVIATIONS   xiii

HURRICANE KATRINA: *A Quick Timeline*   xv

1. Hurricane Katrina Revisited: Reflecting on Success and Failure 1

2. Why Didn't They See It Coming? The Challenges of
Timely Crisis Recognition 21

3. Understanding the Unimaginable: Why Collective Sense
Making Failed 46

4. Who's in Charge Here? Coordinating a Multilevel Response 79

5. Meaning Making in Crisis: The Detrimental Effects of Missing
Narratives and Escalating Blame Games 118

Conclusion: Lessons of a Mega-disaster 153

APPENDIX I: *Timeline on Levee Breaches*   179

APPENDIX II: *Emergency Management in the American Federal System*   183

NOTES   187 | BIBLIOGRAPHY   237 | INDEX   261

PREFACE

So why another book about Hurricane Katrina?

Much has been written on Katrina. In the summer of 2015, a decade after the storm, the bookshop at the Louisiana State University campus featured a long, overloaded table on this mega-disaster. Apart from the congressional reports and many other official documents, the years after Katrina have seen a wave of memoirs, journalistic accounts, documentaries, and academic analyses.

We had originally planned this book to be in bookstores around that time. But it has taken us much longer to complete our research than we anticipated. The fact that so much happened in that first week of the disaster alone meant that we spent many months just fact-checking what we and others had written.

We pressed on because we believe there are still lessons to be learned from this disaster, especially for practitioners operating at the strategic level of crisis management systems. Our envisioned contribution is twofold.

First, we offer a clear and theory-based evaluative framework that allows for a fair assessment of crisis management performance. In the months and years after Katrina, the performance of strategic actors (the mayor of New Orleans, the governor of Louisiana, the Federal Emergency Management Agency director, the president of the United States) has been panned. If all the books and reports out there are to be believed, these authority figures acted sloppily, sluggishly, and with a disregard for their responsibilities. Our framework moves the analytical focus from these individual leaders to the system that was designed to produce an effective and legitimate response. Our analysis is more fine grained and subtle than the political reports and emotional memoirs.

Second, we study the response to this disaster with an eye on improving the response to future mega-disasters no matter where they might strike. We are facing new threats, ranging from climate change to cyberattacks. We have no doubt that new threats will at some point produce new types of "rude surprises" (a phrase coined by the brilliant Todd LaPorte). Hurricane Katrina, like the 9/11 attacks, can be viewed as a mega-disaster laboratory. What went wrong in 2005 may well go wrong in the near future. For this reason alone, learning from Katrina is a critical task for public administration and crisis scholars alike.

Our team packs expertise on exactly these two areas. Arjen Boin is a crisis scholar with a public administration background. Christer Brown combines scholarly crisis expertise with the experience of a crisis management practitioner. Jim Richardson is a public administration scholar who knows Louisiana government and politics like few others.

We experienced Katrina from very different vantage points. Arjen had just arrived in Chapel Hill for a sabbatical at the University of North Carolina. Coming from the Netherlands, he closely followed the unfolding disaster like most Americans did (through radio, television, and newspapers). It was only much later, after he had moved to Baton Rouge to take a job at Louisiana State University, that he learned about the complexities of the disaster. Talking to many people who had suffered through Katrina, professionally or personally (often both), he slowly began to understand that the received wisdom on the response was uninformed, incomplete, and shallow.

Christer happened to experience Katrina during a visit to his hometown, Houston, which received tens of thousands of New Orleanians after Katrina and then was partially evacuated ahead of Hurricane Rita less than a month later (as we write these words, a massive flood produced by Hurricane Harvey is bringing Houston to its knees). Dozens, many elderly, would die in the evacuation ahead of Rita. Upon returning to Sweden and completing his studies, Christer joined the National Center for Crisis Management Research and Training at the Swedish Defence University, where his first assignment was to dissect the crisis decision-making that occurred during Katrina. This and other hurricane-related projects formed the foundations for his doctoral work at Radboud University Nijmegen in the Netherlands. In his thesis, Christer studied why organizations sometimes struggle to respond to foreseeable complex threats, focusing on FEMA and Katrina.

Jim Richardson was in Louisiana when it all happened. Just before Katrina, Jim and his wife had moved into the Lod Cook Hotel on the LSU campus while his house was being renovated. His daughter was working for Senator Mary Landrieu and happened to spend the week with her parents.

Then Lod Cook became a place for families fleeing New Orleans, Jefferson Parish, and St. Tammany Parish. There was much fear and deep uncertainty about their homes, schools, businesses, and so on. Soon families began to look for schools and housing in the Baton Rouge area. Driving around the city, Jim saw families standing in line at Walmart and Target, buying new clothing for their children—from underclothes to socks to shirts and pants. These families had lost everything. People were scared and absolutely unsure of what might happen to them next.

Katrina affected the rich and the poor, but the ability to cope with the storm favored the rich. The people at Lod Cook were for the most part affluent. They had the financial ability to take care of themselves for the next three to six months, and most of them had jobs that they could restart quickly. Others who did not have much financial support or who had jobs that were physically connected to the New Orleans area were *really* scared.

The disaster of Katrina was of incredible depth. Typically in a hurricane, families are out of their homes for a couple of days or weeks (such as when Rita put families out of their homes for up to two weeks). Katrina put families out of their homes for at least five to six months and some much longer. Moreover, Katrina fundamentally changed New Orleans and St. Bernard Parish. New Orleans's population is now about 80% of its pre-Katrina level, and St. Bernard Parish's population is now about 45,000, compared to about 65,000 before Katrina.

A NOTE ON SOURCES

This study makes use of a wide range of sources, including media reports, official statements, interviews, public reports and investigations, internal evaluations, academic works, and popular literature, as well as think-tank, interest-group, and industry evaluations.

Many of these sources have proven helpful in capturing developments at key junctures during the crisis. We found particularly useful Christopher Cooper and Robert Block's *Disaster: Hurricane Katrina and the Failure of Homeland Security* and Douglas Brinkley's *The Great Deluge.*[1] Survivor accounts helped us understand what people went through during that first week (and the months and years thereafter).

We made extensive use of media reporting.[2] Looking back, we can see what information was available and how, if at all, it shaped perceptions of the situation in the eyes of decision makers, storm victims, and the wider public. With hindsight, we can see that many of these reports contained inaccurate or exaggerated information.

We have also made heavy use of the various public investigations of the Katrina response. Some consider the overall response. Others examine very specific elements of the crisis, such as the levee failures, search and rescue operations, the medical response, or the financial implications of the storm. Many of these reports provide granular detail of the response that is helpful in capturing the essence of the crisis. All these reports were written in a highly politicized environment, which influenced how information was interpreted.

In the years since 2005, we have interviewed several dozen individuals involved in the Katrina response. The majority of these interviews were conducted in 2006 and, later, in 2008, during a study of the response to Hurricane Gustav sponsored by the Swedish Emergency Management Agency. The majority of our respondents worked at the local or state level at the time of Katrina or were employed by nongovernment organizations or private companies; most of the federal officials we contacted were unavailable. These interviews have helped fill in various gaps in the empirical record and contextualize reports from other sources. We have also spoken with many people who lived through the storm. We do not use excerpts from these interviews, but they did inform our understanding of the disaster and the response to it.

ACKNOWLEDGMENTS

We first of all want to thank all those people who talked to us about their experiences during that first week of the disaster. It is through these conversations that we learned of the many things that went well but also went underreported. These conversations also provided a constant source of motivation to make our research count: we aim to help practitioners build better systems that will help protect citizens from threats, ancient and new ones alike. In addition, we thank our colleagues at Leiden University, Louisiana State University, the Swedish Defence University, Utrecht University, and the University of Hong Kong for providing feedback to presentations of research findings.

We benefited from the help of several young people who vaguely remembered Katrina but became obsessed with it, at least for a while. Charlotte Boin started years ago assisting with this project, typing out notes on the congressional reports. Tim de Jongh and Juul Kwaks spent many months doing research and checking facts—they now know everything there is to know about the response. Adinda van de Broek, Daphne de Groot, Rianne Kleinveld, and Manouck Schotvanger helped with the manuscript preparation. Lavinia Cadar oversaw the entire process, applying her sense of perfection as always.

We thank all the good people of Louisiana State University Press who have worked so hard to turn our manuscript into a book. Margaret Lovecraft kept faith in us. Catherine Kadair oversaw the production, and George Roupe cast a sharp eye on the manuscript (saving us from many errors).

Arjen would like to thank colleagues at the Stephenson Disaster Management Institute at LSU. Joey Booth and Brant Mitchell provided useful feedback on earlier drafts of this manuscript (they were there when Katrina unfolded). Jared Llorens of LSU's Public Administration Institute has been especially supportive in facilitating research visits to the university. Arjen's contribution to this project was made possible by his colleagues at Crisisplan BV. He is especially grateful for the faithful support of Werner Overdijk, director of Crisisplan BV.

Christer extends his thanks to the National Center for Crisis Management Research and Training at the Swedish Defence University for supporting his research through the years. Particular thanks are in order to Eric Stern, Fredrik Bynander, and Anna Fornstedt, as well as Bertjan Verbeek, Kerstin Eriksson, Anders Johansson, Kjell Mo, and Annika Brändström.

Jim wishes to thank all the state and local officials, and citizens, who worked tirelessly during Katrina. They worked around the clock to assist all of the evacuees. Many officials endured criticism but never let it stop them. Jim also wants to highlight the activities of the administration of Louisiana State University and especially then-chancellor Sean O'Keefe. LSU immediately opened up its facilities and never once worried about how the university was going to pay for it. Jim was very proud of LSU.

ABBREVIATIONS

CDC	Centers for Disease Control and Prevention
DHS	Department of Homeland Security
DMAT	Disaster Medical Assistance Team
DOD	Department of Defense
DOT	Department of Transportation
DOTD	Louisiana Department of Transportation and Development
EMAC	Emergency Management Assistance Compact
EOC	emergency operations center
ERT-A	Emergency Response Team—Advanced
ERT-N	National Emergency Response Team
ESF	Emergency Support Function
FCO	federal coordinating officer
FEMA	Federal Emergency Management Agency
FPS	Federal Protection Service
HLT	Hurricane Liaison Team
HSC	Homeland Security Council
HSOC	Homeland Security Operations Center
ICS	Incident Command System
INS	Incident of National Significance
JFO	Joint Field Office
JTF-Katrina	Joint Task Force on Hurricane Katrina
LANG	Louisiana National Guard
LDWF	Louisiana Department of Wildlife and Fisheries

LOHSEP	Louisiana Office of Homeland Security and Emergency Preparedness
LSU	Louisiana State University
MERS	Mobile Emergency Response Support
NDMS	National Disaster Medical System
NHC	National Hurricane Center
NOPD	New Orleans Police Department
NORTHCOM	US Northern Command
NRCC	National Response Coordination Center
NRP	National Response Plan
NRP-CIA	Catastrophic Incident Annex of the National Response Plan
PFO	Principal Federal Official
RTA	Regional Transit Authority
TMOSA	Temporary Medical Operations and Staging Area
TSA	Transportation Security Administration
USACE	US Army Corps of Engineers

HURRICANE KATRINA

A QUICK TIMELINE

Friday, August 26: After hitting Florida and moving back into the Gulf, Hurricane Katrina aims for Louisiana. Preparations begin in Louisiana, Mississippi, and Alabama. In New Orleans there is little concern among the public. On Friday evening, the New Orleans Saints play a preseason game in the Superdome.

Saturday, August 27: The evacuation of New Orleans begins. In Baton Rouge, Governor Kathleen Blanco works with FEMA to pre-position resources. Blanco and the mayor of New Orleans, Ray Nagin, discuss evacuation and preparation issues.

Sunday, August 28: Hurricane Katrina is now a Category 5 storm. Mayor Nagin, Governor Blanco, and President Bush call on citizens to leave New Orleans. FEMA director Michael Brown arrives in Baton Rouge. New Orleans empties out. Thousands of "remainers" go to the Superdome to seek shelter from the storm. The anxious wait for Katrina begins.

Monday, August 29: Katrina makes landfall in the early morning. Flood waves devastate coastal areas of Louisiana, Mississippi, and Alabama. The levees in New Orleans are breached, and the city begins to flood. The bowl is filling up, unbeknownst to most people. First responders save many lives.

Tuesday, August 30: The United States wakes up to a mega-disaster. A massive response is initiated. Outside help begins to arrive. The first rumors of looting and violence reach the media. In Washington, DC, federal agencies struggle to get accurate information about the unfolding disaster.

Wednesday, August 31: Disturbing pictures from New Orleans dominate the news. People are stuck on highways or in the Superdome or the Ernest N. Morial Convention Center or wandering the streets. Anarchy and violence reportedly reign in New Orleans. Federal and state leaders struggle to produce a clear message.

Thursday, September 1: The response is increasingly described in the media as "too little, too late." FEMA becomes a household name for failure. Meanwhile, the evacuation of the Superdome has started.

Friday, September 2: The Superdome is evacuated, as is most of the city. President Bush visits New Orleans and confers with Nagin, Blanco, and Brown. Many military resources arrive, as do federal agencies. The worst is almost over. In the media, the blame game is in full swing.

Saturday and Sunday, September 3–4: The Convention Center is evacuated. New Orleans is now mostly empty. While the ordeal is far from over for survivors, authorities can now start to focus on the long-term task of bringing the city back to normal.

MANAGING HURRICANE KATRINA

1

HURRICANE KATRINA REVISITED

REFLECTING ON SUCCESS AND FAILURE

What went wrong? Just about everything . . . hesitancy, bureaucratic rivalries,
failures of leadership from city hall to the White House and epically bad luck.
—EVAN THOMAS, "WHAT WENT WRONG"

THE SHAME OF KATRINA

In late August of 2005, Hurricane Katrina struck the city of New Orleans and
several nearby parishes. In a matter of 24 hours, much of the city was covered
by floodwaters as deep as eighteen feet in places. Hundreds drowned, trapped
in their homes. Thousands were stranded on roofs, raised berms, highway overpasses, at a darkened, sweltering stadium, and in an empty Convention Center.
Live images showed desperate residents calling for help from rooftops, people
looting stores, and lifeless bodies floating facedown in the floodwaters. Journalists broadcasting on live television were shaken to tears by reports of rape
and violence.

Hurricane Katrina produced a mega-disaster, the largest in US history. Katrina was not just a natural disaster. It was also a *man-made* disaster in at least
two ways. First, Katrina could wreak havoc because of a woefully inadequate
protective levee structure. This failure to protect the Crescent City has been
scrutinized and rightly so.

1

But it was also, and perhaps foremost, the *response* to the event that turned Katrina into a disaster. In the first days after landfall, local, state, and federal authorities seemed incapable of doing anything. Images of helpless victims and violent looters dominated the news. Mayhem and anarchy appeared to reign in New Orleans.

Public and political assessments quickly branded the response as a deep failure: government officials failed, the president failed, the Federal Emergency Management Agency (FEMA) failed, the system failed. One report found "a litany of mistakes, misjudgments, lapses, and absurdities all cascading together."[1] These dire assessments undermined the legitimacy of the nation's crisis response system. They also undermined the legitimacy of key institutions, ranging from local government agencies to the presidency of the United States. The response, today, is still considered so poor that "Katrina" has become shorthand for shameful government performance.

This is a powerful indictment, which we will carefully consider and dispute. For starters, we can say that this assessment does not take into account the many things that actually went well right before, during, and after Katrina. To be sure, the response to Katrina was not as good as one might have hoped or expected. Mistakes were made. Some actors failed; some failed miserably. But many things went remarkably well, especially given the circumstances.[2]

For instance, the pre-landfall evacuation of New Orleans and the surrounding areas was well organized and went smoothly. After the city flooded, a flotilla of heroic rescuers saved many lives. In addition to first responders (residents and local officials), personnel from all over the United States joined the search and rescue effort and provided medical assistance to the wounded and the displaced. Federal troops helped, as did churches, volunteer associations, and corporations. Within six days after landfall, the authorities had evacuated tens of thousands of survivors from the drowned city. The federal government sent an unprecedented amount of resources to Louisiana and other affected states in the first two weeks after landfall and earmarked a massive amount of funding to support the recovery of the stricken areas.

The indictment does not take into account the circumstances under which government agencies were asked to respond. This was the first time that government agencies faced the challenge of a major US city being almost completely flooded. There were no plans for this contingency, and there was very little experience to adequately guide public agencies in their crisis management efforts.

So if the management of this disaster is rated as woefully inadequate, as it has been, we must ask ourselves: How could things have worked better, realistically speaking? Here we encounter a rarely noticed but deeply important problem: we lack a clear and agreed-upon framework for assessing the response to a mega-disaster (or for any sort of crisis for that matter). It is striking to see how a range of official committees and investigative bodies have boldly passed judgments and prescribed remedies in the aftermath of the storm without such a framework. Fast assessments that serve political ends do little to enhance public trust in those systems and processes that should protect society from the impact of future disasters.

This book aims to offer a more balanced way to study and assess the response to a mega-disaster. Unlike other assessments, we make use of an explicit framework that guides our analysis of the response. We assess the quality of the response in terms of four performance indicators on which, we argue, citizens may expect high scores from their government before, during, and after a disaster. We refer here to the strategic tasks of crisis management—those tasks that research has shown enhance the quality of the crisis response.[3] These tasks make up our framework for assessment, which we outline later in this chapter. In this study, we identify the factors that affected the capacity of government organizations to fulfill these tasks. Each task will be discussed in a separate chapter.

This is a book on managing a mega-disaster. Hurricane Katrina was a unique event, a "black swan" event, which required a response developed more or less on the fly.[4] We seek to learn the lessons from this response—lessons that help governments at all levels to better prepare for the next mega-disaster. Before we lay out our analytical framework, let's first briefly recount what happened during that first week after landfall of Hurricane Katrina.

WHAT HAPPENED
New Orleans: The City That Care Forgot

The focus of this book is confined to New Orleans, though we recognize that it was by no means the only community affected by the storm. Areas of Mississippi, Alabama, and Florida also suffered tremendously. Nevertheless, New Orleans was the single largest metropolitan area affected by Katrina and saw the largest loss of life.

The city of New Orleans is coextensive with Orleans Parish and covers 118 square miles. The city is situated between the Mississippi River and Lake Pontchartrain in a low coastal plain, dipping to as much as 14 feet below sea level in places. Prior to Hurricane Katrina, the city was home to 454,000 residents, making it the nation's thirty-first-largest city. A total of 1,330,000 people resided in Greater New Orleans, a region encompassing eight parishes.

New Orleans has been called "the impossible but inevitable city"—inevitable to the extent that a city must exist near the mouth of the Mississippi River, impossible in light of the region's inhospitable climate and challenging geography. In order to make the area more comfortable and economically viable, residents have altered the landscape over the course of centuries.[5] Many of these interventions increased the vulnerability of the city and its inhabitants to forces of nature.[6]

Until the Louisiana Purchase transferred New Orleans into American hands, the city's Creole and African slave populations were confined to what today is the French Quarter, a small neighborhood on high ground near the banks of the Mississippi River. The arrival of additional residents during the 1800s prompted growth into low-lying areas protected by natural levees. Subsequent technological advances made possible the construction of artificial flood control measures, allowing the local population to move into low-lying areas that were more susceptible to flooding.

Over time, ethnic animosities and structural discrimination would lead to the division of the city into three self-governing "municipalities," namely the French Quarter, the American Faubourg St. Mary, and a third district that in later years would come to include the Ninth and Lower Ninth Wards.[7] This was where most of the city's African American population settled. According to geographer Peirce Lewis, "Drainage was bad, foundation material precarious, streets atrociously maintained, mosquitoes endemic, and flooding a recurrent hazard."[8]

During the Great Flood of 1927, when the Mississippi jumped its banks and flooded much of the lower Mississippi valley, a group of businessmen had area levees dynamited in order to protect their business interests, properties, and homes.[9] According to the New Orleans native and author Kalamu ya Salaam, "The white city fathers of New Orleans—the men of the Louisiana Club, the Boston Club, and the Pickwick Club—won permission from the federal government to dynamite the Caernarvon levee, downriver from the city, to keep their interests dry. But destroying the levee also insured that the surrounding poorer St. Bernard and Plaquemines Parishes would flood. Thousands of the trappers who lived there lost their homes and their livelihoods. The promise of compensation was never fulfilled."[10]

During Hurricane Betsy (1965), New Orleans mayor Victor Schiro was accused of ordering water to be pumped out of his well-to-do subdivision (Lake Vista) into the Ninth Ward. It was rumored that the mayor "cut the Industrial Canal to drown the colored people so that they would not vote in the coming election."[11] The 1965 flooding of low-lying neighborhoods was a lingering memory in the minds of many African American residents when Katrina flooded New Orleans.[12]

Following World War II, the geographic and social isolation of the city's African American population increased as white residents began moving to the city's expanding suburbs, which were made possible by improvements in water management technologies and federally funded transportation initiatives. New roads and bridges allowed the city to "explode into the swamp."[13] The exodus of white residents and a significant segment of the African American middle class continued over the decades to come.[14] They fled from corruption within local government and the police, one of the nation's highest violent crime rates, an anemic criminal justice system, poor public health services, and failing schools.[15]

In the years before Katrina, the local economy was underpinned by the shipbuilding, aerospace, and port industries. Many major oil companies had begun to retreat from the region, but the tourism industry was booming.[16] The medical services and telecommunications sectors were also expanding; New Orleans was striving to become one of the centers for advanced health care in the South.

Despite being an engine of the state's economy and a major tourist draw, New Orleans was not what we would call a resilient city. The city hosted only one Fortune 500 company and had a bleeding tax base as the local population continued to shrink (by as much as 2.5% on an annual basis in the years prior to Katrina dating back to the 1970s).[17] The city was wracked by heavy debt that crippled public services.

New Orleans was a predominantly poor and African American city with a large elderly population.[18] The overall poverty level was as high as 27.9%. More than a quarter of households did not have access to private transportation (an obvious limiting factor in the event of evacuation).[19] The city's public transit system was inadequate for the population.[20] Its nativity rate (the percentage of the population born in the city) was high. As much as 75% of the population had never journeyed beyond southeastern Louisiana. Many residents were thus neither willing nor able to evacuate.[21] New Orleans was arguably in a state of financial, social, and legal crisis long before Hurricane Katrina appeared on the horizon.

Enter Hurricane Katrina

Hurricane Katrina destroyed not only a major city but also a large area around it. Katrina first visited Florida, leaving a trail of devastation in the Sunshine State. After passing over Florida in the early hours of Friday, August 26, the hurricane swerved back into the Gulf, gaining renewed strength from the warm water. That afternoon, the National Hurricane Center forecast that the eye of Hurricane Katrina would pass just east of New Orleans on Monday, August 29.[22] This prediction, remarkably accurate in hindsight, gave federal, state, and local officials approximately 56 hours' advance notice. Over the weekend, Katrina would go on to develop into a Category 5 storm with the city of New Orleans squarely in its crosshairs.

Government officials at all levels prepared for the monster storm. Louisiana, Mississippi, and Alabama initiated unprecedented evacuations, successfully moving millions out of the storm's path. The states prepared their crisis headquarters, and the federal government pre-positioned large quantities of resources. It was the biggest response ever mounted in the face of a hurricane.

During the afternoon of Sunday, August 28, Katrina announced herself to residents of southeastern Louisiana with heavy rains. Katrina came ashore at 6:10 a.m. the following morning near Buras, Louisiana (an unincorporated community in Plaquemines Parish) as a Category 3 hurricane.[23] The South had certainly seen stronger hurricanes than Katrina.[24]

The damage caused in Alabama, Mississippi, and southern Louisiana was staggering. The 115–130 mph winds created a storm surge as high as 27 feet from Mobile, Alabama, to New Orleans, impacting nearly 93,000 square miles—an area roughly the size of Great Britain.[25] Storm surge flooded over six miles inland in many parts of coastal Mississippi and up to twelve miles inland along rivers and bays.[26] Entire coastal communities were obliterated. In St. Bernard Parish, a few miles east of downtown New Orleans, only four houses avoided catastrophic damage.[27] Dauphin Island, near Mobile, was nearly wiped out. Hurricane-force winds and tornadoes reached Jackson, Mississippi, and that state's northernmost counties, transforming 28,000 square miles—or 60% of the state—into a disaster area. After surveying the region from the air, Mississippi governor Haley Barbour likened the scene to a nuclear detonation, stating, "I can only imagine that this is what Hiroshima looked like sixty years ago."[28]

On Monday, August 29, the nation's attention was initially focused on Mississippi and Alabama. Along with the rest of the country, many officials in Louisiana thought that the Crescent City had dodged the proverbial bullet. But in the early morning, a number of levees had in fact been breached. Unbeknownst to all but a few, the city of New Orleans was beginning to fill with water.

New Orleans has always been vulnerable to flooding, as the city is surrounded by water and most of it is below sea level. The federal levees and floodwalls in place before Katrina were designed so that individual breaches would not lead to catastrophic flooding. The compartmentalized design, with four main basins, was intended to minimize the threat of flooding to the entire system. The city had 22 pumping stations in place. Had only one basin experienced a breach, it would have been possible to avoid the catastrophic flooding New Orleans subsequently experienced.[29] Unfortunately, the city experienced multiple breaches in the wake of Katrina (see map).

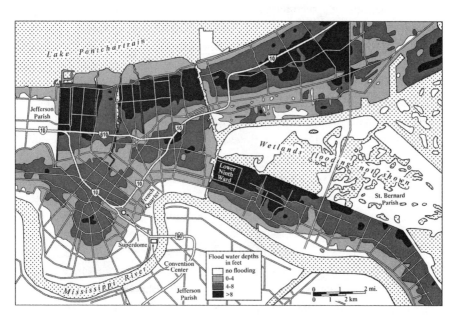

Levels of flooding in New Orleans. Map by Mary Lee Eggart, based on map by C&C Technologies Survey Services (originally published on nola.com; http://media.nola.com/hurricane_impact/photo/graphic-katrina-flooding-1jpg-b37680dbc82e6ffb.jpg).

Many people had not evacuated. An estimated 100,000 residents—including intensive-care patients, nursing home residents, and visitors—still remained in New Orleans when Katrina made landfall. In low-lying neighborhoods such as the Lower Ninth Ward, houses were completely inundated by floodwaters, forcing remaining residents into attics and onto roofs. Within 24 hours, nearly 80% of the city was flooded with between 6 and 20 feet of water.[30]

The Final Toll

The human cost of the tragedy was immense—estimates vary from 1,200 to 1,800 people losing their lives in the storm and its aftermath.[31] Katrina left one million people without power or drinking water.[32] The region's health care infrastructure sustained extraordinary damage.[33] Katrina destroyed or made uninhabitable an estimated 300,000 homes.[34] In addition, the storm caused an environmental nightmare that would take years to fully recover from.

Hurricane Katrina became America's most expensive disaster—natural or man-made, causing $108 billion in damage.[35] The overall destruction wrought by the storm vastly exceeded that of other major disasters in the nation's history, including the Chicago fire of 1871, the San Francisco earthquake and fire of 1906, and Hurricane Andrew in 1992.[36]

Government officials mounted a massive response effort. In the first week after landfall, government agencies saved many lives, fed survivors, brought in thousands of uniformed officers, and organized a large-scale evacuation that emptied the city of all but a few thousand holdouts. Around 770,000 people were displaced—the largest figure since the Dust Bowl migration during the 1930s.[37] Officials around the country faced the challenge of housing hundreds of thousands of homeless New Orleanians.

UNPACKING FAILURE

When President George W. Bush visited New Orleans on September 15, 2005, speaking on Jackson Square, he acknowledged that "the system, at every level of government, was not well-coordinated, and was overwhelmed in the first few days."[38] To many observers this seemed an understatement. The president was battling broad consensus that the immediate response to Katrina had been far below expectations. Over a decade after the disaster, the response is still considered shameful and unbefitting of the United States.

Focusing on New Orleans alone, an iconic set of failures has come to define the response in the collective memory of many Americans. Let's briefly revisit some of the most memorable of these.

Suffering in New Orleans

Located near the French Quarter, where the media had set up camp, the Superdome was the Crescent City's designated shelter of last resort. It was not intended or designed as a long-term shelter but could serve as a safe place to ride out the storm. It was never advertised as anything else but a last resort. By Sunday evening, 10,000 people had made it to the Dome.[39] Many more would find their way to the Superdome after the city flooded. Various reports suggest that around 25,000 people spent at least a few days in the Superdome.

In the many media stories about suffering survivors, the Superdome featured prominently. To be sure, Mayor Nagin and Governor Blanco had emphasized in their public messaging just how uncomfortable the Superdome would be and that residents would be better off leaving the city.[40] But many people did not want to leave, preferring the comfort of home or a hotel room. Others who had no other option began lining up outside the Superdome on Sunday. They ended up staying at the Dome far longer than anticipated.

The Superdome soon became a very unpleasant place. On Sunday, a reporter for the *New York Times* spoke with foreign tourists stranded in the Dome who were appalled by the situation.[41] It would get worse. The power went out early Monday morning. Later that morning, winds blew part of the roof off, and rain soaked the field of the Dome. It was hot, and the sanitation soon became nasty. Portable toilets were in short supply. Thousands of people had to go without working plumbing for nearly a week.[42]

Later in the week, media reports would describe the situation at the Superdome as anarchic. Many reports gave the impression that there were no law enforcement officials in or around the Superdome. This is not true: the New Orleans Police Department and Louisiana National Guardsmen were on duty around the clock in and around the facility.[43] The Superdome was much safer than the media suggested.[44] Moreover, there was never a shortage of food and water; simple meals were distributed twice a day.[45]

The Superdome was not the only place where survivors waited to be evacuated from the drowning city. Thousands of survivors were stranded on the main interstate (I-10) running through New Orleans, suffering from the heat, an acute shortage of supplies, and with nowhere to go. Television viewers across the world watched in disbelief as large groups of mostly black people sat around in the heat for days, lacking access to potable water and working toilets. What viewers did not know was that the unfortunate situation on I-10 was the unintended result of a very successful search and rescue operation that had been ongoing since immediately after landfall.[46] When boats and helicopters dropped survivors off at the high points in the city (including the overpasses over I-10), there was no organization in place there to move them to a more hospitable environment. As a result, many were forced to remain there for hours or even days.[47] The Senate report described how the process *should* have worked: "In particular, during Hurricane Katrina, a 'lily-pad' type of search-and-rescue operation was implemented. By using this methodology, victims were rescued and transported to a safe area on high ground. The idea was that from there another group would transport them to a Temporary Medical Operations Staging Area (TMOSA). There, the rescued would undergo a medical-triage screening process to determine individuals' medical-care needs."[48]

A few blocks away from the Superdome, thousands of people awaited evacuation at the Convention Center.[49] Situated in the downtown area near the river, the Convention Center was not formally predesignated as a shelter (as the Superdome was).[50] Nevertheless, people began to congregate there either late Monday or sometime Tuesday.[51] The emerging situation at the Convention Center caught state and federal officials by surprise, even though the media were set up right around the corner and soon began to broadcast from the area.[52] There was no electricity, water, or food. Except for the ill or injured, no one was evacuated from the overcrowded Convention Center until Saturday, September 3.[53]

Many survivors were scared. Rumors of crime were rampant. The media reported anomie. Initial reports suggested that 100–200 people had died at the Superdome.[54] The local *Times-Picayune* reported that National Guard troops found 30 to 40 decomposing bodies piled in a freezer at the Convention Center.[55] As we will see in chapter 5, many media reports were inaccurate at best and provocative at worst. The Louisiana National Guard would later state that "the vast majority of the sheltered evacuees were good people who were trapped in a bad situation."[56]

A very serious situation did emerge on Thursday when some 200 people who had grown tired of waiting for evacuation from New Orleans attempted to cross the bridge over the Mississippi leading into the town of Gretna. Threatening force, the Gretna police closed off the bridge and turned them back.[57] The mayor of Gretna, Ronnie Harris, later explained that local police had acted on rumors about the situation in New Orleans: "We were going to protect the lives of our residents. It's impossible to know what happened unless you were here. At the time, you don't know what to believe, but you don't want to be in a place to find out if what you heard is true."[58]

Those who were just trying to get away from the mayhem were understandably shocked and dismayed by the reception of their neighbors across the river. As one witness recounted: "The only two explanations we ever received was, one, 'We're not going to have any Superdomes over here,' and 'This is not New Orleans.' To me, that was code language or code words for 'We're not having black people coming into our neighborhood.'"[59] The Gretna incident points to the racial dimensions of the Katrina crisis (which we will return to later).

How Hard Can It Be? Waiting for the Buses

To many Americans, one of the most baffling failures witnessed in the days after landfall was the authorities' apparent inability to evacuate those stuck in the submerged city. Even if they took into account (and few actually did) that it is not an easy task to move 25,000 people out of an inundated city, many found it hard to understand why the evacuation took so long to organize.

It was not for a lack of trying. When Governor Blanco visited the Superdome on Tuesday, she realized that the stadium needed to be cleared "as soon as possible."[60] FEMA director Michael Brown agreed. By all accounts, the operation was set in motion immediately, albeit haltingly. By Wednesday night, the first convoy of buses entered New Orleans, but they were filled before they could reach the Dome.[61] It was not until midday on Thursday that the evacuation of central New Orleans began in earnest.[62] Over the course of the response, the US Department of Transportation delivered a total of 1,100 buses to the region.[63] Many of these were used to evacuate the Superdome, which was empty by Friday. The Convention Center was evacuated the following day.

The Plight of Patients

The major hospitals in New Orleans did not evacuate, following common practice. Many privately owned nursing homes opted not to evacuate either.[64] Some would later blame Mayor Nagin for not explicitly ordering them to evacuate. But Louisiana hospitals and nursing homes were responsible for having and implementing their own emergency evacuation plans. Evacuation was not a requirement.

Most of the hospitals in the area pursued a "shelter in place" strategy ahead of Katrina.[65] The costs associated with evacuating a hospital are astronomical and, in the case of for-profit hospitals, were not reimbursable by either the state or FEMA.[66] More importantly, it was considered too dangerous to hastily move patients from one location to another.[67] Moreover, hospital facilities with their thick walls and backup generators were comparatively safe places in which to ride out a hurricane. In fact, hospital staff had made it a habit of bringing their families to the hospitals during hurricanes. A similar tradition existed among nursing home personnel.

In the case of Katrina, the decision to stay put would have terrible consequences. In all too many cases, emergency power generators situated at ground level were flooded. Without power, hospitals and nursing homes quickly became dark, damp hothouses without access to life-sustaining medical equipment.[68] Flooding forced personnel to hurriedly evacuate patients upward into the facilities (oftentimes in the dark by stairs once the power failed). Residents at single-story nursing homes were placed on mattresses that their caretakers hoped would remain afloat.[69] Douglas Brinkley describes the situation at one particularly ill-fated facility, Memorial Hospital: "The staff at Memorial Medical Center, which was surrounded by six feet of water, couldn't properly care for its 260 patients. When people swam or paddled to the hospital seeking help, they were turned away. Memorial was in fact trying to evacuate its own patients, even though, as CEO Rene Goux would later write, 'there was no sign of any organized rescue effort, just these people who came out of nowhere.' Remarkably, no government agency made any effort to canvass the hospitals or coordinate an evacuation effort."[70]

It has been alleged that a number of patients at Memorial Hospital were euthanized by staff apparently believing they were too ill to survive the evacuation.[71] Chaos reigned in many other hospitals as well.[72] At St. Rita's nursing home, thirty-five patients died.[73]

Anarchy in the City

There is a long-standing adage in the disaster literature that looting rarely occurs in the immediate aftermath of a disaster. Reports of looting and violence usually prove incorrect.[74]

In New Orleans, there was looting. According to Brinkley, it was more than looting—he called it malicious vandalizing.[75] But the media exaggerated the amount of looting and spiced their stories with suggestions of violence. Most of the looting took place downtown along Canal Street, which was in full view of the media.[76] Instances of looting and violence were breathlessly reported. The resulting perception was that New Orleans suffered from a collective sense of insecurity if not outright anarchy during that first week of the disaster.

And then there were the rumors. New Orleans police officers were looting a Cadillac dealership. Women were raped and people were randomly attacked. There was shooting everywhere, and in some instances it was even directed at rescue helicopters overhead. An NBC crew was intimidated by gang members. Babies were being raped in the Superdome. Thugs ruled the Convention Center.[77]

All these rumors turned out to be false.

The perception of anarchy in New Orleans had real consequences, however. The media reports scared first responders and survivors, who then sought protection from the violence. Citizens armed themselves. Helicopters were grounded and buses were delayed. The militarized approach of federal responders, in turn, alienated victims who had been waiting a long time for help.

Looking Back at Failure

The stories about perceived failures described above are still repeated—in detail or offhandedly—in academic, popular, and governmental discourse. Katrina has become a byword for shameful failure. But a more complex view emerges with the advantage of hindsight. When we take into account the challenges posed by Katrina for citizens and government alike, a different and more informed picture of the response emerges. We see that, in fact, a great deal was accomplished in the first 48–72 hours after Katrina made landfall.

That is, of course, a very long time if you are waiting for a bus and you are tired, sick, thirsty, hot, scared, and scarred by the experience of disaster. The question is whether the response could have been much better. Taking into account the circumstances, as we will do in this book, leads to a more measured assessment. When we consider what needs to be done and what is actually possible in a mega-disaster, we can see that there were also success stories.

SUCCESS STORIES

Not everything went badly after Hurricane Katrina. In fact, some things went remarkably well. One would never know it from the relentless media reporting, but the response network did chalk up some major accomplishments.

We single out two of these accomplishments here to make the point. First, the evacuation of New Orleans prior to landfall was a real and in our view underappreciated success. The evacuation of a large city is very hard and rarely done.[78] The timely evacuation of New Orleans likely prevented a disaster of biblical proportions (the Hurricane Pam scenario, which we will discuss in chapter 2, predicted over 50,000 deaths for a Katrina-like disaster). Second, the search and rescue operation that was launched immediately after the storm had passed was much more effective than commonly assumed and saved many lives. Both state and federal organizations performed outstandingly, as did the many volunteers who assisted.

Evacuating New Orleans: A Triumph of Learning and Planning

In the face of a hurricane, there are essentially two options for people living in its path: shelter in place or move out of its trajectory. Given the vulnerable position of New Orleans, disaster management professionals in federal government as well as the Red Cross considered evacuation the safest and most logical precautionary response.[79] In line with this consensus, city authorities had opted not to organize many evacuation centers. They did not want to encourage sheltering in place.

If evacuating a large city is hard, evacuating one surrounded by water is even harder. Indeed, officials have long struggled to evacuate New Orleans and surrounding communities. When Hurricane Georges (1998) threatened New Orleans, the evacuation wrought chaos on the roads, in large part because no plan existed to help authorities.[80] The poorly executed evacuation turned "roadways [into] virtual parking lots as traffic snaked and stalled from New Orleans to Baton Rouge."[81] After Georges, officials resolved to develop a regional evacuation plan.[82] Nevertheless, the kinks had yet to be worked out in 2004, when Hurricane Ivan prompted yet another chaotic evacuation.[83]

After Ivan, Governor Blanco ordered the Louisiana State Police, the Louisiana Department of Transportation and Development (DOTD) and the Louisiana Office of Homeland Security and Emergency Preparedness (LOHSEP) to revise the state's evacuation plan in order to guarantee that this did not happen again.[84] The Southeast Louisiana Hurricane Evacuation and Sheltering Plan that the agencies developed was still a work in progress, as the evacuation for Hurricane Dennis (a good month before Katrina) demonstrated. Many residents vowed to stay home the next time a hurricane came around.[85]

Yet the majority of New Orleans residents were evacuated before Katrina made landfall. Governor Blanco later estimated that 1.2 million people, 92% of the affected population, left the area prior to landfall.[86] In fact, it was one of the largest emergency evacuations in history.[87] One senior LOHSEP official later proudly explained: "We estimate that over 1 million people, or approximately 90% of the affected parishes' populations, evacuate[d] in about a 40-hour period. I don't know of any other evacuation that has occurred with that many people under these circumstances with that high of percentage of people being evacuated in that short of a time period."[88]

The evacuation was carefully planned. On Saturday, two days before landfall, the Louisiana State Police superintendent, Colonel Henry Whitehorn, and the DOTD secretary, Johnny Bradberry, recommended to Governor Blanco that she implement the state's contraflow plan, which would reverse the flow of traffic on inbound lanes to facilitate the evacuation of the New Orleans metropolitan area. She then notified Governor Haley Barbour in neighboring Mississippi to expect thousands of guests from Louisiana in the hours to come.[89] By all accounts, the contraflow scheme coordinated with authorities in Mississippi worked very well.[90]

After the disaster, Mayor Nagin of New Orleans was blamed for the high number of drowned New Orleanians. It was asserted that the evacuation of the city had started too late. More importantly, Mayor Nagin was accused of being late in issuing a *mandatory* evacuation order. In its long hurricane history, New Orleans had never issued such an order. Mayor Nagin issued one on Sunday.[91]

The question is whether it mattered: a mandatory evacuation order does not mean much without the means to enforce it. City officials were powerless against citizens who chose to disregard the order by remaining in their homes.[92] Moreover, many people in New Orleans did not own a television, so they did not learn about the order until it was too late.[93] Many simply did not want to leave.[94] Others did not have the means to evacuate. Leaving town, even for a few short days, is an expensive proposition, and Social Security and welfare checks would not be sent out until August 31. Poor and elderly people living from month to month could not be expected to leave without adequate funds.[95] Many of those who might have wanted to leave could not because they had no car. Some of the poorest areas of New Orleans (such as the Lower Ninth Ward) were not well served by public transportation.[96]

Search and Rescue: Improvisation, Emergent Collaboration, and Heroism

When New Orleans and the surrounding areas flooded, thousands of people were stranded in their homes. With the water rapidly rising, many were forced upwards into attics and onto roofs. Hundreds drowned, but many more were saved—by both fellow residents and uniformed personnel.

The rescue operation was immediate, massive, and effective. Federal, state, and local agencies rescued approximately 60,000 people (most but not all from New Orleans). US Coast Guard missions alone accounted for 33,000 rescues.[97] The Louisiana Department of Wildlife and Fisheries (LDWF), with the assistance of out-of-state agencies, accounted for an additional 21,000 rescues. Their performance "stand[s] out as a singular success story of the hurricane response."[98]

Thousands more were rescued by fellow citizens. An improvised network of citizens started rescue operations immediately. Some people had stayed behind to help and started search and rescue with their boats.[99] The "NOLA Homeboys" and the "Cajun Navy" were colorful examples of highly effective self-organization.[100] Drawing on deeply anchored family structures (common to Louisiana), they organized in a remarkably efficient way.[101]

There were other notable performances that received little attention, then or later, apart from local recognition and the occasional byline in a report. Consider the following cases:

LSU becomes a center for medical assistance. The chancellor of Louisiana State University, Sean O'Keefe, did not hesitate when he learned how badly New Orleans had been hit. He made available LSU's Pete Maravich Assembly Center in Baton Rouge for medical triage; helicopters landed on the nearby athletic fields, and wounded were brought into the center, where volunteers were waiting. Dorm rooms were provided to FEMA personnel and other responders.[102] "With a capacity of 800 beds to provide medical care, the TMOSA at the LSU campus in Baton Rouge was the largest temporary emergency facility ever built," according to Dr. Jimmy Guidry, medical director for the Louisiana Department of Health and Hospitals.[103]

States helping each other. The states worked together under the Emergency Management Assistance Compact, a critical part of the national emergency management framework. The compact provided a quick and effective process that moved significant resources into the region after landfall. Some 68,000 personnel (19,481 civilians and 48,477 members of the National Guard) were deployed to Louisiana and Mississippi.[104] Texas opened the Reliant Dome in Houston, where it hosted thousands of exhausted evacuees from the New Orleans Superdome.[105]

Corporations to the rescue. Many large corporations played a positive role in the response.[106] Walmart provided a particularly noteworthy story. Often reviled in media stories, Walmart made available critical goods and used its logistics expertise to bring these goods to stricken areas.[107] Home Depot donated money and materials such as tarps, bottled water, and flashlights for the emergency response. IBM and Lenovo donated computers, while Coca-Cola and American Airlines helped out in other ways.[108]

There were more success stories. For instance, there was the frantic effort to save the animals in New Orleans's famous Audubon Zoo.[109] There were the medical heroes who "met with overwhelming demand for patient assessment and treatment, operating under extreme fatigue with limited medical supplies, inadequate amounts of food and water, intermittent electricity, and no air-conditioning."[110] There were the people of Acadian Ambulance Service, who kept the ambulances running. There were the many faith-based, nonprofit, and volunteer organizations, which mobilized quickly and continued to provide essential support to Katrina victims long after landfall.[111] When we read about Katrina, it is hard not to be struck by the many examples of heroic, improvised, and sadly unnoticed success stories.

STUDYING A MEGA-DISASTER:
HOW TO ASSESS SUCCESS AND FAILURE

We have recounted well-remembered response failures and pointed to some clear if less-well-known successes. It is critical that we understand exactly what failed and why. It is also important to identify what did work and how lessons can be learned from these performances.

In describing the failures, we hint at exculpatory explanations: we mention the immense and unsuspected scale of the disaster, we note the general willingness of officials to do good and do well, and we suggest that their overall performance was not so bad in light of the limited time between the realization that New Orleans had flooded and the complete evacuation of the surviving population. In describing the successes, we also touch upon inadequacies and inefficiencies. If the boundaries of the success and failure categories appear blurry at times, it is because they are.

This prompts a set of questions: How can we fairly assess the performance of a cobbled-together response network that must perform under dire if not nearly impossible conditions? If government failed massively, as the critics assert, how can we account for the successes? If government agencies performed well in carrying out some tasks (as we have suggested), why did they fail at other tasks for which they had more time and resources?

The assessment of crisis and disaster management is a subjective affair.[112] One reason is that we often do not have all the information needed to pass judgment. Another reason is that we do not have a thorough understanding of the causal relations between actions and outcomes. What, exactly, did New York mayor Rudy Giuliani do in the aftermath of the 9/11 attacks that made him a celebrated crisis manager? And why was President Bush's crisis management after 9/11 assessed in a much more favorable light than his efforts in response to Katrina? Why was the British response to the London bombing attacks (2005) widely viewed as exemplary? Was the French reaction to the Paris shootings (November 2015) exemplary, insufficient, or perhaps over the top?

To answer these questions, we need what we don't have: a widely shared normative framework that specifies what we may expect from our leaders in times of crisis. When elections roll around, there is lots of discussion about visions of governance, society, and the role of leadership. But society rarely discusses expectations of crisis leadership until after a crisis. At that stage, the negative outcome of the crisis is often equated with bad leadership (even though we do not have an evidence-based theory that connects leadership actions with outcomes).

Our approach in this book combines a set of clearly explicated expectations of government performance with a keen understanding of the "impossible" constraints that crises and disasters tend to impose on such performance. We offer, in other words, a theory of crisis management that relates expectations to performance while taking account of conditions.

Our theory of crisis leadership is based on years of crisis research.[113] Building on empirical findings, this theory proposes that if government leaders engage in a selected set of crisis management tasks, they will initiate a response that is likely to minimize the effects of a large-scale crisis or disaster. These strategic tasks are as follows:

- *Detection and preparation:* Working together to prepare for known and unknown threats; organizing to detect and act upon credible signals of emerging threats.

- *Sense making:* Organizing to collect, interpret, and disseminate critical information that enables a shared understanding of an unfolding crisis.

- *Coordination and critical decision-making:* Identifying critical decisions that must be made at the strategic level; enabling vertical and horizontal collaboration between all parties of the response network to save lives and limit the damage.

- *Meaning making:* Formulating and communicating a convincing and enabling narrative that explains what has happened and what is being done to minimize the consequences of the crisis.

An assessment of government performance during crisis must take account of the circumstances in which strategic crisis management plays out. We must consider what is actually possible in the case of a superdisaster.

In a superdisaster such as Katrina, there are clear limits to what crisis management can achieve. A superdisaster not only creates huge challenges; it also renders many coping capacities useless. Most disasters happen in vulnerable places, where we find weak institutions and less affluent populations.[114] All this was true in the case of Katrina: the floods destroyed pre-positioned goods and hit one of the most underprivileged regions of the United States.

We therefore define successful crisis management in terms of doing the best that can be expected given the circumstances. Viewed from this perspective, *a successful crisis response is one where government writ large makes an honest attempt to fulfill various strategic tasks in a timely and legitimate manner.*

We can now formulate explicit expectations with regard to the joint performance of local, state, and federal government organizations before and during Hurricane Katrina. Given what was known (or could realistically have been known) before the disaster and given the immediate impact of the superdisaster, we formulate the following expectations with regard to the strategic tasks outlined above:

- *Detection and preparation:* Governments at all levels must take the threat seriously and act as best they can to prepare and protect the population. *Our finding: Government agencies did take Katrina seriously and prepared as well as could be reasonably expected.*

- *Sense making:* Governments at all levels should cooperate to share and analyze information; they should share their emerging picture(s) of the situation. *Our finding:* Apart from a few isolated successes, *the authorities lacked a system or set of procedures that might have enabled them to put all available information together in an accurate and timely fashion.*

- *Coordination and decision-making:* Governments at all levels should work together to ensure that critical tasks are being performed by those who are best placed to perform them (and that decisions are made at the appropriate levels). *Our finding: The federal disaster structure proved very complex and was not geared toward managing a catastrophic event like Katrina.*

- *Meaning making:* Governments at all levels should cooperate to formulate and communicate a shared frame to survivors and the general public. *Our finding: The politics of crisis management played out in a vicious and dysfunctional way, undermining and reversing the positive dynamics that marked the initial phase of this disaster.*

We will devote a chapter to each task outlined above. We will delve into the empirics, establish what went right and what went wrong (in accordance with the framework described above), and identify the factors that explain success and failure. In the final chapter, we discuss what these findings imply for the management of mega-disasters everywhere.

2

WHY DIDN'T THEY SEE IT COMING?

THE CHALLENGES OF TIMELY CRISIS RECOGNITION

My gut hurts on this one.

—FEMA DIRECTOR MICHAEL BROWN

SURPRISE!

On Wednesday, August 31, America woke up to a superdisaster. The message that initially dominated the national news held that New Orleans had "dodged a bullet." For instance, the *Washington Post* reported on Tuesday morning: "Some experts predicted the storm could become one of the worst catastrophes in U.S. history. But the city managed to avoid the worst of the worst. The Mississippi River did not breach New Orleans's famed levees to any serious degree, at least in part because Katrina veered 15 miles eastward of its predicted track just before landfall. 'We believe we were spared,' said Jacquie Bauer, a spokesman for Jefferson Parish, La., which lies next to New Orleans."[1]

It slowly became clear later the same day that no bullet had been dodged. ABC News opened its Tuesday evening broadcast by reporting, "Last night we began this broadcast saying Katrina was bad, very bad. Last night, we didn't know the half of it. . . . In New Orleans we have a major American city under water. New Orleans thought it had been spared the worst."[2]

The *New York Times* asserted on Wednesday that "the scope of the catastrophe caught New Orleans by surprise."[3] In truth, the entire nation had been caught by surprise. But that's not the way most people remember it.

According to members of the US House of Representatives, "Perhaps the single most important question the Select Committee has struggled to answer is why the federal response did not adequately anticipate the consequences of Katrina striking New Orleans."[4] Or as Chairman Tom Davis stated during a Select Committee hearing in December 2005, "That's probably the most painful thing about Katrina, and the tragic loss of life: the foreseeability of it all."[5] The House committee's final report flatly states that "this crisis was not only predictable, it was predicted [and the] government failed because it did not learn from past experiences."[6]

Most crises and disasters may appear predictable in hindsight, but actually foreseeing superdisasters like Katrina is in fact very difficult.[7] It is fairly easy to offer general predictions ("San Francisco is due for a big earthquake"), but it is quite something else to foretell when and how a disaster will happen.

Some types of threats—the *known* risks—can and should be expected. Known risks are threats that materialize with some sort of regularity and play out in more or less similar ways. Examples include river floods, earthquakes, epidemics, financial crises, and hurricanes. While these may occur regularly, it is still difficult to predict exactly when and where they will occur. So while we may know that hurricanes are a likely occurrence during the summer months, we have no idea which state or states (if any) will be affected in any given summer or exactly when.

But there is a different category—the *unknown* risks—that defies this type of forecasting. They are unique events for which no statistical base rate exists. Examples of unknown risks include the outbreak of mad cow disease, the 9/11 attacks, the Iceland ash cloud event, and the Fukushima disaster. Not only is it nearly impossible to predict these types of events, because they occur so rarely (or may never have occurred at all), it is also very hard to adequately *plan* for unique events.[8] Hurricane Katrina produced such a unique event: the flooding of New Orleans.

If prediction is impossible, the best we can hope for is *timely detection* of the threat: authorities recognizing that something potentially dangerous and out of the ordinary is unfolding. But early recognition turns out to be difficult as well. People are not well equipped to make sense of uncertainties; they tend to make use of mental shortcuts ("heuristics" in the parlance of psychologists) that are not very effective when it comes to sniffing out unfamiliar threats. They do much better when it comes to known threats.[9]

We might expect organizations to compensate for the cognitive limitations of their employees. Unfortunately, that is not what typically happens.[10] It turns out that organizations fail often and easily in collecting, recognizing, and puzzling together pieces of information that in hindsight turn out to be critical. The research identifies many factors that help to explain this pattern (institutionalized mind-sets, organizational cultures, limited capacities), but the upshot is that organizations are not very good at detecting the unimaginable. Organizations may become well versed at collecting and analyzing the information that has been shown to detect crises in the past; they don't know how to recognize the signals of impending anomalies.

This means that the recognition of an unknown crisis is not a fair evaluation standard for organizational performance. If we cannot demand the impossible (predicting a disaster), and if we take seriously the research lessons that point out how hard it is to detect a "black swan," the following question emerges: *What can we reasonably expect from government agencies operating in the domain of crisis and disaster management if a disaster cannot be accurately predicted and a "black swan" is hard to recognize in time?*

We propose three fair expectations to help us assess how well government organizations handled the preresponse phase ahead of Katrina; we offer these expectations in terms of evaluative questions:

- Did authorities willfully ignore clear and unambiguous signals of an impending disaster?

- Did they take adequate preparatory measures in light of what could reasonably have been foreseen or expected?

- Did they warn people in a timely fashion and try to move them out of harm's way?

The remainder of this chapter is structured around these questions. We examine and weigh the empirical evidence and conclude with an overall assessment of the nation's preparation for Katrina.

*   *   *

DID AUTHORITIES WILLFULLY IGNORE CLEAR AND
UNAMBIGUOUS SIGNALS OF AN IMPENDING DISASTER?

After Katrina, a pervasive story line depicted how local, state, and federal authorities had ignored clear signals that a storm like Katrina would produce a superdisaster for New Orleans. There were indeed plenty of warnings that it could happen. In the years preceding Katrina, *Popular Mechanics, Scientific American, Civil Engineering* magazine, the *Natural Hazards Observer,* the *American Prospect,* and the *Philadelphia Enquirer* highlighted the city's vulnerability to hurricanes, some in more sensationalistic terms than others. Sample headlines included "New Orleans is sinking" and "New Orleans faces doomsday scenario."[11]

The unfortunate confluence of the city's unique physical and social vulnerabilities has always made the possibility of catastrophe real. Hurricane Betsy (1965), in the words of Louisiana senator Russell Long, "picked up [Lake Pontchartrain] . . . and put it inside New Orleans and Jefferson Parish," prompting widespread flooding.[12] Four years later, Hurricane Camille, a Category 5 storm, barely missed New Orleans and flattened large swathes of coastal Mississippi. In 1992, Hurricane Andrew made landfall in Louisiana as a Category 3 storm, barely missing the city of New Orleans.[13]

In 2000, the director of Louisiana's emergency preparedness agency penned a 22-page letter to then-FEMA director James Lee Witt requesting funds for a catastrophic hurricane exercise. Louisiana, he argued, was in no position to respond to a major storm, and the federal government seemed unprepared to provide for the needs that state officials envisioned.[14] In August 2001, FEMA compiled a list of the three most likely catastrophic events in the United States, one of which was a hurricane hitting New Orleans. FEMA foresaw that as many as 250,000 residents would be stranded and that another 25,000 would be killed.[15] Soon after, FEMA director Joe Allbaugh ordered FEMA planners to assist Louisiana in developing a regional catastrophic hurricane response plan.[16]

In November 2003, LSU researchers found that approximately one-third of New Orleans residents would be unable or unwilling to evacuate ahead of a major hurricane. Limited access to personal or public transportation and congestion on major evacuation routes were cited as primary determining factors.[17]

The following year, a study by University of New Orleans researchers predicted that even a moderate hurricane would devastate the city.[18] LSU researcher Ivor Van Heerden predicted thousands and thousands of casualties in the case of a hurricane strike.[19] A *USA Today* story warned in 2004 of "a modern

Atlantis."[20] The *Picayune*'s Pulitzer Prize–winning series of articles "Washing Away" sketched a relation between coastal erosion and the increased vulnerability of urban centers to hurricanes.[21] On cable television, a docudrama broadcast in early 2005 depicted the aftermath of a hurricane strike on New Orleans. It wasn't a pretty sight.[22]

Upon returning from a tour of tsunami-affected areas of Indonesia in early 2005, the new FEMA director, Michael Brown, reportedly ordered planners to prepare for a large-scale disaster in the United States. According to one official, "New Orleans was the number one disaster we were talking about. We were obsessed with New Orleans because of the risk."[23]

After Katrina, many reports brought out the smoking gun: Hurricane Pam.[24]

Hurricane Pam

Hurricane Pam never happened. A Category 3 storm, Pam was the centerpiece of a fictitious disaster scenario designed by nationally recognized disaster management consultancy IEM, then based in Baton Rouge. In the summer of 2004, local and state authorities in Louisiana worked with FEMA to explore the consequences of the scenario. The aim was to assess and improve the state of preparedness for a hurricane strike.

The exercise was the culmination of significant efforts on the part of state and federal officials to develop an overarching catastrophic hurricane plan for southeastern Louisiana. According to a joint statement issued by FEMA and Louisiana officials at the time, "The gravity of the situation [in New Orleans] calls for an extraordinary level of advance planning to improve government readiness to respond effectively to such an event."[25] The participants used Pam to create a workable regional plan, what came to be known as the Southeast Louisiana Catastrophic Hurricane Plan.[26]

The Pam scenario bore some resemblance to Katrina. Pam was a big hurricane, just like Katrina. It even followed the same path. So when it became known after Katrina that officials had worked on a similar scenario, the reactions were understandably incredulous. How could the authorities not have been more prepared? Critics charged that public authorities, especially FEMA, had not learned from—or did not act on the lessons learned from—the Pam exercise.

That's too simple, however.

First of all, Pam was not a simulation but a planning exercise. This is more than a semantic difference. Officials typically use interactive disaster simulations to practice decision-making, cooperation, and coordination under stress. A simulation helps them test their plans, skills, and capacities. However, that was not the purpose that Hurricane Pam was intended to serve. There was no plan that officials wanted to test. They did not "practice." Rather, they were trying to *develop* a set of plans. The consensus at the time was that "existing plans, policies, procedures and resources" were inadequate to effectively manage a mega-disaster as depicted in the scenario.[27] The Pam exercise aimed to help officials address the deficit.[28]

The exercise was intended to explore the types of issues that might emerge during a hurricane.[29] Pam was "designed to be the first step toward producing a comprehensive hurricane response plan . . . to provide general guidance, a sort of 'to do list' for state and localities."[30] Many actors worked for days on the scenario, thinking through their aims and what they would need in order to achieve them. The participants focused on issues ranging from search and rescue and temporary sheltering to dewatering, debris removal, and medical care. These issues were then compared to existing plans with an eye to identifying weaknesses and strengths.

Second, Hurricane Pam *as a disaster* was in some ways very different from Hurricane Katrina. In fact, the Pam scenario was considered a bit unrealistic at the time.[31] Hurricane Pam did not breach any levees; there were only the usual overtoppings.[32] Yet the scenario envisioned approximately 175,000 people injured, 200,000 falling ill, and more than 60,000 killed.[33] It is hard to see how such a scenario in real life could possibly result in the envisioned number of casualties.

Furthermore, some issues highly relevant during Katrina were not covered at all. For instance, the scenario did not address law and order or breakdowns in communications.[34] The CEO of IEM later explained that while these issues were slated to be addressed during the exercise, the development of a plan to coordinate the displacement of schoolchildren took precedence.[35]

Third, many lessons *were* learned. Although the participants may have failed to generate a comprehensive, integrated, and actionable plan in time for Hurricane Katrina, the various workshops that were held during the exercise yielded concrete outcomes. Numerous action plans ranging from debris removal to sheltering to search and rescue were developed. State transportation officials took the lessons learned from the Pam exercise and previous hurricanes and revised the state's contraflow plan.[36] They also developed the Evacuation Liaison Team concept, which worked well during Katrina. The contingency plan for the medical component, almost complete when Katrina made landfall, proved invaluable to the response effort.[37] The excellent performance of Louisiana Department of Wildlife and Fisheries officials was at least in part due to the Pam exercise: rescue teams applied a model that had been developed during the exercise.[38]

Importantly, the Pam exercise facilitated personal relationships among officials across government.[39] To quote one official: "The workshops and planning process—knowledge of inter-jurisdictional relationships and capabilities, identification of issues, and rudimentary concepts for handling the consequences—have been beneficial to all involved in the hurricane response."[40] En route to Baton Rouge on Saturday, the federal coordinating officer, Bill Lokey, reportedly reviewed documents relating to the exercise.[41] Upon landing, he requested that representatives from IEM be invited to the state's emergency operations center (EOC) in Baton Rouge and that a summary of the draft plan be distributed to members of the FEMA staff.[42] According to FEMA director Brown, "The Hurricane Pam book was flying everywhere. It was all over FEMA."[43]

To be sure, the Pam exercise was not perfect. The plan had still not been finalized as of August 2005.[44] The search and rescue group developed a transportation plan for retrieving and evacuating stranded residents, but this plan clearly did not work (or was never applied).[45] FEMA officials made promises at the time that they subsequently did not or could not keep.[46] Funding shortfalls limited participation at and shortened the length of both the Pam exercise in 2004 and several follow-up meetings.

Late Predictions

As many critics have pointed out, Hurricane Pam did not help the authorities foresee the flood disaster that came on the heels of Katrina. But if, as critics claim, Pam is to be taken seriously as a predictor of impending doom and an indicator of failure, we can only conclude that Katrina was handled much better than the fictitious Pam: Katrina was, in effect, a worse disaster (a flooded city) but saw far fewer casualties.

Few people saw *this* disaster—a New Orleans flooded for weeks—coming. Even fewer offered specific warnings to this effect. There was plenty of talk about the possible *topping* of levees, but few if any predicted that any levees would breach and the city would flood as a result.[47] The National Hurricane Center (NHC), for instance, issued advisories warning only that the levees in New Orleans could be overtopped by waters from Lake Pontchartrain.[48] It was reported that the NHC director, Max Mayfield, had cautioned senior officials that the levees could breach, but no such warning was in fact ever issued. "What I indicated in my briefings to emergency managers and to the media was the possibility that some levees in the greater New Orleans area could be *overtopped* [emphasis added], depending on the details of Katrina's track and intensity," Mayfield later explained.[49]

As Katrina closed in on New Orleans, a few experts gave increasingly dire assessments of the storm's possible consequences. But their predictions came late and seemed over the top. Sunday evening, the Department of Homeland Security's (DHS's) National Infrastructure Simulation and Analysis Center issued its "Fast Analysis Report," which predicted that the storm *would* breach the levees and leave at least 100,000 people stranded on rooftops; the computer simulation further predicted widespread and persisting power outages, $2.2 billion in direct economic losses, and $20 billion in property damages. The report reached the White House Situation Room just hours before landfall.[50] But it came very late in the game. The White House received a copy in the early hours of Monday morning. That same evening, the National Weather Service issued an uncharacteristically stark warning, suggesting that Katrina would render "most of the area . . . uninhabitable for weeks . . . perhaps longer."[51]

Also on Sunday evening, the *Seattle Times* reported that New Orleans was at risk of becoming "a vast cesspool tainted with toxic chemicals, human waste and even coffins released . . . from the city's legendary cemeteries. . . . The storm threatened an environmental disaster of biblical proportions, one that could leave more than 1 million people homeless."[52] In that same *Seattle Times* article, LSU's Van Heerden was quoted, predicting that "vast swaths of New Orleans could be under water up to 30 feet . . . We're talking about in essence having—in the continental United States—a refugee camp of a million people."[53] Despite the flurry of dire predictions on the eve of landfall, there were relatively few warnings of a flooding city.[54]

DID AUTHORITIES TAKE ADEQUATE PREPARATORY MEASURES IN LIGHT OF WHAT COULD REASONABLY HAVE BEEN FORESEEN OR EXPECTED?

FEMA is not going to hesitate at all in this storm. We are not going to sit back and make this a bureaucratic process. We are going to move fast, we are going to move quick, and we are going to do whatever it takes to help disaster victims.

—FEMA DIRECTOR MICHAEL BROWN

Even though authorities did not recognize a superdisaster in the making, they did take Hurricane Katrina very seriously. There was no downplaying or ignoring the potential effects of the hurricane. Quite the contrary: authorities warned that a very dangerous storm was coming, and they prepared accordingly.

There was initially little to suggest that Katrina would be particularly extraordinary. On Wednesday, August 24, a tropical depression in the Caribbean (TD 12) was upgraded to a tropical storm named Katrina. This prompted the activation of the Hurricane Liaison Team (HLT) at the NHC, as well as the National Response Coordination Center (NRCC) at FEMA headquarters in Washington.[55] In the following days, the HLT would coordinate conference and video conference calls among officials at the NRCC, the Florida Division of Emergency Management, and other federal and state offices of emergency preparedness within FEMA Region IV, which includes eight US states (but not Louisiana, which was part of neighboring FEMA Region VI).

At the NRCC, FEMA officials arranged for the first Katrina-specific conference call with Department of Defense (DOD) and National Guard Bureau officials. The bureau's joint operations center began coordinating the activation of National Guard units in likely affected states. Because of the storm's track toward Florida (and because Louisiana was in a different FEMA region), Louisiana lacked representation during these discussions.

On August 25, Katrina was upgraded to a Category 1 hurricane and later in the day made landfall along Florida's southern Atlantic coast, causing widespread power outages and at least 11 deaths. At the same time, staff at the state EOC in Baton Rouge began conducting communications checks with local parishes in the event that Katrina swung to the west toward Louisiana.[56]

The military's Joint Forces Command issued an advisory to all forces to be prepared to assist civilian authorities.[57] Soon after, the DOD ordered the deployment of defense coordinating officers to those states likely to be affected by the storm.[58] Full Defense Coordinating Elements were prestaged outside the region for deployment where appropriate.[59]

Until midday on Friday, August 26, NHC forecasters predicted that Katrina would head north, through the Florida Panhandle and into Georgia. By early afternoon, however, the storm began to shift westward and increased in intensity far more quickly than predicted, prompting serious concerns that the storm was headed toward southeastern Louisiana instead.[60] According to the NHC director, New Orleans in particular had at this stage entered the NHC's "cone of uncertainty," prompting a round of urgent late-afternoon calls to alert local, state, and federal officials in the region.[61]

That Friday night, the New Orleans Saints played a preseason home game against the Baltimore Ravens at the Superdome (the Ravens won 21–6). No mention was made of the storm either at the game or during the televised broadcast of the game beamed into homes across the state and the wider region.[62]

Nevertheless, major preparations had started. Louisiana governor Kathleen Blanco had by midafternoon on Friday canceled a planned trip to Atlanta. During the evening, she declared a statewide state of emergency (a full 24 hours earlier than her counterpart in Mississippi). The governor also made a formal request for a federal declaration of emergency for Louisiana. In her request, Blanco wrote that an "effective response will be beyond the capabilities of the state and the affected local governments and that supplementary federal assistance will be necessary."[63]

Now on an emergency footing, LOHSEP organized its first statewide conference call during the late afternoon. The call focused on the evacuation of Greater New Orleans.[64] LOHSEP and state police officials announced plans to activate their respective emergency operations centers the following morning.[65] Furthermore, state and local agencies placed critical personnel on standby and canceled all scheduled leave.[66] LOHSEP hosted five such conference calls on Saturday, four on Sunday, and one on Monday before communications were disrupted by the storm.[67]

Blanco's emergency declaration authorized the immediate mobilization of 2,000 Louisiana National Guard (LANG) troops to support the evacuation effort.[68] The following day, a further 2,000 troops were mobilized, and all three of the LANG's joint operations centers went into 24-hour operation.[69] Since some LANG assets were at the time deployed in Iraq, the Louisiana Air National Guard requested additional airborne capabilities via the Emergency Management Assistance Compact, which was in the process of deploying a so-called A Team to Baton Rouge to facilitate state-to-state requests for military and civilian response assets.[70]

Late in the evening on Friday, the NHC released an advisory suggesting that Katrina, now a Category 4 hurricane, posed a threat to Louisiana (though it did not refer to New Orleans specifically). However, the cone of uncertainty remained imprecise, with various storm track models "clustered between the eastern coast of Louisiana and the coast of Mississippi."[71]

On Friday, the mayor of New Orleans, C. Ray Nagin, stated that "this storm really scares me."[72] By late evening, national news outlets had initiated coverage of the storm. Local officials announced that any decision regarding the evacuation of the city would be made the following day. Saturday morning, New Orleans started preparing for landfall. The city's EOC, located on an upper story in the city hall complex, was activated.

A Frantic Weekend

On Saturday, August 27, the NHC reported that the storm, after weakening somewhat during the night, had again increased in intensity and was headed toward southeastern Louisiana. By late Saturday afternoon, the state EOC in Baton Rouge was staffed by 40 full-time personnel working 12-hour shifts. By this time, LOHSEP officials had joined regularly scheduled HLT conference calls. Governor Blanco joined one such call, during which an NHC forecaster explained that Louisiana could expect hurricane-force winds over New Orleans by 9:00 a.m. on Monday, August 29, preceded by storm surge as high as 18 feet.[73]

The FEMA director, also on the call, appeared worried; he had "learned over the past four and a half, five years, to go with my gut on a lot of things, and my gut hurts on this one." He encouraged officials to "take this one very, very seriously" and "lean forward and get right to the edge of the envelope" in preparing for the storm. They should not expect any "flak" from him.[74]

President Bush, vacationing at his ranch near Crawford, Texas, reportedly first discussed Hurricane Katrina during an afternoon meeting on Saturday, August 27. A senior White House adviser, Dan Bartlett, met Bush to raise Governor Blanco's request for a federal emergency declaration.[75] During this meeting, the two men discussed whether the president should cancel a planned speech regarding identity theft in order to free up room in his schedule to visit the Gulf Coast during the coming week.[76] Bush resolved to stick to his prearranged schedule for the coming days, which included appearances in Arizona and California on August 29 and 30.[77]

The president approved Blanco's request for an emergency declaration in Louisiana. This order designated Bill Lokey, a senior FEMA official, as the federal coordinating officer. His job would be to liaise with the state coordinating officer in Louisiana, Jeff Smith.

FEMA field deployments began on Saturday. But FEMA was undermanned.[78] An Emergency Response Team—Advanced (ERT-A) was sent from Boston to FEMA Region VI headquarters in Denton, Texas. This unit was tasked with "establish[ing] a Unified Command, [making] contact with the highly affected parishes, and [setting] up a base of operations for FEMA."[79] Upon arriving in Texas, the head of the ERT-A, Phil Parr, and a FEMA public affairs officer, Marty Bahamonde, were ordered by Michael Brown to proceed directly to New Orleans. Bahamonde, who had worked closely with the FEMA director in the past, was to facilitate public media appearances involving federal officials after landfall.[80] Bahamonde arrived in New Orleans late on Saturday.[81] Few federal and no state officials appear to have been aware that a FEMA representative had arrived in New Orleans prior to landfall.[82] Parr, meanwhile, was delayed by deteriorating weather conditions; he would not make it into the city until Tuesday.[83]

After receiving notification of the president's emergency declaration, FEMA approved the deployment of a National Emergency Response Team (ERT-N), led by federal coordinating officer Bill Lokey, to the state EOC in Baton Rouge.[84] Deployment of ERT-N members to the state EOC in Baton Rouge was incomplete as of landfall.[85] The shortage of FEMA staff at the site was immediately apparent and frustrating to FEMA officials both with the ERT-N in Louisiana and at FEMA headquarters in Washington.[86] Only after landfall would FEMA ease restrictions on the deployment of FEMA personnel to the region, thus expediting the augmentation of the ERT-N staff and other undermanned FEMA teams throughout the region.[87]

Also on Saturday, FEMA established an operational staging area in Alexandria, Louisiana, to support post-storm response and recovery operations. Emergency supplies readied at FEMA's logistics centers around the nation would be received there in the coming days.[88] Meanwhile, the US Army Corps of Engineers began pre-positioning supplies in areas north of the likely strike zone.[89] At the EOC in Baton Rouge, a work group was formed from representatives of FEMA, the US Coast Guard, the Louisiana Department of Transportation and Development, and the Louisiana Department of Wildlife and Fisheries to coordinate search and rescue operations after landfall.

Louisiana officials identified three medical staging areas on university campuses in the region to tend to emerging medical needs. The head of the National Disaster Medical System (NDMS) ordered the deployment of at least twenty medical teams of various sizes to the region.[90] Only one team, based in Oklahoma, was directed to Louisiana.[91] Senate investigators later found that "although a number of teams were mobilized and began moving into the Gulf region, this effort fell far short of needs."[92] This number was also far below that envisioned by those present during the Pam exercise.[93] At the same time, the Centers for Disease Control and Prevention was preparing to use the nation's Strategic National Stockpile for only the second time in history (the first being after the 9/11 attacks).[94]

The Coast Guard had been on standby in the region since Friday; nonessential personnel and family members were being relocated to safety.[95] In New Orleans, federal law enforcement agencies worked to secure their offices at the Boggs Federal Office Building and made arrangements in the event that operations needed to be relocated after landfall.[96]

As the storm moved closer to the Gulf Coast, Lieutenant General Russel Honoré of the US First Army ordered that a number of specific capabilities be readied for deployment to the region.[97] Soon after, Honoré personally requested that US Northern Command formulate a list of likely required assets that could be deployed to the region *without* a request from FEMA. The Pentagon was slow to respond.[98] Honoré resolved to stage an "exercise" that would take the First Army's command element to Camp Shelby, Mississippi, on Tuesday.[99] Navy commanders independently placed numerous assets, including two large amphibious assault ships, on standby as of Sunday.[100] In Baltimore, Maryland, the USNS *Comfort*, a hospital ship, was prepared for deployment to the region.[101] The US Transportation Command alerted air units to be prepared for heavy-lift air transport orders, while specialized Air Force units tasked with quickly reestablishing airport operations were placed on standby.[102]

The American Red Cross had launched its own prestorm preparations. On Friday, the organization reported to DHS officials that "[Hurricane Katrina would] be the most intense storm to hit the [US] mainland" in some time. Red Cross officials established for the first time ever a "[mass care, housing, and human services] coordination center at American Red Cross national headquarters to coordinate the delivery of mass care services with our governmental and nongovernmental organization partners."[103] Simultaneously, Red Cross representatives were sent to FEMA's National Response Coordination Center in Washington, the Region VI Regional Response Coordination Center, and the state EOC in Baton Rouge.[104]

The Red Cross did not have a presence in New Orleans prior to landfall because the city's shelter of last resort at the Superdome did not meet the organization's shelter criteria.[105]

FEMA Is Worried

Claims that senior FEMA officials underplayed the threat facing New Orleans are not solidly defensible.[106] Senior officials exhibited a clear recognition that Hurricane Katrina was potentially extraordinary and that the federal government's capabilities could be inadequate. On Friday, FEMA's Leo Bosner, in charge of an early warning unit, recognized Katrina as a "nightmare scenario."[107] He collected information about the storm and sent a report around on Saturday morning, with a clear warning that the storm's impact might be big.[108] FEMA's deputy director of response, Michael Lowder, told his staff that "if [this] is the 'New Orleans' scenario, we are already way behind. Let's don't hold back. . . . This may be IT!"[109]

FEMA director Brown clearly understood the potential of Katrina.[110] During one conference call with FEMA staff and the various relevant EOC representatives in attendance, he admonished those under his command to "lean forward as much as possible [as] this is our chance to really show what we can do."[111]

These were more than just words: House investigators found FEMA's pre-landfall staging activities to be unprecedented in scale.[112]

Preparation at the State and Local Levels

State agencies mobilized resources ahead of the storm.[113] The LDWF moved supplies and equipment, including high-water vehicles and boats, to Jackson Barracks, a National Guard facility located in central New Orleans that officials assumed would be safe from flooding.[114] LDWF also had 200 agents with boats in a ring around New Orleans.[115] LOHSEP officials in Baton Rouge worked to secure additional boats through FEMA and directly from other states.[116] Called-up Guard personnel converged on New Orleans during the weekend to assist with law enforcement, traffic control, shelter support, and security operations at the Superdome. Emergency responders were standing by to begin search and rescue.[117]

Officials in New Orleans reacted a bit slower, initially sticking with a business-as-usual approach. At a Saturday meeting of the New Orleans City Council at city hall, one council member suggested that the city would survive Katrina as it had so many storms in the past.[118] Later in the day, Mayor Nagin and other local officials attended a three-hour funeral for a prominent local political figure. Nagin left the service at 2:30 p.m. to return to city hall, where he briefly met with the lieutenant governor.[119]

The superintendent of the New Orleans Police Department (NOPD), Eddie Compass, warned that Katrina would cause substantial wind damage and "possible street flooding."[120] According to at least one NOPD commander, subsequent NOPD preparations using the department's own Emergency Preparation Plan were "pretty much the same" as they had been ahead of hurricanes in the past.[121] A deputy chief of police explained to reporters that the NOPD's four boats would be sufficient to carry out any necessary rescue missions.[122] Most local police vehicles were pre-positioned in designated areas on higher ground, including parking garages in central New Orleans. An NOPD request for high-water vehicles to be deployed to various local police precincts was reportedly denied by National Guard officials, who had decided to consolidate all assets at Jackson Barracks for the time being.[123]

The New Orleans Fire Department did what it could to prepare for landfall. Even though it was formally responsible for search and rescue at the local level, the department in fact had no rescue boats of its own. For this reason, firefighters reportedly pre-positioned their own boats in the city just in case.[124] In a last-ditch effort to boost the city's capacity, Mayor Nagin's office and the NOPD superintendent worked to rent or purchase additional boats. The boats that they did manage to acquire were moved to Jackson Barracks prior to landfall.[125]

Final Preparations

Early on Sunday morning, Hurricane Katrina was upgraded to a Category 5 storm. At this point, FEMA director Brown was preparing to depart Washington, DC, for Baton Rouge. He was, at the same time, dealing with wildfires raging in California.

In Baton Rouge, Governor Blanco was growing increasingly concerned about the looming storm's catastrophic potential and, as a result, sought to bypass the standard federal disaster declaration request process. In a communication to the president, Blanco took the rare step of requesting an expedited disaster declaration for all parishes in the state.[126]

At 11:00 a.m., the HLT organized a teleconference. FEMA Region VI officials were joined on the call by FEMA director Brown, DHS secretary Michael Chertoff, DHS deputy secretary Michael Jackson, NHC director Mayfield, and President Bush. Governor Blanco and a number of LOHSEP officials were also included in the video conference.[127] The call commenced with a weather report from Mayfield. After comparing Katrina to Hurricane Andrew, Mayfield suggested that "the wisest thing to do here is to plan on a Category 5 hurricane."[128]

Despite later reports to the contrary, Mayfield at no point in the days prior to landfall suggested that the levees around New Orleans would be "breached" by Katrina. In fact, he predicted "minimal flooding in the city of New Orleans itself."[129] However, the NHC director did foresee the possibility of some levees being "overtopped" should the storm shift more to the west, as it ultimately did. Mayfield seemed, in fact, more concerned about Mississippi and Alabama.

The FEMA director then welcomed the president to the call. Bush assured Louisiana officials that the federal government and FEMA in particular were "fully prepared" to assist the states. He then signed off the call.[130]

Jeff Smith (the director of Louisiana's Department of Emergency Preparedness) said he was "happy enough with the supplies FEMA had en route to the region." His colleague, William Doriant, explained that the EOC was operating at the highest state of readiness and that evacuation efforts were in full swing. In response, the FEMA director urged his people to "jam up" the supply chain: "just keep jamming those lines full as much as you can with commodities."[131]

Excerpts of the Sunday noon video conference:

> *Colonel Jeff Smith:* . . . I can tell you that our Governor is very concerned about the potential loss of life here with our citizens, and she is very appreciative of the federal resources that have come into the state and the willingness to give us everything you've got, because, again, we're very concerned with this.

Colonel Bill Doriant: The Emergency Operations Center is at a Level 1, which is the highest state of readiness. We've currently got 11 parishes with evacuations, and climbing. . . . Evacuations are underway currently. We're planning for a catastrophic event, which we have been planning for, thanks to the help of FEMA, when we did the Hurricane Pam exercises. So we're way ahead of the game here.

Colonel Smith: We're also taking a look at our sheltering needs, long-term sheltering needs, looking at sites to start bringing in the temporary housing. So we're not only fighting the current battle, managing expectations here with our local parishes, but we are also working with FEMA and our other federal partners to have the most effective response and recovery that we possibly can during this time. . . . I think that at this point in time our coordination is as good as it can be.

Mike Brown: Colonel, do you have any unmet needs, anything that we are not getting to you . . . ?

Colonel Smith: Mike, no. [inaudible] resources that are en route, and it looks like those resources that are en route are going to—to be a good first shot. Naturally, once we get into this thing, you know, neck deep here, unfortunately, or deeper, I'm sure that things are going to come up that maybe some of even our best planners hadn't even thought about. So I think flexibility is going to be the key. . . . We appreciate your comments. I think they were to lean as far, far as you possibly can, you know, without falling, and your people here are doing that. And that's the type of attitude we need in an event like this.

Mike Brown: Any questions? [Inaudible] on the commodities that I want to see that supply chain jammed up just as much as possible. I mean, I want stuff [inaudible] than we need. Just keep jamming those lines full as much as you can with commodities.[132]

Brown worried about New Orleans. He noted that the Superdome "is about 12 feet below sea level" and expressed concern about the roof (which in fact would be blown off hours later). "They're not taking patients out of hospitals, taking prisoners out of prisons, and they're leaving hotels open in downtown New Orleans. So I'm very concerned about that." This, he explained, could be "the catastrophe within a catastrophe."[133] The FEMA director subsequently urged everyone participating in the call to take Katrina "very, very seriously." He rounded off the call by claiming that his "gut tells me this . . . is a bad one and a big one."[134]

Marty Bahamonde, the sole FEMA official to reach New Orleans prior to landfall, sent several reports to FEMA headquarters from the city on Sunday. In one email, Bahamonde wrote that the situation at the Superdome was "going to get ugly real fast."[135] At least 1,000 special needs patients would reach the Superdome by Sunday night. Many patients had needs that could not be met with the limited supplies available at the Superdome. Several hundred patients were subsequently moved late Sunday evening to the LSU campus in Baton Rouge. Despite these last-minute efforts, the total number of special needs patients at the Superdome still far exceeded officials' expectations, putting considerable pressure on the limited medical resources available at the site.

Federal officials worked all day Sunday to send additional emergency medical teams and supplies to the Superdome, though most of these would only arrive after landfall.[136] The storm happened to coincide with a national emergency medical services convention in the city. At least some attendees were recruited to support medical operations at the Superdome.[137]

By late afternoon, all official evacuation efforts were called off as the storm crept closer to the coast. By 6:00 p.m., a curfew had been imposed in the city.[138] Officials at the state EOC in Baton Rouge, including the recently arrived FEMA director, were hunkering down. In late-night television appearances, Brown asserted that federal, state, and local officials were ready.

Just hours before landfall, the city had completed its preparations. Many local institutions—universities, the Audubon Zoo, the Aquarium of the Americas, the D-Day Museum—were closed.[139] Many of those who had not evacuated were filing into the Superdome. Approximately 300 city and state officials were available to deal with the evacuees. Several hundred National Guard troops and police provided security.[140]

If there was one organization that did not properly prepare, it was the local prison service. Sheriff Marlin N. Gusman was by law obligated to evacuate detention facilities under his authority "whenever [these became] unsafe or unfit for the security of prisoners."[141] Gusman told reporters before landfall that Orleans Parish Prison facilities in the city were "fully staffed" and in compliance with their emergency operations plans.[142] Gusman explained at the time that he had decided to "keep prisoners where they belong"—in their cells.[143]

Gusman's decision was noteworthy, given early warnings that at least some of these facilities were at risk of flooding in the event of a Category 3 hurricane.[144] The Juvenile Justice Project of Louisiana later found that the Orleans Parish Prison failed to implement its own hurricane/flood contingency plan, which Gusman referred to during press appearances before landfall.[145]

The onset of strong winds early Monday morning, August 29, prompted the conclusion of all operations, including all police patrols. Soon after, authorities began experiencing power outages and disruptions to emergency communications systems.[146] At 4:30 a.m., FEMA issued what would be its final pre-landfall National Situation Update. The report suggested that "conditions will continue to steadily deteriorate. . . . Coastal storm surge flooding of 18 to 22 feet above normal tide levels, locally as high as 28 feet . . . can be expected. . . . Some levees in the greater New Orleans area could be overtopped."[147]

DID AUTHORITIES WARN PEOPLE IN A TIMELY FASHION AND TRY TO MOVE THEM OUT OF HARM'S WAY?

After the storm, critics blamed the number of deaths and the general desperation on local administrators, claiming that they had failed to warn local residents of the approaching storm and evacuate those who could not make it out of the city by themselves. In hindsight, there is no doubt that a more complete evacuation would have saved more lives. It is also clear, however, that local government did try to warn residents and move them out of the city.

Preparing the Evacuation

On Friday, the decision was made to implement the state's contraflow plan the following morning. Mississippi officials were subsequently notified that they could expect a large influx of Louisianians within the next 24 hours. By Saturday afternoon, all coastal parishes to the south of New Orleans had been evacuated. The evacuation of Greater New Orleans could begin—slightly earlier, in fact, than planners had envisioned.

On Saturday, Governor Blanco, Mayor Nagin, and other local officials held a joint news conference in New Orleans to warn people of the approaching storm.[148] Katrina, Nagin explained, "is the real deal. . . . As of right now, New Orleans is definitely the target for this hurricane." Residents were encouraged to "treat [Katrina] differently because it is pointed toward New Orleans."[149] Mayor

Nagin and the president of neighboring Jefferson Parish subsequently issued voluntary evacuation orders to their constituents.

Meanwhile, NHC director Mayfield worried that state and local officials were underestimating the storm's catastrophic potential. Mayfield later explained that "sometimes politicians are isolated. I just thought it would be good to let them know." He called the governor.[150] Blanco recommended that Mayfield also contact Mayor Nagin.[151] Mayfield did just that, reportedly reaching Nagin a few moments later on his cell phone.[152] At some point soon after this conversation, Nagin remarked to a local councilwoman that "Max Mayfield [had] scared [him] to death." Later that evening, Nagin decided that a mandatory evacuation order needed to be finalized by the following morning. He also requested that Blanco again travel to New Orleans to appear with him during his televised announcement of the order.[153]

Throughout Saturday evening, federal, state, and local officials urged residents to leave the city during interviews on the radio and on local and national television.[154] Behind the scenes, officials worked to ensure that their message was being conveyed through other, less traditional channels as well.[155] In an attempt to reach as many citizens as possible, Governor Blanco and her staff contacted clergy throughout Saturday night and early Sunday morning to ask them to urge their parishioners to evacuate immediately.[156] LSU meteorologists made numerous media appearances, invoking the 2004 tsunami as a point of comparison in order to "dramatize the damage that could result."[157]

During the early evening, Mayor Nagin reappeared before the television cameras in New Orleans, the governor by his side. Nagin declared a state of emergency and suggested that he might issue a mandatory evacuation order the following day, the first ever in the city's history.[158] The mandatory evacuation order was issued Sunday morning.

Evacuation and the Special Needs Population

The mayor's decision to issue a mandatory evacuation order for New Orleans was unprecedented. For this very reason, the city first had to determine the legality of the order.[159] The mayor's staff decided that existing law permitted such an order, but they worried about its implementation. The already strained NOPD lacked the resources to forcibly remove residents from their homes, and officers might find themselves in dangerous encounters with stubborn and, in many instances, armed residents. It was unclear if the order should apply to hospitals and nursing homes. Most hospitals that had not already been evacuated would have little time to summon adequate resources to relocate remaining patients at such a late hour.[160] For this reason, the mayor and his staff chose to exclude hospitals from the order.[161]

The city's Comprehensive Emergency Management Plan made provisions to assist in the evacuation of as many as 100,000 residents without access to vehicles of their own.[162] According to the plan, local officials were expected to "utilize all available resources [including buses] to quickly and safely evacuate threatened areas."[163]

The city's emergency planning had somehow failed to account for nursing homes. Many nursing homes in New Orleans were not in compliance with the emergency standards set out by the federal government and the state.[164] Even if inspection regimes had been more robust, nursing home administrators were not required to demonstrate the workability of their emergency evacuation plans.[165] As a result, emergency generators at many facilities were vulnerable to flooding, and contracts with busing companies were not finalized. In many instances, administrators had failed to pre-identify facilities for patient relocation in the event of an evacuation.[166]

State and local government lacked the capacity to assist both patients and other segments of the population at the same time. Nursing homes thus came to rely on the Louisiana Nursing Home Association, which had by 6:30 a.m. Saturday swung into 24-hour operation in support of nursing homes in need of transport assistance.[167] The nursing home association would play a key role in coordinating the evacuation of patients from numerous at-risk facilities both before and after landfall.[168]

Ultimately, only 21 of 36 nursing homes in Greater New Orleans were completely evacuated prior to landfall.[169] Over the course of the weekend before landfall, there was little the city or state could do but move at-risk residents from these facilities to the Superdome. The majority of remaining residents sheltered in place alongside staff members and, in many cases, their families.

On Sunday, the day before landfall, the governor rose at 4:00 a.m. in order to appear on a variety of local and national television news programs. During one interview, she explained that evacuation was critical, as those remaining in New Orleans would "not survive" if storm surge overtopped the city's levee system.[170] At 5:00 a.m., Mayor Nagin contacted officials in neighboring parishes to urge them to evacuate any remaining residents as quickly as possible, as he would be issuing a mandatory evacuation order shortly.[171]

While it is clear officials tried to warn citizens, it is not clear how effective these warnings were. A survey of residents evacuated to Houston after landfall found that only one in three had "heard an evacuation order but that it had not provided clear information about how to evacuate." Another third were unaware that any evacuation order had even been issued.[172]

Final Preparations

At 9:25 a.m. Sunday, nineteen hours before projected landfall, Mayor Nagin, accompanied by Governor Blanco and other officials, ordered the mandatory evacuation of New Orleans on live television.[173] In his address, Nagin granted local authorities special powers, including the right to commandeer vehicles required to evacuate remaining residents. Hospitals, prisons, public officials, tourists, and journalists were exempted from the order. The mayor argued that "New Orleans has never seen a hurricane of this strength to hit it almost directly."[174] Remaining residents were encouraged to have axes at hand in case they needed to smash their way onto their roofs in the event of flooding.[175]

President Bush issued a warning during his televised speech to the nation. The topic of his speech was actually the referendum on a new Iraqi constitution. Bush nevertheless took a moment to report on what he had heard during the recent HLT call.[176] Bush emphasized "the danger this hurricane poses to Gulf Coast communities" and urged citizens in the area to heed state and local officials' instructions and to move to "safe ground" if directed.[177]

Nagin instructed remaining residents to gather at collection points throughout the city. From here, local buses would transport them to the Superdome. Residents were asked to bring a three- to five-day supply of food, bedding, medications, diapers, and batteries, as well as "patience and a positive attitude."[178] Immediately after the order was issued, NOPD personnel began canvassing the city, their public address systems blaring instructions.[179] Churches and community associations also played a significant albeit largely ad hoc and informal role in spreading the word.[180]

The bus service promised by the mayor was sporadic. According to the city's hurricane evacuation plan, "Transportation [would] be provided to those persons requiring public transportation from the area." This responsibility fell to the Regional Transit Authority (RTA).[181] One obvious problem was that hundreds of bus drivers employed by the RTA had already left the city.[182] LOHSEP officials in Baton Rouge proposed that Guard personnel drive the buses instead, though this turned out to be unrealistic—the Guard in the city was occupied with providing security, directing traffic, and administering emergency medical care at the Superdome.

By midafternoon, the service was canceled outright, along with the city's regularly scheduled local streetcar and bus services.[183] After making their final runs to the Superdome, the buses were fueled and then parked on a lot near downtown New Orleans.[184]

City officials acted to augment existing supplies at the Superdome as the numbers of those seeking shelter exceeded expectations. Besides medical supplies, these included essentials like food and water, fuel, and portable toilet facilities. The National Guard made a number of deliveries, drawing on stockpiles at its Jackson Barracks facility.[185]

By 10:30 p.m. on Sunday evening, between 8,000 and 12,000 residents (excluding those with special needs) were sheltered at the Superdome. Every person was searched for weapons, drugs, and other contraband before entering the facility.[186] Local hospitals were sheltering thousands more.[187] Unbeknownst to officials, residents elsewhere in the city had established informal shelters in hardened structures, including local schools. Residents stocked these sites with supplies and established communal dining rooms and sleeping areas. One such shelter housed as many as 200 people.[188] At least some of these might have been residents with pets, which were not welcome at the Superdome.[189]

Late on Sunday evening, officials estimated that at least one million people, a full 80% of the area's total population, had left southeastern Louisiana. Most had driven out of the area in their own vehicles. No critical fuel shortages or major accidents were reported along major evacuation routes. The Louisiana authorities had done it: they had successfully evacuated an area that had never been effectively evacuated before.[190]

HOW MUCH PREPARATION IS ENOUGH?

Many observers later claimed that authorities did not properly prepare. We have shown that these claims are largely unfounded. Given the evidence, it would be difficult to argue that the authorities did not take Katrina seriously, that they failed to prepare, or that they did not warn the local population.

There is no doubt that key players took this storm very seriously. Governor Blanco demonstrated a deep personal engagement in the crisis, both operationally and symbolically. She presided over many statewide teleconferences in preparation for and during the evacuation of New Orleans. Blanco also stayed in close contact with parish officials throughout this period. She traveled to New Orleans on two occasions during the weekend to appear with Mayor Nagin in televised press conferences.

Federal authorities (FEMA in particular) were undermanned but also "leaning forward." The FEMA director had in early 2005 toured tsunami-affected areas on northern Sumatra in Indonesia. The scale of the destruction reportedly motivated him to ensure that FEMA was better prepared for a hurricane strike on New Orleans. After Katrina, some officials in Washington suggested that "the FEMA leadership" took an insufficient number of steps to ensure that adequate preparations had been made in the face of one of the agency's own worst-case scenarios. But transcripts from video teleconferences during the weekend prior to landfall do not bear this out. If anything, Brown's willingness to travel to Baton Rouge before landfall suggests a personal engagement in the issue.[191]

During media appearances on Saturday, officials at all levels of government encouraged residents to flee the approaching storm. By Sunday, officials were crystal clear in their messaging. Nagin called Katrina "a once-in-a-lifetime event."[192] Blanco stated that "this storm is bigger than anything we have dealt with before." President Bush in a televised speech urged people to leave.[193]

That does not mean people acted on those warnings. As is often the case in the Gulf Coast states, many people seemed unconcerned about the impending storm.[194] Saturday night witnessed the usual hurricane parties.[195] While most people left, thousands stayed behind. Some of these showed up at the Superdome just in case this was the Big One everyone had been dreading. Others hunkered down in their homes.

Based on what authorities thought they knew, we conclude that *preparatory efforts at the federal and the state level were more than adequate.* These preparatory efforts included nearly all the activities one would expect. There was a well-executed evacuation for car owners; FEMA had prestaged resources; the state of Louisiana and the US Coast Guard had boats ready; shelters were organized.

After the storm, some people would claim that FEMA did not do enough in the face of the Big One. There is some truth to this observation, as FEMA was operating in routine mode—routine for a large-scale hurricane, that is. During the 2004 hurricane season, four major hurricanes and one tropical storm hit Florida. Both DHS and FEMA received good marks for their responses. FEMA had been lauded for very similar actions during the busy storm summer of 2005.[196] In the face of Katrina, the agency positioned an unprecedented number of resources in the area.[197]

Preparations in New Orleans initially followed a business-as-usual approach. But when it began to dawn on local authorities that Katrina was not a "usual" hurricane, they upped the ante and tried to move more people out of their houses, away from the city, or at least into the Superdome. By any measure, New Orleans had shifted to the highest gear ever, at least when compared with past experiences.

The city prepared for a hurricane, not a flooded city. The director for the local Office of Homeland Security and Public Safety would later explain: "We're thinking [48] hours and this'll all be over. Nobody's going to starve by then."[198] The truth of the matter is nobody did.

The real lesson here—lost to many—is that the pre-landfall preparations saved lives. We can only imagine what would have happened if the authorities had been as unprepared, uninterested, and uncaring as they were made out to be in hindsight. If there had not been any warnings, no evacuation, no pre-staging of boats and medical teams, the 60,000 deaths predicted in the Pam scenario may well have become reality.

3

UNDERSTANDING THE UNIMAGINABLE

WHY COLLECTIVE SENSE MAKING FAILED

I don't want to alarm everybody that, you know, New Orleans is
filling up like a bowl. That's just not happening.
—SENATOR DAVID VITTER, PRESS BRIEFING, BATON ROUGE, AUGUST 29, 2005

THE INFORMATION CHALLENGE

Tuesday morning, August 30, 2005. The epic disaster named Katrina was just beginning to attract national attention. Despite the availability of aerial footage of the flooded city, the presence of journalists in New Orleans, and official reports confirming levee breaches, the morning editions of many newspapers suggested that New Orleans had once again escaped the worst-case scenario.[1] A sigh of relief set the tone across America.

It took a remarkably long time to *recognize* that a mega-disaster was unfolding. The media were slow to realize the full scale of the disaster. Most federal officials were not much faster to grasp the extent of the devastation caused by Katrina. In the days after landfall, officials continued to be surprised by new developments that demanded an immediate response.

The disaster started as a surprise packaged in a highly anticipated event. Hurricane Katrina came ashore in Louisiana on Monday morning at 6:10 a.m. Flooding was reported as early as 4:30 a.m.[2] By 6:30, outlying areas of Orleans

46

Parish were already underwater. At 6:50 a.m., waters along the Industrial Canal leading through central New Orleans began to spill into residential areas, including both the Lower and Upper Ninth Ward. Before 8:00 a.m., at least two sections of the canal would fail, "send[ing] a wall of water into the Lower [Ninth] Ward."[3]

By midmorning, several more canals and levee walls were breached in both Orleans and St. Bernard Parishes.[4] Thousands were trapped in their homes and other buildings, including hospital facilities and prisons. The French Quarter and the Garden District, both on higher ground, stayed dry. Floodwaters in most other areas of the city would continue to rise for hours to come.

In hindsight, it is overwhelmingly clear that all the puzzle pieces needed to form an accurate picture of the situation were available by Monday evening. There were many messages that, together, painted a detailed picture of the evolving situation (see appendix I). Hundreds of 911 calls reported people on rooftops and clinging to trees. Throughout the morning and stretching into the afternoon, the National Weather Service offices, first responders in New Orleans, Coast Guard personnel, and LOHSEP all released reports suggesting (but not confirming) that at least some levees had been breached and that the city was flooding.[5]

Yet it took the Department of Homeland Security nearly thirty-six hours to officially conclude that the levees had been breached in New Orleans and that the city was underwater.[6] It would take yet more time to grasp the immediate social consequences of the rising water in the Crescent City. Three issues in particular posed nasty surprises to authorities during the first week:

- *The plight of "city refugees."* When the water began to rise, people in New Orleans were forced to move. They ended up on highways, waiting for buses; many made it to the Superdome or the Convention Center. When the Convention Center came into focus on Wednesday, it came as a "total surprise" to both FEMA director Brown and DHS secretary Chertoff.[7] In one of the most memorable moments of the crisis, Chertoff admitted on national radio that he did not know anything about the Convention Center. This was Thursday.[8]

- *The forgotten ones.* While New Orleans was being evacuated, hospitals and nursing homes did the opposite: patients and residents, staff members and their families, sheltered in place. When the city flooded and the generators failed, hospitals quickly became hellish places. Their plight went mostly unnoticed by authorities.

- *Mayhem in the city.* On Wednesday, the media sketched a dire picture of New Orleans, a city where chaos reigned. Authorities had no idea whether this was true or not. Reacting to the alarming reports, people in New Orleans began to arm themselves. First responders from out of state were soon afraid to enter the city.

In their detailed description of the federal response to Katrina, Christopher Cooper and Robert Block concluded that "pertinent, accurate and real-time information flowed in great waves through government agencies."[9] They were right: key officials at all levels possessed detailed information about the flooding and the situation on the ground. In theory, that information should flow through the system and result in a shared picture of what was transpiring.

In practice, it did not work that way. Different actors had different pieces of information; they did not manage to put the pieces together and see the bigger picture. In this chapter, we investigate how and why that happened.

––––––––––

A common (and accurate) picture can only emerge if response organizations work together to understand the evolving situation. Crisis managers must collect information, analyze it, establish a picture of the situation, share that picture, and then update it as new information becomes available.[10] They must do this quickly and accurately.

We call this *joint sense making*, which is critically important to effective crisis management: if decision makers do not have a shared and accurate picture of the situation, they cannot make informed decisions and communicate effectively with partners, politicians, and the public.

The various official inquiries found the sense-making performance of all government organizations wanting in one way or another. At DHS, "early situational awareness was poor, a problem that should have been corrected following identical damage assessment challenges during Hurricane Andrew."[11] The military faced a similar problem: the biggest challenge for US Northern Command (NORTHCOM) was in "gaining and maintaining situational awareness as to the catastrophic disaster."[12] The White House and FEMA, as well as authorities in New Orleans and Baton Rouge, also encountered this problem. Simply put, everyone found it difficult to get a handle on what was going on in and around New Orleans.

This observed shortcoming suggests that these organizations, with all their investments in sense-making capacities, failed at an essential facet of their job description. This prompts the question of why some officials and some organizations *did* have an accurate picture of the situation.

In hindsight it is, of course, always possible to reconstruct in detailed fashion what happened when (and who knew, or could have known, about it). This "hindsight bias" is known to affect the assessment of crisis researchers and especially crisis evaluators; as a result, they tend to underestimate the sense-making challenge as experienced by decision makers.[13]

Sense making in times of crisis is much harder than often imagined. Crises are characterized by deep uncertainty.[14] And as crises evolve, they frequently produce additional negative surprises.[15] The "accurate information flowing in great waves through government agencies" is rarely recognizable as such.[16] It must be culled from an abundance of irrelevant, ambiguous, or false information. Moreover, for some critical events there may be no information available whatsoever (no news is not always good news).

Routine information-processing mechanisms do not suffice.[17] Normal processes of information collection and communication tend to fall apart in a crisis; organizational chains often fragment. Key information is hard to locate. It takes precious time to survey a disaster site, collect critical information, summarize that information in an understandable way, and get the right information to the right person in the chain. Moreover, first responders have other priorities.

We should therefore *expect* collective sense-making failures in the initial phase of a complex and catastrophic crisis like Katrina. Many crises—ranging from 9/11 to the Boston Marathon attack, from Fukushima to the Paris attacks—have shown how hard it is to make sense of a fast-moving threat that defies plans and challenges experience. Virtually every inquiry report on large-scale crises and disasters asks why it takes so long for authorities to figure out what is happening. All these reports show that relevant information was indeed available but authorities nevertheless did not comprehend how bad the situation was. This is the rule rather than the exception.

It is fair to expect improvement during the course of a disaster, however. One might expect to see governments trying to adapt, finding ways to improve their sense-making capacities. As we will see, that did not happen in the case of Katrina. The authorities did not manage to "up their game" during that first week. As a result, confusion reigned at all levels of government.

As we try to shed light on why the authorities did not act adequately to collect, verify, share, and appreciate critical information, we will consider three areas of explanation:[18]

- *Limited capacity to collect and verify information.* The crisis literature describes a pattern of technical failures, due to destruction, that prevent effective communication. It also documents how the failure of local institutions undermines the quality of the communication process.

- *A breakdown in the communication chain.* The public administration and organization theory literatures help us understand why critical information travels slowly across organizations, or not at all, in times of crisis.

- *A failure of collective imagination.* The psychological literature helps us understand why even trained officials find it hard to grasp information about events that they cannot imagine. The information may be right in front of them, but they cannot see it.

CAPACITY TO COLLECT: COMMUNICATION BREAKDOWN AND WEAK INSTITUTIONS PUT TO THE TEST

Effective sense making should begin at the *local* level, near the scene of the disaster. In New Orleans, however, there was no collective sense-making effort at the local level. There were individual nodes where information collected, but the information from those nodes was not brought together, either in New Orleans or at a higher level. There were two reasons for this: a breakdown of communication means and the malfunctioning of local institutions.

Collecting and Transmitting Information

One of the most common explanations for sluggish sense making is found in the *failure of communication means.* As happens so often in disasters, officials in New Orleans quickly discovered that they were unable to communicate through normal channels. According to House investigators, communication challenges delayed "the delivery of direct assistance where it was most needed, and it hindered the ability to forward requests to state or federal agencies that might have been able to help."[19]

Shortly after the eye of Hurricane Katrina moved across the area, a massive communications failure occurred in New Orleans. By 7:00 a.m., most stationary and mobile telephone and internet services were down throughout much of southeastern Louisiana.[20] Approximately three million customers were affected.[21] Still-operational communications systems, including towers and transponders, transitioned to generator power. The only problem was that many of these generators were located at ground level and were thus susceptible to flooding as water levels rose.[22] The flooding prevented technicians from gaining access to many sites in need of repairs or fuel, meaning that the outage lasted for days instead of hours. When repairs were finally possible, crews received orders to prioritize units located at "pumping, sanitation, medical, and housing facilities."[23]

State and local officials immediately felt the effects of the communications failure, starting with the nearly total collapse of multiple emergency call centers throughout the region.[24] The call center in New Orleans failed when NOPD headquarters in central New Orleans was flooded. Before it shut down, though, the center had already received hundreds of emergency calls, mostly from residents trapped in their flooded homes. Operators were unable to dispatch units to respond to the vast majority of these calls.[25] The state police was experiencing "severe and debilitating" communications problems with its own statewide communications and data transfer system.[26] The system, last upgraded in 1996, had approximately 10,000 subscribers, including at least 70 state and local agencies.[27]

First responders in New Orleans had to rely on two-way radios to speak with one another. The system lacked range, was unreliable, worked at the whim of the weather, and would quickly become overburdened.[28] It was only on Thursday that first responders were able to transition to other, more stable long-range communications systems provided by state and federal authorities.[29]

Though numerous means of communications (telephone, mobile phone, fax, email, etc.) were available to state and federal officials at the state emergency operations center in Baton Rouge, communication proved problematic after landfall. In fact, "The communications problems were so severe that state officers could not reliably communicate with local officials, others in the state government, or federal officials, exacerbating the already severe problems with situational awareness."[30]

According to FEMA officials, maintaining a common operating picture was severely hampered due to the loss of communications. Like local officials in New Orleans and elsewhere, FEMA officials working in the region came to rely on satellite phones and BlackBerries to communicate. Data transfer was still limited and call quality was poor.[31]

The small FEMA contingent in New Orleans (at the Superdome) experienced difficulties contacting colleagues until Wednesday. They turned to the National Guard to make calls and send emails. When they were unable to get information directly to Washington or Baton Rouge, they could sometimes reach staff at the FEMA Region VI office in Texas instead, who relayed their messages. The team even had trouble communicating with local officials at the Hyatt Regency hotel just one block away.[32]

It was immediately clear to FEMA officials that state and local communications capabilities needed to be augmented. According to the National Response Plan, FEMA and the US Forestry Service are tasked with supporting the National Communications System, which aims to ensure emergency communications capability at the federal level through the use of assets like Mobile Emergency Response Support (MERS) units.[33]

FEMA had mobilized all but one of its MERS units prior to landfall.[34] The flooding in New Orleans prevented the agency from moving these units into the city.[35] FEMA's Red October communications unit (more capable than MERS) was eventually moved to the city hall complex in the middle of New Orleans, where it effectively augmented local, state, and federal communications capabilities in the city. But that did not happen before Saturday. Brown was hard to reach during the week, due as much to communications issues as to the fact that he was constantly on the move, trying to get more information. The FEMA director remarked later that he "wish[ed] [he] had [moved Red October to New Orleans] four days earlier."[36]

It was later estimated that FEMA's effectiveness in the city was reduced by as much as 90% because of communications issues. This goes some way in explaining why the agency was unable to get a good read on the situation from the beginning.[37] It is important to keep in mind, however, that FEMA had few boots on the ground at the time of landfall. While the FEMA advance team may have communicated more effectively had the MERS been predeployed, they still would have been undermanned and lacking staff with a good understanding of the city and its unique geography.[38]

Louisiana state senator Robert Barham, chairman of the State Senate's homeland security committee, summed up the situation in the state: "People could not communicate. It got to the point that people were literally writing messages on paper, putting them in bottles and dropping them from helicopters to other people on the ground."[39]

Difficulty moving around the city also made it hard to gather basic facts. For instance, the US Army Corps of Engineers (USACE) needed to determine the status of the levee system. However, the USACE district commander in New Orleans would have to wait until Tuesday morning before a helicopter could take him up for an aerial survey of the levees. This helps to explain why levee repairs did not begin until the middle of the week—it took the Corps a long time to figure out what had happened and what needed to be done to remedy the situation.[40]

Even reporters found it hard to communicate their information. For instance, a *New York Times* photographer had produced an illustrated story by Tuesday morning (he hitched a ride on a helicopter surveying the damage). But the reporter could not immediately get the story to the *Times* offices for publication.[41]

One official who managed to collect and transmit information relatively quickly was Marty Bahamonde, the sole FEMA official in New Orleans immediately after landfall. Bahamonde got an aerial view of the flooded city aboard a Coast Guard helicopter late Monday afternoon.[42] He took photographs of the various breached levees around the city, including the one along the Seventeenth Street Canal.[43] However, because Bahamonde lacked access to reliable communications, his photos only reached the Homeland Security Operations Center (HSOC) on Tuesday (a written report of his observations, which came to be known as the "Bahamonde report," made it to the HSOC just hours after the flight).[44] Bahamonde was able to set up a number of teleconferences to share his observations (see below).

City under Siege: The Breakdown of Local Institutions

The headquarters of both the local fire department and the National Guard at Jackson Barracks were flooded, as were the lower floors of the city hall complex. This unforeseen development would make it difficult to reach the city's EOC, which was also located at the facility. The loss of many of the city's command facilities and communications systems effectively cut the mayor of New Orleans off from the outside world.[45]

On Sunday evening, Nagin together with many other city administrators, the NOPD leadership, and Entergy executives withdrew to the Hyatt.[46] The Hyatt was across the street from both the city hall complex and the Superdome. The hotel's main ballroom would become the city's informal meeting space for representatives of organizations in the response network.[47]

Mayor Nagin spent much of his time at the Hyatt or visiting sites around the city. He was hard to trace and even harder to reach.[48] According to Bob Mann, Blanco's communications director, "For a week or more, the only way Blanco and Nagin could speak was if the governor flew to New Orleans and hunted him down. . . . Nobody knew where he was."[49]

The city's EOC was cramped and without power but still operational.[50] The mayor's absence from the EOC coupled with persisting communications problems forced local emergency management officials to assume many of the mayor's formally mandated responsibilities.[51] Nagin did make an attempt to move the EOC to the Hyatt at some point, but the move was abandoned.[52] As a result, "the Mayor was neither able to effectively command the local efforts, nor was he able to guide the State and Federal support for two days following the storm."[53]

Due to limited mobility and the ongoing communications breakdown, local officials were unable to adequately assess the situation, let alone communicate their needs to the state EOC in Baton Rouge. Nagin certainly knew that a disaster was unfolding, but he never became a source of structured information flows. Given that neither FEMA nor the USACE had significant numbers of personnel on the ground during those first days, the failure of local institutions to provide adequate information about the evolving situation was especially jarring.

The performance of the NOPD did not help matters. In times of disaster, the police usually deliver a stream of critical situational reports, becoming the "eyes and ears" of the city administration. The NOPD never became such an information node. By all accounts, the NOPD simply fell apart.[54] "As an institution . . . the New Orleans Police Department disintegrated with the first drop of floodwater."[55]

The troubled reputation of the NOPD undermined its information position. Its history was marred by incidents of police brutality.[56] Residents had little trust in the NOPD. This distrust made rumors about the behavior of "dozens" of NOPD officers, some reportedly engaging in violent or racist behavior, others looting, all the more believable.[57] While it is impossible to assess how many officers did act improperly, the reputation of the NOPD was undeniably dealt a major blow when MSNBC looped footage of looters, including local police officers, apparently ransacking a local Walmart.[58] On September 4—the city was mostly empty by then—several NOPD officers were involved in the fatal shootings of two residents, one of whom was mentally disabled.[59]

Other organizations in the response network quickly shied away from the NOPD, a tendency that further weakened the agency's already limited information position. For instance, FEMA reportedly refused to work with the NOPD, as did guardsmen from both Louisiana and Oklahoma.[60] The Louisiana Department of Wildlife and Fisheries did coordinate patrols with the NOPD, though their efforts were hampered by distrust and suspicion.[61] The result was organizational isolation.

The NOPD was further hampered by the loss of its headquarters building, which was flooded within hours after landfall. NOPD officers set up an operational command post at the entrance to a casino in downtown New Orleans.[62] However, the absence of reliable communications with the local EOC, other first responders in New Orleans, and the state EOC minimized the effectiveness of the command post.[63]

It is important to note that the NOPD did not fail completely. Many officers performed heroically.[64] We should also note just how hard the force was hit by Katrina: according to NOPD deputy chief Warren Riley, "some 80 police officers— 5 percent of the city's force—were stranded at home."[65] Many lost their homes.[66] Two officers committed suicide.[67] While some officers did walk off the job, most remained on duty.[68]

BOTTLENECKS IN THE INFORMATION CHAIN

Understanding what is happening in a large-scale crisis typically requires sharing information between a large number of actors, operating at different levels of the system. Sense making takes place in different units, at different organizational levels, across organizations; this gives rise to multiple, conflicting interpretations, all of which may be plausible. Such a variety of perspectives makes it hard to collectively puzzle together available information into a complete picture of a dynamic situation. The more actors and the more variety in organizational stripes, the harder it becomes to establish a shared picture.

Many barriers within and between organizations can prevent the necessary flow of critical information and the sharing of perceptions. In his classic *Man-Made Disasters*, Barry Turner explains how specialization and division of labor in modern organizations create and institutionalize different ways of seeing, which, in turn, can create collective "blind corners" (ways of *not* seeing).[69] These cognitive blinders make it hard to understand which information might be relevant for other organizations.

Another divide often opens between first responders and strategic crisis managers.[70] These actors operate at different levels (and in different worlds). The strategic layer of decision makers typically gathers at an EOC and manages a given crisis from that location. The first responders operate at the heart of the crisis: where the explosion occurs, the shooting happens, or the levees break.

At both levels, individuals are trying to order information and understand the situation, drawing from a cacophony of voices and images, comparing notes in an atmosphere marked by stress and chaos. The sense making is done "on the side," as most people in the chain of command have other responsibilities that they must tend to: making decisions, calling partners, dealing with media, and coping with unforeseen problems. The perceptions of both worlds must all add up somehow, quickly and correctly.

The United States has a system in place to overcome this divide between the strategic and the operational. In theory, the division of labor is quite simple. The states have the primary responsibility for managing a disaster that occurs in their territory. If a state cannot cope on its own, it can request assistance from the federal government. Information flows in the federal response system follow a similar logic. The response organizations close to the scene of the disaster report upward in a chain of command. Information from the states is channeled to various crisis rooms at the federal level in or near Washington. The DHS maintained such a center: the Homeland Security Operations Center was designed to collect and "deconflict" information and then create a common picture of the situation.

The White House had a similar, albeit much smaller center, the Homeland Security Council (HSC). The HSC was responsible for "circulating information throughout the White House during a catastrophe. It serves as a gate-keeper to mitigate duplicative information requests to other agencies."[71] In addition, the HSC was formally responsible for coordinating homeland security activities between and among federal departments and agencies.[72]

During that first week, the information that reached Washington did not necessarily follow these preconceived paths. That's to be expected in times of crisis. The real problem was that critical information that reached Washington got bottled up in the HSOC.

HSOC: The Bottleneck in Washington

On Tuesday morning, Governor Blanco knew that "the dreaded 'big one' ha[d] arrived" and that the city was "in dire trouble."[73] Blanco and members of her staff traveled to New Orleans multiple times during those first days. As soon as it was safe on Monday, the governor was in the air over Louisiana observing the situation firsthand. She would return to the EOC in Baton Rouge and then head straight back to the Superdome.[74] It was clear to her that extensive resources would be required to carry out all manner of missions in the coming days.

By Tuesday, FEMA director Brown also realized that the situation was out of control. At this point, Brown had apparently been convinced by his federal coordinating officer (FCO) in Baton Rouge, Bill Lokey, that the disaster was too big for FEMA and that the Pentagon should be asked to step in.[75] In one newspaper interview, Brown claims that he asked the White House to take over the Katrina response effort on Tuesday: "By the time of that call, he added, 'I was beginning to realize things were going to hell in a handbasket' in Louisiana."[76] In Louisiana, senior officials understood that a major disaster was unfolding.

Officials in Washington would later complain that they did not receive adequate and timely information from the disaster area. There is little evidence indicating that critical information was withheld or bottled up in Louisiana. In fact, waves of information (not all of it accurate) reached Washington in that first week. In addition, various centers in Washington were collecting, interpreting, analyzing, summarizing, and sharing information.

Much of this critical information got bottled up in the HSOC. The HSOC had been designed to "connect the dots" during a disaster: it was responsible for information collection at the national level and subsequent information sharing through a number of means, including National Situation Updates, spot reports, and National Situation Reports ("sitreps").[77] Representing over 35 agencies, it was established on July 8, 2004, and operated with a $70 million annual budget and a staff numbering 300. With hundreds of trained people paying close attention to an emerging disaster, one might expect collective sense making to be speedy and effective.[78]

The HSOC director, Matthew Broderick, would later claim that the HSOC had been just that during Katrina, speedy and effective. Although he later complained that "we were getting nothing out of Louisiana," he asserted that HSOC officials "were able to successfully monitor operations and . . . provide accurate and timely situational awareness to the nationwide stakeholders."[79]

The evidence does not bear this out, however. On the day of landfall, the HSOC did not confirm any breaches. Secretary Chertoff and other senior DHS officials later stated that they did not learn of the collapse of the levees until Tuesday, 24 hours after it happened.[80]

Monday's early reports of flooding did reach the HSOC (see appendix I). Around 9:00 a.m., DHS protective security adviser Louis Dabdoub, stationed in New Orleans, sent an email to the HSOC directly. Dabdoub wrote that "flooding is worsening every minute. . . . The bad part has not hit here yet." A subsequent report from Dabdoub described "lower parishes of [Louisiana] . . . under water." In another example:

> At 10:41 a.m., the HSOC received a copy of an 8 a.m. "Katrina Brief" created by the Transportation Security Administration (TSA), which stated, in part, that "the National Weather Service has reported that a levee broke on the Industrial Canal near the St. Bernard–Orleans Parish line, and 3 to 8 feet of flooding was possible. . . . In the uptown area of New Orleans on the south shore of Lake Pontchartrain, floodwaters by [sic] have already intruded on the first stories of some houses and some roads are impassable. . . . There is heavy street flooding throughout Orleans, St. Bernard, and Jefferson parishes."[81]

Reports from the HSOC suggest that at least some officials there grasped the significance of this incoming information. An early spot report, issued by the HSOC at 10:22 a.m., described rising waters across the city (but made no mention of levee breaches).[82] At 11:16 a.m., Insung Lee from the HSOC emailed Kirstjen Nielsen at the HSC to report that Mayor Nagin had announced that there was "water coming over the levee system in the Lower Ninth Ward"; that the head of LANG, Major General Bennett Landreneau, had confirmed that water was rising in the Lower Ninth Ward; and that local officials had said that "floodwaters are encroaching on roads in the lower-lying parishes of St. Bernard and Plaquemines."[83]

At 2:20 p.m. on Monday, an HSOC report stated that some Louisiana parishes had 8 to 10 feet of water and that people were stranded in flooded areas in both Louisiana and Mississippi. The Bahamonde report reached the HSOC on Monday evening; it was sent on to the White House (received 12:02 a.m. Tuesday).[84] The report described "a quarter-mile breach in the levee near the 17th Street Canal about 200 yards from Lake Pontchartrain allowing water to flow into [New Orleans]. . . . Between 2/3 to 75% of the city is under water. . . . A few bodies were seen floating in the water."[85]

The HSOC received reports of levee breaches throughout the day. Yet the HSOC, amazingly, failed to conclude that levees had been breached.[86] As late as 6:00 p.m. that day, the HSOC informed senior DHS and White House officials that, "Preliminary reports indicate the levees in New Orleans have not been breached," but noted that "an assessment is still pending."[87] It was not until around noon on Tuesday that the HSOC finally confirmed that some levees had been breached, but only after receiving word from the local USACE district commander.[88]

On Thursday, the HSOC again missed the story of the day: the Convention Center. Again, there was plenty of available information to flag the emerging situation. A group of Federal Protection Service (FPS) officials, in town to secure federal buildings in New Orleans, had communicated how they stumbled on a "spontaneous gathering" in front of the Convention Center as early as Tuesday evening.[89] Unfortunately the HSOC staff was "operating under its mistaken impression that the convention center and Superdome—about a mile apart— were in the same complex."[90]

As a result, HSOC sitreps on Wednesday and Thursday (when the HSOC was still "sorting out" the distinction between the two facilities) did not refer to reports in the local media and from the state police that thousands were gathered at the Convention Center.[91]

Source of Failure: HSOC's Way of Working

Why did the HSOC not provide timely and accurate assessments during that first week? One explanation is that the HSOC did not have a method to effectively make sense of a mega-disaster.

The HSOC did have a working philosophy, but it proved problematic. Only fact-checked information counted. But there was very limited capacity to check facts. DHS and FEMA had few boots on the ground (and of those, few if any actually knew the city).[92] The HSOC apparently did not monitor local media. But even if it had, it is not at all clear that the HSOC's official assessments would have been based on these reports, skeptical as its staff was about the accuracy of unofficial sources of information.

The HSOC director, Matthew Broderick, personally had to sanction information before it was passed on to his superiors ("They wouldn't know until I passed it on").[93] A former military officer, Broderick insisted on personally "making sense" of incoming data. He had learned in Vietnam that in the fog of war it was rarely immediately clear what the "hard facts" were.[94] He did not want to commit the error of relaying mere impressions; he only wanted to pass on verified facts. Broderick summarizes his operational philosophy: "We should not help spread rumors or innuendo, nor should we rely on speculation or hype, and we should not react to initial or unconfirmed reports, which are almost invariably lacking or incomplete."[95]

Even though Broderick "knew we had a catastrophe" on Tuesday morning, he "needed a few hours to get some ground truth" before he would confirm the levee breaches.[96] According to the HSOC director, any reports of flooding needed to be "put . . . in context. . . . We have floods in Pennsylvania all the time. We have floods in New Jersey all the time. Every time there's a hurricane, there's a flood. So, you know, to say that there is flooding in a particular part of town is a normal expectation of what's happening in a hurricane. Flooding does occur, and sometimes significant flooding in a certain part."[97]

He asked the National Geospatial Agency "to start overflying and giving us whatever picture they could."[98] When Broderick saw the Bahamonde report (based on the latter's helicopter ride), he still discounted the report months later because it was not factual enough: "You know, you can see why we go in and try to get clarification. . . . It says . . . 'Downtown, there is less flooding.' Yet, he says, '75 percent of the city is underwater.' You know, that's hyping something that you would go back and check. A quarter-mile breach in a levee: again, is it a breach or is it overspilling?"[99]

The HSOC director viewed the USACE as the sole source of confirmation concerning the state of the levees. All other reports were to his mind merely "personal observations."[100] FEMA reports of breached levees were treated as mere rumors or "impressions" until they could be verified.[101] So it was not until around noon on Tuesday, after speaking personally with the local USACE commander in New Orleans, that Broderick felt confident enough to confirm a number of breaches in and around New Orleans. At this point, he immediately called the DHS secretary to inform him of the HSOC's new assessment of the situation.[102]

Broderick was personally involved in the work of confirming incoming reports. Brown recalls that the "pings" from DHS were driving him "nuts" as "we had operations to run."[103] Interestingly, for all this "pinging," Broderick lacked the ability to review the information that came in as a result. For instance, he had little time to read his emails: "Probably during this thing [Hurricane Katrina] I think I tried to answer when I could, but I probably had 700 or 800 emails backlogged by then. I kind of skipped the e-mail unless someone tells me 'I sent you an e-mail, and it's important,' or I'm looking out for something. I don't get too wrapped up in it."[104]

Broderick later admitted that FEMA accurately informed him Monday night, by email, about the situation in New Orleans. But Broderick never saw the report containing Bahamonde's observations on the extent of the flooding (he went home before the report arrived).[105]

Broderick assumed that Brown or others at FEMA would call him directly with news of any significant development.[106] Here it is worth recalling that it was often impossible to make voice calls during those first days. Officials had better luck with email and therefore came to rely on that medium.[107]

By the time the HSOC finally did begin reporting the "facts" of the disaster, its reports no longer had much value.[108] According to Senate investigators, the process of compiling sources, confirming information, and then formulating the sitrep resulted in a final product that "was, at a minimum, five hours old" upon release.[109] That's not very helpful in a fast-evolving disaster.

A House report would later conclude that the HSOC "failed to provide valuable situational information to the White House and key operational officials."[110] The HSOC's failure to quickly deconflict available reports as well as the lengthy process by which the center refined sitreps prior to release helps to explain why President Bush and DHS secretary Chertoff retired on Monday evening assuming New Orleans had dodged the bullet. If the HSOC's 5:00 p.m. sitrep was the last thing they read on Monday, Chertoff and other senior DHS officials would have been under the impression that no levees had been breached. The president characterized the mood among members of his staff on Monday evening as "relaxed."[111] As far as the president knew, this was a "normal" hurricane and the situation was under control.[112]

That would also explain why senior DHS and DOD officials kept to their regular schedules until midday on Tuesday, August 30.[113] On Tuesday morning,

Chertoff flew to Atlanta, where he was participating in a conference on avian flu. Given his early-morning departure from the capital, it is unclear if Chertoff received either a daily briefing or at the very least a so-called briefing book that would have contained the HSOC's most recent 5:00 a.m. sitrep (see appendix I).[114]

Push or Pull?

An essential factor explaining sense making during Katrina was the diametrically opposed expectations with regard to how critical information should be flagged. A "push" philosophy expects lower-level administrators to send critical information upward along the chain of command. A "pull" philosophy, on the other hand, expects strategic decision makers to *ask* for particular types of information that they deem to be critical. The HSOC appears to have operated on the basis of a "push" philosophy, although this was not evident to other actors. The HSOC *waited* for information to emerge through the bureaucratic layers.

Broderick thought a "pull" philosophy to be detrimental to the effectiveness of the response: "Our standard operating procedure is not to disturb the operations of field commanders in the middle of a crisis."[115] In most crises, "pull" is not necessary; time clears things up. The HSOC operated as if Katrina was a normal crisis: "Prior experience had shown that as the storm cleared over the next day or two, the ground truth would begin to crystallize and a common operational picture and more frequent and accurate reporting would emerge."[116]

If something really important happened, Broderick counted on officials to actively bring this information to his attention: "We relied on the good judgment of the information providers in the field to push relevant, pertinent information to the HSOC."[117] Broderick expected to be contacted directly to alert him about new pieces of critical information: "If they were urgent messages that needed to be conveyed, I would have thought they would have called and not sent an e-mail."[118]

The HSOC leadership came to suspect that FEMA's senior leadership was intentionally *restricting* the flow of information to the HSOC.[119] That was not true. FEMA sent through "numerous daily reports [that were] automatically transmitted to HSOC."[120] HSOC staffers could get the latest picture of the situation through regularly scheduled conference calls; Brown had little sympathy for the argument that FEMA should create a separate dedicated channel for information for the HSOC specifically. "All they had to do was to listen to those VTCs [video teleconferences] and pay attention to those VTCs, and they would have known what was going on."[121] Brown thus favored the "pull" method: HSOC officials should actively select information from the streams of operational communications that they could easily access.

FEMA kept the HSOC in the loop via the National Response Coordination Center, FEMA's information hub. In one example, when FEMA deputy director Patrick Rhode first heard reports about "issues with the levee" during the early hours of Monday morning, he made sure that the information was fed up to the NRCC, where it should be fed onward to the HSOC. It doesn't appear to have crossed Rhode's mind at the time to contact the HSOC directly; in his mind, the existing routine sufficed.[122]

FEMA did not *flag* critical information. Brown neglected at one point to reach out to the head of NORTHCOM, assuming that a DOD liaison officer present at the state EOC would provide him with the information he needed.[123] Nor did he take steps to personally apprise Chertoff of the situation on Monday: "If the secretary wants information about something, he can either call me directly or reach out to HSOC to get that information."[124] Brown explained later that there was "no reason for me to talk to them. I had a disaster to run."[125]

So Broderick was right that "Brown was not giving the HSOC the information."[126] Brown made an exception for the White House. Other officials could get updates via established routines, liaisons, and the relevant crisis centers and their regular reports.

We can thus conclude that HSOC's "push" philosophy did not work in practice. The HSOC failed to switch to a "pull" mode as soon as it realized it was operating in the dark. As a result, it was deprived of relevant information while sitting on the information it had.

Sense Making in the White House

The White House also had a small sense-making center. The Homeland Security Council commenced 24-hour operations on Monday morning.[127] Over the coming days, HSC staff solicited regular situation reports from almost every federal agency for their own use and on behalf of the White House Situation Room.

The HSC, like the HSOC, had access to information on Monday about a disaster unfolding in New Orleans. For instance, on Monday morning, at

10:13 a.m., the HSC released a spot report stating that "flooding is significant throughout the region and a levee in New Orleans has reportedly been breached sending 6–8 feet of water throughout the 9th Ward area of the city."[128] The report also relayed that water was rising at one foot per hour and pumping stations had failed.[129]

Yet White House officials did not believe that they had confirmation of any levee breaches, even when, at 12:02 a.m. on Tuesday morning, the White House received the Bahamonde spot report.[130] Only after receiving an updated sitrep from a DHS watch officer at 10:23 a.m. would White House officials consider the breaches confirmed.[131] The sitrep included maps depicting the locations of the different breach sites, highlighting two areas of concern, the levee at Tennessee Street and the levee at Seventeenth Street.[132] A House report later concluded that "the White House failed to de-conflict varying damage assessments and discounted information that ultimately proved accurate."[133]

As mentioned earlier, Michael Brown communicated directly with officials in the White House close to the president (thereby bypassing both the HSOC *and* the HSC).[134] Several times on Monday, for instance, Brown spoke by phone with White House deputy chief of staff Joe Hagin. Around noon that day, Hagin, who was traveling with the president on *Air Force One,* participated in a conference call with state and local officials who reported severe flooding in St. Bernard Parish. Brown claimed that he informed Hagin no later than 6:00 p.m. central standard time on Monday that "New Orleans is flooding, it's the worst-case scenario." Brown recalls the conversation as follows: "I think I told him that we were realizing our worst nightmare, that everything we had planned about, worried about, that FEMA, frankly, had worried about for ten years was coming true."[135]

Given the information that was making its way to the White House (via Brown, the HSC, and the HSOC), it is puzzling that President Bush did not seem to be more in the know during those first few days (we return to this point later in the chapter). Brown testified that he was certain that the information that he had relayed to Hagin and others ultimately reached the president: "I never worried about whether I talked directly to the President because I knew that in speaking to Joe [Hagin], I was talking directly to the President."[136] However, the president did not take part in any of those calls. Hagin did inform the president's chief of staff, Andy Card. In a 9:51 p.m. email, Card confirmed to Brown that Hagin was keeping him informed about the situation.[137] It appears that the president began to realize on Tuesday how bad the flooding was. But during the week, he did not seem to realize how badly people suffered.

Conventional wisdom now has it that the president and his staff were slow to realize the extent of the disaster unfolding in New Orleans. Questions as to how slow, whether they were too slow, and what difference it made in determining the quality of the response consumed the immediate postdisaster debate.

We will probably never know when exactly the president fully realized the extent of the unfolding disaster. From an accountability perspective that may be unsatisfactory. But we can certainly see that the president was not the only one who was slow in arriving at an accurate assessment. For us, the more interesting question is why it took so long to *collectively* realize that a massive disaster was unfolding in New Orleans. To answer that question, we must adopt a psychological perspective.

A FAILURE OF COLLECTIVE AWARENESS

Many officials had access to accurate information. A critical problem was that at times these same officials did not *understand* the meaning or implications of the information they had. We argue that this was due to a combination of stress and fatigue, conceptual confusion, and "imaginary limitations."

Stress, Emotions, and Stamina

Psychological research tells us that even under the best of circumstances we overestimate what we think we know. It also teaches us that the brain's sense-making capacities quickly deteriorate under stress. When we get tired, many routine tasks become more difficult.[138] It becomes harder to make accurate assessments, switch tasks, and gauge risks. We are also more likely to make selfish choices, use improper language, and make superficial judgments. For this reason, it is fair to argue that fatigue and stress are among the most common dangers for decision makers in disasters.

The exact impact of stress and fatigue on decision makers is, of course, hard to assess in hindsight. But we know that many of the key actors in Baton Rouge and New Orleans were very tired that first week. Consider this interchange on

Wednesday morning between Generals Steven Blum and Clyde Vaughn of the National Guard Bureau in Washington and General Bennett Landreneau, head of LANG:

General Blum: Benny, how are things going?

General Landreneau: Sir, we've had a difficult night.

General Blum: What do you need?

General Landreneau: We need 5K soldiers to help out. The armory is flooded. My command and control is at the Superdome. We have a lot of undesirables here trying to cause trouble.

General Vaughn: Hey Benny, can we drive to the Superdome?

General Landreneau: No sir, we are cut off by the rising water, along with the armory.

General Vaughn: Where do you want us to send the incoming soldiers?

General Landreneau: Sir, send them to the intersection of Interstate 310 and State 10.

General Blum: Benny, when's the last time you got any sleep?

General Landreneau: Well sir, I think two days ago.

General Blum: Listen, you need to get some rest, you sound exhausted.

General Landreneau: I'll try, sir, but every time I lay down someone gets me up for a little emergency.

General Blum: Try and get some rest; this is an ongoing effort and we need your energy.[139]

Key actors looked stressed and emotional. Governor Blanco was visibly affected by the scale of the disaster, tearing up on television several times. When Bahamonde briefed Mayor Nagin on Monday at the Hyatt, the tone was reportedly very emotional. The mayor was "stunned" by what he and his staff had heard.[140] They became deeply frustrated when the buses did not materialize as promised and the levees had still not been fixed.[141]

There was speculation after Katrina that Mayor Nagin had succumbed to stress. Lieutenant Governor Mitch Landrieu reportedly described finding Nagin "shell shocked" in his hotel room.[142] Douglas Brinkley writes that Nagin had grown "paranoid" by Thursday, apparently believing that the Superdome crowd was after him.[143] Governor Blanco asserted that Nagin "was falling apart. He was near nervous breakdown."[144] Nagin later explained that he was "emotionally spent" when he gave his now-famous interview on Thursday (discussed in chapter 4).[145]

His agitation was fed by his close friend and the city's police chief, Eddie Compass, who related numerous graphic accounts of looting and violence. Compass told the mayor that his officers "had run out of ammo" in battles with looters.[146] On Thursday, Compass stated, "We have individuals who are getting raped; we have individuals who are getting beaten."[147] Compass reportedly claimed that he almost got kidnapped in the Convention Center.[148] At one point, Compass broke down in front of the cameras.[149]

While Michael Brown started the week strongly (in terms of sense making), he too would begin to display irrational behavior as the days passed. On Thursday, a visibly exhausted Brown appeared on TV all day to convince America that "things are going relatively well."[150] That was obviously not true. It was also around this time that Brown began firing off "goofy" emails "exposing his vanity and embarrassing FEMA."[151] For instance, Bahamonde on Wednesday emailed Brown to report how desperate the situation was from his vantage point at the Superdome. He received a reply three hours later stating that Brown needed time to eat.[152] While some of these emails appear in a particularly bad light when taken out of context, they do suggest that Brown became increasingly focused on bureaucratic politics rather than making things happen as the crisis deepened.

Conceptual Confusion

House investigators found that both the HSOC and the HSC "appeared to discount information that ultimately proved accurate, and failed to provide decision-makers, up to and including the president, with timely information."[153] One explanation we explore here is the prevalence in crisis of "conceptual confusion"—people misunderstanding basic terms of information or texts without realizing their mistake. Time and again we see that what may appear obvious in hindsight is often ambiguous or misleading to the participants as events are unfolding.

One widely shared source of confusion concerned the difference between levees being *breached* and being *overtopped*.[154] Overtopping refers to water spilling over the top of a levee, while the levee itself remains intact and structurally sound. Overtopping is normal and potentially dangerous but in the end not disastrous (as the water can be pumped out). A breach, on the other hand, is an actual break in the levee, allowing water to pour through unimpeded and at full force. It was unclear to officials during Katrina if the flooding being reported in New Orleans was caused by the normal combination of heavy precipitation and overtopping or by levee breaches. Many officials (and not a few journalists) failed to understand the difference.

The HSOC, according to Broderick, its director, "spent a lot of time on what was a breach and what was overtopping and what's the significance of either one."[155] Further complicating matters, it appears that to Broderick a breach was only a breach when it could not be repaired.[156]

The lack of shared definitions gave rise to ambiguity. By late Monday morning, Governor Blanco, state coordinating officer Smith, FCO Lokey, and Michael Brown, in Baton Rouge, signed onto a video teleconference attended by DHS secretary Chertoff and at least one deputy secretary, as well as a White House representative.[157] State officials went into the teleconference having just received reports of at least one levee breach. FCO Lokey briefly summarized the situation as he understood it: "In New Orleans [*sic*] Parish, we have got water in the eastern part. And down in the Ninth Ward that borders St. Bernard Parish, we're going to have serious search and rescue efforts that are going to need to take place once we can get back in. . . . We are pretty much inundated right now, and our next priorities are going to be search and rescue and saving lives."[158]

Looking back, we can see that Lokey described a disaster in the making. But when asked by a White House official about the state of the city's flood protection system, the governor explained that the state EOC continued to receive "reports in some places that maybe water is coming over the levees." She went on to explain that officials had "heard a report unconfirmed [that] we have not breached the levee. I think we have not breached the levee at this time. . . . That could change, but in some places we have floodwaters coming into New Orleans."[159] Max Mayfield, the National Hurricane Center director—the Cassandra of previous days—agreed with the governor during the call, saying that the "federal levees" did not appear to have been breached.

No attempt was made at the time to correct Governor Blanco during the call. It seemed to Smith that "she conveyed the important information, which was that there was so much water in the neighborhoods that people were swimming in it."[160] While it might have seemed obvious to Smith that the levees had been breached, the governor did not say so. She actually downplayed the possibility. The DHS secretary later explained that the governor's claim that no levees had been breached informed many federal officials' initial understanding of what had happened in New Orleans: "I, and the other participants [in the call], heard [that] the levees had not been breached." Nobody involved in the conference call, he explained, asserted that "the flooding was extraordinary or out of the norm for a significant hurricane with substantial rainfall or whether the more than thirty pumps in the city of New Orleans would be able to channel the excess water appropriately."[161]

The USACE office in New Orleans released its first post-landfall report to the USACE command and the HSOC concerning the situation in New Orleans late on Monday. According to Cooper and Block, "If officials were seeking confirmation about levee breaches, the news was buried and cloaked in jargon": "On page five of the six-page report on conditions in New Orleans, just after recounting the 'positive media' the Corps had been receiving . . . the report devoted five brief sentences to the matter of levee failures. 'At this point, the Corps of Engineers has no confirmed reports of levee breaching or levee failure of any kind during Hurricane Katrina,' the report said. 'We are investigating for the possibility of any breaching, and we are also investigating whether levees have been overtopped at any point.'"[162]

Only sentences later, the report "confirmed a floodwall failure on the Industrial Canal." The report went on to describe "floodwalls [that] were overtopped on the east side of the 17th Street Canal and the east side of the [Industrial Canal]. Sections of wall failed in each area."[163]

Even when reports did relay the news that New Orleans was flooding, the language was often ambiguous or the salient details were hidden somewhere further down the page. For example, a 10:52 a.m. National Weather Service report noted "some levees overtopped." A 1:54 p.m. report from the Corps of Engineers mentioned a "small breach reported at 17th Canal" and "some level of widespread flooding."[164] These reports did not sound very alarming. A FEMA email (1:38 p.m.) contained the following: "North side of City under est. 11′ water in heavy residential area."[165] This meant that the north side of the city was flooding; this was only possible if a levee had been breached. But you wouldn't know that by reading the report.

Or consider how FEMA's Patrick Rhode, in his email to DHS's Michael Jackson on Monday at 11:05 p.m., downplayed the Bahamonde spot report. Where Bahamonde's spot report estimated that "2/3 to 75% of the city" flooded, with some homes "with water to the first floor and others completely underwater," Rhode merely stated that "approximately 60 percent of the city is under water to some degree."[166] Rhode did not mention the small fires where natural gas lines had broken, nor did he describe the failure of the pumps essential to the task of "deflooding" the city.

When something is not clearly communicated, it may not get through during a crisis.

Imagining the Inconceivable: Inherent Limitations

State and federal officials interpreted initial reports of a breach in a canal wall in downtown New Orleans in various ways. The governor's chief counsel, for instance, recognized these reports as "very, very bad news" and assumed that "everybody else would recognize that." A USACE official at the state EOC reportedly "discounted" the news of the breach.[167] It appears that many state and local officials were ultimately "lulled into a sense of security by the continual assurance by the [USACE leadership in Washington] that the levees were never going to fail."[168] Broderick would later explain that watching television reports about the French Quarter "led us to believe that the flooding may have been just an isolated incident . . . because we were not seeing it."[169]

A common problem in crisis situations is the difficulty of appreciating the importance of information about an event that seems inconceivable.[170] In his book *Thinking, Fast and Slow,* Daniel Kahneman explains that people don't see what they don't expect to see and that they are more likely to see what they expect to see. An inherent limitation of the mind, according to Kahneman, is "our excessive confidence in what we believe we know, and our apparent inability to acknowledge the full extent of our ignorance and the uncertainty of the world we live in."[171] When people cannot conceive of what might be going on, "they are very likely to believe arguments that appear to support what they think they know, even when those arguments are unsound."[172]

When the levees gave way early on Monday morning, we can safely assume that few officials conjured up a mental picture of a submerged city or anticipated the magnitude of the destruction that such a flood might entail.[173] Brown later made an excellent point when he suggested that if the flooding had been couched in terms of terrorism, "everybody would have paid attention."[174]

But as it was, many officials did not "get it."

The extent to which officials were familiar with the local environment appears to have played a role in shaping their perceptions. For example, officials kept confusing the Superdome with the Convention Center. In another example, "Phil Parr and the small contingent of FEMA officials at the Superdome knew absolutely nothing about the city they were sitting in. . . . Parr thought his team was trapped by floodwaters at the Superdome, and he did not realize that the dry section of the city sat only about a block away from where they were camped."[175] The local USACE commander, Richard Wagenaar, had only recently arrived in New Orleans from his previous posting—in South Korea. By his own account, he "didn't even know where the Seventeenth Street Canal was."[176]

But even those who knew the city well initially failed to grasp the extent of the disaster. Trymaine Lee was reporting for the *Times-Picayune* from downtown New Orleans:

> I was here, you know, the entire time they were evacuating, with a small group of reporters. I think just the level of despair when you realize *on day two* [emphasis added] when these huddled masses of people were stranded out on the interstate, you know, slept overnight and, you know, people were trapped in their attics and on their rooftops. The sheer magnitude of the crisis, that's what astounded me because I wasn't prepared for that. You know I figured the storm would blow by and there would be some wind damage. But once the levees broke and you realize that eighty percent of the city was underwater and that people in some sections of the city were unable to or didn't have the wherewithal to leave, or resources to leave. I realized that, O.K., this is serious, serious business. People are drowning and people are trapped in attics. Seeing that—the first body I saw in the street—I realized that this is serious.[177]

Two of Lee's colleagues found out how bad the situation was on Monday when they went out to survey the city on bicycle. Seeing the devastated neighborhoods (including his own), James O'Byrne began to realize the extent of the disaster: "As it happened, Doug [the other reporter] and I were the only reporters who made it to the edge of Lakeview that day and were the first reporters to grasp the extent of the catastrophe that would soon engulf us."[178] O'Byrne understands why others did not grasp the situation right away:

A symphony of national media reports was trumpeting the fact that New Orleans had lucked out again. . . . National news programs were broadcasting
that the city had, quote, "dodged a bullet," words that became a virtual media
catchphrase for the rest of Monday and well into Tuesday.

But these national media outlets had sent to town in most instances a single
reporter, and from where each of them stood, in their downtown and French
Quarter hotels, on the high ground close to the Mississippi River, the phrase
seemed to fit. It was all they could see.[179]

Professional reporters looking for a story, who were on the ground in the middle
of a flooded city, did not realize that a superdisaster was unfolding.

One official who did have a fairly comprehensive view of the situation early
on was Marty Bahamonde, FEMA's lone representative in New Orleans. Monday morning around 11:00 a.m., the New Orleans EOC (where Bahamonde
was at that time) received a "very specific" report from the local fire department describing "the location . . . and the size" of a canal breach in downtown
New Orleans.[180] Bahamonde emailed the firefighters' report to a FEMA deputy
director in Washington, who in turn forwarded the email to FEMA director
Brown.[181] Brown replied immediately on his BlackBerry, thanking Bahamonde
for the report before explaining that the consensus in Baton Rouge was that the
"water over [the levee] was not a breach."[182]

Later in the day, Bahamonde took in the scale of the disaster during two
brief helicopter rides (the first one on Monday at 5:15 p.m.), taking aerial pictures of the breached levees.[183] He was "struck by how accurate" the firefighters' report had been. Upon returning to the Superdome, he called Brown. Bahamonde also called the FEMA Office of Public Affairs to arrange a conference
call among FEMA officials "so that [he] could make as many people aware of
the situation that faced FEMA and the city of New Orleans [as possible]."[184]

During the subsequent call with several senior DHS officials, including the
DHS secretary's chief of staff, Bahamonde described, among other things, damaged or impassable roadways in and leading out of the city, stranded residents,
supply and personnel shortages at the Superdome, and emerging public health
risks.[185] Bahamonde "believed that [he] was confirming the worst-case scenario
that everyone had always talked about." Bahamonde later reported feeling that
the assembled officials were not impressed by his account of the situation.[186]
He was right. As deputy assistant to the president for homeland security Ken

Rapuano said: "This was just Marty's observation, and it's difficult to distinguish between a [levee] overtopping and a breach."[187] Bahamonde's reports were met with incredulity, in part because, according to Brown, he had a reputation within the agency for "hyperbole."[188]

But the bigger problem was that Bahamonde's report conflicted with other trusted sources. As Brown later explained: "The real problem that was going on while Marty was down there is that I'm sitting in Baton Rouge, Marty's giving us these reports, and the governor's staff is getting conflicting reports. And I'm trying to balance those two reports. Marty's down there, a guy that I know. The governor's telling me she has people down there that she trusts, and there are two conflicting reports. So I'm trying to synthesize those two reports."[189]

Brown is a case study in the limitations of imagination. This was the man whose "gut was hurting," warning others Katrina was the big one. He then received plenty of information to confirm his worst fears. On Monday morning, Brown received at least four emails describing levee breaches. The first was based on the 8:14 a.m. report from the National Weather Service. At 10:20 a.m., Bahamonde reported "severe flooding on the St. Bernard/Orleans parish line" and that the "area around the Superdome is beginning to flood" (his eyewitness report).[190] At 11:57 a.m., Brown received a report containing the firefighters' report from earlier in the day about a 20-foot-wide breach on the Lake Pontchartrain side levee.[191]

Yet, despite all that information, Brown initially assumed that New Orleans had dodged the bullet: "There was a point where I felt we had dodged a bullet, too, because we had conflicting information within the EOC about whether there been a breach of the levees or the levees had been topped. That did go on for a couple of hours. But then later in the day, it became abundantly clear, as Marty got his photographs to us and the phone calls, that indeed the levees had been breached and we know that."[192]

It took the HSOC director much longer to understand how bad it was. When Broderick turned on the radio on Tuesday morning during his drive in to work and learned how bad the situation was in New Orleans, he could not believe his ears.[193] Yet Broderick continued to dismiss incoming reports of major flooding and levee breaches as "hype."[194] Broderick reportedly informed the DHS secretary early in the day on Tuesday that his people had yet to confirm any reports of levee breaches.[195]

It appears that even President Bush, a former Texas governor who had himself faced down hurricanes in Blanco's position, was slow to grasp the scale and urgency of the unfolding disaster. On Monday evening, the White House was briefed on Bahamonde's assessment of the situation. By then, one would expect the White House to understand the severity of the situation. Early the following day, both the HSOC and the HSC confirmed the levee breaches and issued reports to that effect.[196] At least some of the president's advisers had begun to realize by early morning that the print media's claims that New Orleans had "dodged the bullet" did not match well with the images being broadcast on the 24-hour news channels.[197]

On Tuesday morning, the president was in consultations with Vice President Dick Cheney, the White House homeland security adviser, DHS secretary Chertoff, and FEMA director Brown by telephone. If the FEMA director's later recollections are any indication, the president was still coming to terms with the magnitude of what had happened. Brown informed the group that at least 90% of the local population had been displaced and that responders needed military assets. "This was the 'Big One,'" Brown said. During the discussion, Brown outlined FEMA's needs and suggested the possible "federalization" of operations.[198]

Brown thought this was the turning point in the president's understanding of the situation: "And as I recall my first statement to him was, you know, Mr. President, I estimate right now that 90 percent of the population of New Orleans has been displaced. And he is like, My God you mean it is that bad? Yes, sir, it was that bad."[199]

By 4:00 p.m. Tuesday, the White House was "getting it," pressing the DHS secretary into action.[200] Later that evening, Chertoff declared Katrina to be what is referred to in the National Response Plan as an Incident of National Significance.[201] Looking back, Bush admitted that he had missed early cues about the scale of the disaster:

> When that storm came by, a lot of people said we dodged a bullet. When that storm came through at first, people said, whew. There was a sense of relaxation, and that's what I was referring to. And I, myself, thought we had dodged a bullet. You know why? Because I was listening to people, probably over the airways, say, the bullet has been dodged. And that was what I was referring to. Of course, there were plans in case the levee had been breached. There was a sense of relaxation in the moment, a critical moment. And thank you for giving me a chance to clarify that.[202]

Bush's former press secretary, Scott McClellan, later rejected the notion that the White House lacked information that might have led to a more proactive response. He argues that the president had grown "numb" and "perhaps a little complacent":

> The potential seriousness of the storm had been clearly conveyed to us in advance by Max Mayfield. . . . And while the information we received after Katrina's landfall . . . was fragmentary, chaotic, and sometimes inaccurate, we were getting enough data to know that this was a very bad storm—possibly "the big one" residents of New Orleans and emergency managements professionals had long worried about. *The problem lay in our mind-set* [emphasis added]. Our White House team had already weathered many disasters, from the hurricanes of the previous year all the way back to the unprecedented calamity of 9/11. As a result, we were probably a little numb . . . and perhaps a little complacent. . . . We assumed that local and federal officials would do their usual yeomen's work at minimizing the devastation, much as the more seasoned Florida officials had done the year before, and we recalled how President Bush had excelled at reassuring and comforting the nation in the wake of past calamities. Instead of planning and acting for the potential worst-case scenario, we took a chance that Katrina would not be as unmanageable, overwhelming, or catastrophic as it turned out. *So we allowed our institutional response to go on autopilot* [emphasis added].[203]

Default Expectations and Confirmation Bias: Explaining Blind Corners

Psychologists tell us that we are wont to (subconsciously) seek out information that confirms what we think we know. Looking back, we can see that there was indeed plenty of information that seemed to confirm that New Orleans had dodged the bullet. Let's look at a few data points (see appendix I for an overview of relevant messages).

Early on Monday morning (at 7:33 a.m. to be exact), Bahamonde reported that there was "no widespread flooding yet." In an interview with national media, around 8:10 a.m., Senator Mary Landrieu (then at the state EOC in Baton Rouge) did not mention floods.[204] According to a 10:32 a.m. HSOC report, "Major General Landreneau [adjutant general for Louisiana] said that emergency personnel stationed at Jackson Barracks have confirmed that the waters are rising, although he could not say whether the cause was a levee breach or overtopping."[205]

The HSOC spot reports released on Monday cited "unconfirmed, conflicting, or unreliable" reports of breaches.[206] They described "typical," "expected," "standard," or "normal" hurricane flooding, which, according to investigators, blinded many readers to the "horrific devastation" that the storm had in fact wrought.[207]

Broderick left DHS headquarters on Monday evening believing that no levees in the city had been breached. He had watched people on television partying on Bourbon Street, leading him to believe that New Orleans had dodged the bullet.[208] To his mind, Hurricane Katrina had been a "normal hurricane situation" in which the federal government "may have to go in and help with search and rescue for a certain amount of people but it's the regular hurricane drill."[209] As the HSOC head later explained:

> There were no urgent calls or flash messages coming up from anyone during the day of Monday that gave us any indication [that the levees had collapsed]. We did get reports that there was breaching and overtopping. However, we had other conflicting reports that said there were no breaches and that only certain parts of the city were taking water. Lastly, we finally got a report that I remember at—I think it was the last SITREP of that evening that said there were no breaches to the levee systems in New Orleans, and that's what came up to us.[210]

Brown knew how bad the situation was on Monday night. On television, he was still struggling to be clear about how dire things were. During an appearance on CNN that evening, Brown explained that FEMA was preparing to house "at least tens of thousands of victims that are going to be without homes for literally months on end. . . . FEMA folks who have been with the agency for . . . 15 or 20 years . . . talk about how this is the worst flooding they've ever seen in their entire lives."[211] At the same time, the FEMA director maintained that the city actually "got off easy." Similar ambiguity was reflected in other statements made by various state officials throughout the evening.[212]

Most media were late to grasp the enormity of the disaster.[213] Early on Monday afternoon, MSNBC set the tone when reporters suggested that the storm had missed New Orleans by "this much." MSNBC's reporter, broadcasting from the French Quarter, correctly noted that there was "not much floodwater." The French Quarter never flooded. Later that afternoon, NBC reported high water levels, but snakes, alligators, and exposure to contaminants were the primary concerns (rather than people drowning). NBC twice broadcast footage of teens dancing in the dirty water.

NBC's *Nightly News with Brian Williams* reported from the Superdome. Williams said Katrina was "not even as destructive as predicted" and seemed to worry more about flooding in Tennessee. According to Williams, the "number of people killed is low and New Orleans had been 'spared from disaster.'" The people of New Orleans were being advised to make sure to boil any water they took from the taps. Bill O'Reilly on FOX News focused primarily on nearby St. Bernard Parish, which in his words had been hit (there was "colossal devastation") but was "not very populated." There was footage from New Orleans as well, but it was mostly of people walking through shallow floodwater.[214]

On Monday night, CNN's Larry King spoke of "massive floods"—he talked to correspondents everywhere but in New Orleans. As mentioned earlier, the FEMA director briefly made an appearance during the broadcast. When Brown talked about a "catastrophic disaster," King countered that Katrina's "little move to the right" saved downtown New Orleans. Brown explained that everything east of downtown had been decimated, mentioned flooding everywhere, and predicted that it was only going to get worse. But there were no pictures to illustrate his story. And, astonishingly, he then said that *there were no breaches*. He must have misspoken, because he knew better. Regardless, it did not help to raise awareness about the unfolding disaster in New Orleans.

On Tuesday, the *New York Times* reported that while parts of New Orleans were inundated, the majority of the confirmed deaths were in neighboring Mississippi. "Most of the levees held" in New Orleans, but "40,000 homes had been flooded in St. Bernard Parish." Midway through the piece, almost as an aside, the reader was informed that "on the southern shore of [Lake Pontchartrain], entire neighborhoods were flooded to the roof lines." One had to know the geography of New Orleans to understand the implications of this sentence.

The *Washington Post* described the damage and devastation in Louisiana and Mississippi as severe but, like the *New York Times*, indicated that New Orleans had been spared the worst-case scenario.[215] The *Wall Street Journal*, too, saw that an even larger catastrophe in New Orleans had been averted because the storm had turned at the last minute.[216]

By Tuesday evening, it was clear. ABC News opened its evening broadcast by stating, "Last night we began this broadcast saying Katrina was bad, very bad. Last night, we didn't know the half of it."[217] By Wednesday, the United States was in disaster mode.

SEEING THE ELEPHANT IN THE ROOM

When we look back on that first week, it is still baffling to see how long it took many federal officials to realize that they were in the middle of an unfolding mega-disaster. In this chapter, we considered the various factors that help to explain this key failure.

Communications breakdowns—a common feature of disasters everywhere—undermined officials' ability to quickly reassess the situation. On the day of landfall, authoritative reporting from the field was nearly impossible because of the widespread destruction of communications infrastructure. It is no wonder, then, that analysts in crisis centers far removed from the scene needed more time to grasp the enormity of events.

In their efforts to understand the situation, officials were dependent on conflicting reports from media, government, and private sources, many of which continued to provide inaccurate or incomplete information throughout Monday and into Tuesday.

The HSOC's failure to make sense of the increasingly dire reports emerging from New Orleans has been cited as one of the primary reasons why senior federal officials in Washington only belatedly understood that levees had been breached. Critical pieces of information flowed upward but were offset by contradictory reports. Simply put, the US disaster management system did not produce an accurate and timely picture of the situation.

If there is one lesson we should take away from this chapter, it is that a bottom-up or "push" approach does not work in a complex disaster. Whereas in relatively minor and routine incidents we may count on the production of timely and accurate situation reports, this becomes an unrealistic assumption in large-scale disasters. The bottom-up approach depends too much on overwhelmed emergency managers to provide accurate and timely information for the next level. We will elaborate on this lesson and its implications in the final chapter.

4

WHO'S IN CHARGE HERE?

COORDINATING A MULTILEVEL RESPONSE

I don't know whether it's the governor's problem, or it's the
president's problem, but somebody needs to get . . . on a plane and
sit down, the two of them, and figure this out right now.
—MAYOR C. RAY NAGIN, INTERVIEW ON RADIO STATION WWL,
SEPTEMBER 1, 2005

The system, at every level of government, was not well-coordinated,
and was overwhelmed in the first few days.
—PRESIDENT GEORGE W. BUSH, ADDRESS TO THE NATION,
SEPTEMBER 15, 2005

THE PERENNIAL PROBLEM OF CRISIS COORDINATION

Mayor Nagin's lament in the foregoing epigraph illustrates his deep frustration
with a core problem of any crisis response: the challenge of coordination. After Katrina, official reports lambasted federal, state, and local actors for their
inability to coordinate with one another. FEMA was singled out as the main
culprit (though other actors received their share of the blame).

A "coordinated response" means that network partners collaborate to solve
critical problems. It entails a clear division of labor with limited overlap, the

79

end result being that the most pressing needs of victims are met in a timely and effective manner. The literature identifies two rather different ways of establishing a coordinated response: a bottom-up and a top-down approach.[1]

A bottom-up approach assumes that much of the required cooperation will just happen in the initial phase: people tend to work together in response to a disaster.[2] This is called "emergent coordination" in the literature. There is no plan, no coordinator. It materializes seemingly without any steering, like an invisible hand.

The top-down approach, or "orchestrated coordination," involves collaboration that is *organized*. There are plans and procedures that set out who is supposed to do what. There are mechanisms for "scaling up"—appointing a coordinator to oversee the coordinators when the span of control widens too far for coordinating officials to handle their task. The underlying assumption is that collaboration does not just happen, or at least not in an efficient way. It must be organized.

A complex disaster typically requires a combination of both approaches. We know that in times of disaster people usually are inclined to work together to help other people. That is critically important, especially in the first hours and days, when help is still on the way. But spontaneous collaboration usually is not enough in the long run, especially when many organizations and large amounts of goods need to be moved into the disaster zone. This requires a combination of intricate multilevel interactions, complex logistics, and swift action that is unlikely to occur without at least some degree of "orchestrated coordination."

The response to Katrina has been criticized foremost as a failure of *orchestrated* coordination. Admiral Timothy Keating, commander of NORTHCOM, observed that "during the first four days, no single organization or agency was in charge of providing a coordinated effort for rescue operations."[3] The House Select Committee "found ample evidence supporting the view that the federal government did not have a unified command."[4] Louisiana's state coordinating officer Jeff Smith commented that "anyone who was there, anyone who chose to look, would realize that there were literally three separate Federal commands."[5] The White House report charged that critical steps in the response were delayed or forgone because "various agencies were unable to effectively coordinate their operations."[6]

As we will see, there were indeed "multiple chains of command" and a "myriad of approaches."[7] This should come as no surprise. Decades of public administration and crisis management research findings suggest that it is not easy to effectively and legitimately orchestrate a crisis response.[8] A response network typically consists of many actors who have their own responsibilities and mandates, which means they cannot be ordered to do something.

In this chapter, we analyze and assess coordination—both emergent and orchestrated—during the first week after Katrina made landfall. We assess coordination in positive terms when it emerges spontaneously during the initial phase of the crisis and is then supported and augmented by official efforts.

FEMA tried to coordinate the response. But at some point during the week, key officials within the agency felt that their organization was no longer up to the task. The city administration of New Orleans was essentially nonfunctioning. The state had tried to step in and make up for the local shortcomings but was quickly overwhelmed in the process. FEMA tried to pass the baton to the military, but this created its own set of problems.

We will discuss coordination in the context of two urgent challenges: the search and rescue operation in New Orleans and the subsequent evacuation of survivors from the city. Paradoxically, the most difficult challenge (search and rescue) was performed spectacularly well, whereas the apparently more simple challenge (organizing buses for evacuation) turned into a dramatic failure. We shall first briefly describe the formal coordination structures that were in place at the time.

THE FORMAL STRUCTURE IN PLACE

R. David Paulison, a senior FEMA official, postulated after Katrina that a "better coordinated plan" would have made for a better response.[9] So let's have a look at the plans that were in place at the time.

At the time of Katrina, the United States had a plan and a system in place to provide a coordinated response to large-scale disasters (for a brief history of the US system, see appendix II). It was described in the National Response Plan (NRP), since replaced by the National Response Framework.[10] The NRP was a new plan, developed in the wake of 9/11 when the US system was revamped to better deal with future disasters.[11] In addition to the new plan, a new organizational constellation was created. This included the new Department of Homeland Security behemoth with a deinstitutionalized FEMA under its wings.

The envisioned system was complex to say the least. Moreover, the new arrangements had never been tested against a mega-disaster. Katrina was the first real test.

This new disaster management system incorporated a deep tension that is inherent to federalism: the tension between federal capacity and state sovereignty. In times of disaster, this tension is often exacerbated.[12] Even when a state is overwhelmed and desperately needs federal assistance, the federal government cannot simply go in and "take over." The federal government can certainly offer its assistance, but it is not in charge. The federal government is mandated to coordinate the efforts of federal agencies and other states that are involved in assisting the overwhelmed state(s).

The NRP described how the federal, state, and local authorities as well as nonprofit and private-sector actors should coordinate their activities with one another in responding to a disaster like Katrina. It introduced the National Incident Management System, providing a nationwide approach for federal, state, and local governments to work together in a consistent manner to prepare for, respond to, and recover from all manner of domestic incidents. The NRP also formulated 15 tasks known as Emergency Support Functions (ESFs) that might need to be carried out in support of the states, depending on the nature of the disaster.[13]

The NRP took effect mid-April of 2005, even though many emergency managers had yet to receive training on the new plan.[14] Senior FEMA officials and state-level emergency managers alike were reportedly hostile to the "very detailed, acronym-heavy document . . . not easily accessible to the first-time user."[15] Furthermore, many officials, including the FEMA director himself, argued that the NRP reflected an institutional preoccupation with terrorism.[16] The fact that "the implementation of the NRP occurred on an aggressive schedule" and only with grudging approval from state emergency managers effectively weakened "buy in" on the part of many stakeholders expected to use the 426-page plan in the event of a crisis.[17]

Assisting an Overwhelmed State

The federal disaster response hinges on two critical principles. First, the Robert T. Stafford Disaster Relief and Emergency Assistance Act, signed into law in 1988, states that disaster response efforts should only utilize federal resources in instances where state and local resources are at risk of being exhausted. Second, the Stafford Act specifies that the overwhelmed state must formally request assistance from the federal government before federal agencies can offer help or begin coordinating assistance. The first step in the request process is a gubernatorial request to the White House for a presidential declaration of emergency or disaster.[18]

FEMA plays a key role in the federal disaster response. After a presidential disaster declaration, FEMA collects state requests for assistance and fulfills them by tasking other federal departments or agencies with the appropriate expertise or resources.[19] The president delegates the *coordination* of response efforts to a federal coordinating officer, typically a FEMA official. Crucially, according to the NRP, the FCO did not have *command* authority over other federal agencies, let alone state and local authorities.[20]

FEMA operated a National Response Coordination Center, a "multiagency center that provides overall Federal response coordination for Incidents of National Significance and emergency management program implementation."[21] Strategic-level coordination and any issues that could not be resolved within the NRCC were passed on to the Interagency Incident Management Group, an interagency body that convened at DHS headquarters and consisted of agency representatives with decision-making authority.

FEMA also had Regional Response Coordination Centers that would coordinate disaster response activities until a Joint Field Office (JFO) could be established. The JFO should make use of state and local incident command structures; it should provide a single location—close to the disaster area—where all engaging federal departments and agencies could acquire situational awareness, receive direction and mission assignments, and interface with one another.[22]

Things became slightly more complicated after 9/11. Homeland Security Presidential Directive 5 (issued on February 28, 2003) made the DHS secretary the Principal Federal Official (PFO) for domestic incident management.[23] If need be, the secretary could delegate this role to others ("In the field, the Secretary of Homeland Security is represented by the PFO").[24] The PFO's responsibilities included ensuring that all federal support was both consistent and effective, interfacing with lower-level officials, providing a primary point of contact and situational awareness locally, and acting as the primary federal spokesperson for media and public communications.

The difference between the FCO and PFO is not self-evident, nor was it well understood by many officials at the time. The PFO was not granted directive authority over the FCOs who would be deployed to each affected state (or any other federal or state official for that matter). This arrangement sat oddly with the formal hierarchy within DHS, as its director (the PFO) might not be able to direct a FEMA subordinate acting in FCO capacity. FEMA's Leo Bosner comments on the arrangement:

> Under the old FRP [Federal Response Plan], a Federal Coordinating Officer . . . from FEMA was in charge of federal disaster responders in the field. Every federal responder in the field knew that and understood that the FCO was calling the shots. But under the NRP, while there was still an FCO from FEMA, now there was also a Principal Federal Official . . . from DHS, who would do . . . well, no one quite knew what, exactly. As the disaster unfolded, it was unclear who was in charge of which things at the federal level . . . the FCO or the PFO. As a result, the NRP was confusing and almost useless and added to the delays in responding to the storm.[25]

Incident of National Significance: A Special Plan for Exceptional Events

The National Response Plan recognized that certain events—such as 9/11 or Katrina—may require a special approach. By creating a new category of "catastrophic events," the NRP's authors introduced an exception to the normal procedure. The NRP defined a catastrophic event as "any natural or manmade incident, including terrorism, that results in extraordinary levels of mass casualties, damage, or disruption severely affecting the population, infrastructure, environment, national morale, and/or government functions."[26]

In these extraordinary events, the federal government should not have to rely on the traditional approach to emergency management, which meant waiting for an overwhelmed state to request specific types of assistance. Rather, the federal government should be able to act proactively by "pushing" its capabilities and assistance directly to those in need.[27]

In the event of a catastrophic event, the DHS secretary could activate the Incident of National Significance (INS) portion of the NRP. This allowed the department to implement the Catastrophic Incident Annex of the National Response Plan (NRP-CIA):[28] "Upon recognition that a catastrophic incident condition (e.g. involving mass casualties and/or mass evacuation) exists, the

Secretary of DHS immediately designates the event an Incident of National Significance . . . and begins, *potentially in advance of a formal Presidential disaster declaration* [emphasis added], implementation of the NRP-CIA."[29]

The NRP-CIA was intended as "an overarching strategy for implementing and coordinating an accelerated, proactive national response to a catastrophic incident." The Catastrophic Incident Supplement (a supplement to the NRP-CIA) offered additional guidelines "to address a no-notice or short-notice incident of catastrophic magnitude."[30] The NRP-CIA and related supplemental guidelines promised accelerated delivery and an "aggressive concept of operations." Unfortunately, neither the NRP-CIA nor the supplement explained what exactly made an event extraordinary or catastrophic.

Furthermore, the plan contradicted itself. For instance, in one section of the supplement, the DHS secretary was described as having the authority to designate an event an INS. It was, in other words, not an automatic designation. The NRP's "Planning Assumptions" section, however, stated that "all Presidentially declared disasters and emergencies under the Stafford Act are considered Incidents of National Significance." Moreover, the NRP failed to specify which actions should be taken and what components should be utilized in the case of a catastrophic incident.[31] Finally, the plan did not account for the fact that some events gradually *develop* into catastrophes. The "push" idea was predicated on the immediate recognition and declaration of a catastrophic event.[32]

Moreover, the INS procedure did not solve the coordination issues that typically accompany involvement of the Department of Defense. An INS declaration opened the door to a much larger degree of DOD involvement than in the case of a "normal" disaster. It permitted the DOD to step in where civilian authorities were unable to manage events on their own.[33] This was expected to occur in only the most exceptional of situations. After all, a core principle of DOD's approach to civilian support holds that "it is generally a resource of last resort."[34] Crucially, neither the FCO nor the PFO had command authority over any DOD units committed in response to an INS declaration. As we will see, this arrangement did little to smooth collaboration between the military and civilian authorities.

The DHS secretary formally declared Katrina an INS on Tuesday.[35] It was the first time that an INS had ever been declared.[36] Why Chertoff did not do so prior to or immediately after landfall is unclear.[37] Regardless, it appears that it would not have made a difference.

A SUCCESS STORY: SEARCH AND RESCUE

Early Monday morning, thousands of people were trapped by the rising flood-waters. As the water kept rising throughout the day and into night, the lives of more and more people came under threat. Hundreds of people ultimately drowned. But thousands more were saved.

The first hours and days after Katrina produced many heroic stories of citizens helping each other to survive.[38] One such informal group of citizen volunteers came to be known as the Cajun Navy: "Volunteers participating in the Cajun Navy were not willing to wait for the government for help and took matters into their own hands. The flat-bottomed fishing boats used by volunteers were ideal for navigating through the flooded city. The Cajun Navy was made-up of 350 to 400 boats and people in Katrina's aftermath. They rescued as many as 10,000 people during the response to Katrina."[39]

Katrina brought together people who had never met before, joining efforts to save lives. The stories about looting and violence, which would come to dominate the media coverage of the storm, did not do justice to the many selfless acts and the innovative ways of cooperation that could be found in New Orleans and across the South.[40]

Jeohn Favors was an emergency management technician from Franklin, Louisiana. Together with friends, he "hotwired empty boats, rescuing 350 people from rooftops by the end of the day":[41]

> Someone like Favors helped Kemberly Samuels, a teacher who sheltered from the storm with her husband at a housing development in St. Bernard Parish, where he worked. "You know, everyone heard about all the young gang bangers in New Orleans, but you didn't hear about the young men who came and found us," she said. "They had to be in their teens or early twenties. . . . They came . . . on Tuesday night with boats. They brought us food and drinks. I asked them where they got it from, they said, 'Don't worry about that, just eat it.' They also said the boats were 'borrowed.'"[42]

There were many more examples of what disaster researchers call self-organization. Solnit describes "improvised communities that took care of each other and made decisions together."[43] Larry Bradshaw and Lorrie Beth Slonsky offer the best summary:

What you will not see, but what we witnessed, were the real heroes and sheroes of the hurricane relief effort: the working class of New Orleans. The maintenance workers who used a forklift to carry the sick and disabled. . . . The electricians who improvised thick extension cords stretching over blocks to share the little electricity we had in order to free cars stuck on rooftop parking lots. Nurses who took over mechanical ventilators and spent many hours on end manually forcing air into the lungs of unconscious patients to keep them alive. . . . Refinery workers who broke into boat yards, "stealing" boats to rescue their neighbors clinging to their roofs in flood waters. Mechanics who helped hotwire any car that could be found to ferry people out of the city. And the food service workers who scoured the commercial kitchens, improvising communal meals for hundreds of those stranded.[44]

State officials later estimated that as many as 60,000 people needed to be rescued after landfall.[45] Responding agencies operating under intense time pressure quickly initiated coordinated search and rescue operations. There was no national plan for search and rescue in a situation like this.[46]

The New Orleans authorities lacked both information and resources to play a central role in orchestrating even their own local response. The flooding (in areas of the city that had rarely if ever flooded before) took local first responders by surprise. Both the New Orleans Fire Department and the New Orleans Police Department headquarters buildings, as well as many local police facilities around the city, were flooded, stranding hundreds of officers at their posts.[47] Hundreds more were stranded in their homes.[48] As many as 300 police cars were either underwater or surrounded by the floodwaters.[49] Downed power lines and trees made it hard for rescue vehicles to move around the city.[50] The NOPD had only three boats (officers commandeered two more in the days to come).[51]

State agencies played a critical if largely unsung role in providing assistance to city authorities. According to US senator Joe Lieberman, the Louisiana Department of Wildlife and Fisheries put on an "extraordinary display of both organization and courage." Rescue crews manning sixty boats began responding on Monday at 4:00 p.m. They had rescued 1,500 people by Tuesday afternoon—21,000 by the time it was all over.[52]

Within hours of Katrina's passing, the Coast Guard activated 31 cutters, 76 aircraft, 131 small boats, and over 4,000 personnel.[53] The Coast Guard's proactive response was in part a reflection of lessons learned during Hurricane Ivan in 2004.[54] Though Coast Guard commanders opted not to fuse their search and rescue command with that of the state and FEMA, they did remain in close contact with their counterparts at the EOC in Baton Rouge and elsewhere.[55] This reportedly worked well.[56]

The Louisiana National Guard also played a critical role during the rescue operation. Gathering during the early afternoon of Monday, Guard members worked through the night. The Guard's swift response was remarkable given that LANG's primary staging area, Jackson Barracks, had completely flooded earlier in the day.[57] This was sheer bad luck: Jackson Barracks was considered to lie outside the projected flood zone and had stayed dry during previous hurricanes. Dozens of prestaged high-water vehicles and boats were flooded or washed away when floodwaters inundated the facility.[58] Four hundred guardsmen were effectively marooned.[59] "For a crucial 24 hours after landfall," the *New York Times* reported, Guard officers "were preoccupied with protecting their nerve center from the waves topping the windows at Jackson Barracks and rescuing soldiers who could not swim."[60] The National Guard relocated its headquarters to the Superdome by boat and helicopter the next morning.[61]

After the move and despite the loss of Jackson Barracks, the National Guard organized troops, helicopters, shelters, and "a triage and medical center that handled 5,000 patients (and delivered 7 babies)."[62] The Guard maintained order at the Superdome and fed thousands of evacuees.[63] It transported and distributed critical supplies, including 300,000 MREs and 397,000 liter bottles of water, as well as ice.[64] Moreover, it coordinated local first responders and made available its communications systems to other organizations.

There were 4,549 Louisiana guardsmen on duty when Katrina hit; by Tuesday, 5,207 guardsmen were on the ground.[65] Nevertheless, it was clear that additional troops would be needed (and this was far before the "anarchic New Orleans" narrative had taken hold). LANG commanders reached out to the National Guard Bureau in Washington to request assistance. By noon the same day, as many as 52 guard commanders around the country were evaluating the LANG's itemized list of needs. According to Lou Dolinar, "Helicopter search and rescue teams began arriving late Monday from as far away as Wisconsin."[66] Hundreds more helicopters would arrive in the coming days.

The performance of the National Guard received little media attention, but its effectiveness cannot be overstated. The Guard had 150 helicopters run 10,244 rescue sorties, saving 17,411 people in the process.[67] It was "controlling more than 200 boats, most of which were run by mixed crews of Guardsmen, police, firefighters and officers of the Louisiana Department of Wildlife and Fisheries."[68] Ultimately, more than 50,000 National Guard troops from all 50 states came to Louisiana to aid in the response.[69] The arrival of Guard units with high-water vehicles in New Orleans on Wednesday greatly improved the ability of authorities to move supplies closer to stranded residents.

FEMA's own urban search and rescue teams played a more modest yet an important role. The first of these units (coming in from Barksdale, Louisiana) did not arrive in the area until Monday evening and did not start working until the following morning. All told, the FEMA teams rescued 6,582 people, even though water rescue was, in fact, not part of the urban search and rescue teams' mission.[70]

During the first days, the different organizations operating helicopters over the city "directed their own aircraft, with the structure changing continuously due to the rapid buildup of assets in the operating area throughout the . . . week."[71] Crews initially operated without any regional air traffic control function in place. They instead relied "on internal pilot-to-pilot communications and standardization of training to maintain order in the airspace."[72] Miraculously, no collisions were reported over the course of the response.[73]

Before landfall, a working group for a search and rescue mission with FEMA, US Coast Guard, Louisiana Department of Transportation and Development, and LDWF representation had been formed to coordinate all search and rescue operations. We can assume that group's work was hampered, given the communications issues that authorities experienced after landfall. It was only on the Saturday after landfall that officials managed to implement a common grid system for first responders, thereby minimizing the number of redundant searches.[74] By that point, however, search and rescue was no longer about saving lives.

CRITICAL FAILURE: EVACUATING SURVIVORS

Ironically, the effectiveness of the search and rescue operation played a significant role in forefronting the problem that arguably came to define how many look back on Katrina today. In its essence, the critical problem was one of transportation: authorities found themselves struggling to quickly and safely move people out of the city and into safety.

In the chaos of the first hours after landfall, volunteer rescuers and government teams created ad hoc drop-off sites on higher ground, including highway overpasses.[75] At the same time and unbeknownst to most officials, stranded residents began to congregate at different sites that were not always easily accessible to rescuers.[76]

People had nowhere to go. Katrina destroyed the homes of many. The Superdome had been rendered unlivable and needed to be emptied as soon as possible. As no transportation had been organized to move survivors to the Superdome (or out of the city), people were effectively stranded in the city. It was hot and humid. There was no food or water and little if any medical support, and conditions deteriorated quickly. The situation grew all the more complicated once officials realized that the Convention Center was also being used as a shelter.

Planners had not envisioned the need for a *secondary* evacuation—from the Superdome and improvised sites to safe accommodations outside the city. Officials estimated that at least 50,000 people needed transportation. This became the challenge of the week.

Buses were the only option. With search and rescue operations still in high gear, helicopters could not be spared (and they lacked the necessary capacity). It would take a few days to organize the buses. Had buses rolled in on Tuesday, the media would not have broadcast images of destitute people waiting for rescue in the sweltering heat. The buses arrived soon thereafter, on Wednesday, but they had taken long enough for images of waiting people suffering to be broadcast around the world.

Where Are the Buses?

Governor Blanco would later refer to the situation at the Superdome and the Convention Center as the "trauma of the week."[77] The state could not organize enough buses, FEMA did not deliver on its promises, and violence seemed to be on the rise. By Wednesday, Blanco began calling for federal troops.

Why did it take so long to organize buses? The solution to the problem appeared deceptively easy: locate (roughly) 1,000 buses, find drivers, assign a driver to each bus, and then send the buses to designated pickup points. One could be excused for thinking that this should be less challenging than locating and then rescuing thousands of people on the verge of drowning in their attics. Yet, while most of those people who could be rescued had been picked up by Wednesday, the evacuation of New Orleans would not be completed before Saturday.

The "bus problem" was not for lack of trying on the part of the authorities. Everybody seemed to recognize early on that the Superdome had to be evacuated quickly. As early as Monday evening, FEMA director Brown assured Governor Blanco that "FEMA had 500 buses on standby, ready to be deployed." The evacuation was again flagged as a top priority when Brown, Blanco, and other FEMA and state officials met with Mayor Nagin in New Orleans on Tuesday morning.[78]

The governor later said she was surprised that FEMA was offering to assist in the collection of buses: "I would [otherwise] have possibly assumed that the [procurement of buses] might have been my responsibility."[79]

Brown's promise was a bit shaky. FEMA did not have buses of its own, nor had it ordered buses.[80] The Department of Transportation (DOT)—as coordinator of ESF-1, Transportation—was tasked with procuring the buses. Preparation ahead of a possible tasking had in effect started before landfall: "Jules Hurst, a FEMA official who participated in the July Pam workshop, gave DOT a 'heads-up' that it would need to check with its transportation contractor to locate between 1,000 and 2,000 buses for evacuations. . . . DOT, in turn, called Landstar, its transportation services contractor, to determine availability, but did not ask Landstar to send buses to the Gulf Coast because FEMA had not given DOT the authority to request it."[81]

The DOT needed a formal request to actually procure buses. It appears that the paperwork got started after Blanco and Brown visited the Superdome on Tuesday. Officials in Baton Rouge worked to formulate a mission assignment for DOT requesting 455 buses to evacuate 15,000–25,000 people from the Superdome.[82] The request traveled slowly to Washington, where it reached DOT in the early hours of Wednesday.[83] Brown could not explain the delay other than to say that the "logistics system in FEMA was broken."[84]

But then things started moving. DOT tasked Landstar, a Jacksonville, Florida–based company, with assembling the required number of buses.[85] Landstar, in turn, asked its subcontractor, Carey Limousine, to order buses. That company then "tapped Transportation Management Services of Vienna, Va., which specializes in arranging buses for conventions and other large events, to help fill an initial order for 300 coaches."[86]

Complex and confusing as this may seem, the arrangement did work. The first buses arrived "at a staging area at Mile Marker 209 (LaPlace, Louisiana) around 6:30 a.m. on Wednesday."[87] By noon, Reggie Johnson from the DOT reported that there were 455 buses under contract and "it looks like we've got about 200 that are currently in place, with the remainder that should be coming in on a staggered basis."[88] Those 200 buses would arrive around midnight, according to DOT's national response program manager, Vincent Pearce: "By 1 p.m. on August 31 . . . roughly 20 buses were already onsite. By midnight, some 200 buses had arrived and were ready for operation, having already outgrown the first two staging areas and moved to a third. Over 200 additional buses were already contracted and en route. By September 5, 2005, DOT had contracted for over 1,100 vehicles."[89]

Meanwhile, the governor had quickly lost faith in FEMA's ability to deliver buses as promised. She took steps to secure buses on her own. The Louisiana Department of Transportation and Development was responsible for emergency transportation according to the state's emergency operations plan. The department, however, had done nothing to prepare for such an eventuality.[90] It is perhaps for this reason that Blanco tasked two of her assistants with finding buses around the state starting on Tuesday. Soon after, the head of the state's Department of Culture, Recreation and Tourism was added to the "bus team."[91] The team was not particularly successful. For instance, the state did not attempt to requisition the 60 buses of the Baton Rouge transit system.[92]

On Tuesday, Louisiana officials began examining the possibility of using school buses requisitioned from around the state.[93] An executive order was signed permitting the National Guard to commandeer, but not drive, any buses that might be found.[94] The governor's orders came long after most school district and church offices in the state had closed for the day.

The state did manage to scrounge together a few buses. By Wednesday, 68 buses had been dispatched to staging areas outside the city. The state suspended its calls for additional buses the same day, given repeated assurances by FEMA—correct as we now know—that large numbers of buses were on their way to the region.

Confusion and Frustration

The first stage of the evacuation started Wednesday afternoon. The National Guard worked closely with the New Orleans Health Department and a FEMA medical team to evacuate the special needs population at the Superdome. Perhaps unsurprisingly, the evacuation of the sick did not go unnoticed. People at the Superdome "figured out that if they were sick they might get out earlier. And so they started having chest pains and they started getting sick so they could get out earlier."[95]

Over the course of Wednesday, Governor Blanco grew increasingly agitated by the lack of buses.[96] It is easy to see why. By Wednesday, the numbers at the Superdome had swollen to approximately 23,000.[97] The media were broadcasting live from the site around the clock. During a conversation with the president's chief of staff, Andrew Card, the governor voiced her frustration.[98] The DHS secretary and the director of the Homeland Security Operations Center subsequently became personally involved in "making sure that sufficient buses were lined up."[99]

FEMA officials continued to assure the governor and her staff that buses arranged by DOT and contractors were close at hand and sufficient in number.[100] The buses were indeed close, but not in sight. During a midday conference call on Wednesday, DOT's Reggie Johnson explained the situation: "There are 300 buses in the New Orleans area. You may not see those because actually they're staging at what's called the Poker Palace Texaco refueling site, and that's in a place in Louisiana, and I understand that they are drawing down from that site. They're bringing in about 40 buses at a time. There are 155 [extra] buses that were requested, and they are en route and should arrive at the truck stop by midnight tonight."[101]

The buses remained out of sight until Wednesday evening, when "significant numbers of federally-contracted buses began to arrive at the Superdome."[102] On Thursday, DOT's Johnson reported that "120 buses . . . departed for [the] Houston Astrodome last night."[103]

So both FEMA and state officials were right: there were buses, but they did not materialize in large numbers at the Superdome. There are two explanations for this frustrating situation.

First, the buses were used somewhere else. The Senate report states that "when government-sponsored buses began trickling into New Orleans on Wednesday evening, they picked up rescuees on highway overpasses like the Cloverleaf."[104] The problem was of Blanco's own making. Flying over the highways, she witnessed people congregating and personally redirected the arriving buses.[105] Blanco reportedly "wanted those buses heading to the Superdome to pick up 5,000 rescuees at the Cloverleaf first."[106]

Second, there was a security issue: many bus drivers refused to enter the city after hearing the sensational reports of looting and violence in New Orleans. For this reason, the governor hastily issued an executive order mandating that the National Guard or police protect the buses.[107] While this decision alleviated the concerns of the bus drivers, it slowed things down even further. An additional problem was that many of the drivers had never been to New Orleans and promptly got lost upon entering the city.

Mayor Nagin created yet more confusion on Thursday. Having little insight into any of the state and federal planning under way, he unexpectedly began advising people stranded in New Orleans—through a statement read on CNN—to head across the Crescent City Connection bridge over the Mississippi River to the city of Gretna, where buses were reportedly waiting to take them to safety.[108]

> Late in the day on Wednesday, a flow of people from New Orleans began to cross the Crescent City Connection on foot. They were told that food, water, safety and shelter could be found on the Westbank. Unbelievably, the Mayor of New Orleans, Ray Nagin, was instructing people to cross the bridge; however he did not tell Gretna officials of his actions. With a crowd massing, Gretna police officers commandeered Westside Transit buses and began the arduous task of transporting busloads of people down the Westbank Expressway to the Huey P. Long Bridge and to safety at I-10 and Causeway, the FEMA-approved evacuation point. It is estimated that approximately 6,000 evacuees were transported by the Gretna Police Department over a period of 12 to 14 hours without a death or injury reported. A fact overlooked by the national media.[109]

Unfortunately, few buses remained in Gretna by the time Nagin started encouraging people to move on Thursday. Moreover, a mall had burned down and reports of violence and looting were rampant, prompting local officials in Gretna to close the bridge to pedestrian traffic from New Orleans. Officials in New Orleans were not informed.[110] In one widely reported incident, police opened fire over the heads of people attempting to cross the bridge.[111] The Gretna leadership was later heavily criticized for its decision to close the bridge and for the behavior of its officers.[112]

The evacuation of the Superdome continued. According to DOT's Johnson, 800 buses were in use on Friday.[113] By Friday morning, "approximately fifteen thousand people had been evacuated from the Superdome, leaving approximately 5,500 remaining. . . . The last 300 [people] in the Superdome climbed aboard buses Saturday."[114]

Many evacuees were not informed as to where they were being sent. Pets were not allowed on board. For these and other reasons, some shelterees refused to board, thereby further slowing the boarding process. Overwhelmed and underresourced officials made no efforts to register evacuees. This would create coordination problems down the road.[115]

Who's in Charge of the Evacuation?

Late on Wednesday evening, General Russel Honoré arrived in Baton Rouge, where he met with Governor Blanco. Honoré headed up the Joint Task Force on Hurricane Katrina (JTF-Katrina). Formed on Tuesday, JTF-Katrina involved units from the US First Army (with command over forces east of the Mississippi River) and the US Fifth Army (commanding forces to the west of the river).[116]

Much to the governor's surprise, Honoré traveled light, with just a small staff contingent in tow. Blanco had assumed that he would bring troops and other resources that could help with the evacuation.[117] Yet Governor Blanco, frustrated with the pace of progress, asked Honoré to assume responsibility for evacuating New Orleans so that the National Guard might "concentrate on saving lives, search and rescue, and law and order issues."[118]

Now in charge of the evacuation mission but without the assets necessary to carry it out, Honoré had to use National Guard forces.[119] Blanco's request blurred established lines of authority, as the central element of the response (evacuation from the city) had been handed off to the federal government. This would play into the debate over federalization that soon emerged (discussed below).

Honoré had already made his mark before receiving the governor's mandate. Unbeknownst to officials in Baton Rouge, the emergency response team at the Superdome, FEMA Region VI in Denton, Texas, and the National Guard operating locally had formulated a plan of their own to empty the shelter using helicopters.[120] When Honoré learned about the plan, he "pulled rank" and canceled the operation.[121]

Early on Thursday morning (at 5:25 a.m.), DOT received word that DOD had been handed "command and control for all evacuation in the New Orleans area and lower LA affected parishes."[122] The buses provided by DOT and its lead contractor, Landstar, would come under DOD command upon arrival at designated staging areas outside the city.

At least four separate bureaucracies (FEMA, DOT, DOD, and the state) thus became involved in the evacuation of the city. These efforts were somewhat unified following the governor's decision to reassign responsibility for coordinating the evacuation effort to the JTF-Katrina commanders. By the time "unified coordination" was established, however, the buses had already started rolling. In other words, it did not really matter.

As flawed as the coordination of the Katrina response appears to have been, it is hard to see in hindsight how the evacuation could have been accomplished any faster. Frustration with the speed of evacuation is certainly understandable. The impatience of key actors, especially Governor Blanco, gave rise to multiple efforts and created new coordination problems (but did not make buses arrive any sooner). Looking back, we may have to allow for the possibility that the evacuation of New Orleans was not as badly performed as today's conventional wisdom would have it.

Evacuating Prisons

Ironically, the evacuation of New Orleans's sizable prison population proceeded quite smoothly and quickly.[123] After landfall, many prisoners were moved from their flooded cells to nearby overpasses. This was only a temporary solution, given the possibility of heat stress and dehydration, not to mention the obvious flight risk. The situation was embarrassing from a public relations standpoint; aerial footage broadcast nationwide showed hundreds of prisoners in brightly colored jumpsuits seated in rows on the concrete.[124]

That these prisoners could not be returned to their now-flooded cells anytime soon was also obvious.[125] The Louisiana Department of Public Safety and Corrections and US Bureau of Prisons on Tuesday established a joint command in Baton Rouge to coordinate the relocation of prisoners. Federal officials agreed to accept "sentenced state prisoners serving felony sentences with no less than six (6) months remaining on their sentences . . . and to undertake their secure custody, housing, safekeeping, subsistence and care."[126] Starting the following morning, 2,500 prisoners were transported on Bureau of Prisons vehicles to federal facilities as far afield as Florida. The remaining prisoners were moved to facilities elsewhere in Louisiana.[127]

Coordinating the Evacuation of Medical Institutions

By midday on Tuesday, first responders had reached two of the largest public hospitals in the city, from which they evacuated a number of intensive-care patients on Coast Guard and National Guard helicopters. Competition soon arose between general search and rescue and medical evacuation coordinators over access to the limited number of helicopters then operating over the region.[128] Even when helicopters and waterborne assets had been explicitly dedicated to medical evacuation missions, they could still be rerouted to other missions.[129]

Out of 27 hospitals in the area, only two remained fully operational and another four only partially so. All other facilities had to be evacuated. Responsibility for the coordination of medical evacuation missions fell to FEMA.[130]

The hospital evacuations happened in a highly uncoordinated manner. There was no plan. Improvisation was the name of the game. This was due in large part to hospital administrators' inability to communicate with rescuers.[131] In fact, hospital administrators "often did not know whom they should contact to communicate their needs."[132]

On Tuesday, FEMA began seeking additional ambulance providers that could support the hospital evacuation effort. FEMA also requested that DOT locate a contractor able to provide additional air ambulance capacity.[133] It is unclear what became of DOT's hunt.

On Tuesday, National Guard officials asked Louisiana-based Acadian Air Ambulance to assume responsibility for "coordinating missions into and out of New Orleans airspace, coordinating requests for air evacuations from many of the New Orleans area hospitals, and also serving as the main contact between civilian providers" and federal contracting officers.[134] Acadian immediately agreed to the request.[135] Helicopters under Acadian's command were typically only used to move patients to collection points in the area before they could be transported to so-called Temporary Medical Operations and Staging Areas (TMOSAs).[136] Ambulances, buses, personal vehicles, and even tractor trailers were used to move patients to these and other, sometimes informal, collection sites, such as elevated roadway intersections and the international airport.[137]

Acadian's politically well-connected CEO helped to mobilize contacts within the Association of Air Medical Services and the federal government to secure additional military helicopters to facilitate the movement of patients from staging areas to health care facilities further afield.[138] Private hospitals received priority as Acadian and other private emergency transportation providers were obligated to honor existing prenegotiated contracts. Those stranded at the city's public facilities with no such contracts would be forced to wait.[139]

On Thursday morning, the US Coast Guard, LANG, other National Guard units, LDWF, NOPD, and the Louisiana State Police launched a concerted effort to evacuate both the Charity and University hospital facilities. By this point, hospital administrators, individual doctors, and patients' families had for two days been harshly criticizing authorities' sluggish response.[140] On television, viewers could see a banner draped from the side of Charity Hospital, exclaiming, "Stop the lying and get us the hell out of here."[141]

The Airport

Thanks to its geography (on dry land) and the ability for helicopters to easily land there, the Louis Armstrong New Orleans International Airport quickly became a drop-off point for residents with special needs. The airport was never designated a TMOSA (like the facility on the LSU campus) and therefore was completely unprepared and sorely underprovisioned. Even with the arrival of additional medical teams throughout the week, at least 26 patients would die while awaiting transport from the airport.[142]

Approximately 800 ticketed passengers were stranded when their flights were canceled prior to Katrina. After the storm passed, "overcrowding at [the airport] was exacerbated by the hundreds of . . . well-intentioned people bringing evacuees to the airport in buses, vans and cars. The unplanned arrivals caused major congestion both outside and inside the airport terminal."[143]

The airport lacked both the resources and the supplies to handle the massive influx of people converging on the site. According to FEMA officials, "Airport management and staff were operating a skeleton crew, and were not provided resources or support from the city or state necessary to facilitate such a large scale evacuation. . . . Given that the airport was not a fundamental part of evacuation or shelter plans . . . it was unprepared for the crowds and resource strains presented in the aftermath of Hurricane Katrina."[144]

By Tuesday it had become clear that the special needs patients at the airport could neither be moved elsewhere by land nor remain much longer at the airport.[145] During the evening of the same day, national medical teams in coordination with the state health authority initiated airborne medical evacuations from the airport using military aircraft.

Officials at FEMA headquarters dispatched at least three Disaster Medical Assistance Teams (DMATs) to the site by Wednesday. Five additional DMATs, four Air National Guard medical teams, American Red Cross volunteers and Public Health Service personnel would arrive in the days to come.[146] The teams worked under chaotic conditions with limited supplies.[147]

By Wednesday, flight operations were once again coming online at the airport, allowing commercial air carriers to evacuate stranded ticketed passengers and at least some residents.[148] The same day, officials began planning for a major airlift from the facility using a mix of military and commercial aircraft.[149] Time was of the essence, as the number of people sheltered at the facility continued to grow by the hour, in spite of officials' pleas to avoid the airport.[150]

On Thursday, a DHS deputy secretary contacted DOT officials, DOT's private emergency transport contractor (Landstar), and the Air Transport Association to notify them that they should be prepared to begin evacuating from the airport.[151] By this point, military transports were already touching down regularly. By noon that same day, empty commercial aircraft (also organized by Landstar) began arriving in New Orleans.[152] The joint airlift involving assets from DHS, DOT, DOD, and the private sector relocated over 24,000 people from the area, making it the largest domestic airlift of civilians in US history.[153]

Nevertheless, there were hiccups in implementation that might have been avoided through better coordination. For instance, the federal Transportation Security Administration (TSA) insisted that all passengers be subject to security screening, that all flights be manifested as per standard procedures, and that air marshals be aboard all departing aircraft.[154] These requirements prompted incredulity on the part of FEMA officials, who wondered aloud if the TSA was prioritizing "helping people or making sure they are not terrorists."[155]

ANALYZING CRISIS COORDINATION

So it took days for the richest nation on earth to organize 1,000 buses to move survivors from a major city. Whether or not this could have been done more quickly, we argue, is up for debate. But it is clear that politicians, the media, citizens, and, of course, those waiting to be evacuated look back at the evacuation as a singular failure.

FEMA was singled out as the main culprit. But, as we have shown, the perceived fiasco was not solely FEMA's, the state of Louisiana's, or local officials' doing. There was a more systemic set of factors at work.

We identify three factors that contributed to this perceived failure. First, we discuss why FEMA found it so hard to fulfill its tasks. We then consider the absence of a backstop for the overwhelmed agency. It took too much time for other federal agencies to assist FEMA after it was overwhelmed. Finally, a combination of bureau politics and politicization—the third factor—undermined the ability of the various actors to achieve effective coordination and collaboration.

Why Did FEMA Fail to Deliver?

We should begin by repeating the obvious: many local actors were overwhelmed from the start. The state for its part did not possess the means to deal with the sheer devastation and suffering. Bill Lokey, FEMA's FCO in Louisiana, characterized the situation as follows: "The locals were overwhelmed. We were going to be overwhelmed. There was no way, with my experience and what I had to bring to the table, I was taking a knife to a gunfight."[156]

According to FEMA officials, state officials were not just overwhelmed but also underprepared. Scott Wells, FEMA's deputy FCO for Louisiana, said, "The state personnel lacked overall discipline, lacked clear control lines of authority, lacked a clearly understood command structure, and lacked consistency in operational procedures."[157] Personnel shortages, an unsettled working environment, and serious communication problems further hampered the state's ability to establish a unified command with federal officials.[158]

FEMA officials complained that the Louisiana Office of Homeland Security and Emergency Preparedness staff was unfamiliar with the Incident Command System (ICS), which FEMA considered a prerequisite for successful interagency coordination.[159] "If people don't understand ICS, we can't do ICS. And if we can't do ICS, we cannot manage disasters," Wells stated in testimony before the Senate.[160]

Brown would later call the state of Louisiana "dysfunctional."[161] The FEMA director looked back in frustration: "I could never get them [Louisiana officials at the EOC] to sit down. I couldn't get the adjutant general and the FCO together. I couldn't even get them to share an office. The [FCO] was down the hallway in another room. The governor was over here in a small anteroom off a conference room. The adjutant general was moving in and out. I couldn't get a team effort together."[162]

But that was all in hindsight. Collaboration between the state of Louisiana and the federal government actually started off well. For instance, DHS secretary Chertoff was generally satisfied with the level of cooperation he received from the governor and her staff: "I had interaction with the governor every day and I think I had a good relationship with her. I didn't have any difficulty in dealing with her or with the state and local authorities that I dealt with."[163]

Accounts from the state EOC in Baton Rouge and the transcripts available from various teleconferences point to a good working relation heading into the storm. When Governor Blanco requested federal assistance on Saturday, asking that President Bush "declare an emergency for the State of Louisiana due to Hurricane Katrina," he did so the same day.[164] On Sunday, in recognition of the potential catastrophic impact of Hurricane Katrina, Blanco asked President Bush to declare an expedited major disaster for Louisiana. Again, President Bush did just as she requested.[165] President Bush, DHS secretary Chertoff, and FEMA director Brown promised to do all that they could to help. During the Sunday teleconference attended by Brown, Bush, and Chertoff, the Louisiana EOC reported that it had no unmet needs and that FEMA was "leaning forward."[166]

At this point, the system appeared to be well prepared (and arguably was well prepared) to deal with a major hurricane. But Katrina was not a "normal" hurricane. Katrina was a mega-disaster that completely overwhelmed all organizations involved in the Louisiana response.

On Tuesday morning, federal-state collaboration remained friction-free as far as we can tell. The mayor, governor, and FEMA director spent quite a bit of time together in New Orleans.[167] They took a chopper ride with Lieutenant Governor Mitch Landrieu and Senator David Vitter, and visited the Superdome with Mayor Nagin and Police Chief Eddie Compass.[168] The atmosphere seemed good.[169] Nagin presented the FEMA director with a list of priorities. The FEMA director remarked that "this [was] the best list [he had] ever seen after a disaster."[170] Brown passed the list to FEMA colleague Phil Parr, the leader of Emergency Response Team—Advanced, who relayed the mayor's list onward to the state EOC in Baton Rouge, where officials set to work fulfilling the mayor's requests.[171] FEMA officials provided every indication that they would deliver.[172]

FEMA's failure to deliver on the expectations of others as well as the agency's own promises was not for lack of trying. In fact, in at least some respects,

FEMA's response was on a larger scale and more robust than ever before.[173] FEMA had pre-positioned search and rescue task forces, two of its five Mobile Emergency Response Support detachments, and eight medical teams.[174] After landfall, FEMA deployed many more resources, including medical assistance teams, search and rescue task forces, and 1,700 trucks of ice, water, and MREs.[175] "From August 31 to September 4, FEMA also deployed ten Disaster Mortuary Operational Response Teams and both of its Disaster Portable Morgue Units."[176] By September 17, FEMA had delivered over $1 billion in assistance.[177]

It would not be enough. There are at least four reasons why FEMA underdelivered.

FEMA did not have enough personnel. Wells later complained that a 90-person FEMA regional office was "woefully inadequate" to perform its two primary disaster functions, namely operating a Regional Response Coordination Center and deploying people to staff emergency response teams in the field.[178] FEMA was also short staffed in Baton Rouge.[179] The sheer number of actors was huge in this disaster, creating tremendous demands on the staff to be in constant communication in order to keep everyone on the same page. Because Hurricane Katrina hit not only Louisiana (part of Region VI) but also Florida, Mississippi, and Alabama (Region IV), both FEMA regions had to conduct response and recovery operations.[180] While this formal division of labor had always worked before, it created internal coordination challenges in the case of Katrina. FEMA's organizational structure did not match the scale of the disaster.

FEMA was unable to establish "joint command" (bringing together representatives of responding organizations). According to the NRP, the activities of federal, state, and local authorities should first be coordinated at a so-called Initial Operating Facility. Once the appropriate infrastructure is in place, a Joint Field Office can be established. The JFO "provides a central location for coordination of federal, state, local, tribal, nongovernmental, and private-sector organizations."[181] According to Senate investigators, "Delays in setting up the JFO made it very difficult for FEMA to coordinate and operate with the state officials, which impeded a unified response."[182] Brown would later blame the absence of unified command on the "unwillingness of the State of Louisiana to participate," but we did not find evidence that would support this claim.[183]

FEMA did not have "eyes and ears" in the disaster zone because of its limited and late deployment of personnel to the region. FEMA officials did not succeed in creating a local command post in New Orleans. This made it difficult to understand what was needed (and where); it also made it hard to orchestrate the logistics of moving supplies into the affected area.

FEMA's logistics chain was overwhelmed. FEMA was unable to deliver what local and state actors were requesting. FEMA had 70 people in Washington calling around for supplies, but despite their best efforts, they could not come up with enough resources to match the rate at which they were being consumed in the field.[184] Moreover, the state's and FEMA's request tracking systems were incompatible.[185] Officials did not know or could not tell where supplies were or when they would arrive.[186] Unsurprisingly, assets were lost or misdirected.[187]

At the Superdome, supply shortages meant that only two meals a day could be served. According to one FEMA official, "It was a struggle from meal to meal, because as one was served, it was clear to everyone that there was not enough food or water for the next meal."[188] Out of concern for staff security, the Red Cross refused to provide mass feeding services in the city, a decision that took FEMA planners by surprise.[189] FEMA personnel would in the coming days seek "commercial sources of extended-shelf-life meals to fill the gap, but the industry was not prepared to supply the quantities" needed.[190]

According to FEMA, shipments were delayed by "endless coordination between the JFO, Staging Area, Mobilization Center, HQ Logistics, DOT/ESF-1, and the Atlanta Emergency Transportation Center," which resulted "in confusion, lost documents, finger pointing, and unfortunately, late or non-deliveries of commodities."[191] Shipments to the region and onward into the hands of victims were delayed by "high winds, flooded roadways, damaged infrastructure, primarily on the roadway system, and widespread debris," as well as still-shuttered or barely operational airports.[192] Much of the city was off limits. Thus the only way to get supplies to people was by helicopter or boat.

Local and state officials expressed frustration that their requests for assistance were not met because they did not follow every step of the formal request process.[193] FEMA logistics personnel were frustrated because they had to play catch-up, filling numerous duplicate orders made earlier by impatient state officials.

Ironically, much of what was requested was actually on offer. But FEMA was not equipped to handle the massive donations and the army of volunteers that descended on the region. Thousands of private citizens came to the city, laden with equipment and supplies. Many were turned away. For instance, FEMA sent out-of-state rescuers and their boats home because they lacked valid licenses to operate in the state.[194] At one point, the FEMA director asked that volunteers only deploy to the region upon receiving an explicit assistance request from authorities.

Companies in the private sector also ran into obstacles when they attempted to donate goods and services to FEMA.[195] There were no arrangements in place that permitted contributions from the private sector. A DHS program aimed at facilitating contacts between emergency managers and major corporations, CEO LINK, went unactivated in the aftermath of the storm.[196] Peter Pantuso of the American Bus Association tried all day Wednesday to call FEMA to help in the search for buses but to no avail.[197] Without any established routines for coordinating private resources, "corporate officials and public servants had to improvise ways of working together, based on personal connections and fortunate coincidences."[198] When a Walmart representative called the agency, a midlevel official made certain allowances enabling Walmart to be brought onboard (only to reportedly be punished for violating internal agency rules).[199]

Katrina prompted an immediate response from dozens of foreign countries and international organizations. Historically a donor nation, the United States had neither the capacity nor procedures in place to receive, vet, and deliver foreign assistance in a domestic setting. FEMA and state officials were privately skeptical that foreign assistance would be of any real utility. President Bush, for example, reported: "I'm not expecting much from foreign nations because we haven't asked for it. I do expect a lot of sympathy, and perhaps some will send cash dollars. But this country is going to rise up and take care of it. . . . You know, we would love help, but we're going to take care of our own business as well, and there's no doubt in my mind we'll succeed."[200]

Though it received little attention at the time, it appears that the Emergency Management Assistance Compact (EMAC) worked better than FEMA's system. EMAC is the mechanism that facilitates emergency support between states (states helping each other).

Early in the week, the state began seeking additional National Guard, rescue, and police resources from other states via EMAC.[201] On Wednesday, officials in Texas agreed to house those sheltered at the Superdome at a sports arena located in central Houston.[202] A total of 680 requests via EMAC for civilian resources were made over the coming days and weeks, prompting the deployment of nearly 28,000 personnel at a cost of approximately $202 million. Members of the US House later remarked that EMAC "provided invaluable interstate mutual aid in support of Hurricane Katrina by deploying nearly 68,000 personnel (19,481 civilians and 48,477 National Guard) to Louisiana and Mississippi."[203]

While EMAC was utilized to great effect, it still had its flaws. For one, the EMAC approval process was considered cumbersome, and therefore ill suited to a large-scale emergency.[204] Louisiana was unable to handle all of the EMAC requests, necessitating that FEMA step in and pick up some of the slack.[205]

When the Existing Structure Does Not Work: The Challenge of "Handing Over"

FEMA was well prepared and well positioned—for a normal hurricane. As hard as FEMA officials tried, they realized by Wednesday that the agency could not deliver on its promises. FEMA turned to DOD for support with the logistics.

When the time came to "scale up" and hand over responsibility to the next level, FEMA encountered a number of challenges. According to Assistant Secretary of Defense Paul McHale, it was on Thursday that FEMA made a formal request "for DoD to accept the responsibility to provide 'full logistic support' throughout the entire area affected by Hurricane Katrina."[206] The Senate report confirms that: "Perceiving an overwhelmed logistics system, FEMA Director Brown 'reached back to headquarters and had discussions about [how he] wanted all logistics turned over to DOD.' On September 1, FEMA headquarters contacted the Department of Defense, requesting that the department take over full logistics operations in Louisiana and Mississippi, thus proposing the transfer of one of its most important functions to another entity."[207]

The midweek breakdown of FEMA came as a surprise. The dominant mindset at FEMA and DHS was that, in the words of Chertoff, "if there is anything that FEMA does and has done over the last twenty years, it's been hurricanes."[208] During his testimony before the House Select Committee, Chertoff freely admitted that he did not have much experience with managing disasters; he certainly did not consider himself an expert on hurricanes.[209] The DHS secretary relied on FEMA. Since joining the department in 2004, the agency had responded reasonably well to multiple hurricanes during the previous summer and in the weeks before Katrina.[210]

DOD had been ready to help for at least two days.[211] On Tuesday, DOD began "leaning forward" in anticipation of any FEMA requests, given "a deep concern that the damage was more severe than was being reported [and possibly] equal or greater in damage than that of Hurricane Andrew in 1992."[212] The Senate report states:

> Through Tuesday morning the Department remained in a posture as dictated by the NRP, to allow FEMA to coordinate the response. At the same time, senior officials within the Department responsible for homeland defense were becoming concerned that they were not receiving requests from FEMA, and that awaiting such requests could further delay the movement of military assets. Assistant Secretary McHale, who that morning met with Deputy Secretary England, and Chairman of the Joint Chiefs of Staff Gen. Myers to discuss the hurricane and the Department's response during the daily morning briefing, said that notwithstanding media reports "that were less sobering than the scope of the actual damage," the leadership recognized that the Department needed to mobilize its assets for the support requests they anticipated.[213]

A DOD deputy secretary, through a seldom-used "vocal command," instructed the chiefs of the armed forces to assist NORTHCOM in identifying and pre-positioning assets that might be requested. This vocal command constituted what one official described as a "blank check" that served to "eliminate . . . much of the internal review and approval process" so as to encourage the swift deployment of DOD assets to the region.[214]

Numerous media reports on Tuesday suggested that available DOD assets were not being used. These reports were largely accurate; the fact that FEMA made no requests for DOD assistance on Tuesday prevented units from engaging directly in the response, blank check or not.

Military officials were reportedly surprised by Brown's "extraordinary" request to take over the entire logistics operation.[215] After all, as Senate investigators point out, FEMA "was asking DOD to take over a role it had not traditionally played in disaster response, and which is not listed as one of DOD's support functions."[216] According to one DOD official, FEMA's request entailed "enormous planning and resource requirements. . . . It may well have been the single most complex civil support mission in the history of the US military."[217]

After clarifying what "full logistics support" would entail, the secretary of defense, Donald Rumsfeld, approved the request on Friday, even though certain questions concerning command structures and the division of labor among DOD, FEMA, and others remained.[218] By the time Rumsfeld approved the request, New Orleans had been almost completely evacuated.

Fresh Coordination Challenges

Bringing in DOD posed two main challenges. First, it introduced new coordination issues insofar as it required that different organizational hierarchies (state, FEMA, DHS, DOD) work together. Second, the involvement of DOD raised questions as to who exactly was in charge of the response. Bringing in the military in the United States (and in most other federal systems for that matter) is a sensitive issue; the military cannot simply "take over" where local institutions fail; at the same time, these same local institutions lack the authority to command military troops literally operating in their backyards.[219]

The National Response Plan offered little guidance. As we have seen, the plan introduced the Incident of National Significance concept. Apart from the fact that nobody seemed to understand what an INS was and what a declaration of an INS entailed exactly, it was equally unclear what should happen when the response "scaled up" to INS level. Critically, the role of the DOD in the event of an INS declaration was underdefined at best.

It would take a considerable amount of time and energy to get answers to these questions. Eventually, work-arounds were created that helped put DOD firmly in the driver's seat. Formally, all assistance requests from state and local authorities still had to go through FEMA. However, as DOD "had the resources to appraise the situation and prioritize its missions more quickly than FEMA could, the Pentagon actually drafted its own requests for assistance and sent them to FEMA, which copied them and sent them back to the Department of Defense for action."[220] Michael Jackson, a DHS deputy secretary, later argued that the request approval process was "one of the best examples of cutting through bureaucratic red tape and getting on with the job that I participated in during the course of these first several weeks."[221]

The commander of JTF-Katrina, Lieutenant General Honoré, coordinated the deployment of DOD assets in what one DOD official claimed was "the largest military deployment within the United States since [the mid-1800s]."[222] Honoré was portrayed on television as the savior of New Orleans, embodying everything Bush, Brown, Chertoff, and the governor were not: action oriented, tough and sure, and cool looking in his sunglasses to boot. Bill Lokey, the FCO in Louisiana, later praised Honoré for "doing what had to be done to get things moving." It helped, of course, that his presence coincided with a turning point in the response—help was finally arriving.[223]

While his appearance on the scene did much to signal that the federal government was (to many, finally) engaging, some observers were less impressed. Retired Coast Guard vice admiral Jim Hull, who later assessed NORTHCOM's response to Katrina, noted that Honoré was constantly on the move, thus making many command decisions away from his headquarters and without the knowledge of his own staff, let alone other authorities. According to one staffer, "We track General Honoré's location by watching CNN."[224] The House report takes a dim view on the JTF-Katrina command's leadership capacity: "The JTF Katrina headquarters never transitioned from the very tactical mindset of life saving to the operational mindset of sustaining and enabling a Joint Force. Since the Forward Command Element (General Honoré) was unable to communicate, they became embroiled and distracted with the tactical and were unable to focus on even the most basic of operational issues. . . . Other units who were responding from outside the area to integrate with what was called a 'Joint' task force expected certain doctrinal norms which materialized very slowly or not at all."[225]

The JTF-Katrina commander and his staff did not always coordinate their efforts with FEMA, which gave rise to redundant response efforts. Not only was Honoré constantly on the move, but he tended to accept taskings directly from the state and even some local parishes, thus circumventing FEMA and the established assistance-request protocol.[226] Lokey suggested that this failure to adhere to protocol prompted "a tremendous amount of duplication and . . . a tremendous amount of gaps."[227] Senate investigators later confirmed that "as of [August 30] the state had established two new avenues, in addition to the traditional processes through the EMAC and the [defense coordinating officer at the state EOC], for requesting military support: (1) through . . . the [National Guard Bureau], and (2) through . . . the Commander of Joint Task Force Katrina. There were now four separate avenues for requests for military support; there would be little coordination among them."[228]

Yet another factor that complicated matters was the dual command structure over DOD units. Rather than one single command, forces arriving in the Joint Operations Area were assigned to separate commands led by the First Army, the Fifth Army, and the Marine Corps. The fact that the JTF did not establish a commander for all land components caused confusion and a lack of coordination between land forces sent into New Orleans.[229] Coordination between the DOD forces and deployed National Guard units could also have been better. Many units never liaised with one another, despite operating in the same areas.[230] In other instances, turf wars reportedly broke out between Louisiana National Guard units and federal troops.[231]

The coordination problems that we have described should not come as a surprise, given that the NRP did not provide clear guidelines as to how the military should relate to civilian authorities. The plan for dealing with a superdisaster did not prescribe how the armed forces should be integrated into a large-scale response network. The structure that worked quite well for "routine disasters" proved inadequate for a mega-disaster. As a result, the largest relief operation in US history was marked by improvisation, redundancies, and tension.

The Detrimental Effect of Bureau-Politism

In a disaster, it is normal that tensions arise between organizations that have little to do with one another on a day-to-day basis and are suddenly forced to work together. When bureaucratic tensions begin to hamper collaboration, we speak of "bureau-politism."[232]

Tensions materialized at different moments between different actors in the wake of Katrina. For instance, there initially was no agreement as to who was in charge of operations at the Superdome. The city maintained that as the Superdome was a state-owned facility, the National Guard should be in charge of security. The Guard argued that it was only working in support of the city's efforts.[233] There were reports about tension between FEMA and the Department of Health and Human Services.[234] NOPD officials complained that FEMA did not want to work with them.[235] There were also tensions between FEMA and DOD officials, while DHS experienced difficulties working with the FBI.[236] Congressional researchers discovered "a pointless 'turf war' between DHS and DOJ [the Department of Justice]" over which department should lead the federal law enforcement effort in New Orleans.[237]

Perhaps one of the biggest and most unproductive sources of tension during that first week was between FEMA (director Brown) and DHS (director Chertoff). In a purely bureaucratic sense, Chertoff was Brown's boss. In practice, Brown had a fair amount of leeway, as he was FEMA's point man in Louisiana.

Despite being a DHS agency, FEMA worked Katrina as if it was still independent.[238] FEMA officials, especially Brown, viewed DHS as an added layer of bureaucracy between the nation's "lead" emergency management agency

(FEMA) and the White House. Brown simply bypassed the DHS leadership and contacted White House staff directly, just as he had done during the 2004 hurricane season.[239] Brown later told Senate investigators that the 2004 hurricane season in Florida demonstrated the unnecessarily bureaucratic nature of DHS and that this had the potential to slow FEMA's response to Katrina.[240]

Brown also sought to defend his autonomy against the JTF-Katrina commander: "When General Honoré and I first got on the telephone together, he already had a litany of things he wanted to do, and I had to back him down and say, 'I may want all of those things done, but until we get federalized, or however we work this out, I am still in control and you need to let me know what you want to do, and we can play this game. I may want you to do all those ten things on your list, but come and tell me before you do them.'"[241]

In a paradoxical confluence of plan and practice, an ostensibly minor bureaucratic procedure would further undermine the relation between Brown and Chertoff. The presidential disaster declaration had automatically designated Chertoff as PFO for the federal response.[242] Then on Tuesday, Chertoff declared Katrina an Incident of National Significance.[243] As per the INS procedure described in the NRP, he appointed FEMA director Brown as PFO. Chertoff later argued that Brown's designation as PFO was merely a formalization of the situation that existed. Chertoff understood Brown to be the de facto PFO throughout the pre-landfall period and claimed that this was clear to others involved in the response.[244] Brown, however, considered the PFO designation to be both a demotion and "an additional layer of bureaucracy."[245] Brown thought the PFO role was a "silly" concept.[246]

Tensions between the two men rose quickly during that first week. The fact that Brown could not be reached by DHS officials was reportedly galling.[247] The DHS secretary made it clear to Brown's chief of staff that "heads were going to roll" if the FEMA director did not get in touch with him soon.[248] When the two men did finally make contact, Chertoff ordered Brown to remain at the state EOC, where he could be more easily reached.[249] In Brown's telling, "So what happens is I get designated as the PFO, which means that I am instructed by Secretary Chertoff to plop my rear end down in Baton Rouge and to not leave Baton Rouge. You can't run a disaster that way."[250] The failure of Brown and Chertoff to communicate was later cited as "evidence of the profound dysfunction then existing between DHS and FEMA leadership."[251]

In bureaucratic terms, FEMA quickly lost clout and relevance during the week. FEMA had already indicated that it was not up to the job. As the days dragged on after landfall and relief had still not arrived in the city, FEMA received increasingly harsh criticism in the media for its performance. This criticism reflected poorly on the White House and fed the growing perception that things were spinning out of control. This gave rise to White House attempts to "federalize" the response, which, in turn, poisoned relations between Louisiana's governor and the White House. The political sideshow soon cemented the general perception that nobody was in control and that officials were either incompetent or only out to save their own skins. In an effort to right the ship, Brown was "sidelined" by the DHS leadership.[252]

A Second Source of Tension: The Federalization Issue

On Friday afternoon, President Bush visited New Orleans. He met with Governor Blanco, Mayor Nagin, and other officials on *Air Force One*. By this point, any signs of solidarity among the officials assembled had all but vanished, replaced by acrimony between the governor and mayor and suspicion on the part of the governor toward the White House. If, as the White House later argued, the president intended to serve as a go-between during this meeting, tempering the coordination problems emerging in the state, he did a poor job. According to Nagin, Bush failed to recognize where the sticking points were and merely "danced" around the command issue.

Governor Blanco and other state officials were very frustrated with what they saw as the inept processing of their assistance requests.[253] The state's continuous complaints, in turn, had prompted questions in Washington as to whether the response in Louisiana should be "federalized."[254] This would become one of the most divisive issues in the days to come, though it largely escaped media scrutiny at the time. The federalization issue dominated the interaction between these leaders during and after Friday's meeting with the president.

When Governor Blanco spoke with President Bush on Monday, Blanco explained that the situation was severe and requested "everything you've got."[255] During the week, Blanco would ask again and again for federal support. Blanco asked her adjutant general to ask Honoré, then in neighboring Mississippi, for troops on Tuesday. She and other state officials hoped that DOD resources could be assigned to the ongoing search and rescue mission, thereby freeing up National Guard units for other assignments, including providing security.

Brown had a different idea. On Tuesday, FEMA director Brown asked the

White House to "federalize" the response effort in Louisiana, possibly by invoking the Insurrection Act.[256] In testimony, Brown explained that "one of the things I was trying to do was to assist the governor in any way that I could in the decision-making process, in trying to help her manage what was going on. And one of my suggestions was that, you know, we could federalize this disaster and take over the National Guard and run the operation through that National Guard."[257] This would mean that all National Guard units operating in the state, including Louisiana units, would come under federal command.[258]

A meeting with FCO Lokey the following day further strengthened Brown's resolve to see the response federalized. Lokey explained to Brown that "[the response] is beyond me, this is beyond FEMA, this is beyond the state." Lokey apparently did not fully grasp what federalization would look like in practice. Later he explained: "What I was talking about was turning this over to somebody that can manage something this size. I've never done something like this. I was trying my best. I wasn't doing very good at it. So [federalization] was just a term I used."[259]

Blanco soon learned of the federalization discussions, leading to a confrontation in the governor's workspace at the state EOC on Wednesday afternoon.[260] "Within an hour" after Lokey and Brown's talk about federalization, Blanco confronted Lokey. "What's this about you taking over my disaster?" she asked Lokey. "I did not want the Guard federalized," Governor Blanco later testified.[261] Federalization, she thought, would not only undermine her authority but might also limit the effectiveness of National Guard units then engaged in law enforcement activities throughout the affected region. This did not even take into account that the Posse Comitatus Act prohibited federal troops from carrying out law enforcement duties.

But the governor was desperate for help. On Wednesday morning, Blanco was overheard ahead of a televised press conference telling her press secretary that she should call "for the military." She seemed to regret not having done so during her first call with Bush.[262] A few hours later, Blanco contacted the White House in hopes of speaking to the president. She had resolved that she would request federal troops. With the president unavailable, Blanco spoke briefly with Bush's homeland security adviser instead.[263]

Later in the day, Blanco again tried to reach Bush.[264] This time she was successful. During their conversation, Blanco explained that she was worried about the security situation. She requested "40,000 troops" along with additional rescue personnel, supplies, and buses.[265] Blanco did not specify which type of troops

(National Guard or active-duty federal troops) she had in mind. Her request was reportedly not based on a completed needs assessment but was intended "to relay the urgency and the magnitude of the need at that point in time."[266] Blanco emphasized during the call that she was not requesting that operations be federalized, only that Louisiana "be a partner in a unified command."[267]

The governor and other state officials were growing increasingly suspicious that the White House was maneuvering to assume complete control over the response. A conversation between US senator David Vitter and the governor's executive council on Wednesday had fed these suspicions: Vitter claimed to have learned from one of the president's advisers, Karl Rove, that *the governor* wanted to federalize the evacuation.[268] Some federal officials were speaking to members of the media as though federalization was already a fact. The DHS secretary, for instance, explained at one point that the federal government was "leading" the response in Louisiana, a statement state officials were unwilling to accept as simply a slip of the tongue.[269]

Honoré did not think more federal troops were needed. The JTF-Katrina commander maintained that he had enough National Guard units. The mission required "thousands of helicopters, not troops."[270] By providing aircraft, DOD would avoid tasking federal troops with law enforcement responsibilities.[271] Honoré would work in the coming days to demonstrate to the governor and her staff that the number of Guard troops in Louisiana was sufficient to carry out most if not all necessary missions.[272]

On Thursday, President Bush and Secretary of Defense Rumsfeld agreed that the National Guard was "responding effectively to the disaster and chose not to federalize the response."[273] But that was not the end of the discussion.

Senior officials at DOD and the White House still preferred that the overall response should be coordinated by the JTF-Katrina commander, not through the dual command structure that existed at the time.[274] On Thursday, a US district attorney and one of the governor's aides met to discuss the state's request for troops. The nature of the discussion suggested to the governor's staff that federal officials were looking for ways to give the JTF-Katrina commander temporary command authority over National Guard units in the state.

In reality, that was already happening. Blanco had asked Honoré to coordinate the evacuation of New Orleans. Since he brought no troops with him, he was obligated to use the National Guard to get the job done.[275] One can see how federal officials were receiving mixed messages from the state. It should perhaps therefore not have come as a surprise when at 7:15 p.m. on Thursday,

Rear Admiral Robert F. Duncan, US Coast Guard, called Blanco to urge the federalization of the response.[276]

That same evening, Blanco reached out to the head of the National Guard Bureau, General Steven Blum, for advice.[277] In Blanco's own words, "On Thursday, and I guess maybe before that, the word 'federalization' had been floating around. I asked General Blum to explain what exactly that would mean."[278] Blum recommended that Blanco retain the existing dual command structure, whereby National Guard units and engaging active-duty federal troops would remain under separate command authorities (one state-led, the other federal).[279]

Pressure on Blanco to cede to a single command structure under the JTF-Katrina commander increased dramatically after a radio interview with a clearly unsettled Mayor Nagin, which was aired on national television that Thursday evening. Nagin exclaimed that federal and state officials "need[ed] to get off their asses . . . and fix the biggest god-damn crisis in the history of this country." He made unfavorable comparisons between the government's engagement in managing this crisis, the September 11 attacks, and the 2004 Indian Ocean tsunami.[280]

Complicating Factor: A Shifting Problem Definition

Early on Friday morning, President Bush chaired a senior-level meeting on Katrina. The president opened the meeting by observing that the federal government was "not winning" before going on to emphasize the importance of getting "New Orleans under control."[281]

What had been a more or less technical debate on coordination now became infused with media-driven politics. The problem was no longer search and rescue and logistics but rather the anarchy that was apparently holding New Orleans in its grip (discussed further in chapter 5).

Discussion then turned to the question of "federalizing the response and asserting U.S. military control over New Orleans." According to the president's press secretary, "Bush believed that the military was the only organization disciplined and organized enough to come in and stabilize the situation quickly. Agreeing that there was an 'issue of confidence' when it came to current response and relief efforts, [the NORTHCOM commander] said the troops were ready if the orders came."[282]

No decision was made during this meeting.[283] Senior DHS, DOD, and White

House officials continued throughout the day to examine various legal means by which to consolidate command with the JTF-Katrina commander. One such option entailed the use of the Insurrection Act and the simultaneous designation of Honoré as commander of all National Guard and federal units in the region—a "dual hat" commander. This option would form the basis for a proposal that Bush presented to Governor Blanco in New Orleans later the same day.[284]

A White House spokeswoman would only say at the time that the White House was "actively trying to find a solution with state officials to bring federal troops as quickly as possible and under a single chain of command." The FEMA director, himself an early proponent of federalization, later suggested that "certain people in the White House were thinking, 'We had to federalize Louisiana because [Governor Blanco] was a white, female Democratic governor, and we have a chance to rub her nose in it. . . . We can't do it to Haley [Barbour, the Mississippi governor] because Haley's a white male Republican governor. And we can't do a thing to him. So we're just gonna federalize Louisiana.'"[285]

It was this federalization issue that so dramatically shaped the Friday meeting on *Air Force One*. According to Blanco, Bush asked her to put the National Guard under General Honoré's command.[286] Blanco agreed "out of respect" to the president to review the proposal.

Late on Friday evening, at 11:20 p.m., a memorandum from the White House with a space for Blanco's signature came through a fax machine at the state EOC.[287] The "midnight memo," as it came to be known, declared the appointment of the JTF-Katrina commander as an officer in the Louisiana National Guard. In this dual-hatted role, Honoré "would . . . be the single military commander for all [DOD] military forces, including active, reserve, and National Guard, providing support to [DHS] as the lead federal agency."[288] According to the *New Orleans Times-Picayune*, this document was followed by calls from the president's chief of staff and the National Guard Bureau chief (now supporting a single command structure), which "dramatically elevated the Blanco team's sense of a political assault from Washington."[289]

Blanco resolved not to sign the memorandum, arguing that the proposed arrangement served no operational purpose at that time. After all, the security situation in New Orleans had improved significantly.[290] But more importantly, Blanco remained suspicious of the White House's actual intentions.[291] According to the *Washington Post*, the governor's refusal came as a surprise to the White House, which scrambled to rewrite the president's remarks ahead of an appearance in the Rose Garden the same morning.[292]

Blanco later explained that it appeared to her that the White House had been angling to federalize the National Guard.[293] All Blanco wanted was to "retain control of the National Guard and for [the president] to send troops in." When Blanco refused to accept federalization, the White House proposed dual-hatting instead.

From a technical standpoint, it is not clear why Blanco refused the White House proposal.[294] As Senator Susan Collins later pointed out, the midnight memorandum did not propose federalization.[295] Honoré would co-command the National Guard, an authority that he technically had already been granted by the state when he accepted responsibility for evacuation.[296]

In hindsight, the memorandum reads as an honest and clever (but also complex) compromise, aimed at establishing joint command. Blanco smelled a rat: "Apparently, they spent all day trying to figure out how to federalize without actually federalizing, I guess. I am not quite sure what the exercise was all about."[297] It appears that the blame game (discussed in chapter 5) was taking its toll.

The governor's late-night no to the White House rounded off a tense week for many senior officials. In a summary of events provided by the state after the dust had settled, Blanco suggested that she was dealing with both a catastrophe and a White House attempting to encroach on her authority as governor.[298] In an effort to counter perceived and real White House attacks in the weeks and months to come, the state hired the services of an emergency management consultancy (headed by former FEMA director James Lee Witt) to aid the state in its dealings with the federal government.

RECONSIDERING COORDINATION OF A SUPERDISASTER

After Katrina, much of the criticism focused on the lack of coordination and the results stemming therefrom. But this chapter gives rise to an important question: can we speak here of a coordination failure? Our research offers a more nuanced assessment.

We have shown that emergent coordination worked well and saved lives. The citizens of New Orleans and those rushing in to help worked closely (and informally) with state and federal organizations in ways that dramatically minimized the loss of life. Viewed from this perspective, coordination worked well.

The seemingly slow evacuation and the absent buses may appear to be clear indicators of failed coordination. The buses, FEMA's imploding logistics system, and the plight of the hospitals have all been held forth as evidence of instances where coordination was lacking. This chapter, again, makes the case that such a verdict is overly simplistic and in fact spurious.

Evacuation was the root problem defining the first week. Neither the state nor FEMA had buses. People had to wait for buses to be driven from elsewhere. If you walked into the Superdome on Sunday afternoon, you wouldn't be leaving again until Thursday at the earliest. This problem—and what a problem it was—took several days to tackle. Even in the best of circumstances, emptying urban centers takes time.

But the fact that people were forced to suffer in safety at the Superdome does not necessarily make the federal response a coordination failure. The evacuation operation was initiated on Monday, which was early given that most officials were slow to realize how serious the situation was. Though buses had to be driven in from across the country, the first convoy reached the outskirts of New Orleans on Wednesday. One can argue whether this is remarkably quick or too slow, but that debate would have nothing to do with coordination.

There was a real failure to reach an agreement on who was in charge during the week. Recognizing that this disaster was too big to handle, FEMA wisely tried to "scale up" early in the week. But upscaling took time and created new problems and dilemmas. The plans in place failed to provide the groundwork for a shift from FEMA to the DOD.

The coordination challenge became further muddled by the political infighting that began to play up during the week. To make things even more complex, the evacuation problem transformed into a law-and-order issue just when the problem seemed solved (the buses were arriving). Coordination was quickly politicized. In the next chapter, we will analyze how this happened.

But there is no compelling evidence that this failure to coordinate across lines of authority directly influenced the quality of the response. The apparent discord was enough to *suggest* organizations did not work together, but that lack of collaboration pertained more to individuals than organizations. The perception of discord did fuel a process of politicization, which in turn sapped the legitimacy of key institutions. We analyze these dynamics in the following chapter.

5

MEANING MAKING IN CRISIS

THE DETRIMENTAL EFFECTS OF MISSING NARRATIVES
AND ESCALATING BLAME GAMES

It's totally wiped out. It's devastating. It's got to be doubly devastating on the ground.
—PRESIDENT GEORGE W. BUSH AFTER FLYING OVER
NEW ORLEANS, AUGUST 31, 2005

I have to tune out the political talking heads. The blame game can get
in the way of protective efforts. It can sap your vitality. It's the vulture mentality.
Woulda coulda shoulda, sitting in their clean spaces, not knowing what's
going on in the trenches. They know not of what they speak.
—GOVERNOR KATHLEEN BLANCO

THE SYMBOLIC DIMENSION OF STRATEGIC CRISIS MANAGEMENT

Much of strategic crisis management is functional in nature: it is about organizing and analyzing information, making decisions, and orchestrating the activities of network partners. We discussed these tasks in the foregoing chapters. But there is also a *symbolic* dimension to strategic crisis management.[1] This pertains to the task of explaining what transpired, communicating what is being done, and offering guidance to survivors, first responders, and citizens.

We call this "meaning making." When citizens look to public leaders to understand what has happened to them, they want guidance. They expect leaders to offer a frame through which the crisis can be understood and through which a way forward can be discerned.[2] An effective "master frame" guides the many actors in a response framework. It not only helps to formulate consistent messages; it can serve as a mission for strategic crisis managers as well.[3]

Leaders do not have a monopoly on meaning making. While crisis leaders may enjoy an initial advantage as media attention focuses on them in the first phase of a crisis, these same media will look for alternative sources (if only to remain "fair and balanced") after the formal leaders have had their say. And there are many others who will have an explanatory frame on offer. Sooner rather than later, a competition between frames is therefore likely to emerge.

Those leaders who perform exceptionally well in this symbolic dimension of crisis management understand that it is not solely about facts and figures. They understand that it does not always matter who is wrong or right. Meaning making is about having the best story that convinces most people—in both the short and the long run.

The outcome of this competition is important. The winning frame not only shapes the common understanding of a disaster; it also clears a path for response strategies and policy changes.

To be sure, meaning making is *not* about blaming other officials or organizations. In fact, the more meaning-making efforts are (perceived to be) infused by politics, the more criticism and alternatives they will invite. As we will demonstrate, the Katrina case is highly instructive in this regard.

Meaning making is different from crisis communication. Meaning making involves formulating a value-based frame that incorporates an explanation of what happened before and during a crisis; it describes a believable future. Once the frame is in place, getting messages to the intended audiences—crisis communication—becomes important. Whereas crisis communication is a profession, meaning making is much closer to the art of politics.

We have noted many times that the response to Katrina was and still is widely viewed as a failure. In this chapter, we argue that this perception of failure is rooted in a failure of meaning making. None of the key actors managed to impose their frame on the general public. As we will show, reputations were tarnished and trust in public institutions suffered as a result.

We start by briefly summarizing the various frames vying for dominance. We delve into the role of the media and the effect of rumors. We discuss the consequences of failed meaning making, which last up until today.

A VARIETY OF FRAMES

The first week of Katrina was characterized by a variety of frames, one dominant frame quickly replacing another (and some frames being more dominant locally than nationally). After proclaiming that New Orleans had dodged the bullet, the media quickly pivoted to describing in graphic detail the level of devastation in the city and elsewhere along the Gulf Coast. The dominant frame then shifted to looting and violence, accompanied by the "absent government" and the "failing FEMA" frames.[4] Let us briefly summarize the various frames that vied for attention during the first week.

New Orleans dodged the bullet. The flooding of a major American city did not capture the headlines on Monday. The first reports on Monday and even Tuesday morning told the story of a monster hurricane that veered away from New Orleans at the last minute. As the gravity of the situation gradually set in (and weather conditions improved), FOX News, ABC, NBC, CNN, and CBS began broadcasting live footage from New Orleans later in the day. While dead bodies could be seen floating in the floodwaters, the extent of the disaster somehow did not immediately became obvious.

OMG—that's terrible! The full scale of the disaster came into focus on Tuesday. When it did become clear that something big had happened after all, media attention ramped up quickly. The frame was one of shocked amazement: a major disaster was in progress and people were dying. Reporters focused on the National Guard troops, private volunteer groups, search and rescue efforts, and FEMA—at this point still cast in a positive light.[5] On Wednesday evening, the NBC *Nightly News* focused on the extensive damage in the region and the "massive response on the way."[6]

It's a war zone down there (the mayhem frame). CNN began reporting on instances of looting, threats to public safety, and anarchy as early as Tuesday evening.[7] By Wednesday, the narrative "began to metaphorically present the disaster-stricken city of New Orleans as a war zone and to draw parallels between the conditions in that city and urban insurgency in Iraq."[8] The narrative was informed by rumors—widely repeated by national media and officials—that painted a vivid picture of chaos and anomie in New Orleans. Looting was depicted as being "widespread, wanton, irrational, and accompanied by violence."[9] This frame was reinforced later in the week by an increased military presence in the city and Governor Blanco's announcement on Thursday that the incoming troops "know how to shoot and kill."[10] Journalists produced many stories describing how the relief effort was being slowed down by gangs and armed looters.[11]

Where is the government? The mayhem frame was soon accompanied by one that decried the slow response of the federal government.[12] The media were reporting on thousands of survivors stranded at the Superdome, the Convention Center, and on highway overpasses. FEMA director Michael Brown claimed repeatedly (but unconvincingly) on live television on Thursday that "things are going relatively well," but images suggested a more dire story.[13] Department of Homeland Security director Chertoff was forced to admit during a live interview on National Public Radio that he did not know thousands of survivors were gathered at the Convention Center.[14] As M. J. Martinko et al. conclude, "The news media had a field day exploiting the apparent incompetence of government officials."[15] By Friday, President Bush had become the object of relentless criticism.[16] His praise for Michael Brown—"Brownie, you're doing a heck of a job"—did not help matters.[17]

Uncaring government. The idea that racism was at play and might explain the tardy response emerged soon after landfall. The underlying theme was that the Bush administration did not care about the plight of the African American community.[18] The Congressional Black Caucus was quick to criticize the federal government's response. During a postlandfall press conference, one caucus member suggested that "poverty, age and skin color" were critical factors in determining who survived the hurricane.[19] On Friday, Kanye West, a well-known hip-hop artist, declared on national television that "George Bush doesn't care about black people."[20] Controversial remarks by former first lady Barbara Bush during a visit to a major evacuation center in Houston (on Monday, September 6) helped to keep this frame alive.[21]

The military comes to the rescue. The military as an institution shone during the end of that first week, appearing as one of only a few functioning institutions (the US Coast Guard was another). Upon arriving in the region, the plainspoken JTF-Katrina commander, General Russel Honoré, attracted lots of media attention. General Honoré, a Louisiana native, became an instant hero in New Orleans. His hands-on leadership style served as a counterpoint to Bush's perceived absenteeism and FEMA director Brown's bumbling. Mayor Nagin referred to Honoré at one point as "that John Wayne dude," a description that resonated with the media.[22] What got lost in this frame was that most of the uniforms seen on television belonged to National Guardsmen, not federal troops.

Ten years after Katrina, the frames that emerged in that first week—and that were fortified in official inquiries—have become the building blocks of a master narrative about dysfunctional government in a time of great need.[23] In this chapter, we investigate how these frames emerged, how the dysfunctional government narrative came about, and what consequences it had.

THE RUMOR MILL

It doesn't appear to be safe now, but it seems that a sniper standing
atop one of the buildings just above us here and firing down at patients
and doctors as they were trying to be evacuated, unbelievable.
—CNN MEDICAL CORRESPONDENT DR. SANJAY GUPTA,
REPORTING LIVE FROM CHARITY HOSPITAL

Rumors always emerge after a disaster. People will fill in the blanks where uncertainty is allowed to exist.[24] An official narrative that is considered plausible and legitimate helps to counter rumors. In its absence, the rumor mill can have a devastating effect on the legitimacy of leaders and institutions.

In a disaster, rumors of looting often emerge. Disaster sociologists have shown that looting rarely occurs, even though media routinely report such rumors during the first phase of a disaster.[25] In the case of Katrina, the first reports of looting in New Orleans reached officials at the state EOC on Monday evening.[26]

And there *was* looting in New Orleans.[27] The local newspaper, the *Times-Picayune*, reported many stories describing widespread looting. On Wednesday, national television ran over and over again a clip of a Walmart being plundered.[28] The *Washington Post* described "looters roam[ing] the city, sacking department stores and grocery stores and floating their spoils away in plastic garbage cans. . . . By nightfall the pillage was widespread."[29]

But the looting was not as widespread as media reports suggested. Television footage was focused on a few stores in a few locations (and was looped over and over again). Overall, as Dan Baum suggests, it was striking just how *few* stores were ransacked.[30] "When responded to, most of the looting calls received by police proved unfounded," according to the Louisiana State Police.[31] The House report found that "major looting was generally limited to the Canal Street area and ended by Tuesday, August 30."[32] The House report also stated that "the extent of crime and lawlessness is difficult to determine."[33] Indeed, the collapse of emergency call centers on the day of landfall made the task of documenting and evaluating suspected cases of looting (not to mention murder and rape) impossible.[34]

Television crews captured on film several police officers looting. Officials later suggested that at least some of these images were misinterpreted. In light of the dire conditions and the lack of desperately needed goods, it probably was not crystal clear to everybody what the difference was between looting and surviving. First responders, including police officers, later argued they had to take food, water, and medical supplies from area stores because their own stocks had been lost or contaminated by floodwaters.[35]

Some of the "looting" was authorized by Mayor Nagin's emergency declaration, which authorized police forces to take (commandeer) things that they needed to do their job. Nagin reportedly directed his staff to take supplies from a nearby Office Depot.[36] Governor Blanco said she "sympathized with people who looted stores to survive."[37]

Reports of looting were accompanied by rumors of violence. First reports of violent crime in New Orleans began to appear in the media on Tuesday. That afternoon, the Louisiana State Police reported that a New Orleans police officer had been shot by a looter. In addition, a gun store had reportedly been sacked. Such reports "set imaginations wild."[38] On Tuesday, Councilwoman Jackie Clarkson declared that "looting is out of control. The French Quarter has been attacked."[39]

Clarkson was not alone in seeing a connection between looting, violence, and anarchy. New Orleans City Council president Oliver Thomas spoke to journalists about "widespread looting in all parts of the city" and "an atmosphere of lawlessness." "People are leaving the Superdome to go to Canal Street to loot," Thomas said. "Some people broke into drugstores and stole the drugs off the shelves. It is looting times five. I'm telling you, it's like Sodom and Gomorrah."[40]

A Sense of Anarchy

Accounts of looting were soon followed by stories describing a city under siege.[41] In these stories, New Orleans was on par with "post-invasion Baghdad" and Mogadishu.[42] The media "featured numerous stories of looting, rape, and lawlessness, continuously 'looping' video of the activities of groups that had already become 'armed, marauding thugs' in the minds of viewers."[43]

Some of the most heinous reports focused on the Superdome and, later, the Convention Center. Media quoted people in the Dome who described drug use and acts of violence including murder inside the facility; riots appeared imminent if these reports were any indication. CNN reported on Thursday that Superdome evacuations were suspended because "someone fired a shot at a helicopter."[44] Chief Lonnie C. Swain, in charge of security in the Superdome, told the *New York Times* that "quite a few of the people died during the course of their time here. . . . I was watching people die."[45] Unnamed officials apparently confirmed to a *New York Times* reporter that ten people had died at the Superdome ("several adults died while walking to the buses").[46]

It got more fantastic. NOPD chief Eddie Compass and Mayor Nagin fanned the fire by repeating rumors of rampant criminality to media representatives, thus suggesting the rumors were true.[47] Compass did not just repeat rumors; he was a *source* of rumors.[48] For instance, he told the *New York Times* that "thugs" had taken control of the Convention Center and were shooting at officers stationed there. In his telling, officers couldn't return fire "because of the families."[49] According to Compass, "eight squads of 11 officers each" were not enough to repel the "thugs." Compass went on to assert that rapes and assaults were occurring "unimpeded in neighboring streets"; the thugs were "preying on tourists."[50] He even claimed at one point that "people tried to kidnap me."[51]

Compass later told Oprah Winfrey on her talk show, "We had little babies in there getting raped."[52] On the same show, Mayor Nagin claimed that "hundreds of armed gang members" were raping women and committing murder in the Superdome. Shelterees, he said, were "in an almost animalistic state . . . in that frickin' Superdome for five days watching dead bodies, watching hooligans killing people, raping people."[53] Nagin speculated that the city's death toll would top 10,000.[54]

There were more tales feeding the rising sense of anarchy. There were reports that police officers, including the NOPD superintendent, had fled the city after landfall.[55] It was rumored that Mayor Nagin declared martial law on Tuesday night.[56] Jefferson Parish president Aaron Broussard reportedly stated: "We're under martial law. And there's only one marshal: Me."[57]

While there was undeniably looting and violence, lawlessness was not anywhere near as pervasive as reports suggested.[58] Accounts of people shooting at helicopters were never verified (no bullet holes were found in any helicopters); the two babies with their throats slit at the Convention Center were never located, nor was the man who heard a rape victim scream and ran outside for help only to be shot and killed by soldiers.[59] Sally Forman, Nagin's communications director, later denied that her boss, as he said, had watched "hooligans killing people, raping people."[60]

In that first week, there were eight gunshot victims (including two suicides)—fairly normal statistics in what was at the time one of the most violent cities in the United States.[61] The House report found that there were six deaths in the Superdome, but none were crime related.[62] On Friday, when FEMA turned its attention to collecting the dead, officials expected to find 200 homicides based on all the media reports—they did not find any.[63] Yet on Saturday morning Scott Wells emailed his FEMA colleagues that "between the super dome and the convention center it looks like about 200 homicide bodies."[64]

Chertoff was correct when he noted that the "Superdome has crowd control issues but is secure."[65] According to the House report, the people in the Superdome "were very unhappy and anxious, but they were never out of control."[66] The Guard troops who secured the Convention Center said they encountered no lawlessness or any resistance.[67] When evacuees from New Orleans arrived in Houston, few problems were reported. "They are nice and courteous," said one senior Houston official.[68]

The Role of the Media

The media played a crucial role in the creation and dissemination of frames. The reporting during that first week helped to shape public opinion and identify culpable parties. In hindsight, we can observe that many of these powerful frames were built on falsehoods.

Experienced reporters did a lousy job fact-checking their stories. Reporters for the *New York Times,* for example, gave lots of room to the wild stories of NOPD captain Jeffrey Winn, who was at the Convention Center.[69] According to Winn, "Violence raged inside the Convention Center. . . . Police SWAT team members found themselves plunging into the darkness, guided by the muzzle flashes of thugs' handguns." Winn claimed that the gunfire became so routine that "large SWAT teams had to storm the place nearly every night." Winn recounted how a number of women had been dragged off by groups of men and gang-raped; he informed the reporters that murders were being committed. Eric Lipton and his *Times* colleagues quoted officials who confirmed that as many as 24 people had perished at the Convention Center alone.[70] None of this turned out to be correct.

The media gave credence to rumors.[71] This led to a simplified, one-dimensional picture of events.[72] In his study of television coverage during Katrina, Frank Durham argues that members of the media shifted away from professionalism toward populism.[73] Robert Littlefield and Andrea Quenette concluded that "the media stepped outside their role of objective observer and assumed a privileged position to point blame toward those with legitimate authority."[74] As an example, consider how CNN's Anderson Cooper interrupted Louisiana senator Mary Landrieu when she dared to praise the efforts of the president and other senior federal officials:

> Excuse me, senator, I'm sorry for interrupting. For the last four days, I've been seeing dead bodies in the streets here in Mississippi. And to listen to politicians thanking each other and complimenting each other, you know, I got to tell you, there are a lot of people out here who are very upset, and very angry, and very frustrated. And when they hear politicians, you know, thanking one another, it just cuts them the wrong way right now, because literally there was a body in the streets of this town yesterday being eaten by rats because this woman had been lying in the streets for 48 hours.[75]

Racial stereotyping crept into the stories. The majority of people still in New Orleans at this stage were African Americans. As a result, they featured heavily in media reports.[76] While they were initially portrayed as victims, the tone of the media's coverage began to shift once footage of looting featuring mostly black people became available and was endlessly looped on television.[77]

Black residents who commandeered supplies during the storm were referred to as "looters," whereas at least one television report described white residents seen engaged in the same behavior as merely "taking" supplies.[78] "In depictions of rescue and aid, two-thirds of the news reports showed only whites helping only African-Americans. . . . There were no instances of African-Americans helping Whites. . . . All looting clips were of African-Americans."[79] The media's portrayal of the city's black population provided a solid foundation for stories (rumors) about depraved behavior in the "Mogadishu" that New Orleans had reportedly become.

Prominent African Americans quickly raised questions about the role that race played in the response. Jesse Jackson leveled the accusation that the federal government did not care about African Americans.[80] Kanye West's suggestion on live television that "George Bush doesn't care about black people" resonated across the country.[81] Tensions were fed by rumors that the levees had been blown up to "wipe out" the city's black population.[82] Author Cedric Muhammad later expressed a similar sentiment: "Any reasonable and rational person with an open mind—not bound by ideology—would have to conclude that there is justification and various forms of evidence for considering the possibility that the levees were breached and the Ninth Ward flooded for reasons other than that provided by the mainstream media and local, state and federal government including the Army Corps of Engineers."[83]

There is no evidence that the media came into Katrina with the intention of pushing certain frames. There is a simpler explanation for the sloppy quality of their reporting. Reporters were working under extremely difficult circumstances. Massive disruptions to communications infrastructure and the unexpected flooding of the city made it difficult to collect reports and then confirm their veracity. Operating from a sliver of dry land near the French Quarter, journalists' perspective on the city was limited. They became particularly reliant on events in the immediate vicinity (which happened to include the Superdome and the Convention Center).

The story then wrote itself: journalists did not have to go far to find subjects willing to vent their frustration. Rumors were taken for eyewitness reports. Journalists had no way to verify these reports. In the absence of any formal (government) sources, they were forced to adapt and seek information from other sources. Accounts became personal in nature; witness reports in many cases remained unverified.[84] Journalistic rigor was abandoned.[85] Unconfirmed reports of looting, violence, and mass rape were perceived as established facts. The reports gave officials, residents, and spectators across the nation a distorted view of what was happening in the city.[86]

With little information of their own, federal, state, and local officials relied heavily on these inaccurate media reports.[87] Local officials then repeated what they assumed to be true (but what were in fact unsubstantiated rumors), which journalists duly reported. In other words, public officials and the media reinforced each other's ignorance through the adoption of unchecked rumors as truths. As we will see, the consequences were very real: "The reputation of a great American city [was], at least to some degree, unfairly tarnished."[88]

CHALLENGES OF MEANING MAKING IN A
DYNAMIC CRISIS ENVIRONMENT

The tone of the media's reporting shifted over the course of a few short days, from relief (Katrina as a near miss) to indignation (the mishandled disaster). This change in tone, from guarded optimism to shock and despair, affected the nature of the response and fueled politicization.

To understand how this shift occurred, we should look at the meaning-making efforts on the part of various key players. One of the central tasks of strategic crisis management is to impute meaning to an event that is widely perceived as a dire threat. Leaders must provide information, address rumors, and inspire hope. A shared understanding of causes, characteristics, and consequences facilitates an effective and legitimate response to the disaster. But a shared frame does not emerge on its own—and when it does, it rarely lasts. Leaders must formulate a frame, ensure that it is adopted by the key players, check regularly to see if it resonates, and then tweak it if needed.

One critical challenge facing leaders lies in managing expectations: they must explain that mistakes are unavoidable in the management of a complex disaster, and that the response will never be fast enough to prevent all suffering. When the response appears slow and looks chaotic, as it inevitably will, officials must be prepared to address the inevitable criticism. The impossibilities of disaster management must be explained.

In terms of meaning making, a "superdisaster" is, paradoxically, the easy case: as there are no external agents to blame (it is hard to blame nature), the "we are all in it together" frame should dominate, at least during the first phase of the disaster.[89]

Another critical challenge is to have key actors "sing from the same sheet." In a multiactor response that unfolds across geographic and policy boundaries, it is never obvious who should communicate what to whom. The logic of the US response system suggests that the bulk of the more functional communication is done by local and state leaders. Federal leaders communicate with the audience at large, if only in ritualistic and symbolic ways.[90] But when different actors communicate at different levels, the risk of mixed messages is real.

In the immediate aftermath of Katrina, none of the key players managed to impose a convincing frame. Federal, state, and local government leaders did not appear to have a communication strategy to "get ahead" of the "information curve."[91] Effectively "initiating, organizing and coordinating all aspects of emergency public information," including rumor control, as described in the National Response Plan, did not happen in the days after landfall. For instance, FEMA's media relations teams "react[ed] to the media coverage rather than [working] proactively to get the right messages out."[92] This was in part due to the fact that a Joint Information Center was not established in Baton Rouge until Wednesday, September 6.

Key players did not get across how difficult it was to organize a rapid response (and how effective they actually were). Adding insult to injury, the various actors communicated different stories, some of which were intended to blame rather than to explain. Moreover, they collectively failed to counter the many rumors that were circulating.[93]

When we revisit the meaning-making efforts of key actors in this crisis, as we do next, it becomes clear that none managed to gain widespread support for his or her preferred frame of the situation. The variety of frames soon became a source of tension.

Mayor Ray Nagin

Mayor Nagin was the perfect candidate to be a winning meaning maker. Charismatic and popular, Nagin had the right set of attributes to craft a story that would have countered the emerging narrative of chaos and violence. While the mayor certainly had plenty to say about Katrina, he failed to offer up a consistent story explaining what was happening in New Orleans.

He repeated rumors and, later in the week, lashed out at state and federal officials. Frustrated by the tardiness of the federal response and tired of hearing Governor Blanco and DHS secretary Chertoff praise the federal effort on Wednesday afternoon, Nagin took to the airwaves on Thursday to deliver an expletive-laden rant (discussed in more detail below).[94]

According to his spokesperson, Sally Forman, Nagin acted impulsively, did not prepare for interviews, and did not tell the truth.[95] His comments were not based on facts. For example, when asked about the number of deaths, he sometimes sounded like he was guessing ("Minimum, hundreds. Most likely, thousands").[96] In one instance, Nagin claimed that his home had been destroyed in the storm, something that turned out to be untrue. Forman asked herself, "Why was the mayor saying he was homeless . . . when Greg had told us his house was fine?"[97] In another instance, Nagin claimed he had personally witnessed "babies dying" at the Superdome. This, too, turned out to be a falsehood.[98]

Looking back, Forman admits that "we were doing a terrible job of keeping the public informed."[99] The absence of a Joint Information Center as envisioned in the NRP did not help. Nagin's spokesperson lamented, "We have so much information that needs to get out to the public and I am the only one here doing it."[100] The first official press conference was not held before September 6, a full week after Katrina's landfall.

Governor Kathleen Blanco

Governor Blanco started the week with a relatively upbeat message, declaring at one point that "the damage has been great; we know it could have been worse."[101] She praised the response, described the damage that had been sustained, and refrained from criticism or grand statements. As the week progressed, she adopted a more forceful "law-and-order" frame. It was not very convincing. Moreover, it reinforced the perception that New Orleans had descended into anarchy.

Blanco was too busy organizing the response in those first few days after landfall to closely monitor how her messaging was being interpreted in the media.[102] She was unwilling to politically exploit the crisis: "Never would I criticize my president in the middle of a crisis."[103] In Louisiana, this gained her praise.[104] Blanco did little to communicate her hands-on engagement in managing the disaster. The governor's office did not allow the media to fly with her into New Orleans. Nor were they allowed near state response operations (the Louisiana National Guard refused to allow reporters to come along on patrol). Her communications director later recognized that this was a mistake: "Now I know I should have urged the governor to order both agencies to make room for reporters and photographers on just a few boats and choppers."[105]

Operating out of the spotlight, the heroic efforts of these two state agencies, the Louisiana Department of Wildlife and Fisheries and the National Guard, went largely unsung. Because the Guard did not "serve" the media, journalists failed to recognize the significant role that the Guard was playing at the Superdome as coordinator, security provider, and mass feeder. Though the LDWF performed just as well as the Coast Guard (which allowed reporters to join rescue missions), it was primarily the latter organization that was celebrated for its efforts.[106] Guard commanders only later recognized that their decision to shun the media came at a steep price. In the words of Major Ed Bush: "I never knew how badly we were being killed in the media."[107]

In the media, there was growing criticism of Blanco, who was depicted as disengaged, incompetent, or some combination of the two. Later in the week, Blanco's staff took steps to arrange public appearances where the governor could be seen "doing something active" while wearing, among other things, "rough-looking shoes." According to the governor's press secretary, Blanco was "doing too many 'first lady' things and not enough John Wayne. Women are easily portrayed as weak, which [Blanco] had a hard time overcoming."[108]

Blanco did not come across well on television: "Blanco was god-awful on television, discouraged and sad."[109] The *New York Times* described the governor as "haggard and shell-shocked before television cameras while blinking back tears and calling for prayers," further commenting that "as a speaker, Ms. Blanco is hardly dynamic, appearing more like a friendly den mother than a seasoned politician."[110]

FEMA Director Michael Brown

At the federal level, FEMA director Brown did most of the talking at the beginning of the week. The initial frame was straightforward: we are doing all we can to help. This frame rapidly lost traction, however, as the effectiveness of federal efforts came into question.

Many actors—not least the media—failed to grasp the limitations on FEMA's role. FEMA failed to explain that it does not own many resources and merely coordinates the allocation of resources made available by other agencies.[111] This created a persistent performance gap in the eyes of the storm's victims. Even though FEMA worked hard to obtain the requested resources, the agency's efforts were quickly discredited. One factor that contributed to the growing perception that FEMA was incompetent was Brown's tendency to make promises that he would ultimately be unable to keep (delivering requested resources, discussed in chapter 4).

Brown's efforts to explain what FEMA was doing to help were undermined by statements suggesting that he did not know what was going on. Early in the week, Brown was one of the few officials who recognized the severity of the situation. However, subsequent days would see Brown lose access to reliable and timely information (due in part to the lack of FEMA personnel in New Orleans).

On Thursday, Brown took to the airwaves. He looked dejected and weary.[112] By this point, it was clear that reporters and victims gravely misunderstood FEMA's role in a disaster.[113] When reporters asked victims if they had received any help from FEMA, they could only answer in the negative. As FEMA had never adequately explained its role (that the agency's personnel were in the most literal sense not first responders), Brown increasingly faced a dominant frame that FEMA was failing.

In perhaps one of the most sensationalized moments after landfall, Brown was asked on national television late on Thursday evening why people at the Convention Center were not receiving more assistance.[114] He replied that "the federal government [had] just learned about those people today."[115] Brown later claimed to have misspoken, blaming stress and fatigue for his error. It was around this time that calls for the FEMA director's resignation were first heard.[116]

One of the few FEMA officials in New Orleans after landfall was Marty Bahamonde, an external affairs officer. There is little to suggest that he did much to "sell" the FEMA story in those first few days. In fact, he seems to have assumed a more defensive posture. Bahamonde viewed the Superdome as an unsuitable venue for senior federal officials to visit. To his mind, the Dome as backdrop would do little to reinforce the "we have things under control" narrative that officials were doing their best to convey.[117] By taking this stance, Bahamonde unwittingly contributed to the growing perception among both officials and the media that the Superdome had descended into anarchy.

DHS Secretary Michael Chertoff

DHS secretary Chertoff initially left the talking to Brown. On Tuesday, he traveled to the Centers for Disease Control and Prevention (CDC) in Atlanta to discuss avian flu preparations; he later claimed he had little information about the situation in New Orleans until well into his meeting at CDC headquarters.[118]

Chertoff became visible upon his return to Washington. On Wednesday, he offered weirdly upbeat and seemingly off-tune praise of the federal effort. The first major blow to his credibility came when he seemed unaware of the problems at the Convention Center during an interview on NPR on Thursday (the same trap Brown had fallen into).[119] Chertoff never produced a convincing storyline that week.

President Bush and His Cabinet

In meaning-making terms, President Bush was never in a leading role. His language was highly scripted, as one would expect from a president in a routine disaster. It did not fit the mega-disaster that was unfolding in New Orleans. His Katrina performance contrasted with his performance after the 9/11 attacks: "As Presidential scholar Clinton Rossiter has written, the President is 'the one-man distillation of the American people.' President Bush showed the power of that role in the wake of 9/11, when he made clear to the nation that he was in control of the response. But in the events leading up to and following Hurricane Katrina's landfall, the President and his staff did not provide early, urgent, and strong public leadership, and the nation suffered."[120]

Before landfall, the president dutifully supported FEMA's routine pre-storm narrative and personally warned of the impending disaster. After landfall, Bush initially left the meaning making to Brown. In other words, he was letting the professionals manage the disaster. Where they deemed it necessary, Bush delivered standard statements of concern and hope. As part of his hands-off approach, the president opted to maintain his official schedule for the following days.

Coming off an extended stay at his ranch in Texas, Bush spent much of Monday in Arizona, where he discussed Social Security reform with senior citizens. From Arizona, Bush traveled to San Diego, where he appeared at a military base to commemorate the victory over Japan in World War II and to meet with wounded veterans. During his public appearances in both Arizona and California, Bush remarked briefly on the severity of Katrina. He assured the people that the federal government stood ready to help the states in any way they might need.[121]

Bush's press secretary, Scott McClellan, offered the standard rhetoric on Monday morning: "The President, this morning, spoke with our FEMA head, Mike Brown. Mike gave the President an update. Katrina remains a dangerous storm. We are coordinating closely with state and local authorities. We continue to urge citizens in those areas to listen to local authorities. Medical assistance teams and rescue teams have been deployed, and we're continuing to coordinate all activities very closely to make sure that the focus is on saving lives. That's where the top priority is right now, and that's where it will remain."[122]

Early on Tuesday, the president's advisers arranged a conference call to discuss the president's communications strategy. One senior adviser emphasized that "it's bad—a worst-case scenario in New Orleans."[123] The consensus within the group was that the president needed to return to Washington.[124] McClellan subsequently informed the White House press pool that Bush intended to return to the White House and visit the region later in the week.[125]

The decision to return to Washington was lost in images of the president celebrating Senator John McCain's birthday in Arizona and, later, strumming a guitar alongside a country-western singer in San Diego.[126] These images were broadcast alongside live footage from New Orleans depicting people on rooftops and scenes from the Superdome.[127] The contrast was jarring. According to McClellan, "It would be a day or two before we would begin to fully grasp it, but we had already blown our initial response to Katrina. In the process, we'd made ourselves vulnerable to exactly the kind of criticism that [the guitar] photo unleashed."[128]

We can now surmise why Bush did not engage more fully in the disaster from the start: he was under the impression that everything was under control. As we saw in chapter 4, Bush admitted that "I, myself, thought we had dodged a bullet."[129] Because the president stuck to his schedule, he conveyed the message that Katrina did not deserve high-level attention. If the images coming out of Arizona and California were any indication, the president did not look like he *wanted* to be in charge of the response. He thus created space for an alternative narrative, the noncaring government frame, to quickly gain traction.

By Wednesday, senior officials at all levels of government had transitioned to full crisis mode. Most of the president's scheduled appearances and meetings, including one with the Chinese president in Washington, were postponed or canceled outright. Before flying back to Washington from Texas, the president's press secretary explained to the assembled journalists that Bush's first priority was to facilitate lifesaving missions and to develop "a long-term strategy for addressing the needs of hundreds of thousands of displaced citizens."[130]

On the way back to Washington, *Air Force One* diverted from its original course, passing over the Gulf Coast region so that the president could see the devastation from the air.[131] The flyover, reportedly Karl Rove's idea and opposed by the president's press secretary, was broadcast live on television.[132]

The flyover did give Bush a better understanding of just how bad the situation was.[133] In an unusual move, members of the White House press corps were invited into the president's private quarters on *Air Force One*, where he was photographed peering down on a flooded New Orleans.[134] The photo of a pensive Bush eying the devastation below[135] backfired quickly, as it suggested that Bush did not care enough to get out of his plane. It fortified an image of a president unwilling to walk among the storm's victims.[136]

The president later defended the flyover, arguing that his presence on the ground would have disrupted ongoing rescue operations.[137] Indeed, the governors of both Louisiana and Mississippi had publicly advised the president against visiting the disaster area until the situation was more settled.[138] The White House did not dispute this point. The president's press secretary later ruminated: "In retrospect, we should have gone straight back to D.C., but no one seemed to feel that the circuitous route back would hurt as long as the president was staying on top of things and the public knew he was cutting short his Texas stay."[139]

When the president did finally assume a more proactive role in meaning making, it was too late to impose his frame on the public. He had lost the initiative. On Wednesday, he delivered a speech on national television in which he emphasized saving lives, federal assistance, and recovery efforts; he did not mention the security situation in New Orleans.[140] The president's narrative was at odds with the rapidly emerging perception of anarchy. The *New York Times* panned the speech:

> George W. Bush gave one of the worst speeches of his life yesterday, especially
> given the level of national distress and the need for words of consolation and
> wisdom. In what seems to be a ritual in this administration, the president ap-
> peared a day later than he was needed. He then read an address of a quality
> more appropriate for an Arbor Day celebration: a long laundry list of pounds
> of ice, generators and blankets delivered to the stricken Gulf Coast. He advised
> the public that anybody who wanted to help should send cash, grinned, and
> promised that everything would work out in the end. . . . And nothing about the
> president's demeanor yesterday—which seemed casual to the point of careless-
> ness—suggested that he understood the depth of the current crisis.[141]

On Thursday, the president engaged in several initiatives aimed at supporting the response and recovery effort. He gave a speech highlighting a fund-raising initiative launched by two former presidents (his father, George H. W. Bush, and Bill Clinton).[142] He wrote a letter to the Speaker of the House asking for an emergency appropriation of $10.5 billion to finance the Katrina response.[143] The White House issued a memorandum allowing federal employees to donate unused leave to colleagues in need of more time on account of Katrina.[144]

On Friday morning, Bush boarded *Air Force One*, bound for the disaster-stricken region. While en route, his advisers showed the president a short compilation of news broadcasts. They did this because they feared that Bush still did not fully understand how the media were portraying the federal government's response at the time.[145]

Before landing in New Orleans, Bush visited several sites in Alabama and Mississippi.[146] During an appearance at a Coast Guard air station in Alabama, Bush turned to the FEMA director, at his side, and told Brown that he was "doing a heck of a job" in responding to the storm. The president's praise of "Brownie" suggested that the response was satisfactory.[147] Looking back on the incident years later, Scott McClellan said, "For Bush to commend [Brown] publicly suggested either that the president's well-known belief in personal loyalty was overwhelming his judgment or that he still didn't realize how bad things were on the Gulf Coast. Either way, the incident said something bad about the Bush administration."[148]

In Biloxi, Mississippi, Bush met with local residents who had been made homeless by the storm, as well as the mayor, the governor, and Republican senator Trent Lott, who had lost his beach house. Here too, Bush's remarks comparing the loss of Lott's house to losses suffered in New Orleans (his point being that they would both be rebuilt) earned him criticism:[149] "Out of the rubble of Trent Lott's house—he lost his entire house—there's going to be a fantastic house. And I'm looking forward to sitting on the porch. Out of New Orleans is going to come that great city again. That's what's going to happen."[150]

At the New Orleans airport, Bush and his staff met with Mayor Nagin and Governor Blanco aboard *Air Force One* (see chapter 4). After their meeting, Bush surveyed the area from a helicopter. Due to security concerns, he did not visit the Superdome or the Convention Center.[151] The *New York Times* took a dim view of the president's decision not to visit the Dome:

> Mr. Bush did not go into the heart of the city's devastation, where thousands of
> largely poor, black refugees have raged at the government's response to one of
> the worst natural disasters in American history. The White House cited security

concerns and worries about causing more chaos as the reasons for keeping Mr. Bush away from the streets and the New Orleans Superdome, where refugees have lived in squalor and lawlessness for days. "The president wanted to see as much as he could without impeding the relief efforts," said Erin Healy, a White House spokeswoman.[152]

Just like his father after Hurricane Andrew (1992), George W. Bush received criticism for not visiting the region sooner.[153] His symbolic performance was later summarized in the House report: "The same President who had flown from Crawford to Washington to intervene in Terri Schiavo's medical case did not visit the devastated areas until his fly-over on September 2nd, the fifth day after landfall, delivering the message 'I am satisfied with the response. I am not satisfied with all the results' at a press conference. The next day, apparently forgetting what he had been told at the August 28th briefing, Bush stated: 'I don't think anybody anticipated the breach of the levees.'"[154]

The actions of his cabinet members did not help the president. Secretary of Defense Donald Rumsfeld was spotted at a baseball game in San Diego.[155] Secretary of State Condoleezza Rice was in New York City, where she attended a Broadway show and was booed by some audience members. Representative Tom Davis, chairman of the House Select Committee, later criticized the absence of federal leaders: "The director . . . of the National Hurricane Center said this was a big one, but when this happened . . . Bush is in Texas, [Chief of Staff Andy] Card is in Maine, the vice president is fly-fishing. I mean, who's in charge here?"[156]

Bush offered a new frame during his weekly radio address to the nation, broadcast on Saturday, September 3. The president noted that Katrina had "strained state and local capabilities." He observed that it was "unacceptable" that "many of our citizens simply are not getting the help they need, especially in New Orleans"—but he talked mostly about law and order, at one point proclaiming that "we will not let criminals prey on the vulnerable."[157]

CONSEQUENCES OF INEFFECTIVE MEANING MAKING

The absence of a shared frame that unified officials at every level of government hurt the response in two significant ways. First, it allowed rumors to proliferate, which directly affected the response. Second, it triggered and fueled a blame game, which in a more insidious way undermined the response.

Rumors and Fear

The rumors were everywhere.[158] There were reports of a downed helicopter. A National Guardsman had been shot at the Superdome.[159] A hostage situation was transpiring at the Tulane hospital. Law enforcement agents said that they had discovered pipe bombs.

None of these reports were true. But the reports went unchallenged and thus reinforced the perception, both inside and beyond New Orleans, of a city overcome by lawlessness.[160] Authorities not only failed to address the rumors; they *acted upon the rumors* without verifying them, thus implicitly validating their content.

Rumors may seem harmless, but in a disaster they are not. As the House report would later conclude, "The hyped media coverage of violence and lawlessness, legitimized by New Orleans authorities, served to delay relief efforts by scaring away truck and bus drivers, increasing the anxiety of those in shelters, and generally increasing the resources that needed to be dedicated to security."[161]

The governor's chief of staff, Andy Kopplin, claimed that 1,000 FEMA employees set to arrive in New Orleans on Wednesday were turned back due to security concerns.[162] FEMA urban search and rescue teams and Coast Guard pilots reported gunfire directed at them.[163] On Thursday, FEMA rescue teams stood down until the security situation had improved.[164] Reports of snipers forced officials to ground helicopters.[165] On Thursday, the evacuation of patients out of New Orleans was put on hold due to "potential harm to rescue workers."[166] At a Friday press conference, Henry Whitehorn of the Louisiana State Police announced that local police officers were quitting because they were being shot at.[167] Officials prevented some nongovernmental organizations, including the Red Cross, from entering the city.[168] Even the Pentagon was reportedly slow to move due to extensive security measures.[169]

A particularly painful example of how rumors influenced the course of events can be found in the Memorial Hospital drama, vividly described by Sheri Fink.[170] Hospital staff were stretched to the limit: without electricity and supplies, they were unable to care for patients, some of them deathly ill. On Tuesday, the airborne evacuation of the hospital was launched. But the helicopters soon stopped coming. Staff members were told that they had been grounded after someone started shooting at them.

The Memorial staff decided to begin evacuating without the helicopters, though they realized that not every patient could be moved. Convinced that the city had been taken over by marauding looters, staff feared for the patients they had to leave behind. The growing fear informed their decision to sedate—some would say euthanize—several very sick patients. Sheri Fink interviewed a doctor who was at Memorial:

> He [John Thiele, a 53-year-old pulmonologist] expected that the people firing guns into the chaos of New Orleans—"the animals," he called them—would storm the hospital, looking for drugs after everyone else was gone. "I figured, What would they do, these crazy black people who think they've been oppressed for all these years by white people? I mean if they're capable of shooting at some-body, why are they not capable of raping them or, or, you know, dismembering them? What's to prevent them from doing things like that?" The laws of man had broken down, Thiele concluded, and only the laws of God applied.[171]

Survivors who were lucky enough to own a home in a dry part of New Orleans rarely saw police officers during the first week: "It felt as if government at all levels had vanished—lurid rumors filled the void."[172] Worried by reports of looting, uptown residents hired private security firms to patrol the neighborhood.[173] According to *New Yorker* reporter Dan Baum, "The phrase on the lips of the guest enforcers was 'martial law.'"[174] Many white residents openly bore arms in self-defense: "The blackout, the crowds of evacuees straggling through their neighborhoods—and, above all, the rumors—persuaded some citizens that an apocalyptic race riot was imminent."[175]

The Nature of the Response Changes

As fear spread, the nature of the response changed. The "civil unrest" lens led policy makers to shift the focus from search and rescue to crime fighting.[176] According to Dan Berger, the media coverage "curtailed rescue attempts and evacuations by helping foster the belief that widespread chaos, carnage and crime ruled New Orleans. Such reportage shifted blame from being primarily institutional to being jointly individual and institutional. In so doing, media coverage created a demand for the military, the police and the prison."[177]

Three days after landfall, Blanco and Nagin ordered public safety officers to prioritize law enforcement over rescue operations.[178] Starting on Wednesday, airborne and land-based search and rescue operations were sporadically suspended or at least temporarily redirected to other areas.[179] Given the "unacceptable" level of lawlessness, Blanco requested thousands of troops from President Bush on Wednesday. In the days to come, more and more troops and police (including SWAT teams and officers trained in riot control) poured into the city.[180]

The perception of widespread looting fed calls for martial law.[181] Nagin reportedly declared it: "During the evening [Wednesday], as officials were completing the evacuation of the sick and disabled from the Superdome, the lawlessness in New Orleans had grown so rampant that Mayor Nagin declared a state of martial law and ordered police officers to abandon rescue efforts in order to focus entirely on controlling the looting. After all, the presence of widespread looting has often led to full-fledged race riots."[182]

Federal and state officials took great pains to emphasize that martial law had in fact not been imposed.[183] Even though martial law was not permitted under Louisiana law, the idea enjoyed wide circulation in New Orleans by the end of the week.[184]

Governor Blanco gave credence to these rumors by issuing "shoot-to-kill" authorization to National Guard units deploying to the city.[185] On Thursday, the governor announced on live television the arrival of 300 National Guard members from Arkansas.[186] In her statement, Blanco explained: "[The] National Guard have landed in the city of New Orleans. These troops are fresh back from Iraq, well trained, experienced, battle-tested and under my orders to restore order in the streets. They have M-16s and they are locked and loaded. These troops know how to shoot and kill and they are more than willing to do so if necessary and I expect they will."[187]

The deployment of numerous private security companies to New Orleans reinforced the perception that martial law had been declared and that public authorities had lost the ability to preserve law and order. Among those companies were DynCorp, Intercon, American Security Group, Blackhawk, Wackenhut, Instinctive Shooting International, and Blackwater USA, the last of which attracted considerable media attention.[188] Blackwater personnel were initially sent to the city to support search and rescue operations. In the days that followed, most of the Blackwater contingent was contracted to provide security in local neighborhoods and area hotels.[189]

Intermezzo: A Military Mind-Set

The *Army Times* reported on Friday that the army would "take the city back."[190] It is worth quoting the article in full to get a good idea of the reigning mind-set at the time:

NEW ORLEANS—Combat operations are underway on the streets "to take this city back" in the aftermath of Hurricane Katrina.

"This place is going to look like Little Somalia," Brig. Gen. Gary Jones, commander of the Louisiana National Guard's Joint Task Force told Army Times Friday as hundreds of armed troops under his charge prepared to launch a massive citywide security mission from a staging area outside the Louisiana Superdome. "We're going to go out and take this city back. This will be a combat operation to get this city under control."

Jones said the military first needs to establish security throughout the city. Military and police officials have said there are several large areas of the city that are in a full state of anarchy.

Dozens of military trucks and up-armored Humvees left the staging area just after 11 a.m. Friday, while hundreds more troops arrived at the same staging area in the city via Black Hawk and Chinook helicopters.

"We're here to do whatever they need us to do," [said] Sgt. 1st Class Ron Dixon, of the Oklahoma National Guard's 1345th Transportation Company. "We packed to stay as long as it takes."

While some fight the insurgency in the city, other[s] carry on with rescue and evacuation operations. Helicopters are still pulling hundreds of stranded people from rooftops of flooded homes.

Army, Air Force, Navy, Marine Corps, Coast Guard, and police helicopters filled the city sky Friday morning. Most had armed soldiers manning the doors. According to Petty Officer Third Class Jeremy Grisham, a spokesman for the amphibious assault ship *Bataan*, the vessel kept its helicopters at sea Thursday night after several military helicopters reported being shot at from the ground.

Numerous soldiers also told Army Times that they have been shot at by armed civilians in New Orleans. Spokesmen for the Joint Task Force Headquarters at the Superdome were unaware of any servicemen being wounded in the streets, although one soldier is recovering from a gunshot wound sustained during a struggle with a civilian in the dome Wednesday night.

"I never thought that as a National Guardsman I would be shot at by other

Americans," said Specialist Philip Baccus of the 527th Engineer Battalion. "And I never thought I'd have to carry a rifle when on a hurricane relief mission. This is a disgrace."

Specialist Cliff Ferguson of the 527th Engineer Battalion pointed out that he knows there are plenty of decent people in New Orleans, but he said it is hard to stay motivated considering the circumstances.

"This is making a lot of us think about not reenlisting." Ferguson said. "You have to think about whether it is worth risking your neck for someone who will turn around and shoot at you. We didn't come here to fight a war. We came here to help."

Ultimately, the federal law enforcement effort in response to Katrina would consist of police officers, SWAT teams, helicopters, monitoring capabilities, and vehicles from a slew of federal agencies, including Immigrations and Customs Enforcement, Customs and Border Protection, the Secret Service, the FBI, the Drug Enforcement Agency, the Coast Guard, and the Bureau of Alcohol, Tobacco and Firearms.[191] As many as 4,000 federal agents were deputized by the state police to enforce state and local law.[192] Organizing these efforts took several days, meaning that much of the federal support would not be in place before the city was almost empty.

As these and other efforts were under way, FEMA's Emergency Response Team—Advanced and medical teams were forced to withdraw from the Superdome on Thursday morning:

> In the absence of FPS [the Federal Protective Service], or of any other dedicated security contingent, FEMA personnel in the Superdome found themselves forced to choose between their mission and their security. The responders' concerns for their safety increasingly distracted them from delivering medical care. On Thursday morning, September 1, concerned for their own safety, FEMA's DMAT and ERT-A teams left the Superdome, leaving behind the team's "cache, equipment, and rental vehicles"—not to mention patients and others taking shelter there. When these teams left, FEMA no longer had a presence at the Superdome, and the medical burden on remaining state and local health-care professionals increased.[193]

General Gary Jones, the Louisiana National Guard commander at the Superdome, remembers that he was surprised by their abrupt departure, leaving behind at least 500 critical care patients with no provisions:

Dr. Lupin came up to me and he said, "Sir"—and he was pretty irate—he said, "You know, how do you expect me to deal with all of these critical care patients here?" And I said, "What are you talking about?" . . . And he said, "All the patients over there on that ramp." And I said, "Why are you dealing with them?" . . . He said, "FEMA left." . . . "They didn't leave any supplies, I don't have charts, I don't know what's wrong with these people, I don't know—they got IVs in their arms, I don't even know really what's supposed to happen, what the plan is or anything else."[194]

Phil Parr, who headed up the ERT-A, claimed that a National Guard commander had advised him to leave as early as Tuesday. In Parr's mind, "The situation in the Superdome was always a powder keg."[195] Early Thursday morning, Parr was again enjoined to leave because a "riot" was being planned.[196] Here's how Parr remembers the situation: "Thursday morning at first light, General Jones, who was the commanding general in place, said to me—I don't remember his exact words, but there are certain phrases that he said that stick out in my mind very clearly. 'I don't believe I can protect you or your people any longer. We are going to be making our last stand,' and he pointed to a portion of the parking lot over there. He says, 'Get behind us, and we will do what we can.' That is when we started making plans to leave."[197]

FEMA personnel at the Dome thought they saw looters going through their personal belongings.[198] Cooper and Block report that the National Guard brought in riot squads to secure the Superdome on Wednesday evening.[199] Parr then learned that his other team was no longer secured by the National Guard: "I was informed by the DMAT team, the medical assistance team that was in the basketball stadium [located next to the Superdome], that the Guard, in shortening their lines, had pulled all security from them. They told me that they did not feel safe and that they were evacuating. And they had high-water vehicles that they used to resupply and that they were pulling out in their vehicles. It was only at that time that I made the decision to leave since if conditions did degenerate, we would have no other way out."[200]

Not everybody shared Parr's assessment of the situation. His colleague in New Orleans, Marty Bahamonde, later said, "It was paranoia on Parr's part. . . . They were the most peaceful 25,000 people in horrid conditions I have ever been around. There was no way they were going to attack anybody."[201] In his testimony before a Senate committee, Bahamonde recounted his opposition: "I strongly voiced my concerns about abandoning the mission and the critical need to continue with medical care and the coordination of food and water into the Dome. I pointed out that overnight, approximately 150 heavily armed forces arrived at the Superdome by helicopter raising the security level."[202]

Lieutenant Colonel Jacques Thibodeaux of the Louisiana National Guard found reports of violence at the Superdome and the Convention Center to be "overblown. . . . For the amount of the people in the situation, it was a very stable environment."[203] Major Ed Bush, a public affairs officer with the Guard, described the situation in the Superdome: "The Superdome itself was its own microcosm. . . . A lot of them [evacuees] had AM radios, and they would listen to news reports that talked about the 'dead bodies at the Superdome' and the 'murders in the bathroom of the Superdome,' and the 'babies being raped at the Superdome,' and it would create terrible panic."[204]

Brigadier General Brod Veillon, assistant adjutant general for the Louisiana Air National Guard, agrees: "The National Guard, we did not stop our rescue efforts for any security issue. It is my experience of Katrina that the National Guard did not experience security concerns. There were a lot of rumors of issues, but we continued our operations and did not experience any problems."[205]

Another official who disagreed with Parr's assessment was Michael Brown. Upon arriving at the state EOC in Baton Rouge after evacuating the Superdome, Parr and Bahamonde reportedly encountered an irate FEMA director. This was the same Brown who had been arguing for days that security at the site was "darn good" and that residents there were "behaving very well." Brown ordered the FEMA teams back to the site immediately.[206] As Bahamonde described the situation: "I do not believe that it was the right decision for us to leave. We were taken to Baton Rouge and the State EOC where I immediately found Under Secretary Brown and again voiced my strong objections about pulling out. He looked at me and he said he was glad I was safe, but I was to 'get my ass back there.' Within hours, another medical team was dispatched to return to the Superdome, and the next day an operational team was sent back. I never went back."[207]

The Convention Center

Thousands of survivors had assembled in front of the Convention Center, located on the Mississippi River, next to the French Quarter and a few blocks from the Superdome. People were milling around, waiting for food, water, and buses. The media had discovered this group of people by Thursday (at one point, Geraldo Rivera did an emotional report from the site with a distressed baby on his arm).[208] Unbeknownst to the survivors, the media began to report on gang activity and violence in and around the Convention Center.[209]

The National Guard prepared to evacuate the Convention Center on Friday. Media reports led National Guard commanders to expect significant resistance: "We waited until we had enough force in place to do an overwhelming force," explained Lieutenant General H. Steven Blum, the head of the National Guard Bureau.[210] A thousand heavily armed soldiers were organized to "retake" the facility—Colonel McLaughlin spoke of "combat assault."[211]

The fears soon proved unfounded.[212] When they arrived on Friday, the Guard found a hungry but cooperative crowd.[213] Mass feeding and triage operations were underway by midafternoon, though those sheltered there would not be evacuated until the following morning.[214] By 6:00 p.m. on Saturday, the facility was almost completely empty.

Exhausted residents were bewildered by the militaristic attitude of incoming forces (police, National Guard, military), which appeared ready to quell an uprising rather than provide the resources (food, water, transportation) they so badly needed.[215] Many survivors expressed their dismay at being subjected to curfews enforced by armed patrols.[216]

FEMA director Brown was one of the few who remained skeptical of the anarchy frame. When given the chance, Brown downplayed reports of violence. On Thursday, he denied receiving any "reports of unrest, if the connotation of the word 'unrest' means that people are beginning to riot or, you know, they're banging on walls and screaming and hollering or burning tires or whatever."[217] Lieutenant General Honoré, the JTF-Katrina commander, also tried to put the situation in perspective, telling one interviewer that New Orleans was "not Baghdad [and that] these are American citizens."[218]

A BLAMING WAR

Leaders in Washington soon discovered that the response was heavily criticized in the media. Nearly one-third of broadcasts in the first week contained blame references. M. D. Barnes et al. found that 40% of newspaper articles blamed the federal government. Only 13.8% of the articles blamed families and individuals.[219] While the attitude toward local governments was mostly neutral, the tone on the performance of federal actors was overwhelmingly negative (and this takes into account positive reporting on the US Coast Guard).

Leaders soon began to blame each other for what happened. Local leaders, the source of the wildest and most vicious rumors, were quick to blame federal officials. Their statements were immediately picked up by the national media. The shift in public perception caught federal and state leaders by surprise. Leaders sought to defend their performance. Sadly but predictably, this sparked a war of words that would determine how many Americans came to see the response to Hurricane Katrina more generally.

The response started off on a—in hindsight surprisingly—positive note. On Monday, Louisiana state coordinating officer Jeff Smith still called FEMA's response "outstanding."[220] At a news conference, Governor Blanco praised the federal assistance that her state was receiving: "Director Brown, I hope you will tell President Bush how much we appreciated—these are the times that really count—to know that our federal government will step in and give us the kind of assistance that we need." Louisiana senator Mary Landrieu, a Democrat, agreed that "we are indeed fortunate to have an able and experienced director of FEMA who has been with us on the ground for some time." Brown reciprocated by recognizing "a team that is very tight-knit, working closely together, being very professional doing it, and in my humble opinion, making the right calls."[221] Blanco appeared to tear up at a Tuesday conference, stating that she was "grateful to have FEMA by our side." She did not criticize anyone.[222]

State leaders would soon have reason to complain about federal support, as the resources promised by FEMA director Brown failed to materialize. Blanco remained measured in her criticism of federal officials—certainly when compared with the emotional outbursts of local leaders.[223] The same was true of her staff. On Wednesday, Jeff Smith was still offering praise for FEMA: "As with any operation there are little hiccups here and there but by and large we're very pleased with the support we're receiving."[224]

Wednesday was the tipping point, after which recriminations would fly and frames shifted. The federal government, in particular FEMA, became the national media's scapegoat.[225] In the background, the federalization issue was simmering. State and local officials began to criticize the federal government's lack of engagement, the tepid response, and the "federal" levee system's evident deficiencies. Mayor Nagin at one point wondered aloud if "people [died] because of the storm or because of the lack of response."[226]

On Thursday, "local officials, describing the security situation as horrific, lambasted the federal government as responding too slowly to the disaster."[227] Colonel Terry Ebbert, in charge of homeland security and public safety in New Orleans, emotionally charged that "the goddamn nation can't get us any resources for security. . . . It's criminal within the confines of the United States that within one hour of the hurricane they weren't force-feeding us."[228]

Mayor Nagin was particularly active in the blame game. He quickly capitalized on the emerging anarchy frame, blaming state and federal authorities for the situation in his city. In a Thursday afternoon radio interview with a well-known local talk show host on WWL, Garland Robinette, Nagin lit up the airwaves with a tirade.[229] Conveniently overlooking his own shortcomings and those of New Orleans institutions, Nagin gave voice to local frustrations over what was happening. The Nagin philippic was soon broadcast nationwide.[230]

Excerpts from the interview demonstrate how Nagin sought to allocate blame:

They don't have a clue what's going on down here. They flew down here one time two days after the doggone event was over with TV cameras, AP reporters, all kind of goddamn—excuse my French everybody in America, but I am pissed.

They're thinking small, man. And this is a major, major, major deal. And I can't emphasize it enough, man. This is crazy. . . .

It's awful down here, man. . . .

You know, God is looking down on all this, and if they are not doing everything in their power to save people, they are going to pay the price. Because every day that we delay, people are dying and they're dying by the hundreds, I'm willing to bet you. . . .

They're feeding the public a line of bull and they're spinning, and people are dying down here. . . .

You have drug addicts that are now walking around this city looking for a fix, and that's the reason why they were breaking in hospitals and drugstores. They're looking for something to take the edge off of their jones, if you will. And right now, they don't have anything to take the edge off. And they've probably found guns. So what you're seeing is drug-starving crazy addicts, drug addicts, that are wreaking havoc. And we don't have the manpower to adequately deal with it. We can only target certain sections of the city and form a perimeter around them and hope to God that we're not overrun. . . .

I don't know whether it's the governor's problem. I don't know whether it's the president's problem, but somebody needs to get their ass on a plane and sit down, the two of them, and figure this out right now. . . .

Don't tell me 40,000 people are coming here. They're not here. It's too doggone late. Now get off your asses and do something, and let's fix the biggest goddamn crisis in the history of this country.

Nagin's angry lament resonated both locally and across the nation.[231] Opinion polls showed that many Americans believed the federal government had failed to provide a timely response.[232] President Bush's frame—"the professionals are handling the situation and help is on the way"—was undermined by questions such as "Where is the government?" and "Why did they not see it coming?"

President Bush had refrained from public criticism during his televised speech on Wednesday. There he made the case that Katrina could not have been foreseen.[233] The administration's argument, however, was undermined by the emergence of more and more evidence suggesting that officials had long been aware of the flood risk.[234] The White House was coming under attack.

When criticism of the federal government began to intensify on Wednesday, the White House had reason to be worried. Katrina played out in a deeply politicized context. President Bush was a vulnerable politician, suffering the consequences of the ongoing intervention in Iraq. Katrina was a golden opportunity for anti-Bush forces to portray him as out of touch and insensitive to the suffering of poor minorities. His flyover on Wednesday helped them to make the point.

Federal officials pushed back by sketching an image of incompetence at the *state* level.[235] For instance, some speculated that one of Bush's key advisers, Karl Rove, tried to cast Blanco, a Democratic governor, as the problem.[236] The governor's communications director, Bob Mann, recalls: "James Carville called me. He said, 'The White House is about to start putting the blame on you guys. It's gonna get ugly.'" Indeed, the tone of some journalists' questions in the following days suggested to the governor's staff that the White House staff was actively working to discredit the state's leaders.[237] Blanco refused to take the bait: "From the beginning, Gov. Blanco emphatically forbade anything that could be interpreted as an attack on President Bush. 'We are going to need this president to help us rebuild the state,' she told the staff. 'Let them politicize this storm. We're not going to do that.'"[238]

In Washington, Louisiana was cast as undeserving of federal help. Federal officials painted a picture of disorganization and irresponsible behavior. They faulted local decision makers for not evacuating their communities earlier. Chertoff lasered in on the state, at one point explaining that "our constitutional system really places the primary authority in each state with the governor."[239]

Chertoff blamed Louisiana for its problems, a familiar refrain.[240] Republican Speaker of the House Dennis Hastert voiced doubts on Thursday as to whether New Orleans should be rebuilt.[241] Senator Rick Santorum, a Republican, blamed local citizens: "You have people who don't heed those warnings and then put people at risk as a result of not heeding those warnings. There may be a need to look at tougher penalties on those who decide to ride it out and understand that there are consequences to not leaving."[242]

A gulf of mistrust soon separated federal, state, and local officials from one another. Furious state officials pointed to FEMA and its "red tape." Senator Mary Landrieu's spokesperson echoed local complaints that FEMA "repeatedly held up assistance."[243] New Orleans City Council president Oliver Thomas rejected the charge that local government had been unprepared: "When you talk about the mightiest government in the world, that's a ludicrous and lame excuse. You're FEMA, and you're the big dog. And you weren't prepared either."[244]

Political tensions reached a boiling point on Friday night when Governor Blanco refused to sign the memorandum creating a dual-hatted command structure for the National Guard. "If I had seen a greater purpose, if I had felt it would make an immediate difference, it would have been a no-brainer, but by Friday, we had everything in control," Blanco later explained.[245] The power struggle would poison relations between Washington and Baton Rouge for quite some time, perpetuating the blame game long after the acute phase had passed and officials were transitioning to the recovery phase.

FEMA was an obvious target for local officials and affected residents, but it also became a convenient punching bag for Bush supporters who needed an outlet to vent their anger with the federal response. For instance, Mississippi senator Trent Lott (who lost his vacation home to Katrina) became a fierce critic of FEMA and its director.[246] In his opinion, Brown had been acting "like a private instead of a general."[247] He had little if anything negative to say about the White House's handling of the crisis.

Michael Brown did not manage to bend this frame. As his own recollections of events make clear, he was focused on the internal workings of the response and bureau politics.[248] Brown went into Katrina upset about the diminished state of FEMA as part of DHS and never got over it.[249]

On Sunday, the *New Orleans Times-Picayune* lashed out at FEMA in an editorial. The editors lambasted the federal government for its argument that New Orleans had been unreachable. They described how "on Thursday morning, that crew saw a caravan of 13 Wal-Mart tractor trailers headed into town to bring food, water and supplies to a dying city. . . . Harry Connick Jr. brought in some aid Thursday . . . yet the people trained to protect our nation, the people whose job it is to quickly bring in aid were absent. Those who should have been deploying troops were singing a sad song about how our city was impossible to reach." They concluded that "every official at the Federal Emergency Management Agency should be fired, Director Michael Brown especially."[250]

The blame game would go on and on, sometimes boiling over into public view and otherwise simmering in the background. It would take a toll on officials. The criticism of the state and local response soon began to annoy Senator Landrieu. During a helicopter tour over New Orleans with ABC's George Stephanopoulos on the Sunday after landfall, Landrieu declared that "if one person criticizes [state and local efforts] or says one more thing, including the president of the United States, he will hear from me. One more word about it after this show airs, and . . . I might likely have to punch him, literally."[251]

A FAILURE OF MEANING MAKING

In times of crisis, a society looks to its leaders for guidance. Leaders are expected to offer an explanation of what happened and a vision of what the future will look like after the disaster. Such a picture (or frame) did not emerge during the Katrina response. What emerged instead was a misinformed but widely shared perception of a situation spiraling out of control, with scenes resembling Dante's *Inferno*.

The government—at all levels—did not manage to convincingly and accurately explain what was going on in New Orleans. The Bush administration never controlled the prevailing narrative. The president had no storyline in that first week (other than "things are going reasonably well"). Governor Blanco remained focused on running the response, forgoing opportunities to craft a frame of her own. When she did finally offer a narrative, it only gave credence to the perception that New Orleans had descended into anarchy. Mayor Nagin, on the other hand, clearly knew how to produce a storyline and sell it to the media. But his frame was informed by rumors and a penchant to blame others.

The meaning-making void allowed vivid rumors to gain traction, creating the impression of mayhem. Across the nation and around the world, it appeared that Katrina had turned New Orleans into a living hell. In New Orleans, officials greatly exaggerated the severity of the situation. The media accepted many of these reports as fact (because, after all, they had come from official sources). At the same time, the media's reporting had an outsized influence on how officials understood the situation. Katrina created a dangerous feedback loop that the key players did not recognize.

Many of the stories that gave rise to the mayhem narrative later turned out to be exaggerated or false. In reality, the problem of law and order was quite limited. It was the *perception* of a law-and-order problem that created a tense situation. Rather than addressing these false images, key actors acted on them. The rapid embrace of military capacities as a solution only reinforced the emerging mayhem frame. Shoot-to-kill orders and law enforcement agents in full battle gear could only mean one thing: the reports were true and, yes, it was just as bad as people feared.

Rumors come easy. As Deputy Police Superintendent Warren Riley later explained: "If one guy said he saw six bodies, then another guy the same six, and another guy saw them—then that became 18."[252] If they are allowed to proliferate, rumors quickly merge into the domain of facts. They proliferate when leaders do not keep them in check.

Theory predicts that ineffective crisis meaning making will have negative consequences for the formal leaders of the response and the key institutions involved.[253] This is especially true if leaders substitute blaming for meaning making. The starkest lesson that springs from Katrina is the warning against blame games. Once it starts, a blame fight is nearly impossible to stop. The blame game did not bring benefits to anybody in this crisis. It merely undermined the legitimacy of the leaders and institutions that were most in need of it. Mayor Nagin, Governor Blanco, FEMA director Brown, DHS secretary Chertoff, and President Bush all lost. The organizational reputation of the White House, DHS, and FEMA also took a serious hit.

This chapter has shown that failed meaning making in combination with a vicious blame game dictated how many still view the response to Katrina. It explains why the response was, and continues to be, widely considered a failure, even though many things went remarkably well (especially given the dire circumstances of this superdisaster). The lessons we can derive from this situation are presented in the conclusion.

CONCLUSION

LESSONS OF A MEGA-DISASTER

KATRINA: A BYWORD FOR FAILURE

The response to Hurricane Katrina is not remembered as a success. Starting almost immediately after landfall, the media highlighted failure. In the months and years after Katrina, the sense of failure was perpetuated by a series of highly critical reports, research findings, documentaries, and memoirs. Congressional hearings were launched within months after the storm.[1] The titles of the Senate and House reports say it all: *A Nation Still Unprepared* and *A Failure of Initiative,* respectively.[2] Both reports found Katrina to be severely mismanaged.

The Senate report charged that "long-term warnings went unheeded and government officials neglected their duties to prepare for a forewarned catastrophe." Government officials "took insufficient actions or made poor decisions in the days immediately before and after landfall."[3] The Department of Homeland Security "failed to create a system to identify and acquire all available, relevant information, and as a result situational awareness was deeply flawed."[4] In short, "government officials at all levels failed to provide effective leadership."[5]

The House report did not pull any punches, either. The main conclusion here was that "DHS and the states were not prepared for this catastrophic event."[6] It found that "critical elements of the National Response Plan were executed late, ineffectively, or not at all" and that "command and control was impaired at all levels, delaying relief."[7] The report further noted that "officials at all levels seemed to be waiting for the disaster that fit their plans, rather than planning and building scalable capacities to meet whatever Mother Nature threw at them."[8]

Blame was apportioned to officials and institutions across the system. The city of New Orleans "had no actual plan provisions" to implement an effective evacuation of those in need.[9] The Louisiana Office of Homeland Security and Emergency Preparedness and the city's Office of Emergency Preparedness were chastised for "chronic staffing problems and employee turnover due to underfunding."[10] The New Orleans Police Department was "ill-prepared for continuity of operations," which led to a loss of "almost all effectiveness."[11]

Katrina was career ending for some officials. Even before the proverbial dust had settled, Michael Brown was portrayed as the main villain. Emails between Brown and members of his staff were used by the media and officials as evidence of Brown's distracted attitude in the midst of the crisis.[12] Much was made of Brown lacking significant emergency management experience.[13] Weeks after the disaster, *Time* magazine cast Brown as a prime example of cronyism in the Bush administration. Brown was soon sidelined.

As additional information came to light through public testimony and document releases, it became increasingly clear that the FEMA director did not bear sole responsibility for the fiasco. The House report charged that Chertoff "executed [his] responsibilities late, ineffectively, or not at all."[14] The Government Accountability Office placed most of the blame for the flawed response at Chertoff's feet.[15]

House investigators also criticized Governor Blanco and Mayor Nagin: "This extraordinary storm required extraordinary measures, which the Governor and Mayor did not take."[16] Blanco was commended for her "urgency and priority on saving lives after the flooding took place," but the committee also concluded that "the same urgency and priority on a more complete evacuation of New Orleans before the flooding would have saved lives."[17]

The White House was chastised. The Senate report stated that "the White House failed to grasp the gravity of the situation as it unfolded. As a result, the White House's initial response appeared halting and inadequate."[18] The local *Times-Picayune* penned an open letter to the president: "We're angry, Mr. President, and we'll be angry long after our beloved city and surrounding parishes have been pumped dry. Our people deserved rescuing. Many who could have been were not. That's to the government's shame."[19] The Senate report pushed the story of the absent leader: "The President did not leave his Texas ranch to return to Washington until two days after landfall, and only then convened his Cabinet, as well as a White House task force, to oversee federal response efforts."[20] President Bush would be dogged by Katrina-related criticism throughout the remainder of his second term.[21] As the *Washington Post* stated, "From the demise of his Social Security overhaul to the war in Iraq, many factors have contributed to Bush's slide in popularity in the past year. But the winds of Katrina may have been the force that finally wrenched the Bush presidency off its moorings."[22]

In all these reports and media accounts, little attention was paid to *successes*. For instance, the unprecedented success of the regional evacuation operation did not get much publicity. Had the evacuation of the New Orleans region not worked as it did, tens of thousands more would have been stranded in the city.

Some major players, including the Department of Defense and the Coast Guard, received glowing commendations, even though available evidence clearly demonstrated that both organizations deviated significantly from the National Response Plan, which was held against FEMA and DHS. One report celebrated "the effective and heroic search-and-rescue efforts by the U.S. Coast Guard."[23] The White House observed: "During the Katrina response, DOD—both National Guard and active duty forces—demonstrated that along with the Coast Guard it was one of the only Federal departments that possessed real operational capabilities to translate Presidential decisions into prompt, effective action on the ground."[24]

Katrina is probably the most widely studied disaster in history, yet it is not clear which lessons should be learned from it. The various official investigations all seemed to agree on a set of abstract lessons: individual initiative-taking and decision-making should be encouraged; roles and responsibilities described in national-level planning documents should be clarified; interagency coordination should be improved; communications should be both more robust and interoperable; and additional resources are required to meet natural and man-made disasters in the future.

It is hard to argue with these lessons. They are almost truisms (and can be found in reports on most other disasters). More money, better plans, improved coordination, perfect communications—these recommendations will not hurt future responses, but it is still not clear how these prescriptions should be applied to improve the response to a Katrina-like event.

More importantly, we think some critical lessons have been *missed*—lessons that will help to strengthen societal resilience in the face of future mega-disasters.[25] In this conclusion, we identify the lessons that we think should be taken from the Katrina response. We arrived at these lessons by applying our theoretical framework, weighing empirical evidence against theoretical findings. Considering all those things that went awfully wrong but also those things that went surprisingly well, we outline here what we can learn from Katrina to prepare societies everywhere for mega-disasters.

We group our lessons according to the strategic crisis tasks outlined in chapter 1. We start with a very brief summary of our key findings and then proceed to formulate our prescriptions.

DETECTING A MEGA-DISASTER

Quick findings:

- Hurricane Katrina was widely recognized as a clear and present danger.

- The flooding of New Orleans came as a surprise.

- There were very few warnings and certainly no clear flood predictions.

- Most officials did *not* see this coming.

- The late detection of levee breaches and major flooding quickly became politicized ("Why didn't they see it coming?").

One of the most damning lines of criticism forwarded in postcrisis analyses was the blunt accusation that "they could have seen this one coming." The implication is obvious: if this disaster *could* have been foreseen, it *should* have been foreseen. By extension, it means that officials failed. This explains the unrelenting search for evidence of authority figures having been warned well ahead of time that this disaster could occur. Long after the disaster, the "failure" to recognize the impending disaster was still hotly debated. It had already become a political football in the first week after landfall.

The Hurricane Pam exercise, held the summer before Katrina, was repeatedly trotted out as the smoking gun. The fact that FEMA had cooperated with state authorities to think through what a hurricane-induced disaster would require from the many partners in the response network was somehow interpreted as proof of forewarning. In chapter 2, we argued that it was not. More importantly, very little attention was paid to the actual accomplishments that flowed from this planning exercise: Hurricane Pam helped improve evacuation, search and rescue, sheltering, and debris removal.

The lesson missed here is that such preparatory exercises are very useful. Hurricane Pam marked the beginning of a comprehensive effort to think through what issues might emerge during a superdisaster. It produced lifesaving results. Hurricane Pam should be considered as a template for best practice rather than a benchmark for performance (which it sadly has become). The politicization of Pam was not only unjustified; it also sent the wrong message. Practitioners will think twice before participating in such events in the future.

This still leaves us with the question of whether authorities could have foreseen that Katrina would turn into a superdisaster. The House report declared, "Federal, state, and local officials recognized the potential for catastrophe and flooding and communicated that potential among themselves and to the public."[26] There is some truth to this statement, but we should not read too much into it.

Here is how we see it. Based on the available data, officials *could* have known that this *could* happen. Had they been provided with detailed and accurate analyses of levee weaknesses and likely or even possible impacts of storm surges, they could have made some sort of risk calculation. But that did not happen. Moreover, we know that most senior policy makers do not have a firm grasp on such risks.[27] By and large, policy makers lack an understanding of threat statistics and "black swans"—those events that we know from blockbuster disaster films or read about in books but do not imagine can or will happen to us.[28] They need expert advice to grasp the risks. But experts did not predict or warn them that New Orleans would flood. We should therefore not be surprised that authorities failed to entertain the possibility that Katrina might demolish the levees and flood the city.

This conclusion has repercussions for discussions on disaster prevention: officials cannot simply assume that people are safe because risk calculations suggest so. Policy makers must realize that seemingly routine emergencies can unexpectedly transition into superdisasters, no matter how unlikely they might seem in terms of risk calculations ("once in a thousand years" may be today). But this admonition has little to do with crisis management. It should inform discussions on local planning, the allocation of scarce resources, and the dialogue between authorities and citizens.[29] These discussions belong in the domain of everyday politics and policy making.

The *lesson* for crisis managers is a bit different: risk objects (such as New Orleans or any sizable city) can and will surprise. It is this realization, above all, that may provide a quick understanding that something is amiss. That does not mean it is easy to detect critical anomalies. Leaders must initiate a determined effort to define "normal" or "expected" pathways and then operationalize the indicators of deviation. This requires a combination of imagination and a willingness to spend resources on detecting something that likely will not happen.

For those leaders who seek to accomplish this feat, the insights from the High Reliability School will surely help. The High Reliability School emphasizes the importance of creating organizational cultures that embrace uncertainty and recognize the pervasive possibility of deadly incidents. It puts a premium on open communication about risks and proactive action by operators to nip emerging risks in the bud.[30]

The bigger point is that we must push for the professionalization of risk management and early detection. Leaders of institutions and societies keep being surprised by black swans. There is an urgent need for approaches that will help societies recognize and address in timely fashion those emerging threats that may develop into mega-disasters.

GETTING READY FOR A MEGA-DISASTER

Quick findings:

- Leading officials took preparations for Katrina very seriously.

- In light of commonly shared expectations about the nature of the threat, preparations were appropriate.

- The evacuation of New Orleans and surrounding areas was well executed.

- FEMA was on the ball: the agency did what it should before landfall.

- The president was involved and informed.

- Leaders communicated clear warnings. The mayor of New Orleans issued a mandatory evacuation order (for the first time ever).

- Low risk awareness of the New Orleans population undermined the effectiveness of the evacuation.

Officials at all levels of government treated Katrina as a very dangerous storm. Wind damage, storm surge, and levee overtoppings were expected. That is exactly what the authorities prepared for and, to their credit, they followed upgraded scripts in their preparatory efforts. FEMA moved an unprecedented amount of resources to the South, well before Katrina made landfall. The president was involved. State and local authorities repeatedly warned citizens of imminent danger. Unfortunately, many citizens chose to stay in New Orleans and sit the storm out.

The evacuation of southeastern Louisiana using contraflow was executed flawlessly. It was a success because authorities had learned from earlier failures (of which there were many). The lesson here cannot be misunderstood: careful planning taking into account previous failures (and successes) makes a difference.

But careful planning means little if you are preparing for the wrong disaster. Preparing for a hurricane is different than preparing for a flooded city. The authorities were ready to deal with wind damage, but they were ill prepared to save residents from drowning and then evacuate tens of thousands of people from the flooded city.

How does one prepare for a superdisaster, especially when it comes as a complete surprise? One obvious answer would be to prepare for the possibility that an emergency might spin out of control and turn into a superdisaster. That can always happen, as we just argued. But it rarely does. How, then, to prevent authorities from overpreparing? After all, if authorities must assume that the worst may happen, not preparing for the worst is tantamount to dereliction of duty. Katrina, in this sense, taught leaders a dangerous lesson: you can be very well prepared and still lose big.

This raises an important question: how much preparation is enough? Western societies rarely engage in this type of debate. There are discussions about prevention (is a one-in-a-thousand-years risk acceptable? Should the state provide for hurricane insurance if private parties do not serve the market?). But politicians, policy makers, and pundits do not ask or engage in answering questions such as, What can we ask from government in times of crisis and disaster? What level of resilience, individual or societal, is desirable? These are *political* questions with huge implications.

Our key lesson: leaders should initiate and engage in serious debate about the role of government and citizens in times of mega-disasters. Many leaders today hide behind resilience strategies. But that is ignoring the question. Politicians should educate citizens about the capacities of the response system and the individual responsibilities of citizens in times of disruption. It is the addendum to the implicit contract that governs the relation between citizen and state. When that addendum is not specified or clear, the resulting confusion will give rise to a blaming environment that pitches citizens against the very institutions that are designed to protect them.

MAKING SENSE OF A MEGA-DISASTER

Quick findings:

- Many officials at one point or another did not grasp certain key events, even if others did.

- Many officials thought they understood certain key events when in reality they did not.

- Most officials were surprisingly quick to adopt the anarchy frame, which guided their sense-making efforts.

- Few officials probed, questioned, or rejected the anarchy frame. Those who did had little effect on other officials.

- Information that fit expectations traveled quickly; information that did not fit expectations got stuck in organizational bottlenecks.

- Officials at higher levels of government did not explicitly seek out information; they waited for information to be brought to them.

- Few efforts were made to ascertain the veracity of rumors.

Even state and local officials, long accustomed to hurricanes, were caught by surprise by Katrina. The flooding, the mayhem, the seeming inability to organize critical resources—the situation they were confronted with bedeviled administrators up and down the chain. Authorities at all levels found it hard to understand what, exactly, was going on in New Orleans.

In our view, the fact that Katrina offered so many unpleasant surprises was due to a lack of joint sense making. In that first week, a shared, accurate picture of the situation did not emerge. In an ideal situation, it might have made use of:

- The many timely and accurate reports about levee failures.

- Information about the various locations where survivors congregated. The situation at the Superdome was known and addressed. Other locations (highways, Convention Center, hospitals) remained under the radar until midweek.

- Information that contradicted the dominant "false positive" of that week: the anarchy story.

Did it have to be this way? Could a more accurate picture of the situation have been pieced together? The information necessary to make joint sense making possible was available. In other words, sense making did not fail because "they could not have known." Key players in the state (including Michael Brown) soon knew and understood that they had a superdisaster on their hands. It took DHS and the White House much longer to grasp the situation.

A complete and fully accurate picture of the situation is, of course, only available long after the crisis. Sense making is difficult: understanding what the critical issues are based on fragmented and muddled data streams is arguably an art in itself.

We have discussed several causes for the glaring inability of officials to identify key issues after Katrina made landfall. The incapacitated administration of New Orleans is one explanation. But that is what happens in disaster: local administrations get overwhelmed (the very reason why state and federal organizations have to step in). Communications breakdowns were another explanation. This also happens during disasters. In the absence of locally sourced information, FEMA and the Homeland Security Operations Center at DHS headquarters had to organize their own information streams. But these federal units had few "eyes on the ground." They did not have the means to independently collect information and verify reports coming in from other sources.

The lesson here is clear: when local administrators are overwhelmed, state and federal organizations must possess the capacity to gather information on their own. The government should create information-gathering units—small groups of trained officials who enter the disaster zone and collect information that is directly relevant for strategic decision-making. Much can be learned from the organizational skills of traditional media organizations.[31] These organizations have trained personnel to descend into any situation in small teams, to make sense of that situation, and to broadcast their analysis quickly.

Interorganizational bottlenecks were another source of sense-making failure. Sense making at the federal level was the core mission of the HSOC. This new organization relied on an inductive or "push" system: organizations in the field (especially FEMA) were expected to push information into the high-tech center in Washington. In other words, the HSOC staff were waiting for crucial bits of verified information to be presented to them, preferably flagged in terms of urgency. Our research shows that this approach does not work in a disaster, if only because response organizations have different priorities (saving lives, for instance).

Central units that rely on critical information to coordinate the efforts of other organizations need a different approach. They must complement the inductive approach with a more deductive one that "pulls" information out of the system on the basis of a clear realization of what information is needed. Information-gathering efforts should be organized to this end. The deductive approach emphasizes the need for the proactive *gathering* of predefined types of information. This, of course, requires imagining what issues might be most salient in a crisis and who is likely to be best positioned to extract the relevant data from the scene.

The HSOC did engage in verification efforts. It dedicated significant energies to deconflicting reports of levee breaches in particular. That the HSOC expended so much energy on confirming levee breaches is understandable. After all, HSOC officials were seeing images on television of street parties in the French Quarter and kids gleefully splashing in shallow floodwaters. It is not clear, however, why the confirmation of incoming information that they required seemingly had to conform to strict academic research standards.

There is also a lesson here concerning internal communication (for the information "pushers" within the network). We know that some key actors had a fairly accurate idea of what was happening in New Orleans, but they did not manage to get their dire assessments across. Michael Brown, for instance, was convinced that he had communicated the gravity of the situation up the chain, all the way to the White House. Looking back at exactly what he and Governor Blanco said at different points during the crisis, however, it is easy to see how their words could have been misinterpreted by those who were not in the know. Those who are in a position to understand that "this is not a standard disaster" must learn to communicate that to people who are far removed from the scene and may have no idea how bad the situation is. A balance is needed between overstatement and sticking with the facts.

A critical question is whether streams of more accurate information would have made an immediate difference. The structural design problems outlined above were exacerbated by what we have called a lack of collective imagination. We noted that policy makers (and many other observers) found it hard to comprehend both the nature and the scale of the disaster. Actors at all levels of government, but also the many media representatives on the ground, found it hard to believe what they were seeing and hearing (either directly or indirectly).

It is tempting to criticize those who did not see what in hindsight seems so obvious. As psychologists have shown over and over again, it is all too easy to miss the "gorilla in the room" or dismiss the black swans.[32] When a certain type of event has never been imagined and does not feature prominently on institutional mind maps, it is understandable that people struggle to connect the dots when they do materialize.

The paradoxical lesson is that crisis managers should *embrace uncertainty*. They should be on constant alert for signs that events are migrating from "zones of expected occurrences" to the domain of the unknown. This starts with an awareness that unexpected things can happen. Based on this acceptance, policy makers should seek out signs that events are beginning to fall outside the domain of expectation. They should be scrutinizing emerging "nodes of certainty" or clusters of "accepted wisdom," which point to sense-making voids or informational black holes that need to be investigated. These can be found in rumors and (social) media reports about bureau-political conflict. Signs of collective amazement or anger, as well as indications of blame games, need to be identified and then investigated. The aim is not just to refute but to establish why these rumors emerge and whether a black swan is triggering them.

Social media are *not* the enemy. Policy makers tend to despise and fear the uncontrollable nature of social media and the waves of incorrect information that traverse cyberspace. That is not a productive approach. If used in the right way, social media can provide a direct link to the concerns and intentions of both survivors and first responders.

Underlying this proposed approach to sense making is the need for a clearly formulated philosophy and accompanying method of prioritization and verification of information. Policy makers need to agree on a common approach in order to answer pertinent questions such as, on what basis can we say that something is true? How long can we wait to receive additional information before we must make critical decisions?

Finally, authorities should realize that sense making has a lot to do with meaning making. What you pay attention to in a crisis is in itself a way of communicating what you consider important. For instance, asking about security, but not about the plight of evacuees, implicitly communicates priorities. Such signals are picked up by others and may be interpreted as reflections of the crisis team's understanding of the situation and what its priorities are. In addition, such lines of inquiry may reinforce a given narrative ("The city must not be safe").

The lesson here runs counter to conventional wisdom. Strategic decision-making units should not wait for urgent messages and complete situation reports to act. The idea that higher levels of government should facilitate and assist lower levels of government when they cannot cope with the situation is sound. But waiting around for information from overwhelmed organizations occupied with the immediate effects of a disaster puts strategic levels of government on a reactive footing. To avoid such a reactive posture requires a vision that spells out what type of information strategic crisis managers should try to acquire. Higher levels of government must actively engage without first being asked to do so. In many crisis and disaster systems, this requires a paradigm shift.

COORDINATING RESPONSE TO A SUPERDISASTER

Quick findings:

- Emergent coordination was very effective.

- Orchestrated coordination was much less effective.

- Existing plans did little to enable or guide orchestrated coordination.

- Improvisation created new coordination challenges.

- Centralization was not the answer. Nor was strong "leadership."

- The involvement of the military introduced new and complex challenges.

We defined the coordination challenge in the following way: a wide variety of citizens, officials, and organizations—many not hierarchically related to one another—must be enticed to work together under difficult conditions. The common goal is to make a number of critically important things happen: save lives, lessen suffering, deliver much-needed supplies, evacuate people, provide safety and security, and start the rebuilding.

Research findings offer two important starting points for understanding crisis coordination.[33] First, we may assume that citizens and frontline organizations will immediately address the emergent challenge of saving lives. Second, we may expect the convergence of organizations, in combination with the rise of new problems, to create new challenges during the course of the disaster.

In line with these research-based expectations, we found that the initial response worked well and required few formal coordination efforts. Search and rescue operations were unquestionably successful. The combined efforts of local, state, and federal agencies, together with private citizens with their own equipment (like the Cajun Navy), saved thousands of lives in the first days after landfall.

The public organizations participating in this emergent search and rescue network by all accounts performed well. The US Coast Guard saved thousands of people and received considerable praise for it. Louisiana's National Guard and the state's Wildlife and Fisheries agency did the same beyond the limelight. Many local organizations contributed, even where they were overwhelmed and lacked essential capacities. The much-maligned FEMA sought to support the emerging response network and largely performed to expectations, at least during the first few days. Collaboration between citizens, between agencies, and between agencies and citizens did not create insurmountable problems.

So why was coordination roundly criticized after the disaster? Our research shows that this is a rather crude and uninformed assessment based on the coordination of certain issues that actually worked and the failed coordination of matters that had little direct relevance to the quality of the response.

In chapter 4, we outlined what effective coordination should look like in the immediate phase of a disaster. After spontaneous lifesaving operations have kicked in, officials must support what works and address any bottlenecks preventing these grassroots efforts from working even better. The challenge for officials is to use their plans in a flexible way: it is no use altering emergent but effective practices just so that they adhere to existing plans; it makes much more sense to support structures and processes that work. There is no evidence that FEMA tried to force response organizations to work according to the NRP or any other plan for that matter during those first days (although they complained afterward about local deviations from the plan). FEMA showed itself willing to support the emerging response.

A core challenge was the lack of buses to evacuate people from New Orleans. FEMA coordinated the procurement of buses (the Department of Transportation did the actual work). Given the nature and extent of the disaster, buses could not have materialized much faster than they actually did. FEMA arguably failed to explain that it would take time to round the buses up and did not seem to know when the buses would arrive. State and local officials, overwhelmed by events and dependent on FEMA, naturally became impatient. In hindsight, we can say that their impatience was a bit unreasonable, but certainly understandable, given relentless media attention to the plight of survivors.

Keeping survivors fed, hydrated, and safe was another pressing challenge that FEMA found harder to negotiate. Disaster logistics are always problematic. But FEMA quickly found itself struggling to live up to the guarantees that it was making to state and local partners.

FEMA officials soon realized that this disaster was too big for their organization. To their credit, they tried to upscale early in the week by involving federal military capabilities. However, this did not work as long as the command authority issue went unresolved. There were no clear, easily executable procedures to help officials integrate the military into their operations. Upscaling (using the Incident of National Significance protocol) may have appeared well organized on paper, but it did not work in practice.

The INS protocol was problematic for two reasons. First, the plan was convoluted. Reading it today, it is not clear how the involvement of DOD and the armed forces could have been executed quicker and with less confusion using the protocol. Second, the INS declaration procedure was underdeveloped and poorly thought through. The underlying ideas may have been sound, but they had not been translated into workable procedures by the time Katrina appeared on the horizon. Moreover, key officials appeared to have no knowledge of the plan or the procedures that it contained.

State agencies actively looked for shortcuts in order to leverage the presence of the armed forces. FEMA, on the other hand, clung to its procedures. Michael Brown had worked to have DOD take over but then proved loath to relinquish control.

Multiple chains of command thus emerged. When new problems arose, it was not always clear which chain of command was best suited to deal with them. For instance, when FEMA was effectively replaced by DOD as the primary federal coordinator on the scene, state and local authorities had to establish new contacts and ways of working with the federal level (a form of emergent coordination that should not have been necessary). One actor that seemed to remain absent during the first week was DHS. The center of coordination authority shifted from FEMA directly to DOD, not to DHS. The idea of a "superdepartment" capable of managing superdisasters lost credibility after its first confrontation with reality.

Our lesson here is that a response network must be able to switch to "megadisaster mode." Two competencies are required. First, the coordinating nodes in a response network must learn to recognize when conventional response mechanisms no longer suffice. Second, procedures for "upscaling" must be in place, practiced, and feasible should key actors (such as FEMA) decide that they need help in coordinating the response. Having a mechanism in place on paper that has never been used before does not suffice.

Exploding Coordination Myths

Reading through the reports on Katrina, it becomes clear that the term "coordination" can have many different meanings. The term is rarely defined. It can relate to collaboration, bureau politics, upscaling, red tape, or network performance (and often in the same report at that). How it is measured generally remains a mystery. But most importantly, discussions about coordination are all too often infused by a set of myths that we need to make explicit and reject. Here are the five most persistent coordination myths.

Coordination is best assessed against a plan. Few reports offer a definition, but it rapidly becomes clear how coordination is assessed. The benchmark: some plan that happened to be in place. Michael Brown was criticized for not sticking to the plan. FEMA was criticized for not organizing a Joint Field Office faster. The state of Louisiana came under fire for not having sufficient numbers of boats and buses, and for not following the Incident Command System and the National Incident Management System.

Plans should *not* be used as a benchmark for coordination. Plans are rarely if ever written to deal with a superdisaster. In the case of Katrina, the parts of the plan that conceivably might have applied had never been tested, and failed to provide proper guidance when it was needed most. Using plans as benchmarks for unrelated events does not make sense and is unfair.

"You get what you pay for" as explanation for coordination outcomes. It has been suggested that a lack of funding explains coordination failures.[34] This in turn

suggests that more funding would lead to better coordination. Our research does not support this line of reasoning. Lack of funding did not significantly undermine coordination efforts. FEMA officials certainly did complain about the number of people available, but there were many other problems that with hindsight appear to have had much more of an impact on their ability to coordinate. The architecture of the system, for instance, proved a greater determinant than any lack of funding.

Red tape as a failure factor. Though formalism ("red tape") did at times prevent officials from orchestrating a swift and collaborated response, we found plenty of examples where federal officials in the field bypassed established procedures in order to provide assistance. They waited for neither appropriate requests from the states nor clear direction from Washington. State and local officials, for example, quickly learned to work with their military counterparts in ways that were completely unforeseen by the plans. FEMA did stick to its rules, but there is no evidence that this directly affected key features of the response.

Coordination as the province of one official. Michael Brown—coordinator in chief—became the national scapegoat for what was widely perceived as a bungled response. The Senate characterized FEMA's director as: "insubordinate, unqualified and counterproductive, in that he . . . circumvented his chain of command and failed to communicate critical information to the Secretary; failed to deliver on commitments made to Louisiana's leaders for buses; failed to organize FEMA's or other federal efforts in any meaningful way; and failed to adequately carry out responsibilities as FEMA's lead official in the Gulf before landfall and when he was appointed as the Principal Federal Official after landfall."[35]

As we have seen, there is some truth to these observations. Intriguingly, though, these criticisms were not heard during previous disasters, when FEMA was said to have performed well.[36] More importantly, the idea that one person can single-handedly coordinate a complex response during a superdisaster is preposterous. Blaming one official for everything that was perceived to go wrong is unfair (even though it may be politically expedient). Moreover, it hides the real lessons from view.

Centralization is the best answer to coordination failure. It is striking how persistent the "centralization reflex" is during and after a crisis.[37] In the case of Katrina, centralization did not provide the solution to the problems experienced in the response. In fact, when FEMA tried to "scale up" the response, the federal network rapidly dissolved into separate hierarchies. From then on, the response became fragmented—new coordination forms had to be invented on the spot. Such forms of improvisation create new coordination challenges, which must be resolved by emergent coordination. Centralization tends to create new forms of circumvention.

How to Work with the Military

In public opinion, the military emerged as the savior. Numerous calls were heard for the military to play a much more central role in the response to disasters.[38] The idea is that the military is better organized, can make quick decisions, and has the logistical capacity to make things happen in a timely manner.

This approach—making the military the primary actor in the response—stands in sharp contrast to academic assumptions concerning how disasters should be managed. Academics tend to advocate local mandates, strengthening community resilience, building public-private partnerships, reaching out to marginalized residents using trusted institutions, and developing consensus-based coordinating mechanisms at the interorganizational, community, and intergovernmental levels.

Granting the military primacy in a response network is not a good idea unless the military is specifically trained to respond to disasters (as China's armed forces are, for instance). As we saw during Katrina, the armed forces typically find it hard to collaborate with civil organizations. By US law, they cannot be subordinated to other agencies.

Interestingly, agencies in the Katrina response network quickly found bureaucratic shortcuts enabling them to work with the military (and vice versa). But these solutions created new coordination challenges in turn. From a distance, this mixture of shortcuts and emerging coordination issues can seem like chaos that must be addressed, preferably in the guise of centralization (and that's what the military is supposedly good at).

The lesson here is that the assistance of armed forces can be necessary, but it is not easy to effectuate. Most emergency management systems have thought-through procedures in place for the use of military forces. In all but the rarest of cases, civilian authorities are in charge. This type of arrangement is unlikely to work in situations where those same civilian authorities are overwhelmed (which is the prime reason for armed forces to play a role in the first place).

A quick "activation" procedure is therefore not enough. The use of armed forces in a mega-disaster requires the articulation of governing principles that explain how they are to be used, what roles they can assume, and the relationship that they will have with civilian authorities in such an event. Developing such principles will require elaborate discussion to establish the coordination arrangement under which armed forces are called in to help—and to define the parameters of their autonomy. It is of critical importance that these principles and procedures are widely known and practiced often.

TOLERATE BUREAU POLITICS, FIGHT BUREAU-POLITISM

Quick findings:

- There were tensions between response organizations.
- Most of these tensions did not have negative consequences for the response.
- Tensions between Brown and Chertoff and between Blanco and the White House fueled the blame game.
- These tensions were not addressed but were left to fester.

There is nothing inherently wrong with some tension between agencies working under pressure.[39] In fact, it is to be expected. In times of crisis, organizations will find that their ideas, priorities, and practices may not always be in sync with those of others. This is fine as long as they work things out in an effective, timely, and constructive manner. The upside is that viewpoints are scrutinized, which prevents destructive phenomena such as groupthink to occur.

But sometimes tensions become embedded and paralyzing; actors cannot seem to get out of their trenches and search for middle ground. This is what Uriel Rosenthal, Paul 't Hart, and Alex Kouzmin refer to as "bureau-politism" (an escalated state of bureau politics).[40] Bureau-politism is very dysfunctional to a response network. It undermines collaboration and fuels blame games.

The tension between Brown and Chertoff quickly went from bad to worse during the first week. There was both a personal and an organizational dimension to the two men's faltering relationship. As far as we can tell, the crux of the matter related to the degradation of FEMA as part of the new DHS organization, coupled with what Brown saw as the department's preoccupation with terrorism over natural disasters. The failure to address this manifestation of bureau-politism undermined a smooth upscaling when FEMA could no longer fulfill its obligations.

Brown correctly understood at a very early stage that FEMA would not be able to handle the disaster on its own. Rather than working with DHS to forge a wider approach, Brown bypassed his boss and floated the idea of federalizing the response (and putting the military in charge) with senior officials at the White House. Not only was this handled in an insensitive way, it did not really offer a solution—certainly not in the short term, which was what was needed.

The lesson is that we cannot assume that bureaucratic tensions, or tensions between bureaucratic leaders, will be temporarily forgotten or ignored because everybody is facing the same disaster. Our findings confirm what other researchers have found: crises and disasters tend to exacerbate preexisting tensions.[41] It is therefore critical that leaders are mindful of the possibility that such tensions can emerge. They should take immediate action to quash them where they are evident.

MEANING MAKING: IT IS MORE IMPORTANT THAN YOU THINK

Quick findings:

- There was no dominant frame during the first week.
- The common denominator of the various frames was failure.
- The lack of an overarching frame had real consequences: it allowed rumors to take hold and ultimately undercut the legitimacy of responding institutions.
- Leaders reacted to "failure frames" by blaming others.
- A proactive leadership effort to shape or "edit" existing frames emerged only after the blame game had started.

The obvious lesson is that leaders must actively formulate a frame that explains the nature of the crisis and provides a fair estimate of what will happen in the near future.

In the initial phase of a crisis or disaster, it is usually relatively easy to establish a common frame: "This is horrible, we are shocked, we stand with the victims, let's all work together." These words come easily and tend to adequately channel the initial sense of distress. But in a superdisaster, this ritualistic framing does not suffice. Ritual phrasings are soon outpaced by events. Leaders then have to explain why things are not happening as soon and as well as victims expect.

Any response to a superdisaster is inevitably marred by failure—there is no such thing as a perfect plan, full information is never available, people make mistakes, and the forces of destruction have unforeseen impacts. In other words, we must expect things to go wrong. Leaders need to explain inevitable failure.

At the strategic level, key actors reacted to failure by blaming each other. Mayor Nagin blamed the federal government, FEMA director Brown blamed DHS, the White House blamed Governor Blanco, and the media blamed government writ large. Governor Blanco and President Bush refrained from public blaming during the first week, but their relationship was nevertheless undercut by mutual suspicion arising, at least in part, out of the escalating blame game.

The blame game supplanted what should have happened: joint meaning making. A shared frame of the situation, enacted by all involved, has a galvanizing effect on a response network. The lack of such a frame creates openings for misunderstandings and antagonizing perspectives, which are the seeds of rapidly escalating blame games.

Nobody was successful in imposing a convincing frame that explained the limits of government response capacities under superdisaster conditions while at the same time offering a believable future. Nobody managed to discount the anarchy frame that took hold in the absence of an alternative frame. The anarchy frame came to dominate the media's reporting on the situation.

The inability of officials to formulate a joint frame had consequences that were immediate and fierce. Media reports perpetuated well-known "disaster" myths that many officials found believable.[42] Reports of looting, rape, and murder in New Orleans, coupled with an inability on the part of officials to validate these reports, resulted in the reframing of the situation in New Orleans from a humanitarian emergency to a law-and-order crisis. This new frame contributed to the rapid delegitimization of the response. Acutely sensitive to the spiraling cycle of distrust, officials felt compelled to (over)respond to the new frame in hopes of conveying action.

We can now see how the governor's "shoot-to-kill" order to the Arkansas National Guard, the call for 40,000 troops, and the presence of private security companies in the city reinforced the anarchy frame in receiving communities, which feared taking in the "thugs" and "gangbangers" that they were hearing about on television. Another critical turning point happened on local radio, when Mayor Nagin spouted off on Thursday. The media loved it, but their reporting of the tirade made federal actors look bad. The White House was forced into a defensive posture, which galvanized the dysfunctional "federalization dance" that absorbed officials' time on Thursday and Friday.

The mayor of New York City during the 9/11 attacks, Rudy Giuliani, understood the importance of meaning making well. Ronald Reagan was arguably the king of the craft. Jimmy Carter, on the other hand, failed miserably in his response to the Iranian hostage crisis (and the botched rescue mission).[43]

President Bush did well after 9/11 but somehow failed after Katrina. It took him a few days to realize that his administration was part of a public relations disaster. For his part, Michael Brown tried but failed to set a narrative. Louisiana traditionally has had very capable politicians—think of "Kingfish" Huey Long—when it comes to meaning making.[44] Governor Blanco, as we learned, found it a much harder challenge.

The lesson here is that if leaders cannot impose an explanatory narrative, they will become the unwitting owners of emerging problems, real or imagined. In the absence of such a narrative, societal expectations will define the way their performance is assessed. As expectations tend to rise and delivery capacity may well dwindle, leaders are likely to quickly suffer the consequences. This is especially true if leaders seek to make up for failed meaning making by engaging in blame games. In hindsight, we can see that *a reasonable claim for joint success could have been produced* had everybody stayed calm for a few days and collaborated on a joint narrative.

It is essential that key actors work together in shaping a dynamic frame that can be updated in response to changing facts or new developments. A frame competition will inevitably invite leaders to oversell their own and undermine those put forward by others. Frame competition then easily turns into blaming, initiating an escalating spiral that feeds on itself: once the blame game gets going, it is hard to stop.

CRISIS COMMUNICATION AND THE MEDIA

Quick findings:

- Technical difficulties made it extremely difficult for authorities to communicate effectively.

- Media representatives in New Orleans had limited access to authority figures.

- Key authority figures communicated in emotional (Nagin, Blanco) or largely ineffective (Brown, Chertoff) ways.

- The media published many stories that were based on rumors.

- There were few efforts to address those rumors.

A crisis narrative must be communicated in an effective way. Regarding this need, this book has revealed a surprising lack of professionalism. Key actors had their message undermined by symbolic mismanagement (Bush's flyover, Brown's television performance, and Blanco's shoot-to-kill rhetoric, to name a few examples). A good start would be to adhere to time-proven rituals: visit disaster sites, embrace victims, and refrain from attending ball games.

A perennial issue in crisis is how authorities should work with the media. This question has become even more urgent with the explosive rise of social media, which was in its infancy at the time of Katrina.

National media stories were overwhelmingly episodic in nature (moving from roof rescues to looting), which "contributed to the perpetuation of racial stereotypes" (white commanders, black victims).[45] The storm's victims were not amused by the "national posturing" of media celebrities such as Geraldo Rivera.[46] The anarchy framework found strong support in the negative stereotype of Louisiana that dominates the American popular imagination.[47]

It has been said that "journalists write the first rough drafts of history."[48] This may be true, but authorities cannot leave it to journalists to produce an *accurate* draft. Even in view of the difficult circumstances, it is still surprising to learn how inaccurate the reporting of major news outlets was. Journalists from respected media organizations repeated the most outrageous rumors, thus granting them a sense of credibility that they otherwise would not have possessed. It is no exaggeration to conclude that many media representatives produced what today might be referred to as "fake news." We can only imagine how bad this may be in the next major disaster unfolding in a "postfactual" world.

Response leaders must work with media representatives *on the ground*. Leaders cannot simply trust them to report in a correct and balanced way. In the absence of a convincing narrative that is brought to media representatives (something they can "work with"), journalists will create their own. It is bound to be overdramatic, focusing on failures rather than successes.

Authorities failed to identify and then address rumors. In many instances, authorities in fact based *their* decisions on the very media reporting that perpetuated some of these rumors. A good example is the call for military involvement. First aimed at remedying logistical problems, bringing in the military came to be seen as a way to achieve a more muscular response that would tamp down the anarchy that had apparently taken hold.

Response leaders must engage in rumor control. Katrina demonstrates the need to prepare officials for the type of information that is sure to emerge but must be actively checked and countered. Some officials (and many journalists) fell for "disaster" myths (widespread violence, panic, etc.). Rumor control requires a particular mind-set. It starts with identifying reliable and accurate sources of information, especially when regular modes of communication are disabled.

Some officials encouraged their counterparts elsewhere to be skeptical of the reports they received.[49] The FEMA director used interviews as opportunities to counter those reports that he considered inaccurate. Still, FEMA officials found that the agency's reactive stance to inaccurate media reporting was "harmful to the overall response." The fact that "most [official] statements seem[ed] like corrections or clarifications of earlier media stories, rather than a clear and consistent message" greatly damaged the agency's credibility and lessened the quality of information being circulated in the media in the days after landfall.[50] Rumor control is no substitute for meaning making.

We argue that the classic relationship between the media and official authorities in times of crisis must be rethought.[51] The idea that authorities do well when they communicate immediately (even if it is to communicate that they do not know anything) and report the facts is outdated. Authorities today have at their disposal communication platforms that hardly existed in 2005. They do not have to rely on journalists working for official media outlets to get their message out. However, the existence of multiple communications channels makes for just as many (if not more) domains in which rumors can spread and then become established fact in the form of "breaking news." In this new media environment, authorities are obligated to actively seek out and correct inaccurate information streams without succumbing to the temptation to control communications (a false illusion).

ASSESSING CRISIS MANAGEMENT PERFORMANCE IN A
MEGA-DISASTER: TOWARD REALISTIC EXPECTATIONS

We started this book arguing that we are in need of a proper and fair way to assess government performance in the face of a mega-disaster. Existing theories do not offer much guidance. Political deliberation does not occur. Citizens do not seem to care until disaster strikes.

The starting point of any discussion should be that managing crisis and disaster is not an easy job. Managing a superdisaster is a contradiction in terms. So what is fair to expect? Based on our research, we suggest a set of expectations that seem both reasonable and feasible.

Early detection: Leaders must pay attention. They should inform themselves of even relatively minor incidents without waiting to be called into action. They should distrust the "everything is under control" storyline. This may seem like a drastic requirement, as leaders are busy people. But many incidents have escalatory potential. To come uninformed is to come unprepared.

Sense making: Leaders need organizational capacity to collect and categorize information. To understand, one must go where the action is. Contact people directly. Probe. Pay attention to rumors. Collect information that leaders need to make decisions that will allow them to stay ahead of the curve.

Decision-making: Once a disaster becomes manifest, leaders should think of the decisions that belong (and eventually will arrive) on their table. It's not a long list. The sooner leaders have it, the sooner they can collect the information they will need to make those decisions. Once they have the information, decisions can be made.

Coordination: It's often extraordinary how well first responders perform in the immediate phase of a disaster. Leaders should support and praise these improvised responses. They should not reinforce paper playbooks in the name of coordination. Rather, they should sniff out bottlenecks and personal conflicts that inhibit collaboration.

Meaning making: Leaders must work together with one another to build a narrative that explains, guides, and inspires hope. They should seek out and address rumors. At the same time, they should consider these same rumors as sources of discontent and uncertainty. They should refrain from blame games.

Communication: Leaders should not leave this task to professional communications experts (who may not know how to communicate during a superdisaster). They should personally monitor national and local media (but not continuously). They should not trust any media reporting to be factually correct. They should make sure that media representatives near the disaster area have access to official spokespersons.

TOWARD A PRAGMATIC APPROACH

Our research findings suggest that key actors in a crisis response would benefit from a shared approach to the challenges they face. We are not referring to a shared language or set of administrative precepts as embodied, for instance, by the National Incident Management System framework that dominates the US response system. We are instead referring to the *philosophical* underpinnings of a shared approach that should offer guidance in dealing with events that have not happened before and for which no navigational map exists.

The prescriptions in this conclusion implicitly build on such an approach. We are inspired by the philosophical school of pragmatism, which offers the building blocks for such underpinnings.[52] This approach prescribes the embrace of uncertainty and offers a distinct approach to problem solving as a form of trial and error.

It is not the only approach and may not be the best approach. But we believe that a shared approach is better than no approach or multiple approaches. The response to Katrina was characterized by multiple approaches, which culminated in a fragmented response.

We see it as a leadership responsibility to guide the thinking and deliberation about the challenges that mega-disasters bring. So if we have one overarching recommendation to leaders, it is this: start thinking about the challenges of mega-disasters and construe the outlines of a shared approach. It is the only way to build a response network that can utilize its capacities in joint fashion and be effective in a time when citizens need it most.

APPENDIX I

MONDAY, AUGUST 29

7:10 a.m. In Baton Rouge, the head of the Louisiana National Guard receives a report of a flash flood hitting Jackson Barracks.[1]

7:30 a.m. During a conference call between local, state, and federal representatives, it is mentioned that "the tidal surge came up and breached the levee system in the canal, so we're faced with major flooding both in the east, East New Orleans, and then out on the lakefront."[2] It is also reported that the "first floor of Charity [Hospital] flooded" and reference is made to "people who are trying to survive on the roofs."[3] 'When state coordinating officer Jeff Smith asks if earlier reports of flooding have been confirmed, a deputy sheriff representing the local parish in question replies that they have and notes that his building was surrounded by "white caps." Smith also states that he is aware of three to four feet of floodwater at Jackson Barracks.[4]

8:00 a.m. Mayor Nagin of New Orleans dials into the *Today* show.[5] He reports that water is coming over the levee system in the Lower Ninth Ward and that pumps have stopped working. "In the Lower 9th Ward . . . [there are] unconfirmed reports of people standing on their roofs."[6]

179

8:14 a.m. The National Weather Service in New Orleans issues a flash flood warning, meaning that "flooding is imminent or occurring." The report further states that "a levee breach occurred along the Industrial Canal at Tennessee Street. 3 to 8 feet of water is expected due to the breach."[7]

8:36 a.m. Matthew Green, a FEMA liaison officer at the National Hurricane Center, reports to Michael Lowder, FEMA's deputy director of response, that the "levee in Arabi has failed, next to the industrial canal."[8]

8:39 a.m., 8:53 a.m., 9:20 a.m., and 10:57 a.m. Email messages received by FEMA director Brown indicate that he was informed of the levee breaches.[9]

9:00 a.m. Louis Dabdoub, a Department of Homeland Security protective security adviser stationed in New Orleans, reports to Homeland Security Operations Center and DHS officials: "It is getting bad. Major flooding in some parts in the city. . . . Flooding is worsening every minute. . . . The bad part has not hit here yet." At 9:36, Dabdoub reports that "the lower parishes of LA, Plaq and St Bernard parish's [sic] are under water."[10] Liz Jackson of DHS is copied on both messages.

10:13 a.m. The Homeland Security Council at the White House reports: "Flooding is significant throughout the region and a levee in New Orleans has reportedly been breached sending 6–8 feet of water throughout the 9th Ward area of the city. Per the governor, water is rising at 1 foot per hour . . . HSOC reports that due to rising water in the 9th Ward, residents are in their attics and on their roofs."[11]

10:32 a.m. A staffer with the HSOC reports during a conference call: "Waters are rising, extensive flooding has been reported."[12]

10:51 a.m. A summary of the Bahamonde report reaches FEMA's Michael Lowder in Washington. In it, Bahamonde states, "New Orleans FD is reporting a 20 foot wide breach on the Lake Pontchartrain side levee."[13]

11:00 a.m. Bahamonde, present in the New Orleans emergency operations center, first receives reports on the levee breaches.[14] "At approximately 11:00 a.m., the worst possible news came into the EOC. I stood there and listened to the first report of the levee break at the 17th Street Canal. I do not know who made the report but they were very specific about the location of the break and the size. And then they added it was 'very bad.'"[15]

11:00 a.m. Captain Mark Willow, a police officer in New Orleans, reports to the Louisiana State Police a "20 foot Levee break at 17th Street Canal."[16]

11:40 a.m. The National Weather Service warns that "widespread flooding will continue . . . continues to be an extremely life threatening situation."[17]

Early to midmorning: Patrick J. Rhode, FEMA's acting deputy director and chief of staff, first hears about issues with the levees.[18]

1:20 p.m. The White House receives an HSOC report stating that some Louisiana parishes had 8 to 10 feet of water and an unspecified number of Louisiana and Mississippi residents were stranded in flooded areas.[19]

4:00 p.m. The Louisiana Office of Homeland Security and Emergency Preparedness reports on the Ninth Ward levee breach, the Seventeenth Street canal levee breach, and flooding in the Lakeview area.[20]

5:00 p.m. In an HSOC report, the White House is advised that "extensive flooding in New Orleans could take months to reverse through the dewatering process."[21]

6:35 p.m. An HSOC spot report mentions breaches first reported in an earlier (2:54 p.m.) email.[22]

7:00 p.m. After conducting a second aerial survey of the city, FEMA's Bahamonde calls Michael Brown and explains what he saw: "I picked up the phone and I called Under Secretary Brown directly, and I began a 10- to 15-minute conversation."[23] Brown listened to Bahamonde's report. He did not ask any questions. "All he said was, 'Thank you. I am now going to call the White House.'"[24]

Brown reports to White House deputy chief of staff Joe Hagin on the developing situation in New Orleans.[25]

On Monday evening, the mayor and his executive staff gather on the ninth floor of the city hall complex to hear Bahamonde describe the devastation he had just witnessed from the air. After the meeting, he asks for a phone in order to brief federal officials in Washington.[26] That same evening, Nagin takes to the airwaves, where he describes a city under water and afire.[27]

8:29 p.m. John Wood, the DHS secretary's chief of staff, receives an email: "The first (unconfirmed) reports they are getting from aerial surveys in New Orleans are far more serious than media reports are currently reflecting. Finding extensive flooding and more stranded people than they had originally thought—also a number of fires."[28]

9:30 p.m. An HSOC spot report describes a "quarter-mile breach," citing Bahamonde's earlier reports.[29]

10:05 p.m. The FEMA acting deputy director informs DHS deputy secretary Michael Jackson about Bahamonde's report via email.[30]

10:47 p.m. An HSOC spot report based on remote sensing imagery suggests that 136,000 housing units have been impacted by flooding.[31]

TUESDAY, AUGUST 30

2:15 a.m. US Coast Guard reports "extensive flooding . . . flooding continues . . . catastrophic damage."[32]

5:00 a.m. An HSOC sitrep describes several levee breaches.[33]

5:00 a.m. The White House Homeland Security Council receives a report from the state EOC in Baton Rouge explaining that large areas in the southern part of the state have no power, the 911 system is out, there is roof damage to the Superdome, and the entire city of New Orleans has flooded.[34]

6:02 a.m. Bahamonde emails DHS. He warns DHS that the area around the Superdome is filling up with water ("now waist deep"). The president "can land and do a presser but then have to leave, there will be no ground tour, only flyover."[35]

APPENDIX II

EMERGENCY MANAGEMENT IN THE
AMERICAN FEDERAL SYSTEM

In the United States, disaster assistance at the local level was provided almost exclusively by local government, charitable organizations, and private citizens until the nineteenth century. According to Saundra Schneider, "Disaster assistance was [before then] not considered a top priority among state governments."[1] Federal disaster assistance was only provided on a case-by-case, piecemeal basis; in principle at least, lawmakers believed that this was something for the states and local authorities to deal with.[2]

The federal government began slowly building up certain response capabilities in order to assist the states as governors increasingly turned to Washington for help when their own resources were overwhelmed. The passage of several federal laws, including the Lower Mississippi Flood Control Act following the catastrophic flooding of the lower Mississippi valley (including much of New Orleans) in 1927, saw the federal government for the first time engaging in disaster mitigation as well.[3]

With the Disaster Relief Act of 1950, Congress sought to improve the federal government's ability to coordinate disaster responses. In part at least, the law reflected growing fears that the United States would come under nuclear attack. The act clearly stated that emergencies should, to the extent possible, be managed locally. Federal resources could be requested where state and local resources were insufficient. The act also urged state and local governments to develop emergency management plans in cooperation with the Federal Civil Defense Administration. According to Schneider, by "delineat[ing] the first general, national-level policy for providing emergency relief, [the act] established a framework for governmental disaster assistance that has essentially remained in place since that time."[4]

Sparked by criticism from the nation's governors, the Carter administration in 1978 created the Federal Emergency Management Agency. According to President Carter, the agency "would be independent, apolitical, and adequately funded." However, the new agency relied on authorization from "a myriad of enabling legislation, appropriation acts, executive orders, and National Security Directives" that would go on to hobble the agency's capacity for effective intraorganizational coordination of effort.[5]

Carter's subsequent defeat in the 1979 presidential election slowed plans to reorganize FEMA. Ronald Reagan, who won office promising to take a more aggressive stance toward the Soviet Union, refocused FEMA's energies on civil defense and ensuring continuity of government. During this period, several senior FEMA officials came under congressional scrutiny for corruption, misuse of public funds, and politicizing the agency's hiring practices.[6]

In 1988, Congress passed the Robert T. Stafford Disaster Relief and Emergency Assistance Act, which further clarified state and local emergency management responsibilities, as well as the federal emergency/disaster assistance request process. For the first time, the importance of effective mitigation efforts in heavily populated, hazard-prone areas was emphasized.

FEMA received poor marks for its management of Hurricane Hugo, a major earthquake in California, and the *Exxon Valdez* oil spill. The agency was also faulted for failing to effectively coordinate federal efforts. In 1992, Hurricane Andrew leveled whole communities in Florida, leaving hundreds of thousands homeless in a critical "swing state" just months before the presidential election. Florida's governor, local emergency managers, victims, and the media responded to the federal government's efforts with scathing criticism. Despite an unprecedented amount of resources being pumped into the state in the days and weeks after landfall, the governmental response was viewed as a failure.[7]

The political fallout after Andrew would have a profound effect on FEMA.[8] Upon taking office, President Bill Clinton appointed as FEMA director James Lee Witt, the former director of emergency management in the president's home state of Arkansas. Witt acted on many of the recommendations made by investigators after Andrew. Furthermore, he worked to secure veto authority over political nominees to the agency, establish closer ties with those committees and subcommittees with oversight over the agency's myriad programs, and improve agency morale.[9] At the same time, pursuant to the Clinton administration's agenda (to "reinvent government"), many FEMA programs were devolved onto state and local authorities. This move was applauded by the Senate, the House, and the National Academy of Public Administrators. In their view, these programs had long disincentivized state and local governments from investing in building up their own emergency management capabilities. State and local authorities welcomed having more discretion to decide how federal grants were spent.[10]

The end of the Cold War provided FEMA with an opportunity to focus its energies more squarely on dealing with nonantagonistic threats, including natural hazards. However, the "new" FEMA's first tests would come in the form of a series of terror attacks during the early 1990s. While generally satisfied with the agency's response to the first World Trade Center attack (1993) and the Oklahoma City bombing (1994), FEMA investigators saw room for improvement in a number of areas, namely: clarifying authorities, roles, and responsibilities; improving interagency plan compatibility; and increasing urban search and rescue capabilities. The agency subsequently clarified certain sections of the nation's emergency response plan, the Federal Response Plan, and ramped up work to strengthen ties with state and local counterparts.

The terror attacks revived a debate concerning the dangers posed by weapons of mass destruction. As Richard Sylves suggests, "The shotgun marriage of civil defense and emergency management" manifested itself in the guise of "civil security."[11] The 9/11 attacks gave the proponents of a more robust national counterterrorism defense the support necessary to push through legislation significantly altering the nation's emergency management system.[12] The Homeland Security Act of 2002 mandated the consolidation of all federal agencies with "homeland security" responsibilities, including FEMA, into a single Department of Homeland Security (DHS).[13]

It has been suggested that FEMA as part of DHS adopted policies and practices aimed primarily at preparing for and managing terror attacks. Nominally at least, the agency retained an "all hazards" focus. However, initiatives intended to strengthen disaster mitigation and postdisaster recovery capabilities suffered dramatic funding cuts and/or were moved beyond FEMA's purview.

Observers worried that the absorption of FEMA into DHS risked eroding the agency's capabilities in dealing with natural disasters and other nonantagonistic incidents.[14]

These concerns did not materialize during the 2004 hurricane season, which saw four major hurricanes strike Florida within the span of a few months. That would be the most costly hurricane season on record and saw the "largest mobilization of emergency response and disaster resources in the history of FEMA."[15] Publicly at least, the FEMA leadership was very satisfied with the response in Florida. In fact, it reportedly intended to build on this success ahead of the 2005 season, one that meteorologists predicted might be even more active.[16]

NOTES

PREFACE

1. Douglas Brinkley's 2006 book was later criticized for being sloppy. We fact-checked this book (and many other hastily written sources) against official reports as best as we could. While we did find errors, we still view Brinkley's book as excellent in portraying the atmosphere in New Orleans in the first week.

2. We assembled our collection of sources at https://www.crisisplan.nl/en/katrina-2.

1. HURRICANE KATRINA REVISITED: REFLECTING ON SUCCESS AND FAILURE

1. Select Bipartisan Committee (2006a: x).

2. Martha Derthick (2007) was one of the first (and few) academics to make this point.

3. See Boin et al. (2016) for a detailed discussion of these strategic tasks.

4. The black swan concept was coined by Taleb (2007) to refer to an event that quickly spins out of control, with extreme consequences.

5. Lewis (1976).

6. S. Jackson (2006).

7. Dyson (2006: 10–11); Lewis (1976: 39).

8. Lewis (1976: 47).

9. Barry (1998).

10. Remnick (2005).

11. Remnick (2005).

12. Brinkley (2006: 43). This rumor was repeated as fact by Katrina survivors in Spike Lee's documentary *When the Levees Broke* (Pollard and Lee, 2006).

13. Bruegmann (2005: 108–109); cf. Hayden (2003).

14. Brookings Institution (2005: 5–12).

15. Brinkley (2006: 47–49, 484); Dyson (2006: 9); Flaherty (2010); Herbert (2005).

16. Brinkley (2006: 31–32).

17. Hurlbert et al. (2005).

18. Strolovitch et al. (2005); McQuaid and Schleifstein (2006: 70). Nearly 12% of residents were 65 years of age or older, which was a greater percentage than in cities of similar size, such as Austin (6.7%) or Boston (10.4%) (Brinkley, 2006: 33).

19. Berube and Raphael (2005); Fussell (2005).

20. Berube and Raphael (2005).

21. Fussell (2005).

22. The White House (2006: 23).

23. The sources are not always clear whether they refer to central daylight time or eastern standard time. When it was unclear to us and triangulation did not create certainty, we used the time that corresponded with the source's place of origin. Despite our best efforts, it may be possible an event took place an hour earlier or later than stated in this book.

24. A few examples of Category 4 or 5 hurricanes before Katrina: Hurricane Andrew (Category 5, August 1992); Hurricane Charley (Category 4, August 2004); Hurricane Ivan (Category 5, September 2004); Hurricane Dennis (Category 4, July 2005).

25. The White House (2006: 1).

26. The White House (2006: 33).

27. Select Bipartisan Committee (2006a: 9).

28. The White House (2006: 34).

29. The White House (2006: 35).

30. The White House (2006: 2).

31. A *USA Today* article from 2015 mentions that 1,833 people lost their lives (N. Scott, 2015). The Senate report mentions a total of 1,577 deaths (Committee on Homeland Security, 2006a: 37), and the White House report (2006: 8) puts the tally at 1,330. The House report does not offer a total number (Select Bipartisan Committee, 2006a). A *Times-Picayune* article mentions around 1,400 victims who perished (Schleifstein, 2009). An article on fivethirtyeight.com from 2015 states that it is still unclear how many people died (Bialik, 2015).

32. Brinkley (2006: 178–179).

33. The White House (2006: 34).

34. The White House (2006: 7). This final toll exceeds the combined damage of the four major 2004 hurricanes—Charley, Frances, Ivan, and Jeanne—which together destroyed or damaged approximately 85,000 homes (ibid.: 7). It far surpasses the residential damage of Hurricane Andrew (1992), which destroyed or damaged approximately 80,000 homes.

35. National Hurricane Center (2005a: 13). The White House's *Lessons Learned* report presents an estimate of $96 billion (The White House, 2006: 7). FEMA also estimates that Katrina caused an estimated $108 billion in damages (Government Accountability Office, 2015: 1).

36. The White House (2006: 5).

37. The White House (2006: 8).

38. Office of the Press Secretary (2005a); Ortega (2014); The White House (2006: 19, 34).

39. Brinkley (2006: 135); Treaster and Goodnough (2005).

40. Cooper and Block (2006: 117).

41. Treaster and Goodnough (2005).

42. Committee on Homeland Security (2006a: 10).

43. Brinkley (2006: 78).

44. Brinkley (2006: 135–136, 192).

45. Select Bipartisan Committee (2006a: 117); Brinkley (2006: 392).

46. Brinkley (2006: 466–467).

47. Select Bipartisan Committee (2006a: 186).

48. Committee on Homeland Security (2006a: 115).

49. Estimates of the number of people at the Convention Center differ, from 19,000 (Committee on Homeland Security, 2006a: 11) to 25,000 (The White House, 2006: 39).

50. It appears that Mayor Nagin did authorize the use of the Convention Center (McQuaid and Schleifstein, 2006: 284). In his prepared statement, the mayor stated that "the swelling crowd at the Superdome and the number of people needing shelter required us to open the Convention Center as another refuge" (Select Bipartisan Committee 2006a: 118). "Tuesday evening, Mayor Nagin had opened the Convention Center as an alternate refuge" (Committee on Homeland Security 2006a: 32). But it also appears that "none of the officials who spoke with the Select Committee staff were willing to take responsibility for the operation of the Convention Center as a 'shelter,' and none claimed that they knew about the situation until Wednesday morning or afternoon, August 31" (Select Bipartisan Committee 2006a: 118).

51. According to the *Washington Post*, people started congregating there on Monday evening (Haygood and Tyson, 2005).

52. The governor's office reported having received notification of the crowds at the Convention Center on Wednesday, August 31 (The White House, 2006: 39).

53. The White House (2006: 39).

54. Brinkley (2006: 193).

55. Select Bipartisan Committee (2006a: 248); Thevenot (2005). An email from within the Department of Homeland Security mentioned an estimate of 200 homicide victims at the Superdome and the Convention Center (Select Bipartisan Committee, 2006b: 320).

56. The White House (2006: 39).

57. Brinkley (2006: 468–470).

58. Select Bipartisan Committee (2006a: 171).

59. Select Bipartisan Committee (2006a: 457).

60. The White House (2006: 39); Cooper and Block (2006: 162).

61. Brinkley (2006: 288–289).

62. Brinkley (2006: 386).

63. Cooper and Block (2006: 210). When the exhausted evacuees were finally loaded on the buses, a no-pet policy was strictly enforced: people were forced to leave their pets behind (Brinkley, 2006: 516–518).

64. Brinkley (2006: 64–65) speaks of 60–70 nursing homes.

65. Select Bipartisan Committee (2006a: 268).

66. Select Bipartisan Committee (2006a: 268).

67. Brinkley (2006: 65).

68. Committee on Homeland Security (2006a: 26–27).

69. Franco et al. (2006).

70. Brinkley (2006: 481).

71. See Sheri Fink's (2013) riveting account in her book *Five Days at Memorial*.

72. Brinkley (2006: 480–492).

73. Brinkley (2006: 221). The White House (2006: 34) states that thirty-four people died in St. Rita's nursing home. For a personal account, see Cobb (2013).

74. Quarantelli (1994); Auf der Heide (2004).

75. Brinkley (2006: 506).

76. Select Bipartisan Committee (2006a: 241).

77. These stories are mentioned in Select Bipartisan Committee (2006a: 246–249).

78. When Hurricane Rita forced the evacuation of Houston (the fourth-largest city in the United States), traffic was a nightmare, and over a hundred people died in traffic accidents (Cooper and Block, 2006: 269–70).

79. Brinkley (2006: 116–117).

80. Cooper and Block (2006: 15–17).

81. Committee on Homeland Security (2007a: 47); Cooper and Block (2006: 6–7).

82. Beamish (2005); Committee on Homeland Security (2007a).

83. Committee on Homeland Security (2007a); Brinkley (2006: 65); Schleifstein (2003).

84. Committee on Homeland Security (2007a); Committee on Homeland Security (2007b: 7).

85. Cooper and Block (2006: 105, 269).

86. The White House (2006: 29); Cooper and Block (2006: 122); Brinkley (2006: 108).

87. Select Bipartisan Committee (2006a: 103).

88. Select Bipartisan Committee (2006a: 102).

89. Select Bipartisan Committee (2006a: 25). Louisiana and Mississippi had jointly revised their respective evacuation plans after encountering problems during Hurricane Ivan in 2004 (ibid.: 26).

90. Cooper and Block (2006: 110).

91. Governors Haley Barbour (Mississippi) and Bob Riley (Alabama) still had not called for a mandatory evacuation (Brinkley, 2006: 77).

92. Brinkley (2006: 62).

93. Brinkley (2006: 53).

94. Brinkley (2006: 45, 46).

95. Brinkley (2006: 66); Select Bipartisan Committee (2006a: 20).

96. Brinkley (2006: 25).

97. Select Bipartisan Committee (2006a: 217); The White House (2006: 38).

98. Committee on Homeland Security (2006a: 8).

99. Brinkley (2006: 138).

100. Brinkley (2006: 302–312, 372); CBS News (2015).

101. Brinkley (2006: 434–435). Louisiana has one of the highest rates of nativity in the United States (77%), behind only Pennsylvania (Horne, 2006).

102. Brinkley (2006: 244). The efforts of LSU are nicely documented in the book *LSU in the Eye of the Storm* (Bacher et al., 2005).

103. Committee on Homeland Security (2006a: 400).

104. Select Bipartisan Committee (2006a: 132, 144, 250).

105. Brinkley (2006: 513).

106. CNN (2005a) offers an overview of corporate donations.

107. Brinkley (2006: 251–252).

108. Brinkley (2006: 252–253).

109. Brinkley (2006: 518).

110. Select Bipartisan Committee (2006a: 272).

111. The White House (2006: 49).

112. Bovens and 't Hart (1996).

113. Rosenthal et al. (1989; 2001); Boin et al. (2008; 2013; 2016).

114. Steinberg (2006); Tierney (2014).

2. WHY DIDN'T THEY SEE IT COMING?
THE CHALLENGES OF TIMELY CRISIS RECOGNITION

1. Whoriskey and Gugliotta (2005).

2. ABC News (2005a). One news source that accurately described the level of devastation on Tuesday was the local *Times-Picayune*.

3. Treaster and Kleinfield (2005).

4. Select Bipartisan Committee (2006a: 137).

5. Select Bipartisan Committee (2006a: 80).

6. Select Bipartisan Committee (2006a: xi).

7. Clarke (1999); Tetlock (2005).

8. Clarke (1999).

9. See Kahneman's *Thinking, Fast and Slow* (2011) on the inaccuracies of these heuristics. See also the fascinating debate between Kahneman and Klein on the differences between recognizing known and unknown threats (Kahneman and Klein, 2009).

10. Turner (1978); Perrow (1984; 1986); Catino (2013).

11. E. Berger (2001); Wilson (2001).

12. Committee on Homeland Security (2006a: 21).

13. Committee on Homeland Security (2007a: 12).

14. Cooper and Block (2006: 7).

15. E. Berger (2001).

16. Cooper and Block (2006: 8).

17. Schleifstein (2003).

18. Cooper and Block (2006: 13).

19. Van Heerden (2005).

20. Brinkley (2006: 81).

21. McQuaid and Schleifstein (2002; 2006: 125–127).

22. Parker et al. (2009).

23. Parker et al. (2009); Shane and Lipton (2005).

24. An article in the *Times-Picayune* explicitly compared the Pam exercise to Katrina and concluded that emergency management officials did not learn enough from the lessons identified after Pam (McQuaid, 2009).

25. Committee on Homeland Security (2007c: 114).

26. Planners resolved not to simulate the evacuation of New Orleans. This, the state argued, was primarily a state and local responsibility that could be exercised separately.

27. Select Bipartisan Committee (2006a: 532).

28. Select Bipartisan Committee (2006a: 81).

29. The "mega-disaster" developed by planners envisioned that "over one million people would evacuate from New Orleans. . . . Hurricane surge would block highways and trap 300,000 to 350,000 persons in flooded areas. Storm surge of over 18 feet would overflow flood-protection levees [and] leave much of New Orleans under 14 to 17 feet of water. . . . It could take weeks to 'de-water' New Orleans. . . . Rescue operations would be difficult because much of the area would be reachable only by helicopters and boats. Hospitals would be overcrowded with special-needs patients. . . . The New Orleans area would be without electric power, food, potable water, medicine, or transportation for an extended time period. . . . Standing water and disease could threaten public health" (Committee on Homeland Security, 2007c: 114–115).

30. Select Bipartisan Committee (2006a: 82).

31. Brinkley (2006: 94).

32. Cooper and Block (2006: 15).

33. Select Bipartisan Committee (2006a: 81).

34. Cooper and Block (2006: 21).

35. Select Bipartisan Committee (2006a: 82).

36. Select Bipartisan Committee (2006a: 82).

37. Select Bipartisan Committee (2006a: 83).

38. Committee on Homeland Security (2006a: 8).

39. Cooper and Block (2006: 16).

40. The White House (2006: 25).

41. A limited number of FEMA officials had been present during the 2004 Hurricane Pam exercise and/or a series of postexercise issue-specific work group meetings. Lokey was one of them (Committee on Homeland Security, 2006a: 115).

42. Committee on Homeland Security (2006a: 115).

43. Committee on Homeland Security (2006a: 115).

44. Committee on Homeland Security (2006a: 115).

45. Select Bipartisan Committee (2006a: 82).

46. Cooper and Block (2006: 20).

47. Cooper and Block (2006: 32).

48. The White House (2006: 28).

49. Select Bipartisan Committee (2006a: 70).

50. Brinkley (2006: 453); Cooper and Block (2006: 123); Select Bipartisan Committee (2006a: 166). The DHS refused to share a copy of this report with us.

51. Brinkley (2006: 79). This warning was written in highly atypical language in an effort to alert officials who had until this point not appreciated the danger. So atypical was this warning that the producers of NBC Nightly News at first doubted its authenticity (Brinkley, 2006: 81, 626).

52. Crenson (2005).

53. Crenson (2005).

54. One of the most vocal critics in hindsight of the "relative ignorance" of government officials, Douglas Brinkley, did not himself evacuate. He booked a hotel room in downtown New Orleans to ride out the storm (Brinkley, 2006: xiii).

55. NRCC responsibilities include "initiating mission assignments . . . to activate other federal departments and agencies; activating and deploying national-level entities such as the National Disaster Medical System (NDMS), Urban Search and Rescue Task Forces, Mobile Emergency Response Support (MERS), and Emergency Response Team (ERT)" and "coordinating operational response and resource allocation planning with the appropriate federal departments and agencies, RRCCs [Regional Response Coordination Centers], and the JFO [Joint Field Office]" (Department of Homeland Security, 2004: 25–26).

56. Select Bipartisan Committee (2006a: 64).

57. It was issued on August 24 (Select Bipartisan Committee, 2006a: 66).

58. Committee on Homeland Security (2006a: 475).

59. Committee on Homeland Security (2007a: 601).

60. Cooper and Block (2006: 96).

61. McQuaid and Schleifstein (2006: 166); Committee on Homeland Security (2007a: 15–16). For instance, NHC director Max Mayfield called Walter Maestri, the director of the Jefferson Parish Office of Emergency Operations. Mayfield urged Maestri to do all that he could to convey to "elected officials" the severity of the approaching hurricane (Committee on Homeland Security, 2007a: 16).

62. The broadcasting team for WWL radio was "still covering the Saints game [on Friday evening, August 26], but during halftime, Dave and his news crew dramatically ramped up their coverage [of Katrina]" (Vaidyanathan, 2015).

63. Select Bipartisan Committee (2006b: 77).

64. Committee on Homeland Security (2006a: 51; 2007a: 15–17).

65. Committee on Homeland Security (2007b: 137); The White House (2006: 24).

66. Committee on Homeland Security (2007a).

67. Select Bipartisan Committee (2006a: 64).

68. Committee on Homeland Security (2007d: 44).

69. Committee on Homeland Security (2007d: 44; 2006a: 150).

70. Select Bipartisan Committee (2006a: 66–67; 2006b: 240; 2005b: 6).

71. National Hurricane Center (2005b).

72. National Hurricane Center (2005b).

73. Committee on Homeland Security (2006a: 52).

74. Cooper and Block (2006: 102).

75. Dyson (2006: 70).

76. Glasser and Grunwald (2005a).

77. The president was scheduled to discuss his administration's Medicare prescription drug benefit plan in Arizona. After staying overnight in San Diego, Bush intended to commemorate the 60th anniversary of V-J Day before visiting wounded military personnel. He would then return to his ranch in Texas (McClellan, 2008: 276). Columnists, pundits, and late-night television hosts had long commented on the length of the president's stays at the ranch. The White House press secretary, Scott McClellan, reportedly encountered significant difficulties in convincing the media

that these stays were in fact "working holidays." More often than not, the press described Bush as "vacationing" when at the Crawford ranch (McClellan, 2008: 275–276). Bush himself argued that being at the "Western White House" did not weaken his decision-making capacity: "being away from Washington doesn't make you not president. You're always president. You're just president with a different feel" (K. Walsh, 2005: 254).

78. McQuaid and Schleifstein (2006: 248).

79. Federal Emergency Management Agency (2006: 61).

80. Cooper and Block (2006: 153); Committee on Homeland Security (2006a: 176, 178).

81. Committee on Homeland Security (2006a: 176).

82. Select Bipartisan Committee (2006a: 190).

83. Committee on Homeland Security (2006a: 176).

84. The emergency response team is the principal interagency group that staffs the Joint Field Office. ERT-A and ERT-N are subcomponents. The ERT-N deploys for large-scale, high-impact events, or as required. The ERT-A is the first team deployed to the field. It thus deploys during the early stages of an incident to work directly with the state to obtain information on the impact of the event and to identify specific state requests for federal incident management assistance (The White House, 2006: 23, 27; Department of Homeland Security, 2004: 40).

85. The ERT-N was intended to comprise 125 to 175 members. However, due to staffing shortfalls, FEMA could allot only twenty-five members per team. Senate investigators found that as a result, "the teams consist of individuals who have not necessarily previously served in these positions, who have not trained, worked, practiced or planned together, and who are sometimes not qualified for the job" (Committee on Homeland Security, 2006a: 177). In June 2004, FEMA's FCO cadre delivered a warning to FEMA director Brown that the ERT-Ns were "unprepared" as the result of "zero funding for training, exercises, or team equipment" and insufficient policy guidance and standard operating procedures (Committee on Homeland Security, 2006a: 219; cf. Cooper and Block, 2006: 87).

86. Committee on Homeland Security (2006a: 177–178, 218–219).

87. Committee on Homeland Security (2006a: 177).

88. Committee on Homeland Security (2006b: 8).

89. Select Bipartisan Committee (2006a: 66).

90. The NDMS is the "coordinated partnership between DHS, HHS, DOD, and the Department of Veterans Affairs established for the purpose of responding to the needs of victims of a public health emergency. NDMS provides medical response assets and the movement of patients to health care facilities where definitive medical care is received when required" (Department of Homeland Security, 2004: 69).

91. Select Bipartisan Committee (2006a: 271); Committee on Homeland Security (2006a: 185–186).

92. Committee on Homeland Security (2006a: 180). Department of Health and Human Services officials had directed the Oklahoma team to Louisiana after speaking with the director of the New Orleans Health Department, who on August 28 requested medical assistance (Committee on Homeland Security, 2006a: 185–186). Only a day earlier, the New Orleans Health Department declined an offer of federal medical assistance, given that the shelter facility at the Superdome was expected to house "a few thousand people" for no longer than two days (McQuaid and Schleifstein, 2006: 181).

93. NDMS team members later attributed deployment delays to poorly articulated deployment procedures and critical personnel shortfalls (Miller et al., 2005; McQuaid and Schleifstein, 2006: 323). Senate investigators found fault with FEMA's training and exercise program and its headquarters- and field-level management support for the NDMS team (Committee on Homeland Security, 2006a: 176–177, 219). These staffing challenges had in fact been recognized during the 2004 hurricane season, though FEMA had been unable to secure adequate funding in the interim to address them (Committee on Homeland Security 2006a: 219).

94. Carmona (2005); Federal Emergency Management Agency (2006); Select Bipartisan Committee (2006a: 268, 273–274); Committee on Homeland Security (2006a: 187, 405, 410, 418, 420–421).

95. Committee on Homeland Security (2006c: 1, 8).

96. Committee on Homeland Security (2007e).

97. This decision was made based on Honoré's general familiarity with hurricanes and his experiences during the 2004 hurricane season. Honoré, a Louisiana native, recognized Hurricane Katrina's catastrophic potential and therefore was intent on being in a position to move quickly into the area after landfall (Committee of Homeland Security, 2006a: 33, 188).

98. Committee of Homeland Security (2006a: 188).

99. Military commanders typically only have the authority to independently deploy units under their command if these moves are designated as exercises (Committee of Homeland Security, 2006a: 188).

100. Committee of Homeland Security (2007d).

101. Committee of Homeland Security (2006a: 419, 425, 479).

102. Committee of Homeland Security (2006a: 480).

103. Select Bipartisan Committee (2006a: 344).

104. Select Bipartisan Committee (2006a: 344).

105. The White House (2006: 29); Brinkley (2006: 17). The Superdome's suitability as a shelter was in question prior to landfall (Dyson, 2006: 59). Numerous problems were reported at the stadium during Hurricane Georges, when the site served as a temporary home to as many as 25,000 residents. Afterward, officials considered sheltering only the special needs population at the site (Hallowell, 2005: 172). The city subsequently made renovations to the facility and augmented stockpiles of emergency supplies. Meanwhile, the Red Cross refused to approve the Superdome as a suitable shelter location, citing the fact that it was situated well within the city's flood zone (McQuaid and Schleifstein, 2006: 146).

106. After the storm, several FEMA officials complained that the agency had seriously underestimated Hurricane Katrina's severity. For instance, interviews with FEMA personnel at the NRCC suggested that preparations were proceeding at a relatively slow pace prior to landfall, despite warnings concerning the storm's catastrophic potential (Cooper and Block, 2006: 100).

107. Cooper and Block (2006: 99); Sullivan (2005).

108. Cooper and Block (2006: 100).

109. Committee on Homeland Security (2006a: 154, 172).

110. Cooper and Block (2006: 101); Brinkley (2006: 37).

111. Brown apparently also talked offline to the governors "to make sure the governors weren't going to tell me something privately that maybe they didn't want to share publicly, and they seemed

satisfied at that point with the help they were getting" (The White House, 2006: 29; Cooper and Block, 2006: 101–102).

112. Select Bipartisan Committee (2006a: 59).

113. Select Bipartisan Committee (2006a: 59, 62, 64).

114. Jackson Barracks is just what its name suggests—a barracks for activated LANG troops. A LANG colonel stationed at the facility during Hurricane Katrina explained that as a boy living there with his family, he did not recall ever seeing any serious flooding in the wake of hurricanes (Van Heerden and Bryan, 2006: 99; McQuaid and Schleifstein, 2006: 195–196).

115. Brinkley (2006: 116).

116. Committee on Homeland Security (2007f; 2006a: 597).

117. The White House (2006: 35).

118. Bender and O'Brien (2005).

119. Brinkley (2006: 42).

120. Committee on Homeland Security (2007e; 12).

121. According to a senior NOPD official, the NOPD's Emergency Preparation Plan "[was] reviewed and revised annually prior to hurricane season. The plan outline[d] the requirements, duties and responsibilities of each respective bureau chief and major command within the department." However, Senate investigators found that most NOPD personnel were unfamiliar with the plan, which was first drafted in 2004 (Committee on Homeland Security, 2007e: 71). The NOPD failed to conduct an "exercise to familiarize officers with the plan" (Select Bipartisan Committee, 2006a: 245).

122. Bender and O'Brien (2005); Brinkley (2006: 117).

123. A senior LANG official explained later that the decision not to deploy high-water vehicles around the city was made on the assumption that Jackson Barracks would not flood (Committee on Homeland Security, 2007f: 26–27).

124. Committee on Homeland Security (2007f: 4).

125. Committee on Homeland Security (2007g: 28).

126. The White House retroactively approved the request the following day. Congressional Research Service (2005: CRS-5, CRS-6); Select Bipartisan Committee (2006a: 63; 2006b: 80–83).

127. Cooper and Block (2006: 112). For a transcript, see Hurricane Katrina Aug. 28, 2005, video conference (2009).

128. Committee on Homeland Security (2007b: 95); Gaouette (2006).

129. Hurricane Katrina Aug. 28, 2005, video conference (2009).

130. Committee on Homeland Security (2007b: 106).

131. Cooper and Block (2006: 114).

132. We were unable to locate the actual video. For the full transcript, see the Senate Committee's hearing of the governors of Louisiana and Mississippi (Committee on Homeland Security, 2007b: 93–131; quotes can be also be found in Select Bipartisan Committee, 2006a: 432–434).

133. Committee on Homeland Security (2007b: 128).

134. Committee on Homeland Security (2007b: 65, 129).

135. Horne (2006: 52).

136. Committee on Homeland Security (2006a: 6, 412–413).

137. Cain (2005); Zuschlag (2006).

138. Brinkley (2006: 627).

139. Brinkley (2006: 40–41).

140. Select Bipartisan Committee (2006b: 89). Brinkley (2006: 78) mentions 900 Guardsmen.

141. Juvenile Justice Project of Louisiana (2006: 10).

142. Juvenile Justice Project of Louisiana (2006: 10).

143. Nagin and Blanco (2005).

144. Juvenile Justice Project of Louisiana (2006: 9).

145. Fox (1997); Juvenile Justice Project of Louisiana (2006: 10).

146. Baum (2006).

147. Cooper and Block (2006: 124).

148. McQuaid and Schleifstein (2006: 172).

149. Becker (2005). As pleasant as the weather was that weekend, Horne argues that dire warnings were incompatible with what local residents were experiencing. Many pursued outdoor activities, ignorant of ongoing media coverage of the storm's approach (Horne, 2006: 14).

150. Cooper and Block (2006: 107). This would be only the second occasion on which Mayfield had ever called a politician. He reportedly "wanted to be able to go to sleep knowing [he] had done all that [he] could" (Carney et al., 2005; cf. Horne, 2006: 30).

151. Immediately after speaking with Mayfield, Governor Blanco called the mayor, then at dinner with his wife and child at a local restaurant, to advise him to expect a call from Mayfield. Nagin, unfamiliar with Mayfield at the time, received a call soon thereafter from the NHC director (Committee on Homeland Security, 2007b: 139–140).

152. Committee on Homeland Security (2007b: 139–140).

153. McQuaid and Schleifstein (2006: 178).

154. Select Bipartisan Committee (2006a: 109); Committee on Homeland Security (2007b: 139; 2006a: 5). Authorities did not provide adequate information in languages other than English.

155. Brinkley (2006: 40); Committee on Homeland Security (2007b: 139).

156. The White House (2006: 26).

157. Van Heerden and Bryan (2006: 50).

158. Brinkley (2006: 625–626). The mayor's tone during this and other appearances on August 27 was less pronounced than that of officials in other parishes. For instance, the mayor of Kenner, Louisiana, west of the city and home to the New Orleans airport, wrote on the municipality's official website, "Residents of Kenner! I AM URGING, I AM BEGGING YOU TO LEAVE TOWN NOW! . . . THIS IS A KILLER STORM" (McQuaid and Schleifstein, 2006: 172).

159. Brinkley (2006: 34).

160. The decision to evacuate hospitals in Greater New Orleans typically rested with the facility administrator. The Louisiana Hospital Association required that all facilities maintain emergency plans but provided little guidance to administrators in making the choice between evacuation and sheltering in place. This decision had been made historically based on the size of the temporal window of opportunity in which evacuation was feasible and on budgetary considerations (Committee on Homeland Security, 2007a; Rodriguez et al. 2006; Committee on Homeland Security, 2006a: 268). The cost of evacuating hospitals, particularly those operated privately, was and remains enormous. Unlike their public counterparts, private facility administrators were not eligible for reimbursement by the federal government for increased operating expenses or lost revenue.

As a result, cost/risk analyses typically yielded the conclusion that "it [made] the most economic sense to ride out [the] storm and protect patients within the hospital rather than evacuate them" (Select Bipartisan Committee, 2006a: 268–269).

161. Committee on Homeland Security (2006a: 248); Nagin and Blanco (2005).

162. Select Bipartisan Committee (2006a: 105).

163. Select Bipartisan Committee (2006a: 105).

164. Levinson (2006: 1, 2–4, 8, 16–17, 20).

165. McQuaid and Schleifstein (2006: 176); Select Bipartisan Committee (2006a: 294).

166. Donchess (2008); Steiner (2005: 40).

167. Committee on Homeland Security (2007a: 33).

168. Committee on Homeland Security (2007a: 33).

169. Committee on Homeland Security (2007a: 33).

170. Committee on Homeland Security (2007b: 140); Select Bipartisan Committee (2006a: 109).

171. Committee on Homeland Security (2007g: 10).

172. Brodie et al. (2006: 1404).

173. CNN (2014a).

174. Select Bipartisan Committee (2006a: 110).

175. Van Heerden and Bryan (2006: 60).

176. Office of the Press Secretary (2005b).

177. Brinkley (2006: 100–1).

178. Bender and O'Brien (2005).

179. Committee on Homeland Security (2007e: 12).

180. Committee on Homeland Security (2007b: 139). A former Office of Homeland Security and Public Safety director helped organize Operation Brother's Keeper, a faith-based hurricane evacuation initiative. However, the program was still in the planning phase as of August 2005 (Horne, 2006: 202; Committee on Homeland Security, 2006a: 248–249).

181. Committee on Homeland Security (2006a: 85). While the city had a considerable degree of administrative control over the RTA, it had none whatsoever over the cash-strapped local school district, which operated a fleet of hundreds of buses. As such, they were not accounted for in the city's planning. At least 200 of the school district's buses would flood after landfall (McQuaid and Schleifstein, 2006: 146; Committee on Homeland Security, 2007g: 31).

182. Glasser and Grunwald (2005b); Committee on Homeland Security (2006a: 85–87). The New Orleans Office of Emergency Preparedness had long recognized the need to designate drivers as "essential personnel," thus precluding them, a full two years earlier, from evacuating ahead of oncoming hurricanes, but had not determined how this would be most effectively accomplished. These efforts might have proceeded more smoothly had the city finalized long-term employment contracts with RTA drivers, who typically worked at low hourly wages. Such contracts might have included clauses requiring drivers to assist during evacuation while at the same time guaranteeing drivers' families transportation out of the city (McQuaid and Schleifstein, 2006: 145). That the city might be faced with a shortage of drivers was common knowledge among state and federal officials present during the Hurricane Pam exercise (Committee on Homeland Security, 2006a: 113).

183. Brinkley (2006: 91, 92); Van Heerden and Bryan (2006: 61).

184. Select Bipartisan Committee (2006a: 64).

185. City officials later claimed that the apparent undersupplying of the Superdome was intentional—an uncomfortable shelter experience, they argued, would be a disincentive for residents to stay around for the next hurricane (Carney et al., 2005; Committee on Homeland Security, 2006a: 152; Select Bipartisan Committee, 2006a: 117, 279–280).

186. At least 50 weapons of various types were seized by the National Guard and police (Brinkley, 2006: 627; Cooper and Block, 2006: 118; Select Bipartisan Committee, 2006a: 117).

187. Arendt and Hess (2006: 13). Those hospitals that would not be evacuated completely by landfall had in the days prior to landfall worked to discharge less critically ill patients; stock up food, water, blood, and medical supplies; and acquire extra fuel for electrical generators. "The general expectation was that the hospital[s] would return to more or less normal operations after four days or so" (Rodriguez et al., 2006).

188. Rodriguez et al. (2006).

189. The Comprehensive Emergency Management Plan made no mention whatsoever of pets. Meanwhile, the state Emergeny Operations Plan as formulated at the time provided an appendix entitled "Animal Management in Disasters," which only recommended that animal health professionals "coordinate with the Louisiana Shelter Task Force on the sheltering of companion animals." The National Response Plan made mention of animals in disaster but only to the extent that they might be carriers of contractible diseases (Louisiana Office of Homeland Security and Emergency Preparedness, 2005: ESF 11-7, ESF 11-9; Department of Homeland Security, 2004).

190. Committee on Homeland Security (2007g: 5–6).

191. See Brown's personal reflections in his book *Deadly Indifference* (Brown and Schwarz, 2011).

192. Treaster and Goodnough (2005).

193. Treaster and Goodnough (2005).

194. The White House (2006: 25).

195. Brinkley (2006: 60).

196. Katrina was preceded that year by Hurricanes Cindy (Category 1), Dennis (Category 4), Emily (Category 5), and Irene (Category 2).

197. Select Bipartisan Committee (2006a: 59).

198. Cooper and Block (2006: 119).

3. UNDERSTANDING THE UNIMAGINABLE: WHY COLLECTIVE SENSE MAKING FAILED

1. For instance, the *New York Times* reported that "Hurricane Katrina pounded the Gulf Coast with devastating force at daybreak on Monday, sparing New Orleans the catastrophic hit that had been feared but inundating parts of the city and heaping damage on neighboring Mississippi, where it killed dozens, ripped away roofs, and left coastal roads impassable" (Brinkley, 2006: 332; Whoriskey and Gugliotta, 2005; Treaster and Zernike, 2005).

2. Van Heerden and Bryan (2006: 83).

3. Marshall (2005).

4. Marshall (2005).

5. For a situational awareness timeline on the day of landfall, see Committee on Homeland Security (2007c: 206–210). The Senate Committee report also gives an overview of the reports received and issued by the National Weather Service, the Homeland Security Operations Center, state police, and the White House (Committee on Homeland Security, 2006a: 304–307).

6. Cooper and Block (2006: 133). It apparently took even longer for government agencies to discover the nearly complete devastation in St. Bernard Parish (this reportedly did not happen until 47 Canadian Mounties arrived on Wednesday, say Cooper and Block [2006: 181]).

7. Brinkley (2006: 395–396).

8. Brinkley (2006: 540); Cooper and Block (2006: 205). See Siegel (2005) for the NPR radio fragment. For a transcript of the interview, see Gura (2010).

9. Cooper and Block (2006: xiv).

10. Weick (1995).

11. Select Bipartisan Committee (2006a: 224).

12. Select Bipartisan Committee (2006a: 224).

13. See Woods (2005) on the hindsight bias phenomenon.

14. Rosenthal et al. (1989; 2001).

15. Leonard and Howitt (2009).

16. Cooper and Block (2006: xiv).

17. Media are the exception: their routine processes are particularly well geared toward crisis sense making (Miller and Goidel, 2009; Miller and Roberts 2014). Yet even the media frequently got it wrong during that first week (see chapter 5).

18. Turner (1978); Boin et al. (2016).

19. Select Bipartisan Committee (2006a: 168).

20. Brinkley (2006: 628).

21. Select Bipartisan Committee (2006a: 163–164).

22. BellSouth lost 33 of its call-routing centers. The company had never previously experienced water damage at even one such center (Committee on Homeland Security, 2006a: 289).

23. Bamberger and Kumins (2005: CRS4).

24. House investigators estimate that as many as "20 million telephone calls did not go through" on August 30 (Select Bipartisan Committee, 2006a: 164). Many 911 operators had themselves evacuated the city with their families, further reducing call management capacity (Committee on Homeland Security, 2006: 292).

25. Committee on Homeland Security (2007e).

26. Select Bipartisan Committee (2006a: 164); State of Louisiana (2006: 34, 40).

27. Select Bipartisan Committee (2006a: 164); Committee on Homeland Security (2006a: 295–296).

28. Committee on Homeland Security (2006a: 290–291).

29. Committee on Homeland Security (2006a: 292–295).

30. Select Bipartisan Committee (2006a: 167–168).

31. Louisiana had received federal funding to supply local offices of emergency operations with satellite telephone capabilities since 1999. Up until 2004, the state paid a $65 monthly fee for each of these units. Among southeastern Louisiana parishes, only Jefferson, Orleans, and Plaquemines

Parishes continued to pay the fee after that date. All other phones were returned to the state and/or the service provider (Select Bipartisan Committee, 2006a: 172–173).

32. Federal Emergency Management Agency (2006: 25).

33. Besides supporting its own responders, FEMA was specifically charged with supporting "the JFO [Joint Field Office] and video teleconferences; coordinating on-site use of federal radio frequencies; disseminating warnings; and coordinating with ESF-2 on the use of DHS telecommunications assets" (Department of Homeland Security, Office of the Inspector General, 2006: 77–78). See also Cooper and Block (2006: 53); Select Bipartisan Committee (2006a: 166, 168–169); Committee on Homeland Security (2006a).

34. Select Bipartisan Committee (2006a: 167–169); Committee on Homeland Security (2006a: 293–294).

35. Committee on Homeland Security (2006a: 294).

36. Cooper and Block (2006: 213). The Senate report (Committee on Homeland Security, 2006a: 178, 294) suggests that Red October never made it to New Orleans due to the flooding. Other reports did place Red October in the city. The discrepancy in reporting may be due to timing: the Senate report may have missed that Red October eventually made it to New Orleans (as we interpret the data). It is not clear when exactly the truck arrived.

37. Committee on Homeland Security (2006a: 178, 288, 378); Federal Emergency Management Agency (2006: 27).

38. Brinkley (2006: 258). FEMA almost moved one of the few officials with a clear idea about the situation out of the city. At the conclusion of the Monday 9:00 p.m. call, the deputy federal coordinating officer to Louisiana ordered Bahamonde to prepare to exit the city; he was to be replaced by a FEMA ERT-A team led by Phil Parr, who was then preparing to deploy to the Superdome (Cooper and Block, 2006: 148).

39. Warrick (2005).

40. Select Bipartisan Committee (2006a: 95).

41. Brinkley (2006: 235–236).

42. Cooper and Block report that the local Coast Guard commander was initially unwilling to allow the use of a US Coast Guard helicopter for any purpose but lifesaving. Bahamonde reportedly resorted to "dropping the president's name" in order to finally persuade the commander to grant him dedicated access to a helicopter for a 10-minute tour of the city on the day of landfall (Cooper and Block, 2006: 144–145).

43. Committee on Homeland Security (2006a: 237, 276).

44. Select Bipartisan Committee (2006a: 140, 56); Committee on Homeland Security (2006a: 56).

45. According to Senate investigators, the telephone in the mayor's hotel room at the Hyatt Regency where he chose to shelter prior to landfall could only sporadically be used to make calls and would not accept any incoming calls. Email capabilities at the Hyatt Regency were also very limited (Committee on Homeland Security, 2006a: 287).

46. Forman (2007: 53–57).

47. LOHSEP director Ebbert could not explain why the mayor decided to move from the 9-story city hall building to the 27-story Hyatt Regency (Brinkley, 2006: 108–109; McQuaid and Schleifstein, 2006: 200). Nagin later argued that relocating was appropriate given the center's outdated

infrastructure and the likelihood that it would become cramped as more federal and state officials converged on the city (Baum, 2006; Committee on Homeland Security, 2007g: 15).

48. Kettl (2006: 285); Thomas (2005b).

49. Mann (2015).

50. Baum (2006); Committee on Homeland Security (2007g). As the phones did not work, some of his aides had to make the swim to reach the mayor (Forman, 2007).

51. Brinkley (2006: 241).

52. Forman (2007: 88).

53. The White House (2006: 37).

54. Brinkley (2006: 205).

55. Select Bipartisan Committee (2006a: 246).

56. Select Bipartisan Committee (2006a: 478). There are many reports on the marred reputation of the NOPD ("Timeline: NOPD's long history of scandal," 2011); Select Bipartisan Committee (2006a: 478–479); Perlstein and Philbin (1994); Mustian (2014). A *New York Times* article described the New Orleans police force as "a loose confederation of gangsters terrorizing sections of the city" (Pennington, 1996).

57. Brinkley (2006: 49, 203, 365, 384–385, 475).

58. Select Bipartisan Committee (2006a: 247).

59. Dewan (2006).

60. Brinkley (2006: 509–511).

61. Brinkley (2006: 300).

62. This police command post was established "absent instructions from superiors" and without any initial coordination with the EOC in Baton Rouge, due to poor communications (Committee on Homeland Security, 2007f: 15; Select Bipartisan Committee, 2006a: 258). Over the coming days, the activities of a number of federal, state, and local authorities conducting land-based search and rescue operations in the city were coordinated from this site (Select Bipartisan Committee, 2006a: 258).

63. Baum (2006).

64. Brinkley (2006: 140–141, 187, 205–206).

65. Committee on Homeland Security (2006a: 23).

66. Brinkley (2006: 207, 300, 509). All NOPD officers are required to reside within the city limits, so a majority of the city's officers were personally affected by Katrina (Select Bipartisan Committee, 2006a: 246).

67. Brinkley (2006: 510).

68. Warren J. Riley testified before Congress that "it is true that about 147 officers abandoned their positions. However, they are no longer a part of the New Orleans Police Department" (The White House, 2006: 37). Ninety percent of the 1,668 force remained on duty (Committee on Homeland Security, 2006a: 441). At a Friday press conference, Henry Whitehorn of the Louisiana State Police explained that NOPD officers were quitting because they were being shot at (Brinkley, 2006: 301, 509; see also chapter 5).

69. Turner (1978); Catino (2013).

70. Boin and Renaud (2013).

71. Committee on Homeland Security (2006a: 239n4).

72. Select Bipartisan Committee (2006a: 141). But this did not happen in the case of Katrina, according to deputy homeland security adviser Ken Rapuano: "We don't do operations at the White House," Rapuano testified. "We're a transit site for information." Select Bipartisan Committee (2006a: 141).

73. Committee on Homeland Security (2007b: 143).

74. Brinkley (2006: 285, 316).

75. Major General Bennett Landreneau reportedly still thought the National Guard could handle the situation (Cooper and Block, 2006: 166–167).

76. Kirkpatrick and Shane (2005). The House report also cites the *New York Times* article when confirming that Brown asked the White House to take over on Tuesday (Select Bipartisan Committee 2006a: 143); see also Brinkley (2006: 370).

77. The HSOC is assigned primary responsibility for information collection and sharing at the federal level. Both the National Response Coordination Center and the FEMA operations center are obligated to feed information upward to the HSOC, which in turn issues National Situation Updates, HSOC spot reports, and National Situation Reports ("sitreps"). Sitreps are issued twice daily, at 5:00 a.m. and 5:00 p.m. (Committee on Homeland Security, 2006a: 303). According to the HSOC director, there was no specific trigger prior to Hurricane Katrina as to when either spot reports or sitreps should initially be issued, nor any guidance as to how often they should be released: "We call the White House [Situation Room] and say, 'Look, it's getting near. How about we give you probably 12 hours or 24 hours out, we'll give you the first SITREP telling you what the preparations are that are taking place for this before it hits?' And then . . . we decide whether it's going to be every six, every 12, or every 24 hours, depending on the size of the storm or the . . . information to be passed" (Broderick, 2006).

78. Ward et al. (2006: 65).

79. Committee on Homeland Security (2007c: 109).

80. Committee on Homeland Security (2007c: 66).

81. All preceding quotes are from the Committee on Homeland Security (2006a: 305).

82. Spot reports were intended to announce "breaking news." According to Senate investigators, numerous spot reports would be issued in the coming days, though decision makers reportedly underutilized them. The reason may have been that "[officials] viewed the sitreps as more authoritative than the Spot Reports" (Committee on Homeland Security, 2006a: 304).

83. Committee on Homeland Security (2006a: 672, 695n33).

84. The White House (2006: 36).

85. Select Bipartisan Committee (2006b: 127–128); Committee on Homeland Security (2006a: 309).

86. Select Bipartisan Committee (2006a: 140).

87. The White House (2006: 36).

88. Cooper and Block (2006: 164).

89. Cooper and Block (2006: 176).

90. McQuaid and Schleifstein (2006: 299).

91. Cooper and Block (2006: 178, 183); Committee on Homeland Security (2006a: 311).

92. Cooper and Block (2006: 183).

93. Committee on Homeland Security (2007c: 70).

94. Cooper and Block (2006: 156).

95. Committee on Homeland Security (2007c: 63).

96. Committee on Homeland Security (2007c: 67).

97. The original source for the quote is an interview conducted by Senate committee staff on January 19, 2006. We were unable to locate this interview. Parts of the quote can be found in different sources: "We have floods in Pennsylvania all the time. We have floods in New Jersey all the time. Every time there's a hurricane, there's a flood" is cited in Cooper and Block (2006: 132). "So, you know, to say that there is flooding in a particular part of town is a normal expectation of what's happening in a hurricane" is taken from Committee on Homeland Security (2006a: 317n50).

98. Committee on Homeland Security (2007c: 72).

99. Cooper and Block (2006: 149).

100. Broderick (2006).

101. Cooper and Block (2006: 132, 133).

102. Cooper and Block (2006: 164).

103. Committee on Homeland Security (2007c: 53). To his credit, Broderick—who initially did not know the difference between the Superdome and the Convention Center—told Wendell Shingler (FPS) on Thursday to keep an eye on the Convention Center. Shingler visited the Convention Center and reported that the people there were tired, scared, and hungry. This may be one instance in which Broderick understood the situation at the Convention Center much better than other administrators.

104. Broderick (2006).

105. Cooper and Block (2006: 149).

106. Note also the following statement made by Broderick during his hearing: "If they were urgent messages that needed to be conveyed, I would have thought they would have called and not sent an e-mail. That person may not, for whatever reason, have been near their computer. I had 500 to 600 e-mails on my computer" (Committee on Homeland Security, 2007c: 75).

107. Committee on Homeland Security (2007c: 75).

108. The White House would grow increasingly impatient with the HSOC as the week progressed. By the morning of September 1, the White House was calling for less "stale" reports, which were seen as wasting the White House staff's time (Cooper and Block, 2006: 182, 197–198, 201).

109. Committee on Homeland Security (2006a: 304).

110. Select Bipartisan Committee (2006a: 3).

111. McQuaid and Schleifstein (2006: 214–215); Office of the Press Secretary (2005c); Office of the Press Secretary (2005b); Committee on Homeland Security (2006a: 236–237).

112. Cooper and Block (2006: 139).

113. Select Bipartisan Committee (2006a: 140); Committee on Homeland Security (2006a: 484).

114. Typically, the HSOC director himself accompanied the HSOC's morning sitrep and a scheduled briefing on weekdays to meet the DHS secretary. On Saturdays and Sundays, the HSOC typically delivered a "briefing book" to the DHS secretary's residence. According to the HSOC director, in the event of an early-morning departure from Washington, Chertoff "should have gotten [a 6:00 a.m. sitrep presented in a briefing book] to read." The sitrep issued during the early morning of August 30 described extensive flooding and levee breaches both in and around New Orleans (Broderick, 2006).

115. Committee on Homeland Security (2007c: 63).

116. Committee on Homeland Security (2007c: 63–64).

117. Committee on Homeland Security (2007c: 63).

118. Committee on Homeland Security (2007c: 75).

119. Broderick (2006).

120. Committee on Homeland Security (2007c: 106).

121. Committee on Homeland Security (2007c: 15).

122. Committee on Homeland Security (2007c: 14).

123. Committee on Homeland Security (2007c: 15).

124. Committee on Homeland Security (2007c: 24).

125. Cooper and Block (2006: 170).

126. Committee on Homeland Security (2007c: 67).

127. Select Bipartisan Committee (2006a: 133).

128. Committee on Homeland Security (2007c: 207).

129. Committee on Homeland Security (2007c: 207).

130. Select Bipartisan Committee (2006a: 142, 377).

131. The importance of speed in the information flow was later downplayed: "Confirmation of a full breach would not have changed anything we would have done," Rapuano said. "We weren't going to repair the levees overnight, and search and rescue was already operating in full gear, regardless" (Select Bipartisan Committee, 2006a: 142).

132. Select Bipartisan Committee (2006a: 377). We assume that the DHS watch officer who sent information to the White House was stationed at the HSOC. We base this assumption on this comment by the Senate Committee: "DHS produced to the Committee documents from the Senior Watch Officer (SWO) at the HSOC on the day of landfall but did not produce documents from the individual desk officers at the HSOC" (Committee on Homeland Security, 2006: 315n12).

133. Select Bipartisan Committee (2006a: 3).

134. Brown later testified that he spoke with White House officials as many as "thirty times." He said he had no trouble getting through to senior decision makers: "I had no problem picking up the phone and getting hold of Chertoff or Andy Card or Joe Hagin, or the President; I don't have those problems" (Select Bipartisan Committee, 2006a: 143).

135. Committee on Homeland Security (2007c: 17); Committee on Homeland Security (2006a: 680).

136. Committee on Homeland Security (2006a: 672).

137. Committee on Homeland Security (2007c: 178).

138. Coates (2012); Kahneman (2011).

139. Select Bipartisan Committee (2006a: 206).

140. Rivlin (2016: 34).

141. Forman (2007: 90, 96).

142. Brinkley (2006: 352).

143. Brinkley (2006: 527).

144. Brinkley (2006: 570).

145. According to Nagin, "I let all my emotions out during that radio interview. Afterward, I said to myself, 'Oh, my God, I have really screwed up.' I have basically called out a President and

a southern governor. Maybe the CIA will swoop in and do some secret poisoning and I'll be dead in two weeks. . . . I was just being real. I was just crying out for all the people of New Orleans" (Fussman, 2006: 100).

146. Forman (2007: 97).

147. Crimes after Katrina may have been overblown (2005).

148. Forman (2007: 125).

149. Brinkley (2006: 388); see also Pollard and Lee (2006). Compass later explained his appearance and behavior: "I was working around the clock with no sleep whatsoever. I was on the front line. I was only human. People started saying I was drunk or on drugs. I wasn't. The only medication I was on was prescription stuff for my glaucoma. And I had recently had a hand operation. I had twenty-some stitches. I was trying to keep it clean but no painkillers" (Brinkley, 2006: 282).

150. Brinkley (2006: 536).

151. Brinkley (2006: 272).

152. Brinkley (2006: 395).

153. Select Bipartisan Committee (2006a: 143).

154. The White House (2006: 35); Cooper and Block (2006: 136–137).

155. Broderick (2006).

156. Committee on Homeland Security (2007c: 66, 78).

157. Committee on Homeland Security (2006a: 306).

158. Committee on Homeland Security (2006a: 306).

159. McQuaid and Schleifstein (2006: 211).

160. Cooper and Block (2006: 139).

161. Cooper and Block (2006: 139).

162. Cooper and Block (2006: 142).

163. Cooper and Block (2006: 142).

164. Committee on Homeland Security (2007c: 208).

165. Committee on Homeland Security (2006d: 66).

166. Committee on Homeland Security (2007c: 288–290).

167. Cooper and Block (2006: 137).

168. Parker et al. (2009: 209).

169. Committee on Homeland Security (2007c: 67).

170. See Dror (2001) on the inconceivability of modern crises.

171. Kahneman (2011: 14); cf. Klayman and Ha (1987); Nickerson (1998); Tetlock (2005).

172. Kahneman (2011: 45).

173. See Brinkley (2006: 172).

174. Committee on Homeland Security (2007c: 15).

175. Cooper and Block (2006: 183–184).

176. Wagenaar had assumed command only six weeks earlier, after serving several years in South Korea. He was still unfamiliar with the local geography and existing flood control infrastructure (Cooper and Block, 2006: 140).

177. Lee and Collins (2006: 1128).

178. O'Byrne (2006).

179. O'Byrne (2006).

180. Committee on Homeland Security (2006b: 6); McQuaid and Schleifstein (2006: 212).

181. Cooper and Block (2006: 136).

182. McQuaid and Schleifstein (2006: 214).

183. Cooper and Block (2006: 144–145).

184. Committee on Homeland Security (2006b: 6).

185. Committee on Homeland Security (2006b: 7).

186. Cooper and Block (2006: 147–148); McQuaid and Schleifstein (2006: 231).

187. Select Bipartisan Committee (2006a: 142).

188. Committee on Homeland Security (2007c: 25); Cooper and Block (2006: 147); McQuaid and Schleifstein (2006: 227).

189. Committee on Homeland Security (2007c: 25–26).

190. For Michael Brown's emails, see Office of US Representative Charles Melancon (2005). It is not clear whether times reported are central daylight or eastern standard time.

191. The original email was sent by Michael Heath to Michael Lowder at 11:51 eastern time (Committee on Homeland Security, 2007c: 207).

192. Select Bipartisan Committee (2006c: 114).

193. Cooper and Block (2006: 155–156).

194. Cooper and Block (2006: 158).

195. Broderick (2006).

196. Select Bipartisan Committee (2006a: 377).

197. McClellan (2008: 273); Select Bipartisan Committee (2006a: 143).

198. Cooper and Block (2006: 161).

199. Committee on Homeland Security (2006a: 674).

200. Cooper and Block (2006: 169).

201. Cooper and Block (2006: 173).

202. Office of the Press Secretary (2005d).

203. McClellan (2008: 280).

204. CNN (2014b).

205. The White House (2006: 36).

206. Committee on Homeland Security (2006a: 310).

207. Committee on Homeland Security (2006a: 310).

208. Cooper and Block (2006: 150–151).

209. Cooper and Block (2006: 150).

210. Committee on Homeland Security (2007c: 66–67).

211. "Tracking Hurricane Katrina" (2005).

212. For instance, LOHSEP's Lieutenant Kevin Cowan suggested at 10:00 p.m. on MSNBC that "there's a lot of heavy rain. There was some breaching of the levee system that pushed the water into St. Bernard Parish and into New Orleans proper itself, flooding neighborhoods. Streets are completely flooded. . . . There were some breaches where water was pushed over the top. I am sure there were areas that the levee did fail. We haven't gotten complete reports" (Committee on Homeland Security, 2006a: 309).

213. Fox News announced Monday morning (10:30 a.m.) that at least one levee had broken. The *Times-Picayune* described the devastation and flood dangers accurately. Most other reports downplayed or underplayed the situation.

214. Pvtjokerusmc (2009).

215. Whoriskey and Gugliotta (2005).

216. Aug. 30, 2005: Hurricane Katrina (2014).

217. ABC News (2005b).

4. WHO'S IN CHARGE HERE? COORDINATING A MULTILEVEL RESPONSE

1. Chisholm (1989); Boin and Bynander (2015).

2. Solnit (2010).

3. Select Bipartisan Committee (2006a: 230).

4. Select Bipartisan Committee (2006a: 189).

5. Select Bipartisan Committee (2006a: 189).

6. The White House (2006: 57).

7. Select Bipartisan Committee (2006a: 420).

8. Boin and Bynander (2015).

9. P. Roberts (2013: 130n10).

10. Department of Homeland Security (2004).

11. On February 28, 2003, President Bush issued a directive mandating the development of a new National Response Plan that accounted for the nation's revised threat spectrum and the presence of the new Department of Homeland Security.

12. Sylves (2008); P. Roberts (2013).

13. Department of Homeland Security (2004: 11).

14. Department of Homeland Security, Office of the Inspector General (2006: 23).

15. Committee on Homeland Security (2006a: 552); Cooper and Block (2006: 82).

16. Tierney (2006); Brown and Schwarz (2011).

17. Department of Homeland Security, Office of the Inspector General (2006: 23).

18. A preliminary damage assessment conducted jointly by the affected state and the relevant Regional Response Coordination Center operated by FEMA typically forms the basis for the governor's request. Gubernatorial requests are relatively rare, and may not necessarily result in approved federal assistance. State and local authorities successfully manage hundreds of emergencies and disasters without any federal assistance (Schneider, 2005: 28).

19. The White House (2006: 18).

20. The White House (2006: 12). According to the NRP, the FCO is appointed by the secretary of homeland security (Department of Homeland Security, 2004: 91).

21. Department of Homeland Security (2004: 25).

22. The White House (2006: 42).

23. The NRP of 2004 stated that "pursuant to HSPD-5, as the principal Federal official for domestic incident management, the Secretary of Homeland Security declares Incidents of National Significance" and that "the NRP bases the definition of Incidents of National Significance on situations . . . set forth in HSPD-5" (Department of Homeland Security, 2004: 4).

24. The NRP describes the PFO as "the Federal official designated by the Secretary of Homeland Security to act as his/her representative locally to oversee, coordinate, and execute the Secretary's incident management responsibilities under HSPD-5 for Incidents of National Significance" (Department of Homeland Security, 2004: 71).

25. Bosner (2011).

26. Department of Homeland Security (2004: 43).

27. The White House (2006: 19).

28. Select Bipartisan Committee (2006a: 36).

29. Select Bipartisan Committee (2006a: 137). Some experts later argued that these documents were designed for no-notice or short-notice incidents where anticipatory preparation and coordination with the state under the Stafford Act are not practicable (Select Bipartisan Committee, 2006a: 427). The implication of this reasoning is that Katrina was not an INS.

30. Department of Homeland Security (2005: 5).

31. The White House (2006: 15).

32. Select Bipartisan Committee (2006a: 137).

33. Select Bipartisan Committee (2006a: 203).

34. Select Bipartisan Committee (2006a: 39).

35. The White House (2006: 14).

36. The White House (2006: 15).

37. Select Bipartisan Committee (2006a: 2).

38. Brinkley (2006); Solnit (2009).

39. "The great Cajun Navy" (2016).

40. CBS News (2015); Ball (2016).

41. Committee on Homeland Security (2006a: 29).

42. Committee on Homeland Security (2006a: 29–30).

43. Solnit (2009: 234).

44. Bradshaw and Slonsky (2005).

45. Committee on Homeland Security (2006a: 331–333).

46. There was a National Search and Rescue Plan, intended to provide guidance "for coordinating civil search and rescue . . . services to meet domestic needs and international commitments" (Committee on Homeland Security, 2006a: 345). However, it was not intended for use in the face of "natural or man-made disasters or terrorist incidents; and typical disaster response operations" (Committee on Homeland Security, 2006a: 345). Search and rescue had been discussed during the Hurricane Pam exercise, and a general strategy had been formulated, but many first responders in New Orleans were unfamiliar with the exercise outcomes. Unsurprisingly, redundant sweep patterns were reported (Brinkley, 2006: 211).

47. Committee on Homeland Security (2007e: 12, 25).

48. Cooper and Block suggest that the number of stranded officers might have been reduced had a different duty schedule been employed: "In the run-up to the storm, instead of putting the entire police department on the clock, the city's officers were split into two shifts. The late shift was sent home to rest—a decision that created a big headache after Katrina hit" (2006: 238). A full 80% of NOPD personnel would lose their homes to wind damage and/or flooding in the storm's aftermath. That so many officers lost their homes is attributable in part to a departmental requirement

that officers live in Orleans Parish. Without higher wages, personnel could in many instances only afford cheaper housing in low-lying, flood-prone neighborhoods (Baum, 2006; Nossiter, 2006).

49. Drew (2006).

50. Baum (2006).

51. Committee on Homeland Security (2006a: 8).

52. Committee on Homeland Security (2007f: 4).

53. Select Bipartisan Committee (2006a: 214).

54. Cooper and Block (2006: 126). The US Coast Guard, in preparation for anticipated operations, placed Disaster Assistance Response Teams on standby for deployment to southeastern Louisiana and evacuated its District 8 New Orleans Command Center to Integrated Support Command in St. Louis, Missouri (The White House, 2006: 28).

55. Select Bipartisan Committee (2006a: 190).

56. Brinkley (2006: 210).

57. Cooper and Block (2006: 125).

58. Cooper and Block (2006: 126).

59. Brinkley (2006: 214).

60. Shane and Shanker (2005).

61. Shane and Shanker (2005).

62. Dolinar (2006).

63. Dolinar (2006).

64. Louisiana National Guard (2005: 7).

65. Louisiana National Guard (2005: 5–7).

66. Dolinar (2006).

67. Dolinar (2006).

68. Dolinar (2006).

69. Committee on Homeland Security (2006a: 10). Reinforcements would not arrive in large numbers before Thursday (Shane and Shanker, 2005).

70. Committee on Homeland Security (2007f: 8).

71. Committee on Homeland Security (2006a: 346).

72. Select Bipartisan Committee (2006a: 215).

73. Committee on Homeland Security (2006a: 346).

74. Committee on Homeland Security (2006a: 26–37).

75. Pilots typically did not have instructions as to where they should deposit residents after being rescued. They had to pick a site. By doing so, they were able to conserve fuel, thereby increasing the total number of rescue missions conducted. Pilots gave little apparent consideration to the feasibility of supplying or evacuating these locations (Select Bipartisan Committee, 2006a: 216). Accounts differ concerning the creation of the drop-off site at the Cloverleaf. The Cloverleaf was originally intended as a triage site or, alternatively, a preliminary evacuation site for patients from local hospitals. It was therefore stocked with limited quantities of food, water, and medical supplies (Dunbar, 2006; Select Bipartisan Committee, 2006a: 215–217; Zuschlag, 2006; Committee on Homeland Security, 2006a: 30). As more and more people gathered at the Cloverleaf, questions arose as to who, if anyone, was in command of the nonmedical situation there (Select Bipartisan Committee, 2006a: 363). All patients would be evacuated from the site by August 31, though the

Cloverleaf would continue to attract helicopters carrying rescued residents throughout the coming days. At one point the overpass was reported to contain between 6,000 and 7,000 evacuees (Select Bipartisan Committee, 2006a: 119).

76. See photo of people waiting for assistance on elevated highways at Nielsen (2005).

77. Committee on Homeland Security (2007b: 24).

78. Committee on Homeland Security (2007b: 142, 144); McQuaid and Schleifstein (2006: 222–223); Committee on Homeland Security (2007g). The need to locate additional buses was immediately apparent to state and federal officials upon learning that hundreds of Regional Transit Authority and Orleans Parish School District school buses located in New Orleans had been flooded (Brinkley, 2006: 286; Committee on Homeland Security, 2006a: 22–25).

79. Committee on Homeland Security (2007b: 142). The city also tried. "On Tuesday, the city tried to obtain Regional Transit Authority . . . buses, but they were believed to be flooded and unusable, as were school buses because they were pre-staged in the flood plain. In fact, as many as 200 buses were pre-staged on high ground at the Poland Street Wharf, but that information was never passed from the RTA to city officials" (Committee on Homeland Security, 2006a: 362).

80. Cooper and Block (2006: 104, 121).

81. Committee on Homeland Security (2006a: 361).

82. The White House (2006: 39); Committee on Homeland Security (2007g: 40). According to state coordinating officer Smith, some "bean counter" at FEMA headquarters had altered the state's request for 500 buses, as the number appeared excessive in light of the number of people remaining in the city (Committee on Homeland Security, 2006a: 362).

83. According to the Senate report, "FEMA did not ask DOT to send buses to New Orleans until 1:45 a.m. on Wednesday, August 31, two days after landfall and 36 hours after Brown's agreement to provide them" (Committee on Homeland Security, 2006a: 362). The House report confirms that "the first task order for buses by the federal government to evacuate New Orleans post landfall was not issued until 1:30 a.m. on Wednesday, August 31" (Select Bipartisan Committee, 2006a: 120). See also the testimony of Vincent Pearce (Committee on Homeland Security, 2007g: 40).

84. Committee on Homeland Security (2007c: 48).

85. The Landstar contract was deemed adequate during the particularly active 2004 hurricane season in Florida (Committee on Homeland Security, 2007g: 40; Shorrock, 2006).

86. Martin and Zajac (2005).

87. Committee on Homeland Security (2006a: 363).

88. Select Bipartisan Committee (2006a: 121).

89. Committee on Homeland Security (2007g: 40).

90. Committee on Homeland Security (2006a: 16).

91. Brinkley (2006: 286, 288); Maggi (2005). The Senate report mentions that "the Governor also turned to state resources, asking Leonard Kleinpeter, a special assistant to the Governor and the head of the Office of Community Programs, an agency with contacts in all the parishes, on Tuesday to locate buses, though without authority to commandeer those buses. Kleinpeter and his staff began to line up buses from local school districts and churches on Tuesday" (Committee on Homeland Security, 2006a: 363).

92. Brinkley (2006: 287).

93. Committee on Homeland Security (2007b: 24).

94. Dyson (2006: 101); Select Bipartisan Committee (2006a: 122).

95. The general population reacted more calmly than expected upon learning of the ongoing evacuation effort. Officials faced significant difficulties sorting through a skyrocketing number of residents who claimed to be sick or injured in hopes of being evacuated more quickly (McQuaid and Schleifstein, 2006: 291; Committee on Homeland Security, 2006a: 403).

96. Brinkley (2006: 392).

97. Select Bipartisan Committee (2006a: 121).

98. Committee on Homeland Security (2006a: 362).

99. Broderick (2006).

100. Committee on Homeland Security (2007g: 7); Shorrock (2006).

101. Select Bipartisan Committee (2006a: 121).

102. The White House (2006: 39).

103. Select Bipartisan Committee (2006a: 121).

104. Committee on Homeland Security (2006a: 364).

105. Committee on Homeland Security (2007b: 146).

106. Committee on Homeland Security (2006a: 365).

107. Brinkley (2006: 291); Select Bipartisan Committee (2006a: 122).

108. McQuaid and Schleifstein (2006: 298, 302).

109. Shearer (2005).

110. Gretna's mayor and chief of police were reportedly concerned about the safety of Gretna residents if thousands of New Orleanians were stranded in the town. There were also concerns that authorities would be unable to provide food and water to these people for any extended period (Brinkley, 2006: 470, 633; McQuaid and Schleifstein, 2006: 298, 302; see also Shearer, 2005).

111. Bradshaw and Slonsky (2005); Kopp (2005); Burnett (2005).

112. CNN (2005h); Kopp (2005).

113. Select Bipartisan Committee (2006a: 122).

114. The White House (2006: 39). "Evacuations of the last remaining [people] at the arena were halted before dawn Saturday as authorities diverted buses to help some 25,000 refugees at the New Orleans Convention Center" (The White House, 2006: 39).

115. Civil Contingencies Secretariat (2006: 20–21); Department of Homeland Security, Office of the Inspector General (2006: 36, 40–41).

116. Committee on Homeland Security (2006a: 26–30).

117. This was for state coordinating officer Smith reportedly one of the most disappointing moments in the days after landfall (Cooper and Block, 2006: 192). The JTF-Katrina commander explained later that "reversing the paradigm" by entering the region before his troops misled many: "This was not a classic military operation. . . . I left my staff at home and went forward on the battlefield, which may have given a perception to people when they saw me that all the federal troops were there, which was not the case" (Committee on Homeland Security, 2006a: 513).

118. During this meeting, the Fifth Army's Brigadier General Mark Graham arrived at the EOC from Texas. Graham was reportedly assigned responsibility for evacuation at this meeting (Committee on Homeland Security, 2007d; Committee on Homeland Security, 2006a: 516).

119. Committee on Homeland Security (2007b: 24).

120. Communications difficulties between Baton Rouge and New Orleans precluded state and federal officials at the state EOC from participating in this planning.

121. McQuaid and Schleifstein (2006: 261).

122. Committee on Homeland Security (2007f: 40).

123. Human Rights Watch (2005).

124. See photo of inmates waiting for transportation to other correctional facilities at Telling Their Stories (2018), specifically http://www.tellingtheirstories.org/wp-content/uploads/2010/08/12_20050830_Pool_Katrina_10.jpg?3af599.

125. Unfortunately, neither the Orleans Parish Prison nor the Louisiana Department of Public Safety and Corrections had identified alternative prison facilities in their respective contingency plans (Committee on Homeland Security, 2006a: 444–445).

126. Select Bipartisan Committee (2006b: 296).

127. Select Bipartisan Committee (2006a: 410).

128. Committee on Homeland Security (2006a: 24–25).

129. Select Bipartisan Committee (2006a: 285–287, 294).

130. Paulison (2006). The nursing homes faced the same dire situation, but by law they were responsible for evacuating their residents. The Louisiana Nursing Home Association set up its own rescue missions using buses that it procured on its own.

131. Franco et al. (2006).

132. Franco et al. (2006).

133. Because FEMA typically relied on state and local first responders to coordinate any necessary medical evacuations, no contingency planning existed at the national level to guide FEMA in quickly identifying additional assets in private hands (Federal Emergency Management Agency, 2006: 55).

134. The state's decision to request Acadian's assistance was reportedly based on a number of factors, including Acadian's familiarity with the local geography, regional medical facilities, and facility administrators; a wide variety of available assets, including helicopters, fixed-wing aircraft, and ambulances; and the fact that Acadian possessed an operational communications system (Acadian Ambulance Service, 2005a; Brinkley, 2006: 458; Select Bipartisan Committee, 2006a: 289; Zuschlag, 2006).

135. As of August 2005, Acadian held exclusive service contracts in all parishes in the greater metropolitan New Orleans region with the exception of New Orleans. In the Acadian CEO's estimation, the company might be in a more advantageous position to negotiate a contract later, if not with the local government then at least with medical centers in the city, assuming it successfully carried out the medical evacuation tasking. For this reason, the CEO was prepared to commit considerable company resources without first receiving any assurances that Acadian would be reimbursed (Zuschlag, 2006).

136. Air ambulances typically have a short range, require large amounts of fuel, and have a limited carrying capacity (Committee on Homeland Security, 2007a).

137. Acadian Ambulance Service (2005b).

138. Operators belonging to the Association of Air Medical Services maintain a full 85% of air medical transport capabilities in the US (Select Bipartisan Committee, 2006a: 289; Acadian Ambulance Service, 2005b; Zuschlag, 2006).

139. Zuschlag (2006).

140. Brinkley (2006: 634).

141. Select Bipartisan Committee (2006a: 284).

142. Committee on Homeland Security (2006a: 412).

143. Federal Emergency Management Agency (2006: 44).

144. Federal Emergency Management Agency (2006: 49).

145. Committee on Homeland Security (2006a: 412, 414).

146. Select Bipartisan Committee (2006a: 271).

147. House investigators found that "medical personnel were operating with a limited amount of supplies and a generator with only partial power." As Dr. Hemant Vankawala noted, "All we could do was provide the barest amount of comfort care. We watched many, many people die. We practiced medical triage at its most basic—black tagging the sickest people and culling them from the masses so that they could die in a separate area" (Select Bipartisan Committee, 2006a: 288).

148. Federal Emergency Management Agency (2006: 47).

149. Federal Emergency Management Agency (2006: 47).

150. Miller et al. (2005); Federal Emergency Management Agency (2006: 47).

151. Select Bipartisan Committee (2006a: 123).

152. Copeland (2005: 4).

153. The White House (2006: 40).

154. Federal aviation regulations require that all passengers be listed on the flight manifest. The fact that most evacuees were not ticketed passengers and/or lacked valid identification made the task of manifesting flights "cumbersome" (Federal Emergency Management Agency, 2006: 48). The TSA initially insisted that it be allowed to fly in generators to power x-ray machines at the airport security controls before any flights could be loaded. The TSA later agreed to allow passengers to be screened by hand (Cooper and Block, 2006: 203). Air marshals were flown to New Orleans to provide security on all departing flights (Cooper and Block, 2006: 203).

155. Cooper and Block (2006: 203).

156. Committee on Homeland Security (2006a: 692).

157. Select Bipartisan Committee (2006a: 193).

158. Glasser and Grunwald (2005a); Department of Homeland Security, Office of the Inspector General (2006: 20–21); Select Bipartisan Committee (2006a: 190–191).

159. Select Bipartisan Committee (2006a: 192–193); State of Louisiana (2006: 37).

160. Select Bipartisan Committee (2006a: 193).

161. Select Bipartisan Committee (2006a: 187).

162. Brown (2005).

163. *All Things Considered* (2005).

164. Select Bipartisan Committee (2006b: 77).

165. Select Bipartisan Committee (2006a: 63).

166. The White House (2006: 29).

167. McQuaid and Schleifstein (2006: 238).

168. Brinkley (2006: 279, 282).

169. Brinkley (2006: 283)

170. Cooper and Block (2006: 161).

171. Cooper and Block (2006: 161–162); McQuaid and Schleifstein (2006: 250); Committee on Homeland Security (2006b). This violated official procedures (Nagin should have gone through the state). Brown later argued that this decision was justified, given the extraordinary nature of the event and his lack of confidence in LOHSEP to swiftly address the mayor's needs. Officials argued that this and similar episodes in the coming days were clear albeit unsurprising deviations from ICS; "the political process is often dominant over the ICS process—resulting in duplicative systems" (Committee on Homeland Security, 2006b: 47). Others argued that at least some bypassing of ICS was "understandable" since the mayor could not communicate reliably with officials at the Superdome and EOC at city hall or the state EOC in Baton Rouge.

172. It was understood that FEMA could not deliver resources out of thin air. Dr. Walter Maestri, the Jefferson Parish director of emergency management, said that "he understood that FEMA may not provide help until 48–72 hours later—but then he expected help" (Select Bipartisan Committee, 2006a: 83).

173. Select Bipartisan Committee (2006a: 151); Committee on Homeland Security (2007f).

174. The White House (2006: 43). FEMA deployed several DMATs after landfall: "FEMA activated OR-2 DMAT from Oregon on August 30 and immediately began treating patients when the team arrived at the New Orleans Airport on the afternoon of September 1." However, "by August 31, three DMATs, WA-1, CA-4, and TX-4, had arrived at the New Orleans Airport, where evacuated patients were being received. Eventually, eight DMATs would be stationed there to help provide medical care during the patient movement operations in New Orleans" (Select Bipartisan Committee, 2006a: 271). The Senate report states that "although a number of [medical assistance] teams were mobilized and began moving into the Gulf region, this effort fell far short of needs. By the night before landfall, only four complete Disaster Medical Assistance Teams (DMATs), two partial teams, and a few small five person strike teams—a total of about 250 personnel—were staged in the entire Gulf region, and only one team was deployed in Louisiana. Thus, fewer than 10% of FEMA's 52 DMAT teams were in the region" (Committee on Homeland Security, 2006a: 180).

175. Bourget (2005: 16). Information on the exact deployment of supplies after landfall is hard to come by. On August 31, 2005, Bush stated in his speech in the Rose Garden that "FEMA is moving supplies and equipment into the hardest-hit areas. The Department of Transportation has provided more than 400 trucks to move 1,000 truckloads containing 5.4 million Meals Ready to Eat—or MREs, 13.4 million liters of water, 10,400 tarps, 3.4 million pounds of ice, 144 generators, 20 containers of pre-positioned disaster supplies, 135,000 blankets and 11,000 cots" (Office of the Press Secretary, 2005e). A fact sheet released by the White House on August 31 states, "To date, the Federal Emergency Management Agency (FEMA) has deployed more than 50 Disaster Medical Assistance Teams, more than 25 Urban Search and Rescue task forces, eight swift water rescue teams, and two Incident Support Teams. FEMA is also working to deliver water, ice, meals, medical supplies, generators, tents, and tarps. There are currently more than 1,700 trucks which have been mobilized to move these supplies into position" (Office of the Press Secretary, 2005f).

176. The White House (2006: 48).

177. The White House (2006: 49).

178. Select Bipartisan Committee (2006a: 157); cf. Bosner (2011).

179. McQuaid and Schleifstein (2006: 248).

180. The White House (2006: 17).

181. Department of Homeland Security (2004: 28).

182. Committee on Homeland Security (2006a: 181).

183. Committee on Homeland Security (2007c: 104).

184. Brinkley (2006: 335); The White House (2006: 44).

185. Committee on Homeland Security (2006a: 30).

186. Cooper and Block (2006: 202).

187. Federal Emergency Management Agency (2006: 38); Committee on Homeland Security (2006a: 379).

188. Committee on Homeland Security (2006b: 8); Cooper and Block (2006: 167, 178); Federal Emergency Management Agency (2006: 16).

189. Federal Emergency Management Agency (2006: 16).

190. Federal Emergency Management Agency (2006: 16).

191. Federal Emergency Management Agency (2006: 20).

192. Department of Homeland Security, Office of the Inspector General (2006: 68).

193. Select Bipartisan Committee (2006a: 139).

194. Brinkley (2006: 250, 254, 334–335, 441, 537, 554).

195. The White House (2006: 45).

196. According to Cooper and Block, CEO LINK was only to be activated in the event of a national catastrophe (Cooper and Block, 2006: 159, 263). To the HSOC director's mind, Hurricane Katrina was only a catastrophe after levee breaches had been confirmed. As a result, no effort was made to activate the program. Alternatively, officials either did not know about or simply forgot to activate the program. Many private actors expressed frustration with difficulties locating points of contact within the federal government to offer assistance of various kinds (Brinkley, 2006: 251–252).

197. The White House (2006: 45); Martin and Zajac (2005).

198. Freedburg (2005). The Louisiana Governor's Office of Homeland Security and Emergency Preparedness brought in University of Louisiana professor Ramesh Kolluru, who worked with his team to create software that would allow quick matching of requested and offered assistance. This effort later informed the need for a unique initiative to facilitate cooperation with the private sector during disasters: the Stephenson Disaster Management Institute Center for Business Preparedness, situated at LSU.

199. Cooper and Block (2006: 260–263). In the days and weeks after landfall, Walmart facilities "sheltered police officers and emergency services workers . . . supported hospitals and communities, fed people, provided pharmaceuticals, changed tires on emergency response vehicles, and provided vaccinations to . . . responders and emergency workers" (Cooper and Block, 2006: 260–263; Freedburg, 2005; Horne, 2006: 35). Walmart independently moved certain supplies to the region, intended as stock in its stores but also as donations to local communities. The arrival of these shipments in the New Orleans area attracted widespread media coverage and some comparisons with the speed of the government response (Troy, 2005). In one nationally televised interview, a parish president stated that "[if the] American government would have responded like Wal-Mart has responded, we wouldn't be in this crisis" (Transcript for September 4, 2005).

200. Kelman (2007: 298).

201. Committee on Homeland Security (2006a: 10).

202. The facility would ultimately hold 17,000 evacuees, necessitating the opening of other shelters, first in Houston and later across the state.

203. Select Bipartisan Committee (2006a: 144). The inspector general of DHS had slightly different figures: "Louisiana submitted 47 requests for assistance through FEMA and 520 requests for assistance through EMAC" (Department of Homeland Security, Office of the Inspector General, 2006: 76).

204. Select Bipartisan Committee (2006a: 227).

205. Select Bipartisan Committee (2006a: 145). The deputy FCO in Louisiana, Scott Wells, noted that some state offers of assistance through FEMA were rejected by Louisiana due to concerns over costs.

206. Committee on Homeland Security (2007c: 55); McQuaid and Schleifstein (2006: 309). Brown claims he reached out to DOD as early as Tuesday: "On August 30, we issued a mission assignment to DOD for airlift and for other capabilities. I don't know whether that mission assignment was ever implemented or ever done. But as early as August 30, I made that request back to headquarters for that to be done" (Committee on Homeland Security, 2007c: 45).

207. Committee on Homeland Security (2006a: 377).

208. Committee on Homeland Security (2007c: 103).

209. Select Bipartisan Committee (2006a: 132).

210. Federal Emergency Management Agency (2004; 2005); Associated Press (2004); Bosner (2011).

211. See Moynihan (2012) for a description and analysis of DOD's "culture shift," which led the department to "lean forward" on Tuesday.

212. Committee on Homeland Security (2006a: 485–486).

213. Committee on Homeland Security (2006a: 485).

214. Committee on Homeland Security (2006a: 483, 486, 602). According to Senate investigators, a vocal command is "extremely rare," in part because it permits the bypassing of requirements that assistance requests be evaluated for legality, readiness, lethality, risk, cost, and appropriateness. According to a senior DOD official, "The message from the deputy secretary of defense . . . was to act with a sense of urgency and to minimize paperwork and bureaucracy to the greatest extent possible" (Committee on Homeland Security [2006a]: 475, 486).

215. Committee on Homeland Security (2006a: 498–499).

216. Committee on Homeland Security (2006a: 499).

217. Committee on Homeland Security (2007d: 70).

218. Committee on Homeland Security (2007d: 30). Many FEMA officials were reportedly frustrated that DOD did not immediately accept FEMA's requests for assistance (Broderick, 2006). However, House investigators argued that DOD had in fact acted swiftly to reach a decision. The FEMA officials' frustration suggests that they were "unaware of the planning already under way . . . and . . . possibly [maintained] an unrealistic expectation that acceptance of such a massive mission would result in immediate action" (Select Bipartisan Committee, 2006a: 214).

219. Federal law allows DOD to refuse mission assignments from FEMA (or any other department or agency) if they are deemed to jeopardize the military's ability to carry out its primary national defense mission.

220. Select Bipartisan Committee (2006a: 204).

221. Committee on Homeland Security (2006a: 502).

222. Select Bipartisan Committee (2006a: 201).

223. Select Bipartisan Committee (2006a: 190).

224. Select Bipartisan Committee (2006a: 225).

225. Select Bipartisan Committee (2006a: 225).

226. Select Bipartisan Committee (2006a: 190, 204–205).

227. Committee on Homeland Security (2006a: 562).

228. Committee on Homeland Security (2006a: 509).

229. Select Bipartisan Committee (2006a: 225); The White House (2006: 43).

230. Select Bipartisan Committee (2006a: 219).

231. Brinkley (2006: 567).

232. Rosenthal et al. (1991).

233. Select Bipartisan Committee (2006a: 186–187).

234. The White House (2006: 47).

235. Brinkley (2006: 509).

236. Cooper and Block (2006: 232).

237. Committee on Homeland Security (2006a: 11–12, 587).

238. Cooper and Block (2006: 90).

239. Cooper and Block (2006: 138); Kirkpatrick and Shane (2005); McClellan (2008: 272); McQuaid and Schleifstein (2006: 253).

240. Cooper and Block suggest that Brown felt as though he had "fought for and won the right to deal [directly] with the White House through Chief of Staff Card, without any interference from [DHS secretary] Ridge" (2006: 87).

241. Committee on Homeland Security (2007c: 33).

242. The PFO element of the NRP had only been tested in terrorism-related exercises before Hurricane Katrina; thus "the response to Hurricane Katrina was the first operational use of the PFO" (Department of Homeland Security, Office of the Inspector General, 2006: 28).

243. The White House (2006: 41). Chertoff was later criticized by state and local officials for belatedly declaring an INS. Doing so sooner, they argued, might have allowed for the more prompt deployment of federal assets to the region. Chertoff later rejected this argument, claiming that the federal government had been proactively engaged to an unprecedented extent prior to landfall. More importantly, Chertoff argued that his INS declaration was superfluous; the federal declaration of emergency on August 27 had already accomplished the same results (Committee on Homeland Security, 2007c: 5, 15–17). Senate investigators contest Chertoff's claim (Committee on Homeland Security, 2006a: 555–556). According to the White House, any confusion concerning when the INS declaration was issued might have been due to unclear wording in the NRP (The White House, 2006: 14).

244. Select Bipartisan Committee (2006a: 135–136).

245. Committee on Homeland Security (2006a: 170). In an email exchange between the FEMA director and a FEMA press secretary, the press secretary wrote, "Demote the Under. Sec. to PFO? What about the precedent being set? What does this say about executive management and leadership in the agency? . . . Why would anyone want to be a PFO when at any moment the Under Sec could be sent to the field?" "Exactly," Brown replied (Hsu, 2005).

246. Committee on Homeland Security (2007c: 44).

247. Cooper and Block (2006: 170).

248. Cooper and Block (2006: 170). By 10:00 p.m. on August 30, the two men spoke by telephone. Brown later recounted the conversation: "I met with [Mississippi] Governor Haley Barbour to find out what he needed in Mississippi. I got back on the G5 jet to head to Baton Rouge, and Chertoff caught me on the phone. He said, 'I've been trying to reach you. I'm tired of you flying around everywhere. I want you to go to Baton Rouge and plop your butt down in Baton Rouge and not leave.' I was in the middle of a disaster, attempting to respond, in this case working with the Mississippi governor, and Chertoff was screaming because I hadn't called him back. . . . I was dumbfounded. It was the most ludicrous order" (Brown, 2006).

249. Cooper and Block (2006: 170).

250. Committee on Homeland Security (2007c: 45). This situation was foreseen. A memorandum observed that the "roles of the PFO [principal federal official] and RD [regional director] are relatively new and the precise parameters have not yet been clearly defined or determined" (Committee on Homeland Security, 2007c: 164). The report further noted "significant potential for duplication, inconsistency and confusion" (Committee on Homeland Security, 2007c: 167).

251. Select Bipartisan Committee (2006a: 166). When Brown was appointed PFO on Tuesday, Patrick Rhode became director of FEMA. Rhode had no idea (Committee on Homeland Security, 2007c: 52).

252. Cooper and Block (2006: 189, 202–203).

253. Select Bipartisan Committee (2006a: 204–205).

254. Committee on Homeland Security (2006a: 513).

255. McQuaid and Schleifstein (2006: 221).

256. Select Bipartisan Committee (2006a: 143); Committee on Homeland Security (2006a: 498, 515).

257. Select Bipartisan Committee (2006a: 143).

258. Committee on Homeland Security (2006a: 506–507).

259. Committee on Homeland Security (2006a: 514).

260. Cooper and Block (2006: 167).

261. Committee on Homeland Security (2006a: 515).

262. McQuaid and Schleifstein (2006: 269).

263. Governor Blanco was transferred a number of times within the White House before speaking with an official at the Office of Intergovernmental Affairs. She soon after received a call from the president's homeland security adviser, Fran Townsend. Blanco reportedly explained that "we're desperate, Fran. The situation is so bad. We've got to have boats, helicopters, and especially buses. We've got to have those buses to get people out of there [the Superdome]. Nobody really understands the magnitude of the problem" (McQuaid and Schleifstein, 2006: 270; Brinkley, 2006: 413).

264. Thomas (2005b).

265. Committee on Homeland Security (2007b: 26, 145).

266. Committee on Homeland Security (2007b: 145).

267. Committee on Homeland Security (2006a: 514).

268. During the day, an aide to the governor reported that a prominent New Orleans businessman had told him that he "ha[d] it on very good authority that Karl Rove is directing an effort to put

blame on [Blanco] for mess saying that the reason feds not on ground sooner was that she refused to give up her authority" (Kromm, 2005). Later, David Vitter, a Republican US senator from the state, explained that the White House had been examining the possibility of federalizing the response since receiving the governor's request for federal troops (Brinkley, 2006: 413). However, Vitter's report was suspect. According to McQuaid and Schleifstein, "Vitter was a loyal Republican and popular among Louisiana voters. . . . But Vitter . . . was viewed with some suspicion by his fellow Louisiana politicians. Many saw him as a habitual freelancer, less interested in teamwork than in advancing his own political fortunes" (McQuaid and Schleifstein, 2006: 274). Vitter later claimed that he was merely acting as a neutral go-between. Scott McClellan later confirmed the state's suspicions: "Throughout the first week, [the White House] focused on how poorly prepared and overwhelmed state and local officials had been in responding to the storm" (McClellan, 2008: 283).

269. Chertoff (2005).

270. Committee on Homeland Security (2006a: 516). .

271. Cooper and Block (2006: 207).

272. Committee on Homeland Security (2006a: 518–519).

273. Select Bipartisan Committee (2006a: 206).

274. Committee on Homeland Security (2006a: 518–520).

275. Committee on Homeland Security (2007b: 145).

276. Committee on Homeland Security (2006a: 519).

277. Committee on Homeland Security (2007b: 27); Committee on Homeland Security (2006a: 519).

278. Committee on Homeland Security (2007b: 28).

279. Committee on Homeland Security (2007b: 147).

280. CNN (2005b).

281. McClellan (2008: 284, 286–287).

282. McClellan (2008: 286–287).

283. McClellan (2008: 286–287).

284. Despite the seemingly ad hoc nature of the deliberations, the "dual-hat" arrangement had in fact been applied in the past, during a G-8 summit held in the United States and, later, at the Democratic and Republican National Conventions in 2004 (Committee on Homeland Security, 2006a: 520).

285. Toosi (2007).

286. Committee on Homeland Security (2007b: 149).

287. Cooper and Block (2006: 213).

288. Select Bipartisan Committee (2006b: 199).

289. R. Scott (2005). After reviewing the document, a member of Blanco's staff called the governor, who was then sleeping (Committee on Homeland Security, 2006a: 26–66). She explained that she was "not signing anything in the middle of the night," though if her staff found that the proposal "could save lives and deliver more resources . . . [she] would want to" sign in the morning (Committee on Homeland Security, 2006a: 522). During a conversation between a member of the governor's staff and the National Guard Bureau head later during the night, it became obvious that he was under political pressure when he advised the governor to sign the memorandum. Early in the morning, the president's chief of staff explained to Blanco during a telephone conversation that it was important that the memorandum be signed by morning ahead of a scheduled White House

press appearance at which the president would announce the deployment of federal troops to New Orleans (Office of the Press Secretary, 2005g). Blanco later explained that "we had come to the end of the most trying week in Louisiana history. We had successfully evacuated [the Superdome and Convention Center] and all the highways, the interstates, and all of a sudden on Saturday morning the president's [going to say] federal troops are coming in to save us? That didn't make a lick of sense to me" (McQuaid and Schleifstein, 2006: 329).

290. NORTHCOM commanders appear to have been relieved by the governor's decision not to accept the command arrangement proposed by the White House. According to NORTHCOM's admiral Timothy Keating, the arrangement "would not have provided an advantage over [the] current situation" (Committee on Homeland Security, 2007b: 523).

291. The need for federal troops was no longer evident, given that the Superdome was almost fully evacuated and the Convention Center had been secured. Louisiana's adjutant general explained that "changing [the processes in place through the dual-hatting of the JTF-Katrina commander] would have only stalled current operations and delayed vital missions and not have provided any additional 'boots on the ground'" (Committee on Homeland Security, 2007d: 115). Early on September 3, Governor Blanco replied by fax to the White House's proposal. Rather than respond directly to the memorandum, Blanco wrote that

> I agree with your idea that—given the unprecedented requests for Federal military assistance that I, and my fellow Governors in Mississippi and Alabama have made—a "single military commander" of "Federal Joint Task Force Katrina" be named for Federal forces. . . . I believe such a decision is critical to improving the timeliness of fulfilling and coordinating the requests for Federal assistance that have already been made. This officer would serve as the single military commander for all [DOD] resources providing support to [DHS] and the State of Louisiana. This could also enhance the contribution of over 25 National Guard states currently being commanded by the Louisiana Adjutant General.
>
> (McQuaid and Schleifstein, 2006: 329; Select Bipartisan Committee, 2006b: 198)

292. Blanco's response reportedly came only ten minutes before the president was scheduled to appear in the Rose Garden, necessitating a frantic effort on the part of the president's staff to rewrite his prepared remarks (Hsu et al., 2005).

293. Committee on Homeland Security (2007b: 23).

294. Committee on Homeland Security (2007b: 28).

295. Committee on Homeland Security (2007b: 34).

296. Committee on Homeland Security (2007b: 132).

297. Committee on Homeland Security (2007b: 34).

298. Committee on Homeland Security (2007b: 143–150).

5. MEANING MAKING IN CRISIS: THE DETRIMENTAL EFFECTS OF MISSING NARRATIVES AND ESCALATING BLAME GAMES

1. 't Hart (1993).

2. Boin et al. (2008; 2009); 't Hart and Tindall (2009); Masters and 't Hart (2012).

3. Cf. Selznick (1957).

4. See Rodriguez and Dynes (2006); Tierney et al. (2006); cf. Brunken (2006); D. Berger (2009); Voorhees et al. (2007).

5. Broder (2005).

6. NBC News (2012). There is not a note of criticism in this 15-minute report.

7. The question "How lawless is New Orleans tonight?" was raised Tuesday evening on CNN NewsNight: https://www.youtube.com/watch?v=t9Y9-RVFJd4#t=6m30s (starts at 6:30). While the reporter says she has not witnessed anything, she relays reports from the New Orleans Police Department that would later be debunked as rumors.

8. Tierney et al. (2006: 61) speak of the "civil unrest lens" in which victims are portrayed as opportunistic, irrational looters and violent criminals.

9. Tierney et al. (2006: 66).

10. Brinkley (2006: 508).

11. D. Berger (2009).

12. Maestas et al. (2008).

13. Brinkley (2006: 535–536).

14. Brinkley (2006: 537).

15. Martinko et al. (2009: 52).

16. Brinkley (2006: 549).

17. Brinkley (2006: 548).

18. Dyson (2006: 181).

19. Barry (1998: 320); Cummings (2005); Dyson (2006: 97).

20. De Moraes (2005).

21. In Houston, Bush's mother suggested that many New Orleanians had little incentive to return to the city: "So many of the people in the arena here, you know, were underprivileged anyway, so this—this is working very well for them" ("Barbara Bush: Things working out 'very well' for poor evacuees from New Orleans," 2005). Mrs. Bush's remarks were condemned by many African American interest groups.

22. "Lt. Gen. Honoré a 'John Wayne dude'" (2005).

23. For instance, Paul Krugman invoked Katrina to warn readers about the potential consequences of President Trump's perceived incompetence (Krugman, 2017).

24. Cf. Larsen (1954); Shibutani (1966); Anthony (1973); Tierney et al. (2006); Liu et al. (2014).

25. Research has consistently shown that myths about looting and violence always emerge in prolonged disaster situations, even if that same research shows that most people behave prosocially during a disaster (Tierney et al., 2006; Wenger et al, 1975; Dynes and Quarantelli, 1968; Quarantelli and Dynes, 1970; Fritz and Marks, 1954).

26. Committee on Homeland Security (2007f).

27. Brinkley (2006).

28. One video depicts police looting (Hammer_Schwert, 2007). A second video depicts looting by residents (NBC News, 2005).

29. Gugliotta and Whoriskey (2005).

30. Baum (2006); see also Cooper and Block (2006: 168). Fox News host Shepard Smith remained in New Orleans through Katrina and its aftermath. Smith told *The O'Reilly Factor* that criminal activity, always a problem in natural disasters, appeared minimal to him: "There's been

some looting, but we've seen a lot more good stories—people who stay behind and help to feed people who didn't have anywhere to go."

31. Cooper and Block (2006: 169).

32. Select Bipartisan Committee (2006a: 243); cf. Baum (2006).

33. Select Bipartisan Committee (2006a: 241); cf. The White House (2006: 40); Tierney et al. (2006).

34. And that was apparently hard enough in New Orleans (Filosa, 2004).

35. CNN (2005i). Regarding looting by police officers, the Bipartisan Committee report had this to say: "At least some police departments were involved in breaking into stores and taking supplies. Plaquemines Parish Sheriff Jiff Hingle said his officers broke into stores and commandeered food, water, and medicine. Some of these items were needed to sustain the sheriff's office and other emergency personnel. Most of the items taken, however, were food and medical items for the growing population at the parish's designated shelter of last resort" (Select Bipartisan Committee, 2006a: 243–244).

36. Cooper and Block (2006: 213); Select Bipartisan Committee (2006a: 241).

37. Select Bipartisan Committee (2006a: 243). But after the worst was over, looting was not always treated with the same understanding by the courts. "A 73-year old church deaconess with diabetes who had never in her long life been charged with a crime" was charged with attempting to loot $63.50 worth of groceries at a deli (Select Bipartisan Committee, 2006a: 478).

38. Cooper and Block (2006: 168).

39. Baum (2006); Lagorio (2005a).

40. Anderson and Moller (2005).

41. For instance, the *Washington Post* reported that "people [are] . . . starting to shoot [at first responders]" (Vendantam and Klein, 2005). Another described "gangs of armed men in the city, moving around the city" ("Blanco says evacuation buses on the way to N.O.," 2005). The *New York Times* on September 2 still reported that "rapes and assaults were occurring unimpeded in the neighborhood streets. . . . Looters set ablaze a shopping center and firefighters, facing guns, abandoned their efforts to extinguish the fires, local radio said" (Treaster and Sontag, 2005).

42. Alexander (2006); Dynes and Rodriguez (2006); Van Heerden and Bryan (2006: 131).

43. Tierney et al. (2006: 68). Network news outlets routinely broadcast scenes from one location while speaking about other locations. This would confuse officials trying to keep abreast of unfolding events (McClellan, 2008: 288).

44. Select Bipartisan Committee (2006a: 247); see also Treaster and Sontag (2005).

45. Lipton et al. (2005).

46. Lipton et al. (2005).

47. Cooper and Block (2006: 193–194, 205–206); Select Bipartisan Committee (2006a: 242).

48. Brinkley (2006: 282, 365).

49. Select Bipartisan Committee (2006a: 248).

50. Treaster and Sontag (2005).

51. Baum (2006).

52. Brinkley (2006: 573). He made this claim in the second week, on September 6, 2005, in an interview with Oprah Winfrey. This claim thus did not affect the meaning-making process in that first week, but it does indicate Compass's perception of the situation.

53. Cooper and Block (2006: 193).

54. Select Bipartisan Committee (2006a: 248).

55. Brinkley (2006: 376). The White House and Senate reports state that 147 officers failed to report for duty or abandoned their posts (The White House, 2006: 37; Committee on Homeland Security, 2006a: 441). While 90% remained on duty, "their ability to carry out their life-saving and law-enforcement missions was gravely compromised by material losses and communication blackouts they suffered in the storm" (Committee on Homeland Security, 2006a: 441).

56. Brinkley (2006: 369); Gold (2005).

57. Finch (2005); see also CNN (2005c).

58. Brinkley (2006: 634); Select Bipartisan Committee (2006a: 281); Treaster and Sontag (2005).

59. Select Bipartisan Committee (2006a: 247).

60. Baum (2006); see also Forman (2007).

61. Cooper and Block (2006: 223).

62. Select Bipartisan Committee (2006a: 169). Five were due to medical reasons and one was a suicide. This number is based on interviews by Select Committee staff with Colonel Mark Mouton and Lieutenant General Jacques Thibodeaux of the Louisiana National Guard. We did not see transcripts of these interviews.

63. Cooper and Block (2006: 223).

64. Select Bipartisan Committee (2006b: 320).

65. Treaster and Sontag (2005).

66. Select Bipartisan Committee (2006a: 248).

67. Select Bipartisan Committee (2006a: 248).

68. Brinkley (2006: 516).

69. Lipton et al. (2005). "Winn, a decorated officer, was initially praised for his leadership amid the post-storm chaos. But he was fired in 2011 after the NOPD's Public Integrity Bureau ruled he broke department rules by failing to tell his superiors that a police officer had set fire to a car holding the body of Henry Glover, who had been shot by another officer" (Grimm, 2015).

70. Lipton et al. (2005).

71. D. Berger (2009).

72. Voorhees et al. (2007).

73. Durham (2008).

74. Littlefield and Quenette (2007: 27).

75. Cooper (2005).

76. Forgette et al. (2008).

77. D. Berger (2009).

78. Select Bipartisan Committee (2006a: 447); see also Bradshaw and Slonsky (2005).

79. Voorhees et al. (2007: 424).

80. Brinkley (2006: 329).

81. De Moraes (2005).

82. This rumor was in fact based on a historical precedent. White city leaders had intentionally flooded a predominantly black section of the city to ease strains on floodwalls backing onto predominantly white areas during the Great Flood in 1927 (Barry, 1998).

83. Select Bipartisan Committee (2006a: 465–466). At an early November forum at Emerson College, Louis Elisa—a former regional director for FEMA under President Clinton—suggested that race *had to be* a factor in the inadequate response. "I am telling you, as a professional, that you could not have had a mistake of this nature . . . if something else was not afoot," the *Boston Globe* quoted Elisa as saying (Select Bipartisan Committee, 2006a: 19–20). He pointed out that most residents of Gulfport, Mississippi, a town whose majority consisted of African American residents, were essentially overlooked by the Red Cross, which according to the Senate inquiry preferred to establish its operations either in white towns or in the white part of town (Select Bipartisan Committee, 2006a: 448).

84. Durham (2008: 111).

85. Durham (2008); Ettema (2005); Langer (1998).

86. Baum (2006).

87. Select Bipartisan Committee (2006b: 295).

88. Welch (2005: 18).

89. Quarantelli (1994) speaks of "solidarity crises."

90. 't Hart (1993).

91. Select Bipartisan Committee (2006a: 242).

92. The NRP contains a Public Affairs Support Annex aimed in part at countering rumors. This annex directs FEMA "to use media monitoring . . . and other techniques to identify rumors, misinformation, inaccurate reports," which should then be corrected. This should be carried out by federal, state, and local officials working out of a Joint Information Center. However, a Joint Information Center was only established in Baton Rouge a full week after landfall (Federal Emergency Management Agency, 2006: 29–30; McQuaid and Schleifstein, 2006: 280–281; Committee on Homeland Security, 2006a: 324).

93. Select Bipartisan Committee (2005a; 2005b).

94. During a press conference around 1:30 p.m. on September 1, Chertoff stated that he was extremely pleased with the response of every element of the federal government and federal partners (CNN, 2005d). See Taddonio (2015, first documentary at 10:40) for Chertoff's statement and Governor Blanco thanking Bush for the aid he promised.

95. Forman (2007).

96. Forman (2007: 115).

97. Forman (2007: 185).

98. Martinko et al. (2009: 53).

99. Forman (2007: 226).

100. Forman (2007: 232).

101. Statement from a press conference with Governor Blanco, Senator Landrieu, Senator Vitter, and Director Brown on Monday, August 29, 2005. See transcript at Malkin (2005).

102. Mann (2015).

103. Brinkley (2006: 289).

104. Brinkley (2006: 225).

105. Mann (2015).

106. Brinkley (2006: 225, 323); Government Accountability Office (2006a: 19); Van Heerden and Bryan (2006: 100); Committee on Homeland Security (2007f); Lacaze (2006).

107. Dolinar (2006).

108. The quote is attributed to Denise Bottcher in Matens (2017).

109. Brinkley (2006: 289).

110. Luo (2005).

111. The White House later explained it well:

FEMA is not, however, the operational provider of most Federal response support. It is a small organization that primarily manages the operational response, relief, and recovery efforts of the rest of the Federal government. FEMA does not, for instance, provide mass care or transportation after a disaster. Instead, pursuant to the NRP structure, FEMA tasks the Departments of Health and Human Services, Defense, and Transportation, as well as the American Red Cross, to perform these operations. Generally, State and local officials and first responders identify necessary missions and required commodities which FEMA—through its organizational structure, coordination practices, and administrative support—will assign to a Federal department or secure from the private sector. The organization exists primarily to coordinate other Federal agencies and departments during emergency response and recovery—acting as an honest broker between departments and agencies, providing a command structure, and serving as the single point of entry for State and local officials into the Federal government. It does not have its own critical response assets, such as buses, trucks, and ambulances.

(The White House, 2006: 16–17)

112. See the interview with Paula Zahn on CNN: http://www.youtube.com/watch?v=Jpm LuIA6DUo&t=1m15s.

113. Rodriguez and Dynes (2006).

114. CNN (2005e). For footage of the interview, see https://www.youtube.com/watch?v= JpmLuIA6DUo.

115. In a later interview, Brown explained his remarks: "We learned about the Convention Center on the afternoon people started going in there. . . . I started doing the shows the next evening. Koppel said, 'What are you doing about the Convention Center?' I instantly said, 'We just learned about the Convention Center.' I couldn't figure out what he was talking about. I mean, 'Yeah, I just learned about it when it started happening.' After that, one after the other, reporters kept asking the same damn question. . . . When I finished the interviews and walked out, my aide said, 'You kept saying you just learned about it, and they were interpreting that to mean that you had just learned about it in the past 30 minutes or hour, while they've been reporting it for the past 24 hours.' . . . It was horrible phrasing, but I repeated it three or four times in a row" (Brown, 2006).

116. After completing one round of interviews on September 1, Brown reportedly received a number of emails from friends, many of whom suggested that he resign (Cooper and Block, 2006: 205). Soon after, media pundits and elected officials would do the same publicly.

117. Cooper and Block (2006: 154–155).

118. Brinkley (2006: 332).

119. Brinkley (2006: 540). This is the link to the NPR radio fragment: http://www.npr.org/ templates/story/story.php?storyId=4828771. For a transcript of the interview on the Convention

Center, see http://www.npr.org/sections/thetwo-way/2010/08/27/129472944/from-the-archives-npr-s-robert-siegel-interviews-michael-chertoff-re-katrina.

120. Committee on Homeland Security (2006a: 668).

121. B. Jackson (2005).

122. Office of the Press Secretary (2006).

123. McClellan (2008: 272–273).

124. McClellan (2008: 273–274).

125. According to McClellan, several factors were considered in deciding when to stage a visit to the region: "The standard practice of the Bush White House was not to have the president rush to the scene of the natural disaster. First and foremost, we wanted to make sure that nothing interfered with emergency response and recovery efforts in the immediate aftermath. . . . Second, President Bush never wanted to give the appearance of capitalizing on a tragedy for political purposes. For these two reasons, leaving a little breathing space between a disaster and his visit always seemed to President Bush the most appropriate thing to do" (McClellan, 2008: 275–276).

126. See photo of Bush strumming a guitar at Naval Base Coronado on Tuesday, August 30, at Raddatz (2005).

127. Froomkin (2005); Transcript for September 4 (2005); Committee on Homeland Security (2006a: 237–238).

128. McClellan (2008: 278–279).

129. Committee on Homeland Security (2006a: 303). The Bush quote is taken from a September 12 press conference. He appears to be referring to an earlier remark in the days before (Select Bipartisan Committee, 2006b: 436–437).

130. McClellan (2008: 280).

131. Brinkley (2006: 633).

132. McClellan (2008: 280–281). The White House press corps accompanying the president on *Air Force One* were permitted to call ahead to their respective news agencies so that cameras could be in place on the ground to record the flyover, which lasted 35 minutes (Cooper and Block, 2006: 191).

133. Some have suggested that airborne search and rescue operations over New Orleans were temporarily suspended during the flyover (Horne, 2006: 63).

134. Cooper and Block (2006: 191); McClellan (2008: 281).

135. See photo at Morse (2005).

136. Horne (2006: 82); McClellan (2008: 283).

137. In the president's own words: "I've thought long and hard about Katrina—you know, could I have done something differently, like land *Air Force One* either in New Orleans or Baton Rouge. The problem with that and—is that law enforcement would have been pulled away from the mission. And then your questions, I suspect, would have been, how could you possibly have flown *Air Force One* into Baton Rouge, and police officers that were needed to expedite traffic out of New Orleans were taken off the task to look after you?" ("President Bush's final news conference," 2009).

138. The governor of Mississippi advised the president to wait with his visit. When Larry King asked Blanco if the president should come to visit, she stated that "he may come for a helicopter tour," but that there were few places he could land because of the devastation (http://www.youtube.com/watch?v=EEcZBNfVa_Y&t=16m40s).

139. McClellan (2008: 273–274).

140. For the full text, see Brinkley (2006: 443–446).

141. "Editorial: Waiting for a leader" (2005).

142. Office of the Press Secretary (2005h).

143. Transcript: https://georgewbush-whitehouse.archives.gov/news/releases/2005/09/2005 0901-6.html.

144. Transcript: https://georgewbush-whitehouse.archives.gov/news/releases/2005/09/2005 0901-7.html.

145. Brinkley (2006: 545); Thomas (2005).

146. Office of the Press Secretary (2005a); Dyson (2006: 94); McClellan (2008: 289); Rosetta (2005).

147. Brown (2006).

148. McClellan (2008: 289).

149. Huffington (2011).

150. For a transcript, see CNN (2005c).

151. Brinkley (2006: 545).

152. See Bumiller (2005).

153. Keeble (1991: 63, 94–95).

154. Select Bipartisan Committee (2006a: 463–464).

155. Cooper and Block (2006: 155).

156. Select Bipartisan Committee (2006a: 463).

157. The White House (2005).

158. Select Bipartisan Committee (2006a: 378–379).

159. His wound was self-inflicted (Chertoff, 2005; Gerhart and Pierre, 2005; Russel and Thevenot, 2005).

160. Voorhees et al. (2007).

161. Select Bipartisan Committee (2006a: 242).

162. Select Bipartisan Committee (2006a: 249)

163. Dunbar (2006); Franco et al. (2006); Government Accountability Office (2006a: 30); Horne (2006: 104); Johnson (2006).

164. Cooper and Block (2006: 197).

165. Brinkley (2006: 508); Select Bipartisan Committee (2006a: 169). The House report referred to the "persistent urban legend of shooting at helicopters" (Select Bipartisan Committee, 2006a: 171).

166. An email between HHS employees that morning confirms this: "Patient evacuation has been hampered by security issues on patient movement. It is unsafe for patient movement to continue without security provided" (Select Bipartisan Committee, 2006a: 285).

167. Brinkley (2006: 509).

168. CNN (2005f); Rodgers (2005); Select Bipartisan Committee (2006a: 350–353).

169. Brinkley (2006: 327); Cooper and Block (2006: 207).

170. Fink (2013); see also Fink's Pulitzer Prize–winning article (2009) in the *New York Times*.

171. Fink (2009).

172. Baum (2006).

173. Brinkley (2006: 342).

174. Baum (2006).

175. Baum (2006); see also Pollard and Lee (2006).

176. Tierney et al. (2006).

177. D. Berger (2009: 493).

178. Committee on Homeland Security (2007f); Blumenthal and McFadden (2005); McQuaid and Schleifstein (2006: 284).

179. Cooper and Block (2006: 197); Lacaze (2006); Select Bipartisan Committee (2006a: 286).

180. D. Berger (2009).

181. Cooper and Block (2006: 168).

182. Belser (2007: 165).

183. Blum (2005).

184. On August 31, the president's spokesman explained during a press briefing that "as you're all aware, martial . . . law has been declared in Mississippi and Louisiana" (Brinkley, 2006: 393). The mayor explained on the evening of September 1 that he had urged Governor Blanco to declare martial law in New Orleans (CNN, 2005b).

185. Sheriff Harry Lee of Jefferson Parish also issued a shoot-to-kill order (Brinkley, 2006: 507).

186. Treaster and Sontag (2005); Brinkley (2006: 508).

187. Select Bipartisan Committee (2006a: 170). The documentary *When the Levees Broke* (Pollard and Lee, 2006) confirms this statement was from September 1 and shows the footage at http://www.youtube.com/watch?v=12xj1sHvIWA&t=75m17s.

188. Scahill (2005).

189. Sizemore (2005); Temple-Raston (2007). On September 4, Blackwater was contracted by the federal government to provide "static guard posts" at disaster recovery centers and disaster medical stations in the region (Temple-Raston, 2007; Scahill, 2005; Department of Homeland Security, Office of the Inspector General, 2006). Blackwater provided a total of 200 personnel in the wake of the storm, 164 of whom carried out duties on behalf of the federal government. Armed personnel from Blackwater and other private security companies remained in the city for months after landfall. There appears to have been confusion among officials and the general public as to what authority private security companies in New Orleans were operating under (Select Bipartisan Committee, 2005; Scahill, 2005; Sizemore, 2005).

190. Chenelly (2005).

191. Committee on Homeland Security (2007e).

192. Select Bipartisan Committee (2006a: 242, 256); Committee on Homeland Security (2006a: 452, 463–464).

193. Committee on Homeland Security (2006a: 182). "The FEMA National DMAT withdrew from the Superdome because team members were concerned about their personal safety and security" (Wombwell, 2009: 62).

194. Committee on Homeland Security (2006a: 405–406); McQuaid and Schleifstein (2006: 292). Ralph Lupin was a doctor working for the National Guard at the Superdome (Lagorio, 2005b).

195. Committee on Homeland Security (2006b: 39). Parr had been making urgent calls to FEMA officials since arriving on the morning of August 30 to request a Federal Protection Service

(FPS) detachment. The FPS would not deploy to the Superdome before the facility was evacuated (Cooper and Block, 2006: 193).

196. Cooper and Block (2006: 193, 196); Rosenblatt and Rainey (2005).

197. Committee on Homeland Security (2006b: 39).

198. Committee on Homeland Security (2006a: 198n229).

199. Cooper and Block (2006: 195). Guard members reportedly spoke of a "final stand" (Cooper and Block, 2006: 196).

200. Committee on Homeland Security (2006b: 39). The LANG Timeline of Significant Events Hurricane Katrina (Louisiana National Guard, 2005: 7–8) confirms that the National Guard received reports of rumors circulating through the crowd that a riot would start if buses did not materialize soon. The timeline does not indicate that any riot squads were sent to the Superdome on either Wednesday or Thursday.

201. Cooper and Block (2006: 197).

202. Committee on Homeland Security (2006b: 4–5).

203. M. Roberts (2005).

204. Wombwell (2009: 62).

205. Committee on Homeland Security (2007f: 33).

206. Cooper and Block (2006: 197); Committee on Homeland Security (2007e).

207. Committee on Homeland Security (2006b: 9).

208. Fox News, http://www.youtube.com/watch?v=moFv2zGF4Gk&t=4m4s.

209. The New Orleans Times-Picayune, for instance, reported that as many as 40 bodies, including that of a young rape victim, were piled in a freezer at the Convention Center (Cooper and Block, 2006: 205; Sontag and Treaster, 2005).

210. Select Bipartisan Committee (2006a: 171).

211. Brinkley (2006: 565); cf. Cooper and Block (2006: 207); Select Bipartisan Committee (2005a); Select Bipartisan Committee (2006a: 171).

212. Cooper and Block (2006: 211).

213. Cooper and Block (2006: 210). Four bodies were found at the site. Three had died of natural causes, while the fourth was a likely homicide (Brinkley, 2006: 476). A Louisiana National Guard colonel found no evidence of widespread rape at the site (Applebaum, 2005).

214. Cooper and Block (2006: 211).

215. See photo of police officers patrolling through New Orleans on an armored vehicle (Select Bipartisan Committee, 2006a: 240).

216. Select Bipartisan Committee (2006a: 453–455, 476).

217. CNN (2005g).

218. Brinkley (2006. 524); "Lt. Gen. Honoré a 'John Wayne dude'" (2005).

219. Barnes et al. (2008: 606).

220. Cooper and Block (2006: 138).

221. Lipton et al. (2005).

222. See https://www.c-span.org/video/?188622-1/hurricane-katrina-relief-efforts, where Blanco says at around 1:20, "We are grateful that FEMA is by our side." She tears up at 1:32.

223. Lipton et al. (2005).

224. Cooper and Block (2006: 186).

225. Schneider (2008); Maestas et al. (2008).

226. Alfano (2005).

227. Treaster and Sontag (2005).

228. Treaster and Sontag (2005).

229. Transcript: http://edition.cnn.com/2005/US/09/02/nagin.transcript/index.html.

230. For a critical analysis, see Brinkley (2006: 530). Transcript: http://edition.cnn.com/2005/US/09/02/nagin.transcript/index.html; audio: https://archive.org/details/WWL_Radio_Interview_New_Orleans_Mayor_Ray_Nagin_ (the date on the audio is wrong).

231. Sommers et al. (2006); Barnes et al. (2008); Nicholls and Picou (2013).

232. Maestas et al. (2008).

233. Preston (2008).

234. Bakker (2005: 795–800).

235. Maestas et al. assert that White House officials were publicly questioning state-level management efforts by August 31: "National political elites and their surrogates continued to question the 'quality' of state and local leadership for months after the storm" (2008: 618). For a critical take on federal efforts to contain blame, see Nahourney and Kornblut (2005).

236. Brinkley (2006: 394, 414); Mann (2015).

237. Mann (2015); Horne (2006: 97).

238. Mann (2015).

239. Roig-Franzia and Hsu (2005).

240. Cooper and Block (2006: 204, 232, 242). See M. Walsh (2014) for a spot-on description of Louisiana's popular image and how Louisianians experience that image.

241. Treaster and Sontag (2005).

242. There are multiple sources for this quote. For an internet source, see https://en.wikiquote.org/wiki/Rick_Santorum.

243. Shane et al. (2005).

244. Roig-Franzia and Hsu (2005).

245. Luo (2005); Roig-Franzia and Hsu (2005).

246. Brinkley (2006: 368).

247. Lehner (2005).

248. Brown and Schwarz (2011).

249. Committee on Homeland Security (2007c: 17).

250. "Editorial: An open letter to the President" (2005).

251. Leibovich (2005). The senator's comments were so remarkable as to later warrant a question to the White House press secretary in Washington: "Louisiana's Senator Landrieu announced on network television, 'I might likely have to punch him, literally.' And my question, since 'him' is the president, and both punching and threatening to punch the president is a felony, have her qualifying words 'might likely' saved her from arrest and prosecution?" (B. Jackson, 2005).

252. Russel and Thevenot (2006).

253. See Boin et al. (2008; 2009).

CONCLUSION: LESSONS OF A MEGA-DISASTER

1. See Preston (2008) for an analysis of the politics behind the initiation of these committees.

2. Committee on Homeland Security (2006a); Select Bipartisan Committee (2006a).

3. Committee on Homeland Security (2006a: 2).

4. Committee on Homeland Security (2006a: 8).

5. Committee on Homeland Security (2006a: 2).

6. Select Bipartisan Committee (2006a: 3).

7. Select Bipartisan Committee (2006a: 2, 3).

8. Select Bipartisan Committee (2006a: 2).

9. Committee on Homeland Security (2006a: 14).

10. Committee on Homeland Security (2006a: 13).

11. Select Bipartisan Committee (2006a: 4).

12. Brown later argued that many of his emails were taken out of context or otherwise misunderstood.

13. Preston (2008: 52); Thompson et al. (2005).

14. Select Bipartisan Committee (2006a: 131).

15. Government Accountability Office (2006b); Neumann (2006).

16. Select Bipartisan Committee (2006a: 109).

17. Select Bipartisan Committee (2006a: 117).

18. Committee on Homeland Security (2006a: 237).

19. "Editorial: An open letter to the President" (2005).

20. Committee on Homeland Security (2006a: 7).

21. K. Walsh (2008, 2015); Alpert (2015); Drennen (2015).

22. Weisman and Abramowitz (2006).

23. Committee on Homeland Security (2006a: 3).

24. The White House (2006: 54).

25. For a discussion on resilience, see Comfort et al. (2010).

26. Select Bipartisan Committee (2006a: 108).

27. Dahl (2013); Masys (2012); Douglas and Wildavsky (1982).

28. Taleb (2007); Kahneman (2011).

29. See Tierney (2014) for a solid approach to policy making on risks.

30. LaPorte (1996); Roe (2011); Schulman (2011); cf. Ansell and Boin (forthcoming).

31. See Miller and Goidel (2009: 17, 4).

32. The phenomenon is known as "inattentional blindness." For a famous experiment, see http://www.theinvisiblegorilla.com/gorilla_experiment.html.

33. For a summary of these findings, see Boin and Bynander (2015).

34. Select Bipartisan Committee (2006a: 158, 193).

35. Committee on Homeland Security (2006a: 593).

36. Brinkley, for instance, admits that Brown "performed ably" in Florida, but he immediately downplays his assessment by remarking that it was election time and Florida was better prepared than Louisiana (2006: 248–249). This is not a very convincing argument.

37. See 't Hart et al. (1993).

38. See White House Fact Sheet: "It is now clear that a challenge on this scale requires greater Federal authority and a broader role for the U.S. Armed Forces—the institution of our government most capable of massive logistical operations on a moment's notice" (quoted in Sylves, 2006: 32–33).

39. See Coser's (1956) classic essay on the functions of conflict.

40. Rosenthal et al. (1991).

41. Rosenthal et al. (1989).

42. Barsky et al. (2006); Freedman et al. (2006); Kaufman (2005); Tierney et al. (2006).

43. Sick (1985).

44. White (2006).

45. Miller et al. (2014: 7, 131–132).

46. Miller et al. (2014: 71).

47. Miller et al. (2014: 5).

48. Miller et al. (2014: 8).

49. For instance, state coordinating officer Smith reminded those present on a September 1 video teleconference that "rumor control . . . is going to be key. Some of the things you hear, some of it has probably partial basis in fact, but there's a lot of exaggeration going on there" (Select Bipartisan Committee, 2006a: 248).

50. Federal Emergency Management Agency (2006: 29–30).

51. For suggestions, see Stern (2017).

52. See Ansell and Boin (forthcoming) for a discussion of a pragmatist approach to crisis and disaster management.

APPENDIX I: TIMELINE ON LEVEE BREACHES

1. Cooper and Block (2006: 126).

2. We were unable to retrieve all the names of the participants. The following officials were named during the call: Mike Deara, National Weather Service; Colonel Jeff Smith, Deputy Director of the Louisiana Office of Homeland Security and Emergency Preparedness; Mayor Camardelle, Grand Isle; Colonel Terry Ebbert, New Orleans Homeland Security Director. The following organizations participated: National Weather Service; Louisiana Emergency Operations Center; Federal Emergency Management Agency Region VI; Louisiana State Police; American Red Cross; Arlene, Ascension, Assumption, Jefferson, Lafourche, Orleans, St. Bernard, St. Charles, Jackson, St. James, St. John, St. Tammany, Tangipahoa, Terrebonne, and Washington Parish officials; Louisiana Department of Transportation and Development; Mississippi Emergency Operations Center (Committee on Homeland Security, 2007c: 206–239).

3. Committee on Homeland Security (2007c).https://www.gpo.gov/fdsys/pkg/CHRG-109shrg27029/pdf/CHRG-109shrg27029.pdf

4. Select Bipartisan Committee (2006a: 94).

5. Forman (2007: 58).

6. "Water tops 9th ward levee system" (2005).

7. Johnson (2006: 19).

8. Committee on Homeland Security (2007c: 206).

9. Office of US Representative Charles Melancon (2005: 5).

10. Committee on Homeland Security (2006a: 305); Committee on Homeland Security (2007c: 207).

11. Committee on Homeland Security (2006a: 305); Committee on Homeland Security (2007c: 207).

12. Committee on Homeland Security (2007c: 207).

13. Committee on Homeland Security (2007c: 207).

14. Committee on Homeland Security (2007c: 13).

15. Select Bipartisan Committee (2006a: 142).

16. Committee on Homeland Security (2007c: 208).

17. Committee on Homeland Security (2007c: 208).

18. Committee on Homeland Security (2007c: 14).

19. Select Bipartisan Committee (2006a: 142).

20. Committee on Homeland Security (2006a: 306).

21. Select Bipartisan Committee (2006a: 142).

22. Committee on Homeland Security (2007c: 209).

23. Committee on Homeland Security (2006b: 12)

24. Committee on Homeland Security (2006b: 12).

25. Committee on Homeland Security (2006a: 236).

26. Forman (2007: 62).

27. Forman (2007: 64).

28. Committee on Homeland Security (2007c: 210).

29. Committee on Homeland Security (2007c: 210).

30. Committee on Homeland Security (2007c: 37, 54).

31. Committee on Homeland Security (2007c: 210).

32. Committee on Homeland Security (2007c: 210).

33. Committee on Homeland Security (2007c: 210).

34. Select Bipartisan Committee (2006a: 377).

35. According to Cooper and Block, he was not referring to the president but to Brown (2006: 154–155). However, the original email states, "The US can land and do a presser." We assume Bahamonde is referring to the president. http://www.nytimes.com/packages/pdf/politics/20051022_FEMA2.pdf, p. 13.

APPENDIX II: EMERGENCY MANAGEMENT IN THE AMERICAN FEDERAL SYSTEM

1. Schneider (1995: 19).

2. For an overview, see P. Roberts (2013).

3. The Flood Control Act created the Mississippi River and Tributaries Project, a large-scale flood protection and river navigation scheme. This arguably constituted the nation's first disaster mitigation initiative (Barry, 1998).

4. Schneider (1995: 20).

5. Funding for and oversight of FEMA was widely dispersed across government. Some 16 congressional committees and 22 subcommittees had jurisdiction over various component programs during the early 1990s (P. S. Roberts, 2013).

6. P. S. Roberts (2013).

7. An embattled White House dispatched Andrew Card, then secretary of transportation, to Florida as the president's "personal representative." Card would lead a task force on Hurricane Andrew recovery. As during Katrina, the FEMA director was effectively sidelined by the White House. With the approval of the Florida governor, Bush directed thousands of troops to assist with humanitarian missions (McQuaid and Schleifstein, 2006: 114).

8. McQuaid and Schleifstein (2006: 114–115).

9. For instance, Witt on his first day on the job stood at the entrance to FEMA headquarters, shaking hands with every arriving employee. "With that one simple act [Witt] wiped away much of the bitterness and dissension, and a nascent union that had been born of all the employees' bitterness dissolved" (P. Roberts, 2013).

10. Department of Homeland Security, Office of the Inspector General (2006: 112–113).

11. Sylves (2006: 42).

12. Department of Homeland Security, Office of the Inspector General (2006: 13).

13. Department of Homeland Security, Office of the Inspector General (2006: 13–14).

14. The most articulate protest was written by Kathleen Tierney (2006).

15. Federal Emergency Management Agency (2005).

16. Federal Emergency Management Agency (2005).

BIBLIOGRAPHY

ABC News (2005a, August 30). "Katrina devastates Louisiana." Video file. Retrieved from http://abcnews.go.com/Archives/video/august-30-2005-hurricane-katrina-9127719.

——— (2005b, September 8). "FEMA was unprepared for Katrina relief effort, insiders say." Retrieved from http://abcnews.go.com/WNT/HurricaneKatrina/story?id= 1108268.

Acadian Ambulance Service (2005a, August 30). "Hurricane Katrina evacuation update." Retrieved from http://www.acadian.com/pressreleases/hurricanekatrinarelease2.htm.

——— (2005b). "Stories of courage, compassion and character." *Acadian Nouvelle Corporate Newsletter.* Lafayette, LA: Acadian Ambulance Service.

Alexander, D. (2006, June 11). "Symbolic and practical interpretations of the Hurricane Katrina disaster in New Orleans." *Understanding Katrina: Perspectives from the social sciences.* Social Science Research Council. Retrieved from http://understandingkatrina.ssrc.org/Alexander/.

Alfano, S. (2005, September 5). "Katrina response sparks outrage." CBS News. Retrieved from http://www.cbsnews.com/stories/2005/09/05/60minutes/main815179.shtml.

All Things Considered (2005, October 19). "Chertoff calls for more hurricane preparedness." Retrieved from http://www.npr.org/templates/story/story.php?storyId=4965914.

Alpert, B. (2015, August 28). "George W. Bush never recovered politically from Katrina." *New Orleans Times-Picayune.* Retrieved from http://www.nola.com/katrina/index.ssf/2015/08/bush_katrina_was_a_setback_to.html.

Anderson, E., and J. Moller (2005, August 30). "Looting difficult to control." *New Orleans Times-Picayune.* Retrieved from http://www.nola.com/katrina/index.ssf/2005/08/looting_difficult_to_control.html.

Ansell, C., and A. Boin (forthcoming). "Taming deep uncertainty: The potential of pragmatist principles for understanding and improving strategic crisis management." *Administration & Society.*

Anthony, S. (1973). "Anxiety and rumor." *Journal of Social Psychology,* 89 (1), 91–98.

Applebaum, A. (2005, October 5). "The rumor mill." *Washington Post.* Retrieved from https://www.washingtonpost.com/archive/opinions/2005/10/05/the-rumor-mill/3bb39988-efd7-4606-9366-8b8466751519/?utm_term=.dccfc2e20110.

Arendt, L. A., and D. B. Hess (2006). *Hospital decision making in the wake of Katrina: The case of New Orleans.* Buffalo: MCEER.

Associated Press (2004, August 26). "Response to Hurricane Charley vs. Andrew is like night and day." Retrieved from http://tdn.com/news/response-to-hurricane-charley-vs-andrew-is-like-night-and/article_6572bb6b-655a-54b1-82f9-a2fa7360c890.html.

Auf der Heide, E. (2004). "Common misperceptions about disasters: Panic, the 'disaster syndrome,' and looting." In M. O'Leary, ed., *The first 72 hours: A community approach to disaster preparedness* (340–380). Lincoln, NE: iUniverse Publishing.

"Aug. 30, 2005: Hurricane Katrina" (2014, August 28). *Wall Street Journal.* Retrieved from https://blogs.wsj.com/wsj125/2014/08/28/aug-30-2005-hurricane-katrina/.

Bacher, R., T. Devlin, and S. O'Keefe (2005). *LSU in the eye of the storm: A university model for disaster response.* Baton Rouge: Louisiana State University Press.

Bakker, K. (2005). "Katrina: The public transcript of 'disaster.'" *Environment and Planning D: Society and Space,* 23 (6), 795–802.

Ball, J. R. (2016, August 15). "'Cajun Navy' sets sail to rescue those trapped by Louisiana flooding." *New Orleans Times-Picayune.* Retrieved from http://www.nola.com/news/baton-rouge/index.ssf/2016/08/louisiana_flooding_cajun_navy.html.

Bamberger, R. L., and L. Kumins (2005). *Oil and gas: Supply issues after Katrina.* Washington, DC: Congressional Research Service. Retrieved from https://pdfs.semanticscholar.org/62ad/a6e0665489bd585d8b8d8e8f026f6fed3530.pdf.

"Barbara Bush: Things working out "very well" for poor evacuees from New Orleans" (2005, September 5). *Editor and Publisher.* Retrieved from http://www.editorandpublisher.com/news/barbara-bush-things-working-out-very-well-for-poor-evacuees-from-new-orleans/.

Barnes, M. D., C. L. Hanson, L. M. B. Novilla, A. T. Meacham, E. McIntyre, and B. C. Erickson (2008). "Analysis of media agenda setting during and after Hurricane Katrina: Implications for emergency preparedness, disaster response, and disaster policy." *American Journal of Public Health,* 98 (4), 604–610.

Barry, J. M. (1998). *Rising tide: The great Mississippi flood of 1927 and how it changed America.* New York: Simon and Schuster.

Barsky, L., J. Trainor, and M. Torres (2006). "Disaster realities in the aftermath of Hurricane Katrina: Revisiting the looting myth." Quick Response Report, no. 184. Newark, DE: Disaster Research Center.

Baum, D. (2006, January 9). "Deluged: When Katrina hit, where were the police?" *New Yorker*. Retrieved from http://www.newyorker.com/magazine/2006/01/09/deluged.

Beamish, R. (2005, September 17). "Money that Congress set aside for evacuation plan went elsewhere." Associated Press. Retrieved from http://onlineathens.com/stories/091805/new_20050918042.shtml#.WWjGuoTyiM8.

Becker, M. (2005, August 28). "Jittery Gulf Coast braces for Katrina." *New York Daily News*. Retrieved from http://www.nydailynews.com/archives/news/jittery-gulf-coast-braces-katrina-article-1.570592.

Belser, M. S. (2007). "Martial law after the storm: A constitutional analysis of martial law and the aftermath of Hurricane Katrina." *Southern University Law Review*, 35 (1), 147–222.

Bender, B., and K. O'Brien (2005, September 11). "Chronology of errors: How a disaster spread." *Boston Globe*. Retrieved from http://archive.boston.com/news/nation/articles/2005/09/11/chronology_of_errors_how_a_disaster_spread/.

Berger, D. (2009). "Constructing crime, framing disaster: Routines of criminalization and crisis in Hurricane Katrina." *Punishment and Society*, 11 (4), 491–510.

Berger, E. (2001, December 1). "New Orleans faces doomsday in hurricane scenario." *Houston Chronicle*. Retrieved from http://www.chron.com/news/nation-world/article/New-Orleans-faces-doomsday-in-hurricane-scenario-2017771.php.

Berube, A., and S. Raphael (2005). "Access to cars in New Orleans." Brookings Institution. Retrieved from http://www.brookings.edu/metro/20050915_katrinacarstables.pdf.

Bialik, C. (2015, August 26). "We still don't know how many people died because of Katrina." FiveThirtyEight.com. Retrieved from https://fivethirtyeight.com/features/we-still-dont-know-how-many-people-died-because-of-katrina/.

"Blanco says evacuation buses on the way to N.O." (2005, August 30). *New Orleans Times-Picayune*. Retrieved from http://www.nola.com/katrina/index.ssf/2005/08/blanco_says_evacuation_buses_on_the_way_to_no.html.

Blum, S. H. (2005, September 1). Press conference. DHS headquarters, Washington, DC.

Blumenthal, R., and R. D. McFadden (2005, September 1). "Higher death toll seen; Police ordered to stop looters." *New York Times*. Retrieved from http://www.nytimes.com/2005/09/01/national/nationalspecial/01storm.html?ei=5090anden=660a515b0f08a83eandex=1283227200andpartner=rssuserlandandemc=rssandpagewanted=print.

Boin, A., and F. Bynander (2015). "Success and failure in crisis coordination." *Geografiska Annaler*, 97 (1), 123–135.

Boin, A., P. 't Hart, E. Stern, and B. Sundelius (2016). *The politics of crisis management: Public leadership under pressure* (2nd ed.). Cambridge: Cambridge University Press.

Boin, A., S. Kuipers, and W. Overdijk (2013). "Leadership in times of crisis: A framework for assessment." *International Review of Public Administration*, 18 (1), 79–91.

Boin, A., A. McConnell, and P. 't Hart, eds. (2008). *Governing after crisis: The politics of investigation, accountability and learning.* Cambridge: Cambridge University Press.

—— (2009). "Crisis exploitation: Political and policy impacts of framing contests." *Journal of European Public Policy*, 16 (1), 81–106.

Boin, A., and C. Renaud (2013). "Orchestrating joint sensemaking across government levels: Challenges and requirements for crisis leadership." *Journal of Leadership Studies*, 7 (3), 41–46.

Bosner, L. (2011). "FEMA and disaster: A look at what worked and what didn't from a FEMA insider." *Truthout*. Retrieved from http://www.truth-out.org/sites/default/files/FEMA-and-Disaster-by-Leo-Bosner.pdf.

Bourget, P. (2005). "Hurricane Katrina: Dimensions of a major disaster." Papers prepared for EMSE 334: Environmental Hazards Management. Retrieved from http://www.gwu.edu/~icdrm/publications/PDF/EMSE334_Katrina.pdf.

Bovens, M., and P. 't Hart (1996). *Understanding policy fiascoes*. New Brunswick, NJ: Transaction.

Bradshaw, L., and L. B. Slonsky (2005, September 9). "Trapped in New Orleans by the flood and martial law: The real heroes and sheroes of New Orleans." *Socialist Worker*. Retrieved from http://socialistworker.org/2005-2/556/556_04_RealHeroes.shtml.

Brinkley, D. (2006). *The great deluge: Hurricane Katrina, New Orleans, and the Mississippi Gulf Coast*. New York: HarperCollins.

Broder, J. M. (2005, August 30). "Guard units shift from combat to flood duty." *New York Times*. Retrieved from http://www.nytimes.com/2005/08/30/us/guard-units-shift-from-combat-to-flood-duty.html.

Broderick, M. (2006, January 19). Interview by US Senate Committee on Homeland Security and Governmental Affairs staff.

Brodie, M., E. Weltzein, D. Altman, R. J. Blendon, and J. M. Benson (2006). "Experiences of Hurricane Katrina evacuees in Houston shelters: Implications for future planning." *American Journal of Public Health*, 96 (81), 1402–1498.

Brookings Institution (2005). *New Orleans after the storm: Lessons from the past, a plan for the future*. Washington, DC: Brookings Institution.

Brown, M. (2005). "The storm." Interview. PBS, *Frontline*. Retrieved from http://www.pbs.org/wgbh/pages/frontline/storm/interviews/brown.html.

—— (2006). Interview by D. Sheff. *Playboy*. Retrieved from http://www.michaelbrown-today.com/File/62f7dad4-6f2b-4cca-8e3c-4c651a58cd66.

Brown, M., and Schwarz, T. (2011). *Deadly indifference: The perfect (political) storm; Hurricane Katrina, the Bush White House, and beyond*. Lanham, MD: Taylor Trade.

Bruegmann, R. (2005). *Sprawl: A compact history*. Chicago: University of Chicago Press.

Brunken, B. L. (2006). "Hurricane Katrina: A content analysis of media framing, attribute agenda setting, and tone of government response." Master's thesis, Louisiana State University. Retrieved from http://digitalcommons.lsu.edu/cgi/viewcontent.cgi?article=2501&context=gradschool_theses.

Bumiller, E. (2005, September 3). "Promises by Bush amid the tears." *New York Times.* Retrieved from http://www.nytimes.com/2005/09/03/us/nationalspecial/promises-by-bush-amid-the-tears.html?_r=0.

Burnett, J. (2005, September 20). "Evacuees were turned away at Gretna, LA." NPR. Retrieved from http://www.npr.org/templates/story/story.php?storyId=4855611.

Cain, S. (2005, September 16). "Hurricane heroes: Cygnus's EMS Expo and Freeman." *Trade Show Executive.* Retrieved from http://www.tradeshowexecutive.com/archive/industry-news/hurricane-heroes-cygnuss-ems-expo-and-freeman/.

Carmona, R. (2005, September 3). Press conference. DHS headquarters, Washington, DC.

Carney, J., K. Tumulty, A. Ripley, and M. Thompson (2005, September 11). "4 places where the system broke down: A TIME investigation shows how confusion, incompetence and, ironically, a fear of making mistakes hobbled the government at all levels." *Time,* 166 (12). Retrieved from http://content.time.com/time/magazine/article/0,9171,1103560,00.html.

Catino, M. (2013). *Organizational myopia: Problems of rationality and foresight in organizations.* Cambridge: Cambridge University Press.

CBS News (2015, August 29). "How citizens turned into saviors after Katrina struck." Retrieved from http://www.cbsnews.com/news/remembering-the-cajun-navy-10-years-after-hurricane-katrina/.

Chenelly, J. R. (2005, September 3). "Troops begin combat operations in New Orleans." *Army Times.* Retrieved from http://www.informationclearinghouse.info/article10100.htm.

Chertoff, M. (2005, August 30). Press conference. DHS headquarters, Washington, DC.

Chisholm, D. (1989). *Coordination without hierarchy: Informal structures in multiorganizational systems.* Berkeley: University of California Press.

Civil Contingencies Secretariat, Cabinet Office of the United Kingdom (2006). *Hurricanes Katrina and Rita: A perspective.* London: Cabinet Office of the United Kingdom. Retrieved from http://cip.management.dal.ca/publications/Hurricanes%20Katrina%20and%20Rita.pdf.

Clarke, L. B. (1999). *Mission improbable: Using fantasy documents to tame disaster.* Chicago: University of Chicago Press.

CNN (2005a, September 15). "Companies pitch in: Major companies—including Home Depot and Ford—pledge millions to hurricane relief efforts." Retrieved from http://money.cnn.com/2005/08/31/news/fortune500/firms_hurricane/.

—— (2005b, September 2). "Mayor to feds: 'Get off your asses.'" Retrieved from http://edition.cnn.com/2005/US/09/02/nagin.transcript/.

—— (2005c, September 1). "Bush tells victims: 'A lot of help coming.'" Retrieved from http://edition.cnn.com/2005/POLITICS/08/31/bush.katrina/.

—— (2005d, September 1). "Homeland security holds press conference on Katrina relief." CNN live event/special [transcript]. Retrieved from http://edition.cnn.com/TRANSCRIPTS/0509/01/se.02.html.

—— (2005e, September 1). *Paula Zahn now* (transcript). Retrieved from http://transcripts .cnn.com/TRANSCRIPTS/0509/01/pzn.01.html.

—— (2005f, September 8). "Red Cross: State rebuffed relief efforts." http://www.cnn.com/ 2005/US/09/08/katrina.redcross/.

—— (2005g, September 2). "The big disconnect on New Orleans." Retrieved from http://edition.cnn.com/2005/US/09/02/katrina.response/index.html.

—— (2005h, September 13). "Racism, resources blamed for bridge incident." Retrieved from http://www.cnn.com/2005/US/09/13/katrina.bridge.

—— (2005i, September 30). "Witnesses: New Orleans cops among looters." Retrieved from http://edition.cnn.com/2005/US/09/29/nopd.looting/index.html.

—— (2014a, June 9). "Hurricane Katrina coverage: Evacuation ordered (8/28/2005)." CNN video file. Retrieved from https://www.youtube.com/watch?v=9upJ1vRCg00.

—— (2014b, June 9). "Hurricane Katrina: Landfall coverage 8:30–9:30 (8/29/2005)." CNN video file. Retrieved from https://www.youtube.com/watch?v=PLKjmHZRHHQ.

Coates, J. (2012). *The hour between dog and wolf: Risk taking, gut feelings and the biology of boom and bust.* New York: Penguin.

Cobb, J. A. (2013). *Flood of lies: The St. Rita's nursing home tragedy.* Gretna, LA: Pelican.

Comfort, L. K., A. Boin, and C. Demchak, eds. (2010). *Designing resilience: Preparing for extreme events.* Pittsburgh: University of Pittsburgh Press.

Committee on Homeland Security and Governmental Affairs (2006a). Senate. *Hurricane Katrina: A nation still unprepared; Special report of the Committee on Homeland Security and Governmental Affairs, United States Senate together with additional views.* S. Rept. 109-322. 109th Cong., 2nd Sess. Washington, DC: US Government Printing Office. Retrieved from https://www.gpo.gov/fdsys/pkg/CRPT-109srpt322/pdf/CRPT-109srpt322.pdf.

—— (2006b). Senate. *Hurricane Katrina: Perspectives of FEMA's operations professionals.* S. Hrg. 109-591. 109th Cong., 1st Sess. Washington, DC: US Government Printing Office. Retrieved from https://www.gpo.gov/fdsys/pkg/CHRG-109shrg26744/pdf/CHRG-109shrg26744.pdf.

—— (2006c). Senate. *Always ready: The Coast Guard's response to Hurricane Katrina.* S. Hrg. 109-527. 109th Cong., 1st Sess. Washington, DC: US Government Printing Office. Retrieved from https://www.gpo.gov/fdsys/pkg/CHRG-109shrg24929/pdf/CHRG-109shrg24929.pdf.

—— (2006d). Senate. *Hurricane Katrina in New Orleans: A flooded city. A chaotic response.* S. Hrg. 109-482. 109th Cong., 1st Sess. Washington, DC: US Government Printing Office. Retrieved from https://www.gpo.gov/fdsys/pkg/CHRG-109shrg24442/pdf/CHRG-109shrg24442.pdf.

—— (2007a). Senate. *Challenges in a catastrophe: Evacuating New Orleans in advance of Hurricane Katrina; Hearing before the Committee on Homeland Security and Governmen-*

tal Affairs. S. Hrg. 109-735. 109th Cong., 2nd Sess. Washington, DC: US Government Printing Office. Retrieved from https://www.gpo.gov/fdsys/pkg/CHRG-109shrg26752/pdf/CHRG-109shrg26752.pdf.

——— (2007b). Senate. *Hurricane Katrina: The role of governors in managing the catastrophe; Hearing before the Committee on Homeland Security and Governmental Affairs.* S. Hrg. 109-804. 109th Cong., 2nd Sess. Washington, DC: US Government Printing Office. Retrieved from https://www.gpo.gov/fdsys/pkg/CHRG-109shrg27024/pdf/CHRG-109shrg27024.pdf.

——— (2007c). Senate. *Hurricane Katrina: The roles of U.S. Department of Homeland Security and Federal Emergency Management Agency leadership.* S. Hrg. 109-829. 109th Cong., 2nd Sess. Washington, DC: US Government Printing Office. Retrieved from https://www.gpo.gov/fdsys/pkg/CHRG-109shrg27029/pdf/CHRG-109shrg27029.pdf.

——— (2007d). Senate. *Hurricane Katrina: The defense department's role in the response; Hearing before the Committee on Homeland Security and Governmental Affairs.* S. Hrg. 109-813. 109th Cong., 2nd Sess. Washington, DC: US Government Printing Office. Retrieved from https://www.gpo.gov/fdsys/pkg/CHRG-109shrg27028/pdf/CHRG-109shrg27028.pdf.

——— (2007e). Senate. *Hurricane Katrina: Managing law enforcement and communications in a catastrophe; Hearing before the Committee on Homeland Security and Governmental Affairs.* S. Hrg. 109-807. 109th Cong., 2nd Sess. Washington, DC: US Government Printing Office. Retrieved from https://www.gpo.gov/fdsys/pkg/CHRG-109shrg27025/pdf/CHRG-109shrg27025.pdf.

——— (2007f). Senate. *Hurricane Katrina: Urban search and rescue in a catastrophe; Hearing before the Committee on Homeland Security and Governmental Affairs.* S. Hrg. 109-757. 109th Cong., 2nd Sess. Washington, DC: US Government Printing Office. Retrieved from https://www.gpo.gov/fdsys/pkg/CHRG-109shrg26751/pdf/CHRG-109shrg26751.pdf.

——— (2007g). Senate. *Hurricane Katrina: Managing the crisis and evacuating New Orleans; Hearing before the Committee on Homeland Security and Governmental Affairs.* S. Hrg. 109-793. 109th Cong., 2nd Sess. Retrieved from https://www.gpo.gov/fdsys/pkg/CHRG-109shrg27023/pdf/CHRG-109shrg27023.pdf.

Congressional Research Service, American Law Division. (2005). *Hurricane Katrina–Stafford Act authorities and actions by Governor Blanco and President Bush to trigger them.* Washington, DC: Congressional Research Service. Retrieved from https://hazdoc.colorado.edu/bitstream/handle/10590/3356/C024052.pdf?sequence=1.

Cooper, A. (2005, September 1). "Special edition: Hurricane Katrina." CNN. Retrieved from http://transcripts.cnn.com/TRANSCRIPTS/0509/01/acd.01.html.

Cooper, C., and R. Block (2006). *Disaster: Hurricane Katrina and the failure of homeland security.* New York: Times Books / Henry Holt.

Copeland, C. W. (2005). "Regulatory waivers and extensions pursuant to Hurricane Katrina." Washington, DC: Congressional Research Service. Retrieved from http://www.au.af.mil/au/awc/awcgate/crs/rs22253.pdf.

Coser, L. (1956). *The functions of social conflict.* London: Routledge.

Crenson, M. (2005, August 28). "Katrina may create environmental catastrophe on an epic scale." *Pittsburgh Post-Gazette.* Retrieved from http://www.post-gazette.com/news/nation/2005/08/28/Katrina-may-create-environmental-catastrophe-of-epic-scale/stories/200508280237.

"Crimes after Katrina may have been overblown" (2005, September 29). NBC News. Retrieved from http://www.nbcnews.com/id/9503449/ns/us_news-%20katrina_the_long_road_back/t/crimes-after-katrina-may-have-been-%20overblown/#.WXjdiISGPRZ.

Cummings, E. E. (2005, September 2). Remarks of Congressman Cummings—Hurricane Katrina press conference. Retrieved from https://cummings.house.gov/sites/cummings.house.gov/files/documents/press/05sep02a.htm.

Dahl, E. J. (2013). *Intelligence and surprise attack: Failure and success from Pearl Harbor to 9/11 and beyond.* Washington, DC: Georgetown University Press.

De Moraes, L. (2005, September 3). "Kanye West's torrent of criticism, live on NBC." *Washington Post.* Retrieved from http://www.washingtonpost.com/wp-dyn/content/article/2005/09/03/AR2005090300165.html.

Department of Homeland Security (2004). *National response plan.* Washington, DC: Department of Homeland Security. Retrieved from https://fas.org/irp/agency/dhs/nrp.pdf.

——— (2005). *Catastrophic incident supplement to the National Response Plan.* Federal Emergency Management Administration. Retrieved from https://www.fema.gov/media-library-data/20130726-1825-25045-3106/catastrophic_incident_annex_2008.pdf.

Department of Homeland Security, Office of the Inspector General (2006). *A performance review of FEMA's disaster management activities in response to Hurricane Katrina.* OIG-06-32. Washington, DC: US Department of Homeland Security.

Derthick, M. (2007). "Where federalism didn't fail." *Public Administration Review,* 67 (1), 36–47.

Dewan, S. (2006, December 29). "Police officers charged in deaths in hurricane's aftermath." *New York Times.* Retrieved from http://www.nytimes.com/2006/12/29/us/29bridge.html.

Dolinar, L. (2006). "Katrina: What the media missed." *Real Clear Politics.* Retrieved from https://www.realclearpolitics.com/articles/2015/08/30/katrina_what_the_media_missed_127932.html.

Donchess, J. A. (2008, November 11). Interview by authors. Baton Rouge, LA.

Douglas, M., and A. Wildavsky (1982). *Risk and culture: An essay on the selection of environmental dangers.* Berkeley: University of California Press.

Drennen, K. (2015, August 28). "MSNBC: Katrina a 'stain' on Bush presidency 'he could never recover from.'" NewsBusters. Retrieved from http://www.newsbusters.org/blogs/nb/kyle-drennen/2015/08/28/msnbc-katrina-stain-bush-presidency-he-could-never-recover.

Drew, C. (2006, June 13). "Police struggles in New Orleans raise old fears." *New York Times*. Retrieved from http://www.nytimes.com/2006/06/13/us/13orleans.html.

Dror, Y. (2001). "Crises to come: Comments and findings." In U. Rosenthal, A. Boin, and L. K. Comfort, eds., *Managing crises: Threats, dilemmas, opportunities* (342–349). Springfield, IL: Charles C. Thomas.

Dunbar, W. (2006, November 9). Interview by authors. Washington, DC.

Durham, F. (2008). "Media ritual in catastrophic times: The populist turn in television coverage of Hurricane Katrina." *Journalism*, 9 (1), 95–116.

Dynes, R., and E. L. Quarantelli (1968). "What looting in civil disturbances really means." *Trans-action*, 5 (6), 9–14.

Dynes, R., and H. Rodriguez (2006, June 11). "Finding and framing Katrina: The social construction of a disaster." *Understanding Katrina: Perspectives from the social sciences*. Social Science Research Council. Retrieved from http://understandingkatrina.ssrc.org/Dynes_Rodriguez/.

Dyson, M. D. (2006). *Come hell or high water: Hurricane Katrina and the color of disaster*. New York: Basic Civitas Books.

"Editorial: Waiting for a leader." (2005, September 1). *New York Times*. Retrieved from http://www.nytimes.com/2005/09/01/opinion/waiting-for-a-leader.html.

"Editorial: An open letter to the President." (2005, September 4). *New Orleans Times-Picayune*. Retrieved from http://www.nola.com/katrina/index.ssf/2005/09/editorial_an_open_letter_to_th.html.

Ettema, J. S. (2005). "Crafting cultural resonance: Imaginative power in everyday journalism." *Journalism*, 6 (2), 131–152.

Federal Emergency Management Agency (2004). *Combined catastrophic plan for Southeast Louisiana and the New Madrid Seismic Zone*. Washington, DC: Federal Emergency Management Agency.

—— (2005, April 28). "Hurricane season 2005: Building on success." Retrieved from https://www.fema.gov/news-release/2005/04/28/hurricane-season-2005-building-success.

—— (2006). *DHS/FEMA initial response hot wash: Hurricane Katrina in Louisiana, DR-1603-LA*. Washington, DC: Federal Emergency Management Agency. Retrieved from https://www.hsdl.org/?abstract&did=467679.

Filosa, G. (2004, February 13). "Scared silent." *New Orleans Times-Picayune*, A-1, A-9–12.

Finch, S. (2005, September 4). "Extraordinary, but not 'martial law.'" *New Orleans Times-Picayune*. Retrieved from http://www.nola.com/katrina/index.ssf/2005/09/extraordinary_but_not_martial_law.html.

Fink, S. (2009, August 25). "The deadly choices at Memorial." *New York Times*. Retrieved from http://www.nytimes.com/2009/08/30/magazine/30doctors.html?pagewanted=all.

———(2013). *Five days at Memorial: Life and death in a storm-ravaged hospital*. New York: Crown.

Flaherty, J. (2010). *Floodlines: Community and resistance from Katrina to Jena six*. Chicago: Haymarket Books.

Forgette, R., M. King, and B. Dettrey (2008). "Race, Hurricane Katrina, and government satisfaction: Examining the role of race in assessing blame." *Publius: The Journal of Federalism*, 38 (4), 671–691.

Forman, S. (2007). *Eye of the storm: Inside city hall during Katrina*. Bloomington, IN: Author House.

Fox, B. (1997, July 22). "Justice besieged: New Orleans juvenile court system is called nation's most troubled." *New York Times*, A1.

Franco, C., E. Toner, R. Waldhorn, B. Maldin, T. O'Toole, and T. V. Inglesby (2006). "Systemic collapse: Medical care in the aftermath of Hurricane Katrina." *Biosecurity and Bioterrorism: Biodefense strategy, practice, and science*, 4 (2), 135–146.

Freedburg, S. J., Jr. (2005, December 22). "Hurricane response shows gaps in public-private coordination." GovExec.com. Retrieved from http://www.govexec.com/defense/2005/12/hurricane-response-shows-gaps-in-public-private-coordination/20867/.

Freedman, T., N. Gossen, M. Lindsey, and N. Gerrish (2006). *Covering Katrina: Trends in Katrina media coverage—initial analysis from the top ten national newspapers and ten Gulf Coast newspapers*. Washington, DC: Partnership for Public Service.

Fritz, C., and E. S. Marks (1954). "The NORC study of human behavior in disaster." *Journal of Social Issues*, 10 (3), 26–41.

Froomkin, D. (2005, May 25). "The ostrich approach." *Washington Post*. Retrieved from http://www.washingtonpost.com/wp-dyn/content/blog/2005/05/25/BL2005052501250.html.

Fussell, E. (2005). "Leaving New Orleans: Social stratification, networks, and hurricane evacuation." *Understanding Katrina: Perspectives from the social sciences*. Social Science Research Council. Retrieved from www.understandingkatrina.ssrc.org/Fussel/.

Fussman, C. (2006). "C. Ray Nagin." *Esquire*, 145 (1), 100–101.

Gaouette, N. (2006, March 2). "Bush is warned on Katrina in video." *Los Angeles Times*. Retrieved from http://articles.latimes.com/2006/mar/02/nation/na-katrina2.

Gerhart, A., and R. E. Pierre (2005, October 5). "News of pandemonium may have slowed aid." *Washington Post*. Retrieved from http://www.washingtonpost.com/wp-dyn/content/article/2005/10/04/AR2005100401525_pf.html.

Glasser, S. B., and M. Grunwald (2005a, September 11). "The steady buildup to a city's chaos." *Washington Post*. Retrieved from http://www.washingtonpost.com/wp-dyn/content/article/2005/09/10/AR2005091001529_pf.html.

———(2005b, December 22). "Department's mission was undermined from start." *Washington Post*. Retrieved from http://www.washingtonpost.com/wp-dyn/content/article/2005/12/21/AR2005122102327.html.

Gold, S. (2005, August 31). "2 states bear the brunt." *Los Angeles Times*. Retrieved from http://articles.sun-sentinel.com/2005-08-31/news/0508300517_1_water-level-nagin-city.

Government Accountability Office (2006a). *Coast Guard: Observations on the preparation, response, and recovery missions related to Hurricane Katrina.* GAO-06-903. Washington, DC: Government Accountability Office.

———(2006b). *Statement by Comptroller General David M. Walker on GAO's preliminary observations regarding preparedness and response to Hurricanes Katrina and Rita.* GAO-06-365R. Washington, DC: Government Accountability Office.

———(2015). *Emergency management: FEMA has made progress since Hurricanes Katrina and Sandy, but challenges remain . . .* Washington, DC: Government Accountability Office. Retrieved from http://www.gao.gov/assets/680/673279.pdf.

"The great Cajun Navy: A voluntary private flotilla comes through in flooded Louisiana." (2016, August 28). *Wall Street Journal*. Retrieved from https://www.wsj.com/articles/the-great-cajun-navy-1472420730?mod=e2two.

Grimm, A. (2015, January 15). "Former NOPD SWAT commander fired after Henry Glover trial, loses latest bid to get job back." *New Orleans Times-Picayune*. Retrieved from http://www.nola.com/crime/index.ssf/2015/01/former_nopd_swat_commander_fir.html.

Gugliotta, G., and P. Whoriskey (2005, August 31). "Floods ravage New Orleans; two levees give way." *Washington Post*. Retrieved from https://www.highbeam.com/doc/1P2-60771.html.

Gupta, S. (2005). "Dr. Sanjay Gupta reports on Charity Hospital." CNN video file. Retrieved from http://edition.cnn.com/videos/tv/2015/08/28/gupta-katrina-charity-2005.cnn.

Gura, D. (2010, August 27). "From the archives: Days after Katrina, Michael Chertoff talks to Robert Siegel." NPR. Retrieved from http://www.npr.org/sections/thetwo-way/2010/08/27/129472944/from-the-archives-npr-s-robert-siegel-interviews-michael-chertoff-re-katrina.

Hallowell, C. (2005). *Holding back the sea: The struggle on the Gulf Coast to save America.* New York: HarperCollins.

Hammer_Schwert (2007, March 29). "Police looting a Wal Mart in New Orleans." *dailymotion*. Retrieved from http://www.dailymotion.com/video/x1kL2e.

Hayden, D. (2003). *Building suburbia: Green fields and urban growth, 1820–2000.* New York: Vintage.

Haygood, W., and A. S. Tyson (2005, September 15). "It was as if all of us were already pronounced dead." *Washington Post*. Retrieved from http://www.washingtonpost.com/wp-dyn/content/article/2005/09/14/AR2005091402655.html.

Herbert, B. (2005, September 8). "No strangers to the blues." *New York Times.* Retrieved from http://www.nytimes.com/2005/09/08/opinion/no-strangers-to-the-blues.html.

Horne, J. (2006). *Breach of faith: Hurricane Katrina and the near death of a great American city.* New York: Random House.

Hsu, S. S. (2005, October 18). "Messages depict disarray in federal Katrina response." *Washington Post.* Retrieved from http://www.washingtonpost.com/wp-dyn/content/article/2005/10/17/AR2005101701230.html.

Hsu, S. S., R. Stein, and J. Warrick (2005, December 5). "Documents highlight Bush-Blanco standoff." *Washington Post.* Retrieved from http://www.washingtonpost.com/wp-dyn/content/article/2005/12/04/AR2005120400963_pf.html.

Huffington, A. (2011, May 25). "President Bush hits the scene, giving hope to . . . uh, Trent Lott." *Huffington Post.* Retrieved from http://www.huffingtonpost.com/arianna-huffington/president-bush-hits-the-s_b_6670.html.

Human Rights Watch. (2005, September 21). "New Orleans: Prisoners abandoned to floodwaters." Retrieved from http://www.hrw.org/en/news/2005/09/21/new-orleans-prisoners-abandoned-floodwaters.

Hurlbert, J., J. Beggs, J. and V. Haines (2005, October 20). "Bridges over troubled water: What are the optimal networks for Katrina's victims?" *Understanding Katrina: Perspectives from the social sciences.* Social Science Research Council. Retrieved from http://understandingkatrina.ssrc.org/Hurlbert_Beggs_Haines/.

Hurricane Katrina, Aug. 28, 2005, video conference (2009, October 30). Transcript. *Popular Mechanics.* Retrieved from http://www.popularmechanics.com/science/environment/a466/2413906/.

"Hurricane Katrina: Blaming the victims." Sourcewatch. Retrieved from http://www.sourcewatch.org/index.php/Hurricane_Katrina:_Blaming_the_Victims.

Jackson, B. (2005, September 16). "Katrina: What happened when." FactCheck.org. Retrieved from http://www.factcheck.org/2005/09/katrina-what-happened-when/.

Jackson, S. (2006, June 11). "Un/natural disasters, here and there." *Understanding Katrina: Perspectives from the social sciences.* Social Science Research Council. Retrieved from http://understandingkatrina.ssrc.org/Jackson/.

Johnson, D. L. (2006). *Service assessment: Hurricane Katrina, August 23–31, 2005.* US Department of Commerce, National Oceanic and Atmospheric Administration (NOAA). Retrieved from https://www.weather.gov/media/publications/assessments/Katrina.pdf.

Juvenile Justice Project of Louisiana (2006). *Treated like trash: Juvenile detention before, during and after Hurricane Katrina.* Retrieved from http://www.jjpl.org/PDF/treated_like_trash.pdf.

Kahneman, D. (2011). *Thinking, Fast and Slow.* New York: Farrar, Straus and Giroux.

Kahneman, D., and G. Klein (2009). "Conditions for intuitive expertise: A failure to disagree." *American Psychologist,* 64 (6), 515–526.

Kaufman, S. (2005, October 20). "The criminalization of New Orleanians in Katrina's wake." *Understanding Katrina: Perspectives from the social sciences.* Social Science Research Council. Retrieved from http://understandingkatrina.ssrc.org/Kaufman/.

Keeble, J. (1991). *Out of the channel: The Exxon Valdez oil spill in Prince William Sound.* New York: HarperCollins.

Kelman, I. (2007). "Hurricane Katrina disaster diplomacy." *Disasters,* 31 (3), 288–309.

Kettl, D. F. (2006). "Is the worst yet to come?" *Annals of the American Academy of Political and Social Science,* 604 (1), 273–287.

Kirkpatrick, D. D., and S. Shane (2005, September 15). "Ex-FEMA chief tells of frustration and chaos." *New York Times.* Retrieved from http://www.nytimes.com/2005/09/15/us/nationalspecial/exfema-chief-tells-of-frustration-and-chaos.html.

Klayman, J., and Y. W. Ha (1987). "Confirmation, disconfirmation, and information in hypothesis-testing." *Psychological Review,* 94 (2), 211–228.

Kopp, C. (2005, December 15). "The bridge to Gretna: Why did police block desperate refugees from New Orleans?" CBS News. Retrieved from https://www.cbsnews.com/news/the-bridge-to-gretna/.

Kromm, C. (2005, December 12). "How the White House delayed the military's response to Katrina." *Facing South.* Retrieved from https://www.facingsouth.org/2005/12/how-the-white-house-delayed-the-militarys-response-to-katrina.html.

Krugman, P. (2017, January 20). "Donald the unready." *New York Times.* Retrieved from https://www.nytimes.com/2017/01/20/opinion/donald-the-unready.html.

Lacaze, K. (2006, November 8). Interview by authors. Baton Rouge, LA.

Lagorio, C. (2005a, August 30). "Crisis deepens in New Orleans." CBS News. Retrieved from https://www.cbsnews.com/news/crisis-deepens-in-new-orleans/.

——— (2005b, August 30). "Safety, frustration in Superdome." CBS News. Retrieved from http://www.cbsnews.com/news/safety-frustration-in-superdome/.

Langer, J. (1998). *Tabloid television: Popular journalism and the "other news."* London: Routledge.

LaPorte, T. R. (1996). "High reliability organizations: Unlikely, demanding, and at risk." *Journal of Contingencies and Crisis Management,* 4 (2), 60–71.

Larsen, O. N. (1954). "Rumors in a disaster." *Journal of Communication,* 4 (4), 111–123.

Lavelle, K., and J. Feagin (2006). "Hurricane Katrina: The race and class debate." *Monthly Review,* 58 (3), 85–66.

Lawrence, J. (2005). "Governors handle crisis in own ways." *USA Today.* Retrieved from http://usatoday30.usatoday.com/news/nation/2005-09-12-two-governors_x.htm.

Lee, T., and M. S. Collins (2006). "Trymaine Lee with Michael S. Collins." *Callaloo* 29 (4), 1128–1138.

Lehner, M. (2005, September 9). "FEMA director relieved of Katrina duties." *People Celebrity.* Retrieved from http://people.com/celebrity/fema-director-relieved-of-katrina-duties/.

Leibovich, M. (2005, September 9). "Senator bears witness to emotions." *Washington Post.* Retrieved from http://www.washingtonpost.com/wp-dyn/content/article/2005/09/08/AR2005090802014.html.

Leonard, H. B., and A. Howitt (2009). *Managing crises: Responses to large-scale emergencies.* Washington, DC: CQ Press.

Levinson, D. R. (2006). *Nursing home emergency preparedness and response during recent hurricanes.* Department of Health and Human Services, Office of the Inspector General (OEI-01-01-00020). Retrieved from https://oig.hhs.gov/oei/reports/oei-06-06-00020.pdf.

Lewis, P. F. (1976). *New Orleans: The making of an urban landscape.* Cambridge: Ballinger.

Lipton, E., C. Drew, S. Shane, and D. Rhode (2005, September 11). "Breakdowns marked path from hurricane to anarchy." *New York Times.* Retrieved from http://www.nytimes.com/2005/09/11/us/nationalspecial/breakdowns-marked-path-from-hurricane-to-anarchy.html.

Littlefield, R. S., and A. M. Quenette (2007). "Crisis leadership and Hurricane Katrina: The portrayal of authority by the media in natural disasters." *Journal of Applied Communication Research,* 35 (1), 26–47.

Liu, F., A. Burton-Jones, and D. Xu (2014). "Rumors on social media in disasters: Extending transmission to retransmission." *PACIS 2014 Proceedings,* 49.

Louisiana National Guard (2005). "Louisiana National Guard timeline of significant events Hurricane Katrina." Retrieved from http://www.columbia.edu/itc/journalism/cases/katrina/Federal%20Government/Congress/U.S.%20Senate/Senate%20Hearings/Senate%20Hearing%202006-02-09/Landreneau%20Timeline%202006-02-09.pdf.

Louisiana Office of Homeland Security and Emergency Preparedness (2005). *Emergency Operations Plan.* Retrieved from http://www.columbia.edu/itc/journalism/cases/katrina/State%20of%20Louisiana/Office%20of%20Emergency%20Preparedness/STATE%20OF%20LOUISIANA%20EOP%202005.pdf.

"Lt. Gen. Honoré a 'John Wayne dude.'" (2005, September 3). CNN. Retrieved from http://www.cnn.com/2005/US/09/02/honore.profile.

Luo, M. (2005, September 8). "The embattled leader of a storm-battered state immersed in crisis." *New York Times.* Retrieved from http://www.nytimes.com/2005/09/08/us/nationalspecial/the-embattled-leader-of-a-stormbattered-state-immersed.html.

Maestas, C. D., L. R. Atkeson, T. Croom, and L. A. Bryant (2008). "Shifting the blame: Federalism, media, and public assignment of blame following Hurricane Katrina." *Publius: The Journal of Federalism,* 38 (4), 609–632.

Maggi, L. (2005, December 6). "Roundup of buses for storm bungled." *New Orleans Times-Picayune.* Retrieved from https://academic.oup.com/publius/article-abstract/38/4/609/1854020/Shifting-the-Blame-Federalism-Media-and-Public.

Malkin, M. "Michael Brown speaks." Retrieved from http://michellemalkin.com/2005/09/15/michael-brown-speaks/.

Mann, B. (2015, August 20). "I worked for the governor of Louisiana during Katrina. Here are 5 things I learned." *Vox.* Retrieved from http://www.vox.com/2015/8/20/9176225/hurricane-katrina-government.

Marshall, T. P. (2005). "Hurricane Katrina damage survey." Haag Engineering Co. Retrieved from https://ams.confex.com/ams/pdfpapers/106926.pdf.

Martin, A., and A. Zajac (2005, September 23). "Offer of buses fell between the cracks." *Chicago Tribune.* Retrieved from http://articles.chicagotribune.com/2005-09-23/news/0509230350_1_mayor-c-ray-nagin-bus-evacuation-buses.

Martinko, M. J., D. M. Breaux, A. D. Martinez, J. Summers, and P. Harvey (2009). "Hurricane Katrina and attributions of responsibility." *Organizational Dynamics,* 38 (1), 52–63.

Masters, A., and P. 't Hart (2012). "Prime ministerial rhetoric and recession politics: Meaning making in economic crisis management." *Public Administration,* 90 (3), 759–780.

Matens, A. (2017). "'Houston should have had a plan' says . . . Kathleen Blanco." *Hayride,* August 29, 2017. Retrieved from https://thehayride.com/2017/08/houston-plan-says-kathleen-blanco/.

Masys, A. J. (2012). "Black swans to grey swans: revealing the uncertainty." *Disaster Prevention and Management,* 21 (3), 320–335.

McClellan, S. (2008). *What happened: Inside the Bush White House and Washington's culture of deception.* New York: PublicAffairs.

McQuaid, J. (2009, September 9). "'Hurricane Pam' exercise offered glimpse of Katrina misery." *New Orleans Times-Picayune.* Retrieved from http://www.nola.com/katrina/index.ssf/2005/09/hurricane_pam_exercise_offered_glimpse_of_katrina_misery.html.

McQuaid, J., and M. Schleifstein (2002, June 23). "Washing away: Worst-case scenarios if a hurricane hits Louisiana." *New Orleans Times-Picayune.* Retrieved from http://www.nola.com/environment/index.ssf/page/washing_away_2002.html.

—— (2006). *Path of destruction: The devastation of New Orleans and the coming age of superstorms.* New York: Little, Brown.

Miller, A., and R. Goidel (2009). "News organizations and information gathering during a natural disaster: Lessons from Hurricane Katrina." *Journal of Contingencies and Crisis Management,* 17 (4), 266–273.

Miller, A., V. LaPoe, and S. Roberts (2014). *Oil and water: Media lessons from Hurricane Katrina and the Deepwater Horizon disaster.* Jackson: University Press of Mississippi.

Miller, H., J. McNamara, and J. Jui (2005). *Hurricane Katrina—after action report OR-2DMAT.* Retrieved from https://www.hsdl.org/?view&did=766144.

Montgomery, C. (2006, June 9). "Ted Koppel interviews FEMA's Mike Brown." Video file. Retrieved from https://www.youtube.com/watch?v=jKtuTV3hNdM&t=0m31s.

Morse, P. (2005). "President George W. Bush looks out over the devastation in New Orleans from Hurricane Katrina as he heads back to Washington D.C." Digital photograph, White House. Retrieved from https://georgewbush-whitehouse.archives.gov/news/releases/2005/08/images/20050831_p083105pm-0117jas-515h.html.

Moynihan, D. P. (2012). "A theory of culture-switching: Leadership and red tape during Hurricane Katrina." *Public Administration*, 90 (4), 851–868.

Mustian, J. (2014, October 15). "A murder 20 years ago marked low point for NOPD: 20 years later, ripple effects still felt." *New Orleans Advocate*. Retrieved from http://www.theadvocate.com/new_orleans/news/article_1c89036b-ab8e-5f5b-863a-e01129b85cbf.html.

Nagin, R., and K. Blanco (2005, August 28). "New Orleans Mayor, Louisiana Governor hold press conference." CNN. Retrieved from http://transcripts.cnn.com/TRANSCRIPTS/0508/28/bn.04.html.

Nahourney, A., and A. Kornblut (2005, September 5). "White House enacts a plan to ease political damage." *New York Times*. Retrieved from http://www.nytimes.com/2005/09/05/us/nationalspecial/white-house-enacts-a-plan-to-ease-political-damage.html.

National Hurricane Center (2005a). "Tropical cyclone report: Hurricane Katrina: 23–30 August 2005." Retrieved from http://www.nhc.noaa.gov/data/tcr/AL122005_Katrina.pdf.

——— (2005b). Katrina's path. Hurricane Katrina discussion number 15. Retrieved from http://www.nhc.noaa.gov/archive/2005/dis/a1122005.discus.015.shtml.

NBC News (2005, August 31). "Officials throw up hands at New Orleans looters." Associated Press. Retrieved from http://www.nbcnews.com/id/9144734/ns/us_news-%20katrina_the_long_road_back/t/officials-throw-hands-new-orleans-%20100ters/#.WagJHrJJaM-.

——— (2012, August 31). "Hurricane Katrina: From the archives." *Nightly News*. Retrieved from http://www.nbcnews.com/video/nightly-news/48864370#48864370.

Neumann, J. (2006, February 2). "Report blames Katrina response on Chertoff." *Los Angeles Times*. Retrieved from http://articles.latimes.com/2006/feb/02/nation/na-katrina2.

Nicholls, K., and J. S. Picou (2013). "The impact of Hurricane Katrina on trust in government." *Social Science Quarterly*, 94 (2), 344–361.

Nickerson, R. S. (1998). "Confirmation bias: A ubiquitous phenomenon in many guises." *Review of General Psychology*, 2 (2), 175–220.

Nielsen, J. (2005). "Conditions deteriorate in aftermath of Hurricane Katrina." Digital photograph. Getty Images. Retrieved from https://www.gettyimages.com/event/conditions-deteriorate-in-aftermath-of-hurricane-katrina-53567814#new-orleans-united-states-hurricane-katrina-refugees-take-shelter-picture-id53913852.

Nossiter, A. (2006, March 30). "As life returns to New Orleans, so does crime." *New York Times*. Retrieved from http://www.nytimes.com/2006/03/30/national/nationalspecial/30crime.html.

O'Byrne, J. (2006, August 22). "Katrina: The power of the press against the wrath of nature." *Poynter*. Retrieved from http://www.poynter.org/2006/katrina-the-power-of-the-press-against-the-wrath-of-nature/76853/.

Office of the Press Secretary (2005a, September 15). "President discusses hurricane relief in address to the nation." Transcript. Retrieved from https://georgewbush-whitehouse.archives.gov/news/releases/2005/09/20050915-8.html.

——— (2005b, August 29). "President participates in conversation on Medicare." Retrieved from https://georgewbush-whitehouse.archives.gov/news/releases/2005/08/20050829-5.html.

——— (2005c, August 29). "President discusses Medicare, new prescription drug benefits." Retrieved from https://georgewbush-whitehouse.archives.gov/news/releases/2005/08/images/20050829-11_p082905pm-0548-515h.html.

——— (2005d, September 12). "President, Lieutenant General Honoré discuss hurricane relief in Louisiana." Transcript. Retrieved from https://georgewbush-whitehouse.archives.gov/news/releases/2005/09/20050912.html.

——— (2005e, August 31). "President outlines hurricane relief efforts. "Transcript. Retrieved from https://georgewbush-whitehouse.archives.gov/news/releases/2005/08/text/20050831-3.html.

——— (2005f, August 31). "Fact sheet: Federal relief for the victims of Hurricane Katrina." Transcript. Retrieved from https://georgewbush-whitehouse.archives.gov/news/releases/2005/08/20050831-4.html.

——— (2005g, August 28). "President discusses Hurricane Katrina, congratulates Iraqis on draft constitution." Transcript. Retrieved from https://georgewbush-whitehouse.archives.gov/news/releases/2005/08/text/20050828-1.html.

——— (2005h, September 1). "President asks Bush and Clinton to assist in hurricane relief efforts." Retrieved from https://georgewbush-whitehouse.archives.gov/news/releases/2005/09/20050901-3.html.

——— (2006). "Setting the record straight: The August 28th Hurricane Katrina videoconference." Retrieved from https://georgewbush-whitehouse.archives.gov/news/releases/2006/03/text/20060302-17.html.

Office of US Representative Charles Melancon (2005). "Hurricane Katrina document analysis: The e-mails of Michael Brown." Retrieved from http://i.a.cnn.net/cnn/2005/images/11/03/brown.emails.analysis.pdf.

Ortega, K. (2014, February 9). "George W. Bush full speech on Katrina from Jackson Square." Video file. Retrieved from https://www.youtube.com/watch?v=YJpcbV6FNc8.

Parker, C., E. Stern, E. Paglia, and C. Brown (2009). "Preventable catastrophe? The Hurricane Katrina disaster revisited." *Journal of Contingencies and Crisis Management*, 17 (4), 206–220.

Paulison, D. R. (2006, May). "FEMA's response to Hurricane Katrina." *Fire Engineering*, 159 (5). Retrieved from http://www.fireengineering.com/articles/print/volume-159/issue-5/features/femarsquos-response-to-hurricane-katrina.html.

Pennington, R. (1996, March 31). "The thinnest blue line." *New York Times*, 32.

Perlstein, M., and Philbin, W. (1994, December 8). "Len Davis, eight other New Orleans police officers, charged in drug sting." *New Orleans Times-Picayune*. Retrieved from

http://www.nola.com/crime/index.ssf/1994/12/len_davis_eight_other_new_orle
.html.

Perrow, C. (1984). *Normal accidents: Living with high-risk technologies.* New York: Basic Books.

—— (1986). *Complex organizations: A critical essay.* 3rd ed. New York: Random House.

Pollard, S. D. (producer), and S. Lee (director). (2006). *When the levees broke: A requiem in four acts.* Motion picture. 40 Acres and a Mule Filmworks.

"President Bush's final news conference" (2009, January 12). *New York Times.* Retrieved from http://www.nytimes.com/2009/01/12/us/politics/12text-bush.html.

Preston, T. (2008). "Weathering the politics of responsibility and blame: The Bush administration and its response to hurricane Katrina." In A. Boin, P. 't Hart, and A. McConnell, eds., *Governing after crisis: The politics of investigation, accountability and learning* (33–61). Cambridge: Cambridge University Press.

Pvtjokerusmc. (2009, April 26). "Hurricane Katrina day 1 vid 2 Fox News live one day after the storm." Video. Retrieved from https://www.youtube.com/watch?v=QBB_PZy4p84.

Quarantelli, E. L. (1994). "Looting and antisocial behavior in disasters." Preliminary paper 205. Retrieved from http://udspace.udel.edu/bitstream/handle/19716/590/PP205.pdf.

Quarantelli, E. L., and R. R. Dynes (1970). "Property norms and looting: Their patterns in community crises". *Phylon,* 31 (2), 168–182.

Raddatz, M. (2005). "Bush playing the guitar with Mark Wills." Digital photograph. Associated Press. Retrieved from http://www.carvinmuseum.com/playersgallery/oddities
.html.

Remnick, D. (2005). "High water: How presidents and citizens react to disaster." *New Yorker.* Retrieved from http://www.newyorker.com/magazine/2005/10/03/high-water.

Rivlin, G. (2016). *Katrina: After the flood.* New York: Simon and Schuster.

Roberts, M. (2005, September 28). "Some violence claims probably exaggerated." *Boston Globe.* Retrieved from http://archive.boston.com/news/nation/articles/2005/09/28/
some_violence_claims_probably_exaggerated/.

Roberts, P. S. (2013). *Disasters and the American state: How politicians, bureaucrats, and the public prepare for the unexpected.* Cambridge: Cambridge University Press.

Rodgers, A. (2005, September 3). "Homeland security won't let Red Cross deliver food." *Pittsburgh Post-Gazette.* Retrieved from http://www.post-gazette.com/pg/05246/565143
.stm.

Rodriguez, H., and R. Dynes (2006). "Finding and framing Katrina: The social construction of disaster." *Understanding Katrina: Perspectives from the social sciences.* Social Science Research Council. Retrieved from http://understandingkatrina.ssrc.org/Dynes_
Rodriguez/.

Rodriguez, H., J. Trainor, and E. L. Quarantelli (2006). "Rising to the challenges of a catastrophe: The emergent and prosocial behavior following Hurricane Katrina." *Annals of the American Academy of Political and Social Science,* 604 (1), 82–101.

Roe, E. (2011). "Surprising answers to rising sea levels, storms, floods, desertification, earthquakes and ever more environmental crises in California's Sacramento–San Joaquin delta." *Journal of Contingencies and Crisis Management*, 19 (1), 34–42.

Roig-Franzia, M., and S. Hsu (2005, September 4). "Many evacuated, but thousands still waiting." *Washington Post*. Retrieved from http://www.washingtonpost.com/wp-dyn/content/article/2005/09/03/AR2005090301680.html.

Rosenblatt, S., and J. Rainey (2005, September 27). "Katrina takes a toll on truth, news accuracy." *Los Angeles Times*. Retrieved from http://articles.latimes.com/2005/sep/27/nation/na-rumors27.

Rosenthal, U., A. Boin, and L. K. Comfort, eds. (2001). *Managing crises: Threats, dilemmas, opportunities*. Springfield, IL: Charles C. Thomas.

Rosenthal, U., M. T. Charles, and P. 't Hart, eds. (1989). *Coping with crises: The management of disasters, riots, and terrorism*. Springfield, IL: Charles C. Thomas.

Rosenthal, U., P. 't Hart, and A. Kouzmin (1991). "The bureau-politics of crisis management." *Public Administration*, 69 (2), 211–233.

Rosetta, L. (2005, September 6). "Frustrated firefighters at Atlanta hold waiting to hand out FEMA fliers." Retrieved from http://www.firehouse.com/news/10499778/frustrated-firefighters-at-atlanta-hold-waiting-to-hand-out-fema-fliers.

Russel, G., and B. Thevenot (2005, September 26). "Reports of anarchy at Superdome overstated." *Seattle Times*. Retrieved from http://www.seattletimes.com/nation-world/reports-of-anarchy-at-superdome-overstated/.

Scahill, J. (2005, October 21). "Blackwater down." *Nation*. Retrieved from https://www.thenation.com/article/blackwater-down/.

Schleifstein, M. (2003, November 22). "Home is where the flood is." *New Orleans Times-Picayune*. Retrieved from http://hurricane.lsu.edu/_in_the_news/1103tp.htm.

——— (2009). "Study of Hurricane Katrina's dead show most were old, lived near levee breaches." *New Orleans Times-Picayune*. Retrieved from https://www.nola.com/hurricane/index.ssf/2009/08/answers_are_scarce_in_study_of.htm.

Schneider, S. K. (1995). *Flirting with disaster: Public management in crisis situations*. Armonk, NY: M. E. Sharpe.

——— (2005). "Administrative breakdowns in the governmental response to Hurricane Katrina." *Public Administration Review*, 65 (5), 515–516.

——— (2008). "Who's to blame? (Mis)perceptions of the intergovernmental response to disasters." *Publius: The Journal of Federalism*, 38 (4), 715–738.

Schulman, P. R. (2011). "Problems in the organization of organization theory: An essay in honour of Todd LaPorte." *Journal of Contingencies and Crisis Management*, 19 (1), 43–50.

Scott, R. T. (2005, December 11). "Politics delayed troops dispatch to N.O.: Blanco resisted Bush leadership proposal." *New Orleans Times-Picayune*, A12.

Scott, N. (2015). "Refuge of the last resort: Five days inside the Superdome for Hurricane Katrina." *USA Today*. Retrieved from http://ftw.usatoday.com/2015/08/refuge-of-last-resort-five-days-inside-the-superdome-for-hurricane-katrina.

Select Bipartisan Committee to Investigate the Preparation for and Response to Hurricane Katrina. (2005a). House of Representatives. *Hurricane Katrina: The role of the Federal Emergency Management Agency.* 109th Cong., 1st Sess. Retrieved from https://www.hsdl.org/?abstract&did=463565.

——— (2005b). House of Representatives. *Hurricane Katrina: Preparedness and response by the state of Louisiana.* 109th Cong., 1st Sess. Retrieved from https://www.hsdl.org/?abstract&did=463505.

——— (2006a). House of Representatives. *A failure of initiative: Final report of the Select Bipartisan Committee to investigate the preparation for and response to Hurricane Katrina.* H. Rept. 109-377. 109th Cong., 2nd Sess. Retrieved from https://www.gpo.gov/fdsys/pkg/CRPT-109hrpt377/pdf/CRPT-109hrpt377.pdf.

——— (2006b). House of Representatives. *A failure of initiative: Supplementary report and document annex.* H. Rept.109-396. 109th Cong., 2nd Sess. Retrieved from https://www.congress.gov/109/crpt/hrpt396/CRPT-109hrpt396.pdf.

Selznick, P. (1957). *Leadership in administration: A sociological interpretation.* Berkeley: University of California Press.

Shane, S., and E. Lipton (2005, September 2). "Government saw flood risk but not levee failure." *New York Times*. Retrieved from http://www.nytimes.com/2005/09/02/us/nationalspecial/government-saw-flood-risk-but-not-levee-failure.html.

Shane, S., and T. Shanker (2005, September 28). "When the storm hit, National Guard was deluged too." *New York Times*. Retrieved from http://www.nytimes.com/2005/09/28/us/nationalspecial/when-storm-hit-national-guard-was-deluged-too.html.

Shane, S., E. Lipton, and C. Drew (2005, September 5). "After failures, government officials play blame game." *New York Times*. Retrieved from https://www.nytimes.com/2005/09/05/us/nationalspecial/after-failures-government-officials-play-blame-game.html.

Shearer, H. (2005). "Gretna responds." *Huffington Post*. Retrieved from http://www.huffingtonpost.com/harry-shearer/gretna-responds_b_8270.html.

Shibutani, T. (1966). *Improvised news: A sociological study of rumor.* Indianapolis: Bobbs-Merrill.

Shorrock, T. (2006, January 22). "Bush-linked Florida company and the Katrina evacuation fiasco." Prisonplanet.com. Retrieved from http://www.prisonplanet.com/articles/january2006/220106fiasco.htm.

Sick, G. G. (1985). *All fall down: America's tragic encounter with Iran.* New York: Random House.

Siegel, R. (2005, September 1). "U.S. aid effort criticized in New Orleans." NPR. Retrieved from http://www.npr.org/templates/story/story.php?storyId=4828771.

Sizemore, B. (2005, September 15). "Blackwater employees create a stir in New Orleans." *Virginia-Pilot*.

Solnit, R. (2009). *A paradise built in hell: The extraordinary communities that arise in disaster*. New York: Viking.

——— (2010, August 26). "Reconstructing the story of the storm: Hurricane Katrina at five." *Nation*. Retrieved from http://www.thenation.com/article/154168/reconstructing-story-storm-hurricane-katrina-five.

Sommers, S. R., E. P. Apfelbaum, K. N. Dukes, N. Toosi, and E. J. Wang (2006). "Race and media coverage of Hurricane Katrina: Analysis, implications and future research questions." *Analyses of Social Issues and Public Policy*, 6 (1), 39–55.

State of Louisiana (2006). *Hurricanes Katrina and Rita: After-action report and improvement plan*. Washington, DC: US Department of Homeland Security. Retrieved from http://gohsep.la.gov/Portals/0/Users/043/43/43/Hurricanes%20Katrina%20and%20Rita%20AAR%20and%20Improvement%20Plan.pdf.

Steinberg, T. (2006). *Acts of God: The unnatural history of natural disaster in America*. New York: Oxford University Press.

Steiner, A. (2005). "Loss of heritage, discovery of justice: Elders and premature babies." In J. B. Childs, ed., *Hurricane Katrina: Response and responsibilities* (39–43). Santa Cruz, CA: New Pacific.

Stern, E. K. (2017). "Crisis management, social media, and smart devices." In B. Akghar, A. Staniforth, and D. Waddington, eds., *Application of social media in crisis management* (21–33). New York: Springer International.

Strolovitch, D. Z., D. T. Warren, and P. Frymer (2005). "Katrina's political roots and divisions: Race, class, and federalism in American politics." *Understanding Katrina: Perspectives from the social sciences*. Social Science Research Council. Retrieved from http://understandingkatrina.ssrc.org/FrymerStrolovitchWarren/.

Sullivan, L. (2005, September 16). "FEMA official says agency heads ignored warnings." NPR. Retrieved from http://www.npr.org/templates/story/story.php?storyId=4849706.

Sylves, R. T. (2006). "President Bush and Hurricane Katrina: The presidential leadership style." *Annals of the American Academy of Political and Social Science*, 604 (1), 26–56.

——— (2008). *Disaster policy and politics: Emergency management and homeland security*. Washington, DC: CQ Press.

Taddonio, P. (2015, August 26). "Katrina, 10 years later: Three documentaries to watch." PBS, *Frontline*. Retrieved from http://www.pbs.org/wgbh/frontline/article/katrina-10-years-later-three-documentaries-to-watch/.

Taleb, N. N. (2007). *The black swan: The impact of the highly improbable*. New York: Random House.

"Telling Their Stories" (2018). Retrieved from http://www.tellingtheirstories.org/exhibit/the-photos/.

Temple-Raston, D. (2007, October 2). "Blackwater eyes domestic contracts in U.S." NPR. Retrieved from http://www.npr.org/templates/story/story.php?storyId=14707922.

Tetlock, P. E. (2005). *Expert political judgment: How good is it? How can we know?* Princeton, NJ: Princeton University Press.

't Hart, P. (1993). "Symbols, rituals and power: The lost dimensions of crisis management." *Journal of Contingencies and Crisis Management,* 1 (1), 36–50.

't Hart, P., U. Rosenthal, and A. Kouzmin (1993). "Crisis decision making: The centralization thesis revisited." *Administration & Society,* 25 (1), 12–41.

't Hart, P., and K. Tindall, eds. (2009). *Framing the global economic downturn: Crisis rhetoric and the politics of recessions.* Canberra: ANU E Press.

Thevenot, B. (2005, September 6). "Bodies found piled in freezer at Convention Center." *New Orleans Times-Picayune.* Retrieved from http://www.informationclearinghouse.info/article10167.htm.

Thomas, E. (2005a, September 12). "What went wrong: The story of Katrina—and a disastrously slow rescue." *Newsweek.* Retrieved from http://www.newsweek.com/what-went-wrong-story-katrina-and-disastrously-slow-rescue-118069.

—— (2005b, September 18). "The government response to Katrina: A disaster within a disaster." *Newsweek.* Retrieved from http://www.newsweek.com/government-response-katrina-disaster-within-disaster-118257.

Thompson, M., K. Tumulty, and M. Allen (2005, October 3). "How many more Mike Browns are out there?" *Time.* Retrieved from http://content.time.com/time/magazine/article/0,9171,1109345,00.html.

Tierney, K. (2006). "The red pill." *Understanding Katrina: Perspectives from the social sciences.* Social Science Research Council. Retrieved from http://understandingkatrina.ssrc.org/Tierney/.

—— (2014). *The social roots of risk: Producing disasters, promoting resilience.* Stanford, CA: Stanford Business Books.

Tierney, K., C. Bevc, and E. Kuligowski (2006). "Metaphors matter: Disaster myths, media frames, and their consequences in Hurricane Katrina." *Annals of the American Academy of Political and Social Science,* 604 (1), 57–81.

"Timeline: NOPD's long history of scandal." (2011, October 6). PBS, *Frontline.* Retrieved from http://www.pbs.org/wgbh/pages/frontline/law-disorder/etc/cron.html.

Toosi, N. (2007, January 20). "Party politics played role in Katrina response, former FEMA leader says." Associated Press. Retrieved from http://www.djournal.com/news/party-politics-played-role-in-katrina-recovery-former-fema-leader/article_6e5c2f32-b3a4-5851-9dcf-96bd9d075a02.html.

"Tracking Hurricane Katrina." (2005, August 29). CNN, *Larry King live.* Retrieved from http://transcripts.cnn.com/TRANSCRIPTS/0508/29/lkl.01.html.

"Transcript for September 4: Michael Chertoff, Marc Morial, Mike Tidwell, Mark Fischetti, David Wessel, Haley Barbour and Aaron Broussard." (2005, September 4). MSNBC,

Meet the press with Tim Russert. Retrieved from http://www.msnbc.msn.com/id/ 9179790.

Treaster, J. B., and A. Goodnough (2005, August 29). "Powerful storm threatens havoc along Gulf Coast." *New York Times.* Retrieved from http://www.nytimes.com/2005/08/ 29/us/powerful-storm-threatens-havoc-along-gulf-coast.html.

Treaster, J. B., and N. R. Kleinfield (2005, August 31). "New Orleans is now off limits; Pentagon joins in relief effort." *New York Times.* Retrieved from http://www.nytimes.com/2005/ 08/31/us/nationalspecial/new-orleans-is-now-off-limitspentagon-joins-in-relief.html.

Treaster, J. B., and D. Sontag (2005, September 2). "Local officials criticize federal government over response." *New York Times.* Retrieved from http://www.nytimes.com/2005/ 09/02/us/nationalspecial/local-officials-criticize-federal-government-over.html?_r=0.

Treaster, J. B., and K. Zernike (2005, August 30). "Hurricane Katrina slams into Gulf Coast; dozens are dead." *New York Times.* Retrieved from http://www.nytimes.com/2005/08/30/ us/hurricane-katrina-slams-into-gulf-coast-dozens-are-dead.html?mcubz=2.

Troy, M. (2005, September 26). "Wal-Mart lauded for Katrina efforts; opposition still wary." *DSN Retailing Today.*

Turner, B. A. (1978). *Man-made disasters.* London: Wykeham.

Vaidyanathan, R. (2015). "The hurricane station: Through deadly winds, rain and floods— the New Orleans radio station that fought to keep listeners alive during Hurricane Katrina." BBC. Retrieved from http://www.bbc.co.uk/news/resources/idt-20ed5228-1f23-4906-9057-ffdd9d5272f2.

Van Heerden, I. (2005, September 10). "Storm that drowned a city." PBS, *NOVA.* Retrieved from https://www.youtube.com/watch?v=R25gjI44Lyo.

Van Heerden, I., and M. Bryan (2006). *The storm: What went wrong and why during Hurricane Katrina—the inside story from one Louisiana scientist.* New York: Viking.

Vendantam, S., and K. Allison (2005, September 3). "You wonder why it didn't kill a million." *Washington Post.* Retrieved from http://www.washingtonpost.com/wp-dyn/ content/article/2005/09/02/AR2005090202170.html.

Voorhees, C. C. W., J. Vick, and D. D. Perkins (2007). "'Came hell and high water': The intersection of Hurricane Katrina, the news media, race and poverty." *Journal of Community and Applied Social Psychology,* 17 (1), 415–429.

Walsh, K. T. (2005). *From Mount Vernon to Crawford: A history of the presidents and their retreats.* New York: Hyperion.

—— (2008). "Hurricane Katrina left a mark on George W. Bush's presidency." *US News & World Report.* Retrieved from https://www.usnews.com/news/articles/2008/12/11/ hurricane-katrina-left-a-mark-on-george-w-bushs-presidency.

—— (2015, August 28). "The undoing of George W. Bush: Hurricane Katrina badly damaged the former president's reputation. And it still hasn't recovered." *Economist.* Retrieved from https://www.usnews.com/news/the-report/articles/2015/08/28/ hurricane-katrina-was-the-beginning-of-the-end-for-george-w-bush.

Walsh, M. O. (2014). *My sunshine away.* New York: Amy Einhorn Books.

Ward, R. H., L. E. Kiernan, and D. Mabrey (2006). *Homeland security: An introduction.* Burlington: Elsevier Science.

Warrick, J. (2005, December 10). "Crisis communications remain flawed." *Washington Post.* Retrieved from http://www.washingtonpost.com/wp-dyn/content/article/2005/12/09/AR2005120902039.html.

"Water tops 9th ward levee system" (2005, August 29). *New Orleans Times-Picayune.* Retrieved from http://www.nola.com/katrina/index.ssf/2005/08/water_tops_9th_ward_levee_system.html.

Welch, M. (2005, December). "They shoot helicopters, don't they?" *Reason.* Retrieved from https://reason.com/archives/2005/12/01/they-shoot-helicopters-dont-th.

Weick, K. E. (1995). *Sensemaking in organizations.* Thousand Oaks, CA: Sage.

Weisman, J., and M. Abramowitz (2006, August 26). "Katrina's damage lingers for Bush." *Washington Post.* Retrieved from http://www.washingtonpost.com/wp-dyn/content/article/2006/08/25/AR2006082501481.html.

Wenger, D. E., J. D. Dykes, T. D. Sebok, and J. L. Neff (1975). "It's a matter of myths: An empirical examination of individual insight into disaster response." *Mass Emergencies,* 1, 33–46.

The White House (2005). "President addresses nation, discusses Hurricane Katrina relief efforts." Retrieved from https://georgewbush-whitehouse.archives.gov/news/releases/2005/09/20050903.html.

—— (2006). *The federal response to Hurricane Katrina: Lessons learned.* Washington, DC: White House. Retrieved from https://www.uscg.mil/history/katrina/docs/Katrina LessonsLearnedWHreport.pdf.

White, R. D. (2006). *Kingfish: The reign of Huey P. Long.* New York: Random House.

Whoriskey, P., and G. Gugliotta (2005, August 30). "Storm thrashes Gulf Coast." *Washington Post.* Retrieved from http://www.washingtonpost.com/wp-dyn/content/article/2005/08/29/AR2005082900206.html.

Wilson, J. (2001, September 10). "New Orleans is sinking." *Popular Mechanics.* Retrieved from http://www.popularmechanics.com/science/environment/a233/new-orleans-is-sinking-640714/.

Wombwell, J. A. (2009). *Army support during Hurricane Katrina.* Retrieved from http://usacac.army.mil/cac2/cgsc/carl/download/csipubs/wombwell.pdf.

Woods, D. D. (2005). "Creating foresight: Lessons for enhancing resilience from *Columbia.*" In W. Starbuck and M. Farjoun, eds., *Organization at the limit: Lessons from the Columbia disaster* (289–308). Oxford: Blackwell.

Zuschlag, R. (2006, November 6). Interview by authors. Lafayette, LA.

INDEX

9/11 attacks, 18, 22, 49, 81, 83, 114, 173, 185

911 system. *See* emergency call centers

ABC News, 21, 77, 120

"absent government" frame, 120–121, 154–155

Acadian Air Ambulance, 97, 213nn134–135

Acadian Ambulance Service, 17

African Americans, 4–5, 121, 126–127, 136, 139, 222n21, 224n82. *See also* race

Air Force One, 64, 111, 134–136, 155, 227n132, 227n137

Air National Guard, 99

airport, 97–99, 214n154

Air Transport Association, 99

Alabama, 3, 6–7, 102, 136

Allbaugh, Joe, 24

American Airlines, 17

American Bus Association, 104

American Faubourg St. Mary, 4

American Prospect, 24

American Red Cross. *See* Red Cross

American Security Group, 140

anarchy frame, 13

    lessons learned, 160–161, 172–175

    meaning making and, 120–125, 130, 135, 145–147, 151, 174–175

media and, 48

military involvement and, 114

animals, evacuation of, 17, 43, 95, 189n63, 199n189

anomie, 10, 120

Arkansas National Guard, 140, 172. *See also* National Guard

armed forces. *See* military involvement

Army Times, 141–142

assessment, 3, 18–20, 176–177. *See also* lessons

Association of Air Medical Services, 97, 213n138

Audubon Zoo, 17

avian flu, 132

Bahamonde, Marty, 32, 38, 67, 132, 143–144, 201n38, 201n42

Bahamonde report, 53, 59–61, 64, 70, 72–75, 180–182

Barbour, Haley, 7, 15, 115, 190n91, 219n248

Barham, Robert, 53

Barnes, M. D., 145

Bartlett, Dan, 31

Bauer, Jacquie, 21

Baum, Dan, 122, 139

BellSouth, 200n22

Berger, Dan, 139
Biloxi, Mississippi, 136
Blackhawk, 140
blacks. *See* African Americans; race
black swan events, 23, 157–158, 163
Blackwater USA, 140, 229n189
blame games
    lessons learned, 163, 170–173
    meaning making and, 116, 118–119,
        128–129, 137, 145–152, 154
    media coverage and, 126, 139, 172
    superdisasters and, 128
Blanco, Kathleen
    coordination and, 90–96, 101, 219n263,
        220n289
    crisis recognition and preparations, 31,
        36, 39–40, 42, 44, 197n151
    criticism of, 148–149, 151, 154
    emergency declaration, 30
    emotional responses, 66–67
    evacuation efforts, 9, 11, 15, 39, 91–96
    federalization and, 90, 111–116, 170–171
    information and sense making, 54, 57,
        68, 123, 162
    meaning making, 129–131, 140, 146,
        150–151, 172–174
    preparations, 31, 36, 39–40, 42, 44,
        197n151
Block, Robert, 48, 68, 143, 201n42, 204n97,
    209n48
Blum, Steven, 66, 114, 145
boats, 34–35, 44, 86–89, 103
Bosner, Leo, 34, 84
Boston Globe, 225n83
Bradberry, Johnny, 15
Bradshaw, Larry, 86
breached levees. *See* levee breaches
Brinkley, Douglas, 12–13, 67, 193n54, 232n36
Broderick, Matthew, 58, 60–62, 68, 70, 73, 76,
    204n103, 204n106
Broussard, Aaron, 124
Brown, Michael, 232n36. *See also* Federal
    Emergency Management Agency (FEMA)

blame games, 172
Bush's praise of, 136
coordination, 100–102, 105–106,
    109–112, 166–168, 170–171, 217n206,
    218n240, 219n248
crisis recognition, 21, 161
criticism of, 149–151, 154, 226n116
evacuation efforts, 11, 91
information and sense making, 47, 57,
    61–64, 67, 70–74, 76–77, 162, 180,
    205n134
meaning making, 121, 131–132, 144, 146,
    174–175, 226n115, 232n12
as PFO, 110, 168
preparations, 25, 27, 31–32, 34–37, 44,
    195n111
tensions with Chertoff, 109–110,
    170–171
bureau-politism, 100, 109–111, 163, 170–171
bus drivers, 43, 90, 94, 138, 198n182
buses, for evacuation, 11, 42–43, 81, 90–95,
    116–117, 166, 198nn181–182, 211n91,
    211nn78–79, 211nn82–83
Bush, Barbara, 121, 222n21
Bush, Ed, 131, 144
Bush, George W., 8, 121, 193n77, 208n11,
    227n125. *See also* White House officials
    9/11 response, 18, 133
    flyover, 118, 134–135, 137, 148, 174,
        227n137, 227nn132–133
    presidential disaster declaration, 31–32,
        83, 85, 101, 110, 218n243
    pre-storm televised warnings, 42, 44, 133

Cajun Navy, 16, 86, 165
Camp Shelby, Mississippi, 33
Card, Andrew, 64, 93, 137, 235n7
Carey Limousine, 91
Carter, Jimmy, 173, 184
Carville, James, 148
Catastrophic Incident Annex of the National
    Response Plan (NRP-CIA), 84–85
Catastrophic Incident Supplement, 85

CBS, 120
Centers for Disease Control and Prevention (CDC), 132
centralization, 168–169
CEO LINK, 104, 216n196
chain of command. *See* command structures
Charity Hospital, 98, 122, 179
Cheney, Dick, 74
Chertoff, Michael, 36, 151, 154
 coordination, 101, 105, 218n243
 information and sense making, 47, 58, 61–63, 68, 74, 204n114
 INS declaration, 85
 meaning making, 121, 125, 129, 132–133, 149, 225n94
 as PFO, 110
 tensions with Brown, 109–110, 170–171
"city refugees," 47–48. *See also* Convention Center; highway overpasses; Superdome
Civil Engineering, 24
Clarkson, Jackie, 123
Clinton, Bill, 184–185
Cloverleaf overpass, 93, 210n75. *See also* highway overpasses
CNN, 77, 94, 120, 124, 126
Coca-Cola, 17
collective sense making. *See* sense making
Collins, Susan, 116
Comfort (hospital ship), 33
command structures, 80, 95–96, 107–116, 149, 167–168
 dual, 108, 113–116, 149, 220n284, 221n291
 joint command, 96, 102, 116
communication. *See also* information; meaning making; media coverage
 compared to meaning making, 119
 between DHS and FEMA, 109–110
 lessons learned, 173–175
 "push" and "pull" approaches, 62–63, 78, 162, 164
 realistic expectations for, 176–177
 of warnings, 42, 44, 133, 158–159

communication infrastructure breakdowns, 200n22, 200n24, 201n45, 202n50
 coordination and, 89
 fact-checking and, 127
 meaning making and, 173–174
 sense making and, 50–55, 78, 161
Compass, Eddie, 35, 67, 101, 124, 206n149, 223n52
Comprehensive Emergency Management Plan, 41, 199n189
confirmation bias, 75–77
confusion, 50, 59, 71, 204n103. *See also* sense making
 conceptual, 67–70
Congressional Black Caucus, 121
Connick, Harry, Jr., 150
contraflow evacuation plan, 15, 27, 39, 159
Convention Center
 authorized as a shelter, 189n50
 conditions in, 10, 13, 125–126, 132–133, 204n103
 confused with Superdome, 59, 71, 204n103
 evacuation of, 11, 90, 145, 221n289
 media reports on, 59, 121, 124, 127, 226n115
 rumors about, 144–145, 189n55, 230n209
 visits from officials, 136
Cooper, Anderson, 126
Cooper, Christopher, 48, 68, 143, 201n42, 204n97, 209n48
coordination, 79–117
 analysis of, 99–116
 bureau-politism and, 100, 109–111, 117
 challenges of, 79–81, 107–109
 command and, 80, 95–96, 107–116 (*see also* command structures)
 emergent (bottom-up), 80–81, 164–169
 evacuation, 81, 89–99, 116–117
 federalization issue, 110–116
 formal structure, 81–85
 lessons learned, 164–170
 logistics, 103–106

coordination (*continued*)
  media-driven politics and, 114–116
  myths about, 167–169
  orchestrated (top-down), 80–81,
    164–170
  realistic expectations, 176
  search and rescue operations, 81, 85–89
  as strategic task, 19–20
Cowan, Kevin, 207n212
Crescent City Connection bridge, 94
crime, 10, 13, 122–123, 139, 222n30. *See also*
  looting; murders; rape; violence
crisis management
  assessment framework, 18–20
  coordination, 79–117
  crisis recognition, 21–45
  lessons learned, 153–177
  meaning making, 118–152
  realistic expectations for assessment,
    176–177
  sense making, 46–78
  strategic tasks of, 3, 19–20
  symbolic dimension of, 118–119
  uncertainty and, 49
crisis recognition, 21–45. *See also* detection of
  mega-disasters; preparation
  known risks, 22
  late predictions, 27–28
  unknown risks, 22–23
  warning signals, 24–25
crisis researchers, 49
critical care patients. *See* special needs
  patients

Dabdoub, Louis, 58, 180
Dauphin Island, 6
Davis, Tom, 22, 137
deaths, 8, 12, 39, 188n31, 190n63. *See also*
  murders
decision-making
  realistic expectations for, 176
  as strategic task, 19–20

default expectations, 75–77
Department of Defense (DOD), 29–30, 57. *See
  also* military involvement
  coordination, 105–109, 114–115, 117,
    166–167, 217n214, 217nn218–219
  evacuation efforts, 95–97, 99
  information and sense making, 61, 63
  INS declaration and, 85
  search and rescue operations, 111
  successes of, 155
Department of Health and Human Services,
  109, 194n92
Department of Homeland Security (DHS). *See
  also* Chertoff, Michael; Homeland Security
  Council (HSC); Homeland Security Operations Center (HSOC)
  coordination, 105, 107–109, 114–115, 167
  crisis recognition, 161
  criticism of, 153–154
  establishment of, 185–186
  evacuation efforts, 93, 99
  "Fast Analysis Report," 28
  FEMA and, 81–82, 185–186
  information and sense making, 47–48,
    61, 68–70, 72–73, 180, 182
  INS designation and, 85
  NRP and, 81–82
  personnel in New Orleans, 60
  PFO role and, 83
  preparations, 45
  reputation of, 151
  tensions with FEMA, 109–110, 170–171
Department of Justice (DOJ), 109
Department of Transportation (DOT)
  buses, 11, 166, 211n83
  evacuation efforts, 91–92, 95–97, 99
detection of mega-disasters. *See also* crisis
  recognition
  lessons learned, 156–158
  realistic expectations, 176
  as strategic task, 19–20
  of unknown risks, 22–23

Disaster Assistance Response Teams (Coast Guard), 210n54

Disaster Medical Assistance Teams (DMATs), 99, 215n174

Disaster Mortuary Operational Response Teams, 102

Disaster Portable Morgue Units, 102

Disaster Relief Act (1950), 183

disasters. *See also* mega-disasters
challenges of, 19–20
man-made, 1–2

"dodged a bullet" frame, 7, 21, 61, 72–75, 120, 134, 199n1

Dolinar, Lou, 88

donations, 103–104

Doriant, William (Bill), 36–37

dual command structure, 108, 113–116, 149, 220n284, 221n291. *See also* command structures

Duncan, Robert F., 114

Durham, Frank, 126

DynCorp, 140

Ebbert, Terry, 147, 201n47

Elisa, Louis, 225n83

emergency call centers, 51, 122, 182, 200n22, 200n24

Emergency Management Assistance Compact (EMAC), 17, 30–31, 104–105, 108

emergency operations center, Baton Rouge (state EOC), 27, 144, 182
Blanco and, 57
communications, 54–55
coordination, 101, 108
preparations, 29, 31–32, 34, 36–38

emergency operations center, New Orleans (EOC), 53–55

Emergency Operations Plan (Louisiana), 199n189

Emergency Response Team—Advanced (ERT-A), 32, 101, 142–143, 194n84, 201n38

Emergency Support Functions (ESFs), 82, 91

emergent coordination, 80–81. *See also* coordination

emotions, 65–67, 206n145

Entergy, 54

evacuation
by air, 97–99, 214n154
of animals, 17, 43, 95, 189n63, 199n189
buses for, 11–12, 42–43, 81, 90–95, 116–117, 166, 198nn181–182, 211n91, 211nn78–79, 211nn82–83
challenges of, 14–15
contraflow plan, 15, 27, 39, 159
failures of, 11–12, 89–99
of highway overpasses, 93, 210n75, 221n289
of hospitals and nursing homes, 12, 97–98, 117, 138–139, 197n160, 228n166
mandatory, 15–16, 40–42, 158, 190n91
medical and special needs, 40–42, 213nn133–136
pre-landfall, 2, 15, 30–31, 38–40, 44, 155, 158–159
prisons, 96
successes of, 14–16
traffic during Hurricane Rita, 190n78

evacuation centers, 14, 43. *See also* Convention Center; Superdome

Evacuation Liaison Team, 27

fact-checked information, 59–61, 125, 127, 162, 174. *See also* information

"fake news," 174. *See also* rumors

fatigue, 65–67

Favors, Jeohn, 86

FBI, 109

fear, 151, 172–173. *See also* rumors

Federal Civil Defense Administration, 184

Federal Coordinating Officer (FCO), 83–85, 208n20

federal disaster management, 20, 183–186
formal structure of, 81–85

federal emergency declaration, 31–32, 83, 85, 101, 110, 218n243

Federal Emergency Management Agency (FEMA). *See also* Brown, Michael; National Response Coordination Center
  communication breakdowns and, 52, 201n33
  coordination, 79, 81, 83, 98, 100–105, 107–111, 165–168, 215n172, 215n175
  criticism of, 2, 100–105, 111, 120, 146, 149–150
  ERT-Ns and, 194n85
  establishment of, 184–186
  evacuation efforts, 11, 91–94, 96–99, 211nn82–83, 213n133
  funding and oversight, 235n5
  hurricane preparation, 25–27 (*see also* Hurricane Pam exercises)
  information and sense making, 48, 52, 62–63, 69–71, 161–162, 180, 201n38
  logistics, 103–106, 117, 166
  meaning making and, 129, 131–132
  NDMS teams and, 195n93
  NOPD and, 55
  Office of Public Affairs, 72
  as part of DHS, 81–82, 170, 185–186
  personnel in New Orleans, 17, 52–54, 60, 102–103
  PFO and, 218n245
  planning exercises, 156–157 (*see also* Hurricane Pam exercises)
  preparations, 32–34, 39, 44–45, 158–159, 195n106
  recognition of Katrina's potential threat, 34
  Region IV, 29, 102
  Region VI, 29, 32, 34, 36, 52, 95, 102
  reports, 39, 60–63
  reputation of, 151
  resources of, 226n111
  security and, 138
  in Superdome, 142–144
  tensions with DHS, 109–111
  upscaling, 105–109, 117, 166–169, 171
  urban search and rescue teams, 89
  White House, relations with, 110–111

federalism, 82

federalization, 95, 110–116, 171, 173, 220n268, 221nn290–291

Federal Protection Service (FPS), 59, 230n195

Federal Response Plan, 185

federal troops. *See* military involvement

Fink, Sheri, 138–139

first responders. *See also* New Orleans Fire Department; New Orleans Police Department; search and rescue operations
  communications and, 51
  flooding and, 87
  priorities of, 49, 56, 162
  reports on breached levees, 47
  supply shortages and, 123

Flood Control Act, 234n3

flooding of New Orleans. *See also* levee breaches
  information on, 46–48, 58–61, 64, 68–77, 204n97, 205n114, 207n212
  predictions of, 27–28, 156–157
  preparations for, 2, 45
  search and rescue operations, 16–17, 47–48
  water levels, 1, 7

Flood of 1927, 4–5, 183, 224n82

floodwalls, 7, 68. *See also* levees

Florida
  damage caused by Katrina, 3, 6, 29
  FEMA operations in, 102
  hurricanes in, 186
  preparations, 29

Florida Division of Emergency Management, 29

flyover, by President Bush, 118, 134–135, 137, 148, 174, 227n137, 227nn132–133

foreign assistance, 104

formalism (red tape), 168

Forman, Sally, 125, 129–130

Fox news, 77, 120, 208n213, 222n30

frames, 119–122, 150–151
    "absent government," 120–121, 154–155
    "dodged a bullet," 7, 21, 61, 72–75, 120,
        134, 199n1
    lessons learned, 171–173
    mayhem (*see* anarchy frame)
    meaning making and, 119–122
    media coverage and, 122–127
    "shock and astonishment," 120
    "uncaring government," 121, 134
    violence as, 120–127
French Quarter, 4, 9, 47, 70, 72, 76, 123, 127,
    162
Fukushima disaster, 22, 49
Full Defense Coordinating Elements, 30
funding, 235n5
    coordination and, 167–168
    federal, 2, 200n31

gangs, 13, 121, 124–125, 145, 172, 233n41
Garden District, 47
generators, 41, 51
Giuliani, Rudy, 18, 173
Glover, Henry, 224n69
Goux, Rene, 12
Government Accountability Office, 154
government response to Katrina, 1–20. *See
    also* local officials; state officials; White
    House officials; *specific agencies*
    assessment framework, 18–20
    coordination, 79–117
    crisis recognition, 21–45
    lessons learned, 155–177
    meaning making, 118–152
    realistic expectations for assessment,
        176–177
    sense making, 46–78
    strategic tasks, 19–20
Graham, Mark, 212n118
Green, Matthew, 180
Gretna, Louisiana, 11, 94, 212n110
Guidry, Jimmy, 17
Gulfport, Mississippi, 225n83

Gupta, Sanjay, 122
Gusman, Marlin N., 38–39

Hagin, Joe, 64, 181
Harris, Ronnie, 11
Hastert, Dennis, 149
Healy, Erin, 137
helicopters
    evacuation of medical patients, 97–98
    rumors of shots fired at, 124, 138, 228n165
    in search and rescue operations, 88–89
    supply deliveries by, 103
heuristics, 23, 191n9
High Reliability School, 158
highway overpasses. *See also* evacuation
    evacuation of, 93, 210n75, 221n289
    media reports on, 121
    prisoners moved to, 96
    survivors on, 10, 47, 90, 97, 210n75
hindsight bias, 49
Hingle, Jeff, 223n35
Home Depot, 17
Homeland Security Council (HSC), 56,
    63–64, 67, 74, 180, 182
Homeland Security Operations Center
    (HSOC), 204n108, 204n114, 216n196
    DHS watch officer at, 205n132
    evacuation buses and, 93
    information and sense making, 53,
        56–64, 68, 73–74, 76, 78, 161–162,
        180–182, 203n77
Homeland Security Presidential Directives, 83
homicides. *See* murders
Honoré, Russel, 33, 195n97
    coordination and, 95–96, 107–108,
        110–111, 113, 115–116
    media attention, 121, 145
Horne, J., 197n149
hospitals
    evacuation of, 12, 97–98, 117, 138–139,
        197n160, 228n166
    shelter in place, 12, 37, 41, 43, 47–48,
        199n187

House of Representatives, 104
  Select Committee, 22, 80, 105
House report (*A Failure of Initiative*), 51, 122,
  125, 138, 153–154, 157, 203n76
Houston, Texas, 17, 104, 125, 190n78
Hull, Jim, 108
Hurricane Andrew (1992), 24, 36, 48, 106, 137,
  184–185, 188n31, 235n7
Hurricane Betsy (1965), 5, 24
Hurricane Camille (1969), 24
Hurricane Dennis (2005), 15
Hurricane Georges (1998), 14–15
Hurricane Hugo (1989), 184
Hurricane Ivan (2004), 15, 87–88, 190n89
Hurricane Katrina (2005). *See also* govern-
  ment response to Katrina
    Category 1 status, 29
    Category 3 status, 6
    Category 4 status, 31
    Category 5 status, xv, 6, 35–36, 188n24
    damage caused by, 1, 6–8, 29, 188n35
    (*see also* levee breaches)
    death toll, 8, 12, 39, 188n31, 190n63
    scale of disaster, 46–47, 70–78, 120, 163
    (*see also* flooding of New Orleans)
    timeline, xv–xvi
Hurricane Liaison Team (HLT), 29, 31,
  36, 42
Hurricane Pam exercises (fictitious scenario),
  14, 25–27, 33, 37, 45, 91, 156–157, 191n24,
  192n41, 209n46
Hurricane Rita, 190n78
Hurst, Jules, 91
Hyatt Regency, as response network head-
  quarters, 54, 201n45, 201n47

I-10 interstate highway, 10, 94. *See also* highway overpasses
IBM, 17
IEM (disaster management consultancy),
  25–27
imaginary limitations, 50, 65, 70–75, 163
inattentional blindness, 232n32

Incident Command System (ICS), 100, 167,
  215n171
Incident of National Significance (INS)
  protocol, 74, 83–85, 107, 110, 166, 208n23,
  209n24, 209n29, 218n243
Indian Ocean tsunami (2004), 114
Industrial Canal, 47, 58, 68, 180
information. *See also* sense making
    accuracy of, 10, 59–61, 78, 125, 127, 162,
      174, 223n43
    bottlenecks in information chain, 55–65
    capacity to collect and verify, 50–55
    challenges, 46–50
    lessons learned, 160–164
information-gathering units, 161–162
Initial Operating Facility, 102
Instinctive Shooting International, 140
Insurrection Act, 112, 115
Interagency Incident Management Group, 83
Intercon, 140
international organizations, 104
internet, 51–52, 61, 201n45. *See also* commu-
  nication infrastructure breakdowns

Jackson, Jesse, 127
Jackson, Liz, 180
Jackson, Michael, 36, 70, 107, 182
Jackson, Mississippi, 6
Jackson Barracks (National Guard facility),
  34–35, 43, 75
    flooding in, 53, 88, 179, 196n114, 196n123
Jefferson Parish, 40, 215n172
    flooding in, 58
    martial law and, 124
    shoot-to-kill order, 229n185
Johnson, Reggie, 91–94
joint command, 96, 102, 116. *See also* com-
  mand structures
Joint Field Office (JFO), 83, 102, 167, 194n84
Joint Forces Command, 29
Joint Information Center, 129–130, 225n92
joint sense making, 48, 160. *See also* sense
  making

Joint Task Force on Hurricane Katrina
(JTF-Katrina), 95–96, 107–108, 110, 113–
115, 121, 145, 212n117, 221n291
Jones, Gary, 142–143
journalists. *See* media coverage
Juvenile Justice Project of Louisiana, 39

Kahneman, Daniel: *Thinking, Fast and Slow,*
70, 191n9
Katrina. *See* Hurricane Katrina (2005)
Keating, Timothy, 80, 221n290
Kenner, Louisiana, 197n158
King, Larry, 77, 227n138
Kleinpeter, Leonard, 211n91
known risks, 22
Kolluru, Ramesh, 216n198
Kopplin, Andy, 138
Kouzmin, Alex, 170
Krugman, Paul, 222n23

Lakeview, flooding in, 181
Landreneau, Bennett, 58, 66, 75, 203n75
Landrieu, Mary, 75, 126, 146, 149–150,
231n251
Landrieu, Mitch, 67, 101
Landstar, 91, 96, 99, 211n85
law enforcement, 140
    federal agencies, 33, 142
    federal troops and, 113–116
    National Guard and, 38, 111–113, 140,
    143–145
lawlessness, 138–140, 172–173, 222n7. *See also*
    anarchy frame; crime
leaders. *See also* government response to
    Katrina; local officials; state officials;
    White House officials; *specific agencies
    and individuals*
    expectations of, 18–19
    meaning making by, 118–119 (*see also*
    blame games)
    stamina of, 65–67
Lee, Harry, 229n185
Lee, Insung, 58

Lee, Trymaine, 71
legitimacy of institutions, 2, 117, 119, 122,
151–152
Lenovo, 17
lessons, 155–177
levee breaches, 1, 7. *See also* flooding of New
Orleans
    definition of, 68
    detection of, 156–157
    as "hype," 73
    information on, 46–47, 58–61, 64, 68–
    77, 162, 205n114, 205n131, 207n212
    timeline on, 179–182
levees
    definitions of breaches and overtopping,
    68
    development of, 4
    predictions of overtopping, 26, 28, 36,
    39, 41–42, 159
Lewis, Peirce, 4
Lieberman, Joe, 87
lifesaving operations. *See* search and rescue
    operations
Lipton, Eric, 125
Littlefield, Robert, 126
local officials. *See also* Nagin, C. Ray
    information and sense making, 161
    meaning making, 128–129
logistics, 103–106, 117, 166, 233n38
Lokey, Bill, 27, 32, 57, 68, 100, 107–108, 112,
192n41
London bombings (2005), 18
Long, Huey "Kingfish," 173
Long, Russell, 24
looting
    martial law and, 140
    media coverage of, 13, 86, 122–123, 172,
    223n41
    by police officers, 55, 123, 223n35
    prosecution for, 223n37
    racial stereotyping and, 126–127
    rumors of, 67, 94, 120–123, 127, 222n25
    in Superdome, 143

Lott, Trent, 136, 149
Louisiana. *See also* state officials
    damage caused by Katrina, 6, 77
    evacuation plans, state-level, 15, 190n89
    evacuations, pre-Katrina, 6
    governor of (*see* Blanco, Kathleen)
    hurricane response plan, 24–27
    nativity in, 190n101
    state police, 51
    Louisiana Department of Culture,
      Recreation and Tourism, 92
Louisiana Department of Public Safety and
    Corrections, 96, 213n125
Louisiana Department of Transportation and
    Development (DOTD), 15
    evacuation buses and, 92–95
    search and rescue operations, 33, 89
Louisiana Department of Wildlife and
    Fisheries (LDWF), 27
    evacuation efforts, 98
    media coverage of, 130–131
    NOPD and, 55
    preparations, 34
    search and rescue operations, 16, 33, 87,
      89, 130–131, 165
Louisiana Hospital Association, 197n160
Louisiana National Guard (LANG), 230n200.
    See also National Guard
    command structure and, 115
    evacuation efforts, 30, 98
    reports of flooding, 58
    search and rescue operations, 88–89
    sheltered evacuees and, 9–11
    at Superdome, 88
    turf wars with federal troops, 109
Louisiana Nursing Home Association, 41,
    213n130
Louisiana Office of Homeland Security and
    Emergency Preparedness (LOHSEP), 15,
    100, 154, 181, 215n171, 216n198
    information and sense making, 201n47
    preparations, 30–31, 34–36, 43, 45
    reports on breached levees, 47, 207n212

Louisiana State Police, 15, 98, 122–123, 138
Louisiana State University (LSU), 190n102
    rescue operations and, 17
    research on hurricane response plans, 24
    special needs patients at, 38
    Stephenson Disaster Management
      Institute Center for Business
      Preparedness, 216n198
Lowder, Michael, 34, 180
Lower Mississippi Flood Control Act, 183
Lower Ninth Ward, 4, 8, 16, 47, 58, 179
Lupin, Ralph, 229n194

Maestri, Walter, 193n61, 215n172
mandatory evacuation order, 15–16, 40–42,
    158, 190n91
Mann, Bob, 54, 148
Marine Corps, 108
martial law, 124, 139–140, 229n184
Martinko, M. J., 121
Mayfield, Max, 28, 36, 68, 75, 193n61,
    197nn150–151
mayhem frame. *See* anarchy frame
McClellan, Scott, 75, 133–134, 136, 193n77,
    220n268, 227n125
McHale, Paul, 105–106
McLaughlin, Colonel, 145
meaning making, 118–152
    blame games and, 116, 118–119, 128–129,
      137, 145–152, 154, 171–172
    challenges of, 128–137
    consequences of failures, 119, 137–145,
      150–152
    frames, 119–122 (*see also* frames)
    by leaders, 128–129, 150–151
    lessons learned, 171–173
    realistic expectations, 176
    rumors and, 119–120, 122–129, 160,
      173–175, 222n7
    sense making and, 164
    as strategic task, 19–20
    as symbolic dimension of crisis manage-
      ment, 118–119

media coverage. *See also* meaning making
blame games, 126, 139, 172
communications and, 53
confusion about levee breaches, 68
criticism of FEMA, 111
early reports, 21–22, 46, 76–77
fact-checking and, 127
frames and, 122–127 (*see also* frames)
inaccuracies in, 10, 223n43
meaning making and, 119
rumors and, 222n7 (*see also* rumors)
sense making and, 71–72, 200n17
medical and special needs evacuation, 40–42,
213nn133–136. *See also* hospitals; nursing
homes
medical staging areas, 10, 17, 33, 97–98
mega-disasters, challenges of, 1–3, 19–20. *See
also* crisis management
Memorial Hospital, 12, 138–139
"midnight memo," 115–116, 220n289,
221nn290–292
military involvement. *See also* Department of
Defense (DOD); National Guard; US Coast
Guard
civilian authorities and, 85
command authority, 195n99
coordination of, 105–109, 164, 169–170
federalization issue and, 111–116
law enforcement and, 13, 113–116
mayhem frame and, 120–121
meaning making and, 121, 139–144, 151
state requests for, 90
Mississippi
Bush's visit to, 136
damage caused by Katrina, 3, 6–7, 77
evacuations, 6, 190n89
FEMA operations in, 102
state of emergency declaration, 30
Mississippi River
Great Flood (1927), 4–5, 183, 224n82
levees on, 21
Mississippi River and Tributaries Project,
234n3

Mobile, Alabama, 6
Mobile Emergency Response Support
(MERS), 52, 102
Mogadishu, comparisons to, 123, 126
MSNBC, 55, 76, 207n212
Muhammad, Cedric, 127
murders, 124–125, 172, 189n55, 230n209,
230n213

Nagin, C. Ray, 9, 12
authorization of Convention Center as
shelter, 189n50
blame games, 146–148, 172–173
coordination and, 79, 101
criticism of, 151, 154
emergency declaration, 40, 123
emotional responses, 66–67, 206n145
evacuation efforts, 39–40, 91, 94
federalization issue and, 111–116
information and sense making, 54, 58,
179, 182, 201n47
mandatory evacuation order, 15–16,
40–42
meaning making, 121, 129–130, 140, 151
preparations, 31, 35, 44, 197n158
rumors and, 124–125
National Academy of Public Administrators,
185
National Communications System, 52
National Disaster Medical System (NDMS),
33, 194n90, 195n93
National Emergency Response Team (ERT-N),
32, 194nn84–85
National Geospatial Agency, 60
National Guard, 17, 203n75. *See also* Louisiana
National Guard (LANG)
command structure, 112–116, 149
communications and, 52
EMAC requests for, 104–105
evacuation efforts, 92, 94–95, 97–99
meaning making and, 121
media coverage of, 130–131
preparations, 35, 38, 43

National Guard (*continued*)
  search and rescue operations, 88–89
  security and law enforcement, 38, 111–
    113, 140, 143–145
  successes of, 165
National Guard Bureau, 88, 108, 115, 220n289
National Hurricane Center (NHC), 6, 28, 30–
  31, 40, 68. *See also* Hurricane Liaison Team
National Incident Management System, 82,
  167, 177
National Public Radio, 121
National Response Coordination Center
  (NRCC), 29, 34, 63, 83, 193n55, 203n77
National Response Framework, 81
National Response Plan (NRP), 52, 74. *See
  also* Incident of National Significance (INS)
  protocol
  on animals, 199n189
  on communications, 129–130
  coordination, 81–85, 102, 106, 208n20,
    208n23, 209n24
  development of, 208n11
  deviation from, 153, 155, 165
  military involvement and, 107, 109
  Public Affairs Support Annex, 225n92
National Search and Rescue Plan, 209n46
National Situation Reports (sitreps), 57, 59,
  61, 64, 182, 203n77, 203n82, 204n114
National Situation Updates, 57, 203n77
National Weather Service
  reports on levees, 47, 58, 68, 73
  warnings issued by, 28, 180–181
Natural Hazards Observer, 24
NBC Nightly News, 77, 120, 192n51
New Orleans
  mayor of (*see* Nagin, C. Ray)
  overview of, 3–6
  population, 4–6, 188n18
  vulnerability to hurricanes, 24–25
New Orleans Fire Department, 35, 53, 87
New Orleans Health Department, 92, 194n92
New Orleans International Airport, 97–99,
  214n154

New Orleans Office of Emergency Preparedness, 154, 198n182
New Orleans Police Department (NOPD),
  224n69
  communication breakdowns and, 202n62
  coordination, 109
  criticism of, 54–55, 154, 202n56
  Emergency Preparation Plan, 35, 196n121
  evacuation efforts, 98
  flooded headquarters, 51, 87
  information position, 54–55
  looting by officers, 55, 123, 223n35
  mandatory evacuation and, 40–41
  preparations, 42
  rumors and, 222n7
  stranded officers, 209n48
  Superdome patrols, 9
New Orleans Saints, 30
New Yorker, 139
New York Times, 9, 22, 53, 77, 88, 124–125, 131,
  135, 199n1, 202n56, 203n76, 223n41
Nielsen, Kirstjen, 58
Ninth Ward, flooding in, 4–5, 25, 47, 64, 68,
  127, 179–181
  Lower, 4, 8, 16, 47, 58, 179
  Upper, 47
NOLA Homeboys, 16
NORTHCOM, 33, 48, 63, 80, 106, 114, 221n290
nursing homes, 12, 41, 190n73, 213n130

O'Byrne, James, 71
Office Depot, 123
O'Keefe, Sean, 17
Oklahoma City bombing (1994), 185
Operation Brother's Keeper, 198n180
orchestrated coordination, 80–81. *See also*
  coordination
O'Reilly, Bill, 77
The O'Reilly Factor, 222n30
organizations, relationships between, 27, 55,
  109–110, 170–171. *See also specific organi-
  zations*
Orleans Parish, flooding in, 46–47, 58, 73

Orleans Parish Prison, 38–39, 213n125
overpasses. *See* highway overpasses
overtopping of levees. *See also* levees
  definition of, 68
  predictions of, 26, 28, 36, 39, 41–42, 159

Pantuso, Peter, 104
Paris shootings (2015), 18, 49
Parr, Phil, 32, 71, 101, 143, 201n38, 230n195
Paulison, R. David, 81
Pearce, Vincent, 92
Pentagon. *See* Department of Defense
performance indicators. *See* strategic tasks of
  crisis management
pets, evacuation of, 43, 95, 189n63, 199n189
Philadelphia Enquirer, 24
planning exercises, 192n29. *See also* Hurricane
  Pam exercises
plans. *See also* National Response Plan (NRP)
  as benchmarks, 167
Plaquemines Parish, 4, 58, 223n35
police brutality, 54–55
politicization, 100, 117
  blame and, 148–149
  detection of disasters, 156–157
  meaning making and, 128
poor people, evacuation of, 16
Popular Mechanics, 24
Posse Comitatus Act, 112
power failures, 12. *See also* generators
pragmatism, 177
predictions, 21–22
  of flooding, 27–28, 156–157
  of overtopping of levees, 26, 28, 36, 39,
    41–42, 159
preparation, 29–45. *See also* crisis recognition
  adequacy of, 29–39, 43–45
  expectations for, 23
  lessons learned, 158–160
  local and state level, 34–35
  in New Orleans, 24–25
  practice exercises, 167 (*see also* Hurri-
    cane Pam exercises)

as strategic task, 19–20
  warnings and evacuation, 39–43
presidency. *See* Bush, George W.; White House
  officials
Principal Federal Official (PFO), 83–85,
  110, 168, 209n24, 218n242, 218n245,
  219nn250–251
prisons
  evacuation of, 47, 96
  preparations, 37–39, 213n125
private sector, 104
private security firms, 139–140, 172, 229n189
public health risks, 72
Public Health Service, 99
pumping stations, 7
"push" and "pull" approaches, 62–63, 78, 162,
  164

Quenette, Andrea, 126

race, 11, 121, 126–127, 224n82, 225n83. *See
  also* African Americans; whites
rape, rumors of, 13, 67, 123–125, 127, 172,
  223n41, 230n209, 230n213
Rapuano, Ken, 72–73, 203n72, 205n131
Reagan, Ronald, 173, 184
recognition. *See* crisis recognition
Red Cross, 14, 99, 138, 225n83
  prestorm preparations, 33–34
  services provided by, 103
  Superdome and, 195n105
Red October communications unit, 52, 201n36
red tape (formalism), 168
Regional Response Coordination Centers, 83,
  208n18
Regional Transit Authority (RTA), 43,
  198nn181–182, 211nn78–79
reporters. *See* media coverage
rescue operations. *See* search and rescue operations
resilience strategies, 159
response networks. *See* government response
  to Katrina

Rhode, Patrick, 63, 70, 181, 219n251

Rice, Condoleezza, 137

Riley, Bob, 190n91

Riley, Warren, 55, 151

Riley, Warren J., 202n68

risk calculations, 157

risk management, professionalization of, 158

Rivera, Geraldo, 145, 174

Robert T. Stafford Disaster Relief and Emergency Assistance Act. *See* Stafford Act

Robinette, Garland, 147

Rosenthal, Uriel, 170

Rossiter, Clinton, 133

Rove, Karl, 134, 148, 219n268

rumor control, 175, 225n92, 233n49

rumors. *See also* sense making
    of breached levees, 60
    consequences of, 13, 137–139, 151
    Convention Center conditions, 144–145,
        189n55, 230n209
    effect of, 119
    of looting, 67, 94, 120–123, 127, 222n25
    meaning making and, 119–120, 122–129,
        160, 173–175, 222n7
    media coverage and, 222n7
    Nagin and, 124–125
    NOPD and, 222n7
    of rape, 13, 67, 123–125, 127, 172, 223n41,
        230n209, 230n213
    of shots fired at helicopters, 124, 138,
        228n165
    Superdome conditions, 77, 121, 123–124,
        127, 142–144, 189n55, 230n200
    of violence, 123, 145, 222n25

Rumsfeld, Donald, 106, 113, 137

Salaam, Kalamu ya, 4

Samuels, Kemberly, 86

Santorum, Rick, 149

scaling up. *See* upscaling

Schiro, Victor, 5

Schneider, Saundra, 183–184

school buses, 92, 198nn181–182, 211nn78–79

Scientific American, 24

search and rescue operations
    coordination of, 81, 85–89
    by DOD, 111
    by LDWF, 16, 33, 87, 89, 130–131, 165
    by Louisiana DOTD, 33, 89
    by National Guard, 88–89
    preparation for, 209n46
    in St. Bernard Parish, 86
    successes of, 2, 16–17, 165
    suspended, 140
    by US Coast Guard, 16, 87–89, 165

Seattle Times, 28

security
    on airlines, 214n154
    blame and, 146–147
    Bush and, 135–136
    evacuation buses and, 94
    federalization and, 111–113, 115
    FEMA and, 138
    National Guard and, 38, 111–113, 140,
        143–145
    private firms, 139–140, 172, 229n189

self-organization, 86–87

Senate report, 93, 102, 106, 200n5, 201n36
    A Nation Still Unprepared, 153–154

sense making, 46–78
    challenges of, 46–50
    communication infrastructure failures
        and, 50–55, 78
    conceptual confusion and, 67–70
    confirmation bias and, 75–77
    default expectations and, 75–77
    imaginary limitations and, 50, 65, 70–75,
        163
    information chain bottlenecks and, 50,
        55–65
    joint, 48, 160
    lessons learned, 160–164
    meaning making and, 164
    New Orleans institutions and, 53–55

psychological aspects, 50, 65–77
"push" and "pull" approaches to commu-
    nication, 62–63, 78, 162, 164
realistic expectations, 176
as strategic task, 19–20
uncertainty and, 49
Seventeenth Street Canal, 53, 59, 64, 69, 71, 181
shared approach, 177. *See also* lessons
shelter in place, 12, 14, 37, 41, 43, 47–48,
    199n187
Shingler, Wendell, 204n103
"shock and astonishment" frame, 120
shoot-to-kill order, 140, 151, 172, 174, 229n185
sitreps. *See* National Situation Reports
Slonsky, Lorrie Beth, 86
Smith, Jeff, 32, 36–37, 68–69, 80, 146, 179,
    211n82, 212n117, 233n49
Smith, Shepard, 222n30
snipers, 122, 124, 138
social media, 163, 174
Solnit, R., 86
Southeast Louisiana Catastrophic Hurricane
    Plan, 25–27
Southeast Louisiana Hurricane Evacuation
    and Sheltering Plan, 15
special needs patients. *See also* hospitals
    evacuation of, 40–42, 92–93, 98–99
    in Superdome, 38, 142–143
spot reports, 57–58, 64, 70, 76, 182, 203n77,
    203n82. *See also* Bahamonde report
Stafford Act, 82–83, 85, 184, 209n29
state officials. *See also* Blanco, Kathleen;
    emergency operations center, Baton Rouge
    (state EOC)
        coordination and, 100–101, 107–109, 167
        criticism of, 148–149
        evacuation and, 96
        meaning making, 128–129
St. Bernard Parish, 4
    damage caused by Katrina, 6
    flooding in, 47, 58, 64, 68, 73, 77, 200n6
    search and rescue operations in, 86

Stephanopoulos, George, 150
Stephenson Disaster Management Institute
    Center for Business Preparedness, 216n198
strategic tasks of crisis management, 3, 19–20
stress, 65–67
St. Rita's nursing home, 12, 190n73
successes, 2, 14–17, 155, 165
superdisasters. *See* mega-disasters
Superdome
    Blanco at, 57
    command over operations in, 109
    conditions in, 9–10, 13, 67, 72, 90, 101, 132
    confused with Convention Center, 59,
        71, 204n103
    evacuation of, 11, 17, 90–95, 104, 117,
        221n289
    FEMA personnel in, 142–144
    flooding around, 73, 182
    FPS at, 230n195
    information on, 59
    media reports and rumors about, 77,
        121, 123–124, 127, 142–144, 189n55,
        230n200
    medical assistance, 194n92
    physical structure, 37
    preparations as shelter, 42–43, 45,
        195n105, 199n185
    Red Cross and, 34, 195n105
    Saints-Ravens game at, 30
    special needs patients in, 38
    supply shortages, 103
    visits from officials, 136–137
supply shortages, 103, 215n175
    looting and, 123, 126
Swain, Lonnie C., 124
Sylves, Richard, 185

telephone services, 51, 61, 200n22, 200n31,
    202n50. *See also* communication infrastruc-
    ture breakdowns; emergency call centers
Temporary Medical Operations Staging Area
    (TMOSA), 10, 17, 97–98

terrorism, 82, 84, 171, 185. *See also* 9/11
Texas, 17, 104, 125, 190n78
't Hart, Paul, 170
Thibodeaux, Jacques, 144
Thiele, John, 139
Thomas, Evan, 1
Thomas, Oliver, 149
thugs, 13, 123–125, 172
Time magazine, 154
Times-Picayune, 10, 25, 71, 115, 122, 150, 154, 191n2, 191n24
Townsend, Fran, 219n263
Transportation Management Services, 91
transportation problems, 89–99. *See also* airport; buses; evacuation
Transportation Security Administration (TSA), 58, 99, 214n154
turf wars, 109
Turner, Barry, *Man-Made Disasters,* 56

"uncaring government" frame, 121, 134
uncertainty, 49, 163
University Hospital, 98
University of New Orleans, 24
unknown risks, 22–23
Upper Ninth Ward, 47
upscaling, 105–109, 117, 166–169, 171
US Air Force, 33
US Army Corps of Engineers (USACE)
    information and sense making, 68, 70
    levee reports, 53, 59–60, 127
    personnel in New Orleans, 54
    preparations, 32
    repairs on levees, 53
USA Today, 24
US Bureau of Prisons, 96
US Coast Guard, 44, 53, 121
    evacuation efforts, 98
    helicopters, 201n42
    media coverage of, 130–131
    preparations, 33, 210n54
    reports on breached levees, 47, 182

search and rescue operations, 16, 87–89, 165
    successes of, 155
US Fifth Army, 95, 108, 212n118
US First Army, 33, 95, 108
US Forestry Service, 52
US Transportation Command, 33

Van Heerden, Ivor, 24, 28
Vankawala, Hemant, 214n147
Vaughn, Clyde, 66
Veillon, Brod, 144
verification. *See* fact-checked information
violence
    evacuation delays and, 90
    as frame, 120–127
    media coverage of, 13, 86, 223n41
    by police officers, 54–55
    rumors of, 67, 94, 123, 145, 222n25
Vitter, David, 46, 101, 220n268
voice calls. *See* communication infrastructure breakdowns; telephone services
volunteers, 103–104

Wackenhut, 140
Wagenaar, Richard, 71, 206n176
Wall Street Journal, 77
Walmart, 17, 104, 122, 216n199
warnings. *See* crisis recognition
Washington Post, 21, 77, 115, 122, 155, 223n41
Wells, Scott, 100, 125
West, Kanye, 121, 127
Whitehorn, Henry, 15, 138, 202n68
White House officials. *See also* Bush, George W.
    coordination, 79–80, 104, 110–116
    crisis recognition and preparations, 158–159, 161
    criticism of, 148, 151, 154–155
    information and sense making, 48, 56–57, 61, 63–65, 73–75
    legitimacy of, 2, 151
    Lessons Learned report, 188n35

meaning making, 133–137, 150, 172,
231n235
Situation Room, 28, 63–64
whites, 4–5, 126
Williams, Brian, 77
Willow, Mark, 181

Winfrey, Oprah, 124, 223n52
Winn, Jeffrey, 125
Witt, James Lee, 24, 116, 184–185, 235n9
Wood, John, 182
World Trade Center attack (1993), 185
WWL radio, 79, 147, 193n62